MUSSAU I

NEW HANOVER I
Taskul KAVIENG
Lavongai

NEW IRELAND

Medina
TABAT ISLANDS

LIHIR GROUP

BOANG I

Sea

NORTH SOLOMONS

NEW IRELAND ISLAND
Ulututur Namatanai

Muliama

FENI
ISLANDS

DUKE OF YORK I
RABAUL
Raluana Kokopo
Navuneram
Kerevat
Warangoi

Rei

GAZELLE
PENINSULA

Open Bay

Wide Bay

BUKA I

WILLAUMEZ
PENINSULA
Talsea
KIMBE Hoskins

LOLOBAU I

Bialla

Pomio

Jacquinot Bay

EAST
NEW BRITAIN

Cape
Gloucester

Sag Sag

Arawe

Kandrian

NEW BRITAIN ISLAND

NORTH SOLOMONS

attelberg
Finchhafen

TAMI I

SSI
ANDS

WEST NEW BRITAIN

Solomon   Sea

Hanahan
BUKA Lonahan
Hutjena
Buka Sohano Teop
Passage Tinputz
Inus
Wakunai

BE

obe

BOUGAINVILLE

Arawa KIETA
Panguna Toboroi

NORTHERN

Ioma
Gona Buna
POPONDETTA
Oro Bay
Lamington Ororo

Tufi

Wanigela

TROBRIAND ISLANDS
KIRIWINA I
Losuia
KITAVA I

GAWA I

Buin

SOLOMON ISLANDS

WOODLARK I
Kulumadau
Guosopa

GOODENOUGH I

FERGUSSON I

Baniara

Esa Ala Salamo
Dawson Straits

kila
Kupiano
Cape Rodney
Magarida

MAILU I

Lagoon

Dogura

NORMANBY I

MILNE BAY

ALOTAU
Mullins Harbour Gurney
Kwato
Fife Bay SUAU I Samarai

East Cape
Milne Bay

BASILAKI I

LOUISIADE
MISIMA I
Bwagoia

CENTRAL

Coral   Sea

Deboyne Lagoon

CALVADOS CHAIN

ARCHIPELAGO

NIMOA I

ROSSEL

TAGULA

PATHWAYS
TO
INDEPENDENCE

First Edition 1984
Second Edition 1985

Copyright © Dame Rachel Cleland 1981
          P.O. Box 156 Cottesloe
          Western Australia

Printed by Singapore National Printers (Pte) Ltd.

National Library of Australia
Cataloguing in Publication Data
Pathways to Independence
Story of Official and Family Life in Papua New Guinea
From 1951 to 1975
ISBN O 9589354 O 8

PATHWAYS
TO
INDEPENDENCE

Story of Official and Family Life
in Papua New Guinea
From 1951 to 1975

RACHEL CLELAND

Portrait by Sir William Darge
End maps   Mark Farrow   Queensland
Line drawings   Jon Dangar   Papua New Guinea
Dust Jacket   Gibneys Graphics   Western Australia

Acknowledgements

Writing this book as I have, mainly from my own memories, I am indebted and give my grateful thanks to the many people with whom I checked details of what I had written, and to those who read all or parts of the manuscript giving me criticism, suggestions and encouragement.

Chief among these were Mr Paul Quinliven who had come to Papua New Guinea before we had and whose knowledge of legal matters extended for a longer time than anyone else. He lent me papers in his possession and carefully checked my accounts of events. Mr Buri Kidu, when Secretary for Law, made his Librarian available to me for checking details from Law Department files. He himself became interested in the period, reading the old files and parts of my manuscript, giving generously of his time. Now Sir Buri Kidu, he is the Chief Justice and Paul Quinliven is also a Judge. I am grateful to them both.

Dr John Ballard, Professor of Administrative Studies at the University of Papua New Guinea, and now Senior Research Fellow of Political Science at the Australian National University, read the first draft and gave me many typed pages of criticism and comment which were an enormous help. Similar assistance was given by Mr Stan Pearsall who worked in daily contact with three Administrators in various capacities. In addition to his own contribution to Chapter 8, he read the first draft and helped elucidate matters which were not quite clear to me. I also greatly value the contribution for Chapter 8 made by Mr David Chenoweth.

I am deeply indebted to Dr John Legge, Professor of History at Monash University for reading the second draft, writing valuable comments and giving me several hours of his time; to Sir David Derham, Vice Chancellor of Melbourne University, for reading Chapter 12 which referred to his report and its fate. Dr Peter Lawrence, Professor of Anthropology at Sydney University and his wife Fancy, both read the second draft, giving me most valuable comments, suggestions and great encouragement, as did Miss Nancy Lutton Librarian in charge of the New Guinea Collection at the Library of U.P.N.G., now executive Librarian, Printed Records at the Battye Library Perth, Mrs Catherine King, Mrs Mavis Montgomery and Mrs Dorrie White.

My thanks also go to Mr John Hohnen, Managing Director of the New Guinea Goldfields Company at Wau, when he was also a member of the Legislative Council at a crucial time and to Mr George Buick, the first Librarian of U.P.N.G., and now of Murdoch University Western Australia, and his wife Barbara who both gave me written criticism of draft three and assisted with discussion. Dr Hank Nelson, historian at U.P.N.G., and now Fellow for the Department of Pacific History at A.N.U. also read the third draft. His criticism, suggestions and encouragement are very much appreciated.

Felicity who typed the first draft in Port Moresby, and Judy Collier who typed the second in Perth both struggled so cheerfully with my writing and re-writing and gave me so much more than the actual work of typing. The days they came were always fun. And lastly, my thanks to my own family in Perth. My sister Barbara Evans helped me peel down my verbosity in the first draft and my brother Bill Evans and his wife Flower went over the third with a fine tooth comb and raised valuable queries.

Finally, in the year of publication when I returned to Port Moresby to work with Jon Dangar, the National artist who drew the delightful chapter headings, my gratitude goes to the Institute of Papua New Guinea Studies. For three weeks Jon Kolia, the assistant director, vacated his office so that Jon Dangar would have a place to work undisturbed. I can imagine no action more generous or supportive. Professor Andrew Strathern, the Director and the Institute staff all tolerated my comings and goings, thus making the experience a very happy one. I thank them all.

And lastly I do appreciate the way my grandson-in-law Mark Farrow, who is a cartographer, coped with my rather exacting requirements when he was drawing the maps for the endpapers.

Rachel Cleland.

* After leaving P.N.G., John Hohnen joined C.R.A., and was manager of the first development in the Pilbara.

FOREWORD

Australian responsibility for the administration of Papua New Guinea came formally to an end when that country became an independent state in 1975. The two countries maintain strong and substantial links and common interests; they share membership of the Commonwealth of Nations and association in other international and regional bodies.

This book is the personal story of one who lived in Papua New Guinea and was intimately associated with the life of the country during the last twenty-five years of Australian administration. Dame Rachel came to join her husband in 1951 in the aftermath of war which had left its heavy mark upon the Territory. Her account is an important record of events and developments, and of the parts played by many people over these important years. As the wife of a man who had major roles in administration, culminating in his appointment as Administrator, she had a special opportunity to observe and to be closely involved.

Sir Donald retired some years before independence, but continued to play a part in the life of Papua New Guinea. He died shortly before independence and was to have been an honoured guest at the ceremonies. Dame Rachel attended them, as she tells in her concluding pages, and the invitation to her was an expression of appreciation to two Australians who had served the two countries principally involved with dedication and distinction.

I have known many of the people about whom Dame Rachel writes, and something of some of the major events and issues. I made two visits to Papua New Guinea, one early in the 1970's when I was Vice-Chancellor of the University of Queensland which had a substantial responsibility for external studies in the Territory. I went to discuss our future role as independence approached. Then in 1982, not long before my retirement as Governor-General of Australia, my wife and I made an official visit. An election was in progress and it must have been an inconvenient time to receive us. We were made welcome; we met and renewed acquaintance with many people and we saw something of the country.

Dame Rachel's book certainly expands my knowledge and understanding of Papua New Guinea and its people, its promise, its prospects and its problems. She tells her story quite fully, she writes clearly, and with affection and candour. I am sure that it will be well received and I am pleased that we have this personal account written by one who was so fully and deeply involved in the life and service of two countries, both of which she would have wished to call her own.

Former Vice Chancellor Brisbane University
Former Governor General of Australia.

CONTENTS

Author's Preface

This book is written almost entirely from my memories of the full, demanding but always interesting life I shared with my husband, Donald Mackinnon Cleland, while he was first, Assistant Administrator and then Administrator of Papua New Guinea.

I did it in six months while still living in Port Moresby. Then most unexpectedly I began to feel that the time had come to return to Australia. I bought a little house just a few minutes walk from the house I was born in and near where my brother and sisters have always lived.

After many months I took the manuscript out again and since then it has gone through three more drafts, which means that publication is some years later. Much has changed, especially in the lives of people but I decided against updating so the present text relates to the end of the nineteen seventies.

When planning the book at the end of 1977, I took the precaution of lodging unread, all Don's official papers and correspondence with the Department of Pacific History at A.N.U. Canberra.

For a memory tickler and dates, I went to the Government House visitor's book, Don's office diary of conferences and interviews, both our engagement books and the collection of itineraries for our District visits as well as those of V.I.P.'s such as Governors General, Ministers and Ambassadors.

Where the text goes beyond my own memories or impressions, I have checked it carefully from public records or with the people concerned, many of whom have read drafts to check the accuracy of my own memory. For the accounts of such chapters as those on Income Tax, the various crises and some parts of those on the law and the courts, I have gone to Don's partly written manuscript, for details of which I had no direct memory.

The impressions, views and opinions so freely expressed are my own; though many reflect what Don thought or were shared by him. I have not knowingly written of things of which he would not approve, although he himself would have been more reticent, for he was a reticent man. I have written frankly of events as I saw them from the unique position of one who was intimately involved.

Rachel Cleland.

Brigadier Sir Donald Cleland Kt., C.B.E., O. St.J.

Appreciation

Sir Donald was a man of great foresight, who saw leaders such as Maori Kiki, Oala Rarua, Peta Simogen, Reuben Taureka, Sinaka Goava, John Guise, as men also with a vision for their country. He consulted them on matters which involved their welfare and well being.

Personally for me, we had learned to admire Don for his vision, vigour and determination and for what he did until his retirement.

Even after retirement he showed his interest in the nation and he decided to live in Papua New Guinea which he loved so much.

Mike Somare
Prime Minister Papua New Guinea

Chapter 1

Arrival at Jackson's Strip

The Beginning—Early Life—The War— Post war Sydney—My Arrival in Port Moresby— Settling in—Lawes Road Progress Association— Opening of Legislative Council—Visit to Vabukori— The Boys Come for the Holidays—Altering the House— Decision on Rabaul

I gave a last look round our bedroom to see if all was in order for my sister, as the horn tooted once more and I ran up the path to my two sons waiting in the car. It was 6.30 a.m. on a fresh spring morning in Sydney and, as I ran, it suddenly came over me how happy we had been in that house — with father and sons slowly coming to know each other after nearly six years' parting during the war. Now here we were breaking up the family again and I was overcome with tears, to the boys' great embarrassment. My husband Don had gone to Papua New Guinea early September, 1951, as Assistant Administrator. It was now October and I was following. My sister Barbara was giving up her flat and coming to live in 'loco parentis' to Robert at the university and Evan, still in school at Cranbrook. At Mascot Airport an icy wind swept across the tarmac as I made my way to the old DC3 aircraft for an 8 a.m. take-off; looking back from the plane to the little group getting smaller and smaller, I struggled with tears again.

A long flight was ahead of me — hedge-hopping up the coast to Townsville by 5 p.m., an overnight stay there and a midday arrival in Port Moresby. A day and a half for what is now three hours in a jet. So I had plenty of time to think ... and my mind went back over the years, remembering so much of the past which seemed to have been pointers culminating in this flight to New Guinea and the unknown life we would live there: back to 1921 when a neighbour and family friend, General Wisdom, became the first Administrator of New Guinea, Australia's new responsibility mandated to her by the old League of Nations: to stories of Rabaul told by Mrs Wisdom when on leave and by various friends who stayed with them. So quite early I was conscious of New Guinea, and also of Sir Hubert Murray in Papua, and that Australia had a trust to the people.

I had been brought up in what was then an 'advanced' political atmosphere. I was the eldest of six children, though only seven years older than the youngest, with twins in the middle. We grew up in a rambly house with a large garden and innumerable animals, in Peppermint Grove on the banks of the Swan River, near Perth. My father did not believe in a lot of toys for children, but in real things. So with ponies to ride and a boat and all the animals to look after, we were a busy and happy bunch and our garden a mecca for other children.

My mother and her sister Bessie Rischbieth were involved in the early women's movement and had been among the founders of the Women's Service Guilds, a non-party-political organisation tackling social questions and legal status problems involving women and children. As my aunt was childless and I was the eldest of four at two and a half, she used to borrow me for weeks at a time. I adored my uncle, who was rather like Don in appearance and character. They lived in a large house full of beautiful old furniture with trained English servants and when they entertained it had a truly Edwardian style. So as a family our childhood was a rich and varied mixture. I grew up hearing endless discussions of social problems of all sorts and the views expressed were ahead of their time. One of the areas of concern was the aborigines and I was very ashamed of the way we had treated them and ardently believed that we should have a different attitude. But I had had no experience myself and did not know how I would react or what I would do when living in a whole country of brown-skinned people.

Don had been a child of the inland. As a mining engineer, his South Australian father had come to the goldfields in the nineties. Don, the eldest of three, was born on historic Bailey's Mine, Coolgardie, and grew up on Kalgoorlie's Great Boulder and Perseverance, which his father managed. In 1914, the family bought a second house at Guildford so that the boys could attend Guildford Grammar School. Here he was greatly influenced by Canon Henn, who inspired a whole generation of boys to seek the responsibilities of leadership and to look to wide horizons in what they did in life.

The Clelands were a solid Scottish border family, early pioneers in

South Australia, while his MacKinnon mother was born in Skye. Don himself was a severe person with the dour and solid qualities of character of his lowland forbears, lightened by flashes of down-to-earth but puckish humour. Though you could not say that from his mother he had inherited the highland 'gift of sight', he did have a strong intuitive streak which gave him an understanding of people and good political nous.

The plane kept coming down to refuel and my mind kept returning to the past. It seemed incredible, but Don might well have been preparing for New Guinea as long ago as 1926 when, shortly after we were engaged, he made a strange remark. He had just been admitted to the Bar and was very much involved in various community and political activities. Law was a second choice of career for him as he had been accepted for Duntroon in 1919, then was failed medically because of a varicose vein in his leg. With his varied interests and activities, I had been puzzled by him seeking the life of a peacetime army officer. He told me that the army gave the best training in administration:

"What I really wanted to do was to administer a country, say, New Guinea."

It always struck me as odd and was the first thing I thought of when he was posted to New Guinea during the war.

He had joined the A.I.F. in September in 1939 as Staff Captain to Brigadier Herring, G.O.C. 6th Division Artillery Brigade, and left for the Middle East on the first convoy. Selected as one of four Australians for the six-month Amberley Staff College course set at Haifa by the British Army, he got his staff training after all.

Graduating in time for the first triumphant North African campaign, he reached Bengazi before being recalled and sent in advance to Greece. Later he was posted to the staff of General Blamey, the Australian Commander in Chief, in battle H.Q. near the Jugoslav border. As movement officer in the retreat, he had to keep troops moving under heavy bombardment down the only primitive road until they were evacuated to Crete on April 25th.

He was back in Egypt in time for the Syrian campaign.

Promoted to Colonel and posted to British headquarters in Singapore in January 1942, to prepare for the arrival of the Australian division, he joined them in Java instead, eventually making it back to Australia, to my immense relief. From Brisbane he organised our evacuation to Leonora near his brother's sheep station, he himself then being promoted to Brigadier and posted to General Bennett's staff in Perth.

Six months later the boys and I returned from Leonora, and in January we took a cottage down the coast with his brother Bill and family. Don was so tired, he just lazed and hardly spoke for the first few days. Then the tiredness fell away and responding to the boys' clamour the two fathers took all the children fishing. Meanwhile the little store sent a message to ring H.Q. and when they all came back chattering and starving, Don went off to the store. Some time later I suddenly thought to ask him what H.Q. had wanted and he said he was to go to New Guinea. Horrified, I asked when, and he said, "Tomorrow". Shortly afterward, a staff car arrived and we sadly packed up and left. The next day he was away.

The telegram had instructed him to report to General Blamey, the G.O.C. at Australian Army Headquarters in Melbourne, prior to taking up special duties in New Guinea. These duties were explained to him by Blamey and Don's original C.O., General Herring, now G.O.C. New Guinea Force, to which he was posted, to get the battle picture. He was then to become the Chief of Staff of Angau, the Australian New Guinea Administrative Unit. General Morris, its C.O., had commanded garrison troops in Port Moresby early in 1941 and had assumed military government of the country after the Japanese invasion.

Don was to be responsible for the day-to-day administration of Angau and was also to set up a 'Production and Control Board' and, as its first chairman, be responsible directly to the Minister for External Territories, then G.F. Fraser and later Eddie Ward. This board of three was to get plantations staffed and producing again, when retaken from the Japanese, if possible with their former managers and staff attached to the army in an Angau unit.

From his letters over the next two years I could see that Don was becoming more and more involved in a very personal way in New Guinea. He loved his work and he loved the country and its people. Home on leave, he spoke glowingly of it and of them. In 1944, he came to Melbourne for top-level talks and conferences and I managed to join him there. Returning by train I found that John Curtin, the wartime Prime Minister, was in the Ministerial car after his visit to London and the celebrated row with Churchill. As he had seen my aunt, caught by the war in London, I sent up a note asking if he could spare me a few minutes to tell me how she was. The result was an invitation for the next afternoon, when he discussed much of great interest, including the wisdom of his earlier insistence that our army be returned to Australia, which had led to the row: he was worried about it. Interestingly, he told me also that he and Blamey had personally selected Don for Angau and setting up the Production and Control Board, later closely questioning me about his post-war plans.

The following January, Don came home on leave. He had recently been approached by A.A. Conlon, Director of Research and Civil Affairs in the Australian Army, who sounded him out on remaining in New Guinea after the war as Administrator. So the reason for Curtin's interest in Don's post-war plans became clear. During leave he anguished over the decision: whether to return to 'law and politics' or remain in New Guinea. Weighing one against the other, with family

First District Officers Conference outside Angau H.Q. Konedobu Feb 1944.

Back row (left): Lt. Kim Kimmorley later Lands Title Commissioner. Second row (left): J.R. Foldi, later District Commissioner, Rabaul, Jack Page, later Lands Title Commissioner, Ian McDonald later Chairman, Copra Marketing Board. Third row (l to r): Major James, Lt. Col. Mack, Lt. Col. Jones, District Services, Brig. D.M. Cleland, chief of Staff, Major Gen. Morris, Officer in Command Angau. Lt. Col. "Sammy" Hall, Major Elliot-Smith, District Services, Major Normoyle, Police. Front row (left): Lt. Eric Flower later District Commissioner.

considerations — five years away from his sons — competing with his love for New Guinea and the chance of being Administrator, the scale was finally tipped just before his return when his senior partner collapsed and died in the office, making it necessary to return and cope with a potentially difficult situation.

In January 1945, he returned to New Guinea and compassionate discharge was granted in May. In the meantime he prepared a complete plan for the handover from military to civil administration and a separate and complementary survey of army installations and equipment which could be taken over by the civil government. In his final interview as he passed through Melbourne, Blamey told him they had hoped that he would have made his post-war career in New Guinea. It was nice to hear.

Rejoining his firm, he found the problems more insoluble than he expected and contemplated the possible need to leave the partnership and start again. Earlier in the year, the then leader of the Opposition, Mr (later Sir) Robert Menzies had founded the Liberal Party and, while still in New Guinea, Don had been elected a Vice-President for Western Australia. So in preparation for the first annual meeting in July, he had put in a month's hard work drafting the new constitution. During this time he had become disillusioned, seeing the problems ahead in rebuilding his legal career, and after two months of civilian life he had turned his mind once more to New Guinea and the proposal made to him in 1944. Exploring the situation, he had written to Reg Halligan, the Secretary for Territories.

One Thursday night Don came home from the Liberal Party Annual Meeting very pleased that his constitution had been passed with only one amendment. Next morning I was awakened by an unusually vehement "Good God".

"What's happened?" I asked, sitting up.

"Curtin's dead."

We both felt quite shattered, as our families, especially the Clelands in Kalgoorlie days, had known and respected him over many years.

As the by-election was fixed just four weeks hence, there was a great flurry in both parties for candidates. A number of men were approached that weekend to stand for Curtin's seat. A good speaker was vital, as it would be the first opportunity to put the Liberal Party platform before Australia. So many were away at the war that those still in Perth were too short-staffed to leave jobs and suddenly they pounced on Don. As we lived in Curtin's electorate, there was nothing for it and although I was apprehensive that standing against Labor would jeopardise his chances for New Guinea, Don thought that his work there and the letter of appreciation he had had from Ward would be enough recommendation when the time came.

Kim Beazley was the Labor candidate and it was a strange election.

Kim was a popular university lecturer in adult education and many of our friends who attended his current affairs discussion groups were horrified at having to choose between Kim and Don. Both sides campaigned madly with a heavy programme of speeches, followed by a large contingent of interstate pressmen.

During that month, three world events had a strong effect on the population, which you could feel in the electorate. The atom bomb was dropped; Churchill lost the British election; the Japanese sued for peace and the war was over. The following week the position of Administrator of Papua and New Guinea was advertised. Don applied at once and was naive enough to think that politics would not come into it as he had worked with Ward on excellent terms for over a year and relied on the eulogistic letter.

The election results were interesting. Don reduced Curtin's majority of 30,000 to 7,000. The blue ribbon parts of the electorate had shown a swing from Liberal to Labor and in the essentially Labor areas Don did surprisingly well. He could go down to the wharves and pubs of Fremantle and yarn to the men, who found him more their kind of man than the intellectual at the university.

The election over, Don went back to the firm and awaited his luck in the New Guinea appointment. Again one morning I was wakened by an exclamation.

"Murray's got the job. Poor old bastard."

"Who's Murray and why is he a poor old bastard?"

Don explained that he was a professor of agriculture and the nicest bloke, but "no match for those wily old Bs in New Guinea. They'll run rings around him."

He was bitterly disappointed, and there followed a period in life when a man must decide a new course. He had realised that rebuilding his legal career would leave no time for politics. After his good effort in Fremantle, a safe Liberal seat was possible but even if he decided that was what he wanted, he was in no financial position to take the risk. Unsettled, he went off to Sydney as one of six delegates to the first Australian Liberal Party Conference where, besides electing an executive and office-bearers, the most important decision was to set up a Federal Secretariat to serve the federal members and to co-ordinate State efforts at election time.

The delegates then went their ways, the new executive remaining for its first meeting. Don was already at Mascot when Mr Ritchie, the new Federal President, found him and at the unanimous wish of the executive, offered him the directorship of the Federal Secretariat with the job of setting up the organisation. He thought it over well. Apart from believing that a good secretariat was vital to building up an Australian as apart from a State outlook, and vital to the effective working of Federal Parliamentarians, he felt the hand of fate.

He left for Sydney in September and I followed with the family in January 1946. I was in despair at leaving our beloved Perth, but we all ended by loving Sydney and made many friends there. By the end of 1948, Don felt that the task of building the secretariat was done and someone else could carry on. In the meantime, he was cured of political ambitions for himself and had realised that the only place he really wanted to be was in New Guinea. But he decided to see the party through the 1949 election, which Mr Menzies had every chance of winning, and would then take the first opportunity of finding a post in New Guinea. The Liberals won with a comfortable majority and Don's work in building the secretariat had made an undoubted contribution to this success.

In October 1950, the post of Deputy Administrator was advertised. Don told Ritchie of his intentions and applied. Percy Spender, then Minister, interviewed him and later intimated unofficially to Don that he would be appointed. Meanwhile, Spender went to the International Court at the Hague and Paul Hasluck became Minister for Territories. Giving himself some months to study the situation, he finally decided to change the post from Deputy to Assistant Administrator and to appoint Don. In actual fact Don had written to Spender in 1950 after applying for the job, pointing out to him that the concept and implications of having 'deputies' was dangerous and that 'Assistant' would be the better term.

These were the happenings running through my mind as we flew north giving me the sense of inevitability. The future was a curious sort of blank, as I did not know what was involved in the work of Administration. I had no idea what lay ahead, but, realising that big demands would be made of me, hoped I would be able to cope. Don was a man of vision, of tremendous capacity for hard work, and just by expecting the same from others, he usually got it. He shared his life fully with me and I used to find myself doing all sorts of unexpected things. Except for the five long years of war, it made our life together full and rewarding. I remember lying back in the plane as we neared Moresby, enveloped in a kind of prayer of dedication that Don and I would be able to meet whatever challenges might come to us. Then I opened my eyes and looked on the gleaming turquoise of the reefs backed by bare brown hills marked with curious burnt patches. Soon we were trundling, clatter, clatter, over the iron of the marsdon matting and came to rest by a small iron shed painted white. Don, also in white, was standing beside it. A blessed sight to see him and nothing else mattered.

Soon my scant luggage was being put into a shabby black Buick by a broadly smiling police driver, smart in the old style navy and red uniform and presented to me as Towoiwoi. The name and the warm

Government House garden in 1952.

Government House Garden 1965.

Donald and I on the terrace of Government House.

smiling personality and hand spontaneously held out to shake mine, caught my imagination; the first Papua New Guinean I had met.

We set off on the dirt track with clouds of dust swirling behind us through some miles of desolate-looking gum-tree savannah. Don's warning that it was the end of the dry season should have prepared me, but it didn't. He should have said that it was like central Australia in a drought. After a few miles, we passed some dilapidated shacks — the Australian Broadcasting Commission. Further on a bulldozer had scarred a hillside for some rows of rooms opening on to verandahs — quarters for the Department of Works. But here the dirt track gave way to bitumen, though still the dreary bush was littered with rusting truck chassis, tins, bottles, old iron, abandoned engines, wheels, tyres, barbed wire and, here and there, slabs of concrete topped by tortured plumbing. Don was telling me how packed it was with men and camps during the war, how the Quanset huts we passed at Murray Barracks were now each divided into two flats for the army officers, even the commanding officer and his family having only half a hut to live in.

Then we popped over Three Mile Hill and the brilliant water and coast was the first beauty I'd seen. Past two more old buildings, then the coconut palms of Koki market, along a road squeezed between sea and hill and, with Don saying "nearly home", we turned up a steep twisting track with little houses on one side, surrounded by a few shrubs thickly covered with dust, and turned into a newly made drive before a small, perfectly square, railway-station ochre and brown house which, becoming vacant, had been hastily bought for us. We climbed a flight of wooden steps to a three-foot-wide verandah. I couldn't believe it and stood stock still, with visions of our Sydney home on the harbour at Darling Point. Inside a room fifteen foot square, newly painted three shades of curry, with a bare wooden floor, stood two easy chairs in khaki plastic, four plain wooden dining chairs and table, and a sideboard with coloured glass in front. Don said "It'll only be temporary; they are going to build us a house". He called and presented an oldish man in a rami (the length of cloth worn round the hips) and his top bare. I unpacked my knife, fork, spoon, and plate to add to Don's for lunch. It was all we had till our household effects arrived. Lunch over, Don went back to the office and I unpacked my two suitcases and took stock of things.

It had seemed so grand to be coming up as the wife of the Assistant Administrator. And now this! I felt utterly miserable and then, luckily, began to laugh. It was so ludicrous, and I laughed helplessly and felt much better. Outside, a huge rain tree in the stony ground was the only one in sight, so that was something and I was touched that Don had begun making a garden by building foot-high walls from the plentiful stone, filling them with soil. Turning inside, I worked to hide the khaki plastic with dress material I had brought up and it looked a bit better by the time Don came home.

There was so much to hear about his work and the Murrays and the men he was working with and the problems and how they were being tackled and about all that had to be done. I was fascinated and realised how much he loved it, and that here was where he really wanted to be and where he felt at home. So here I must fit myself in somehow. The set-up itself was strange, not knowing who was who or what was what. But I gradually got the hang of it, and of the actual daily work of the Administrator and his Assistant, so here is an account of what I eventually learned.

Australian Ministerial responsibility for Papua New Guinea and other dependent people had previously been an extra duty given to the holders of other portfolios. But Menzies' new Liberal government had shown its intention of accelerating Australia's commitment to their development towards ultimate self-government, by creating a new port-folio backed by a new department — that of Territories. Paul Hasluck was the first Minister, with C.R. (Eske) Lambert as the Departmen-tal Secretary. The Minister, advised by his department, formulated policy and, where appropriate, could call for advice or comment from the Administrator. The Minister was responsible to the Australian Parliament, which kept final control at budget time, when Ministerial policy had to be funded.

The Administrator was appointed by the Governor General on ad-vice from the Australian Parliament, his term being 'at the Governor General's pleasure'. He was directly responsible to the Minister for the law, order and good government of Papua New Guinea and for carrying out Ministerial policies. Under a Public Service Commissioner, the country had its own Public Service. All recruiting, however, was done by the department in Canberra. These arrangements were set out in the Papua and New Guinea Act 1949, which was effectively the country's constitution. In 1951 basic government departments ex-isted, each under its departmental head, new departments being formed as new development created new needs.

The daily work of the Administrator and his Assistant was done through and with these departments and in this respect was similar to the Australian pattern. However, in 1951, their personnel was mainly confined to headquarters in Moresby, though some worked in the three main towns. With the exception of the professional services of Health, Education, Agriculture and Forestry, their work in the field was delegated to the staff of the Department of Native Affairs, later renam-ed the Department of District Services, which needs an explanation in itself.

From the end of the 19th century, both the British-Australian and the German governments had adopted the well-tried system by which a dependent country was divided into districts, each with a 'District Commissioner' in charge at District headquarters. Under him was a hierarchy with young Patrol Officers at the bottom, doing just what their name implied. After a careful period of training in such things as Government, Law, Anthropology, they patrolled the area for which they were responsible, visiting all the villages on foot, by workboat or canoe, carrying their much thumbed 'Field Handbook' which outlined the laws and regulations of Papua New Guinea and set out their duties and the limits of their powers. Each district was divided into sub-districts headed by an A.D.O. — Assistant District Officer — living on an outstation with a small hospital, usually a school, a contingent of the Royal Papua New Guinea Constabulary, a small enclosure for a jail, and, to help run the office, some Papua New Guinean clerical staff. In 1951 most buildings were of native materials and thatch, or war-time black iron. There would be several Patrol Officers under the A.D.O., and, as the situation warranted, a P.O. could open a new patrol post, thus spreading influence and authority more widely.

It can be seen then, that District Services was the basic structure by which government was carried out amongst the people and was flexible enough to grow in complexity and in its relationship to the normal departments as various Headquarter Stations grew into towns. District Headquarters in Moresby was staffed mainly by men who had long experience in the field and there was a definite relationship between this department and the Administrator and with the District Commissioners who held certain powers delegated from the Administrator and were his representatives in their districts.

But before I grasped all this, as with other newcomers, I had to try and listen intelligently and keep up with conversation using new terms indicating a different way of life, and found myself always asking questions. In the few weeks after my arrival, I met people and tried to gauge their attitudes, what they did with their time, how they handled their servants, what they did about shopping and all the little domestic things one needs to know in a new country. On my second day, our awful house began to take on perspective, for we attended the opening of the first oil terminal and every woman I met said:

"Oh. You've got the house with the bath."

So the deep mauve bath in the bright green bathroom, which had so repelled me, I now found was unique. Everyone else merely had a shower. Moreover, some still had only bucket showers filled by hand. After all, everything in life is relative. Moreover, this bath had been flown from the U.S. to Manus Island in 1944 especially for Carol Landis, who went to entertain U.S. Marines there — bought, of course, by our predecessor at 'Disposals'. Our house was at least built of timber, for I found that many were still living in frame houses with tarred paper walls.

Through this settling-in time, I was met with much kindliness and given much advice, particularly about servants or houseboys, which tended to be confusing, some of it going against my grain while the ideas of different people were often diametrically opposed. So while I sorted it all out, I let the old man, who had been lent to us by the Murrays, go his own way.

Then I was given the best advice anyone could have. Mick Healy, the District Commissioner, and his wife Molly had both been born in Papua. Realising my confusion, he offered help.

"There are three basic things to remember," he told me. "Firstly, no one needs to work for you — all have their land in their villages and only come to town to work if it suits them. Secondly, your success with staff will depend on the personal relationship you can build up between yourself and each one as an individual. Thirdly, in his eyes, he works with you rather than for you."

This last remark was what I needed to know and I probed into what one could and could not do. He then found me a man from Rigo called Kila, who was an apt and eager pupil and soon learned to do everything in the house and cook most skilfully.

As I met people, one thing was said to me so many times that it was quite frightening. The gist of it was:

"We've been through a terrible time, nothing ever seems to get done, but now your husband has come it will be alright."

Certainly a great many men in the Public Service, then only 1150 people, had served under him during the war and thought highly of him. But I felt that his reputation had grown over the years to a kind of legend and was often quite panicky, thinking: 'no one can live up to those kind of expectations, and when he doesn't bring home the bacon, they will turn against him.'

Two months later we were still waiting for our goods and chattels to arrive. The *Bulolo* on which I was originally booked to travel, had caught fire in Sydney harbour, leaving us to wait two months for the only other ship, the *Montoro*. This also meant that the only three shops were quite literally empty and we were all on short rations, essential things like powdered milk and baby food being flown up. Sitting in an empty house with no resources didn't suit my temperament at all. I didn't like bridge and golf and only enjoyed an occasional morning tea party.

I hated being confronted at every turn by war scrap and the general litter a war leaves behind and hearing everyone saying:

"The Government should clear it up."

The attitude that the Government should do this or the Government should do that distressed me, when I knew they had so few resources and so much on their plate. Then I had an idea, so asked Don what limitations his position imposed on me. For instance, could

I do quite lowly things? He asked what I wanted to do and I said to invite all the women in the road to morning tea and suggest that we ourselves cleared up the scrap round our houses.

"Go right ahead," he said.

So I rang everybody, asking them to come and bring their own teacup, for I had an idea to talk about. They were all intrigued and Mrs. McGowan, wife of the Government Architect, offered to switch it to her house.

I proposed that we and our own house staffs should pick up the scrap round and near our houses, pile it on the roadside and then ask if the rubbish service could collect it, saying that it's so much easier to get people or government departments to do things when you say, "If I do this, will you do that?" They thought it a novel idea and after a lot of discussion and laughter, everyone agreed enthusiastically and all the next week everyone on the road vied with each other as to who could make the highest pile. The Department of Health was happy to send trucks and in no time it was gone.

By then, calling ourselves the Lawes Road Progress Association, we got ambitious and decided to clear the hillsides and waste spaces, but felt dubious about imposing further on our house staffs. Somebody wondered about the stevedores as so few boats came in and enquiries found the department was glad to give them work as long as we supplied an overseer, so we rostered ourselves in pairs. The labour office rang me when a gang was free and from the roster arranged where and under whom they were to work.

Chester Street, Ogoa Street and Davara Road didn't exist then and the whole hillside was a treeless, littered and burnt-out waste and we set to work on it. Meanwhile, we had weekly meetings in each other's houses and I found them a wonderful lot of women. It's always more fun getting to know people doing something together than just sipping tea. When the hillsides were cleared up, Mona Anthony, wife of the Director of Lands, said:

"Why don't we plant trees?"

That caused laughter at the idea of growing trees in dry old Moresby. However, Mona carried the day and got a young surveyor from her husband's department to stake the roadsides and our rosters went on, with the stevedores now digging holes. The next question was soil to fill them and Jean McCubbery wondered about the ration trucks for the police depot at Sogeri, a 2000ft plateau, 30 miles away in the foothills of the Owen Stanley Ranges. Enquiries revealed that they returned empty, but it was alright with the Transport Department to bring back soil if we rewarded the labourers with tobacco. Soon rich Sogeri soil came down every Friday. Forestry supplied trees and after the first rains in January, we had a grand tree planting, and the Director unveiled a plaque still on the crest of the hill. For the first year, everyone watered the trees outside their houses and the huge rain trees and peltophoram now shading the road are the result.

This done, the women couldn't let the ration trucks return empty again and decided that if each household got a load of soil, maybe we could start gardening. Thus, we formed the Lawes Road Garden Club and drew lots for turns to get the soil. Husbands brought back plants from more fertile parts of the country and we had a weekly exchange of cuttings and plants. The results were spectacular and Mona Anthony then began talking of having a Flower Show. By this time two years had passed, the water supply had improved and everyone had flourishing gardens. The first Flower Show was held in the Red Cross Hall in 1953 and was successful beyond our dreams. If ever there was a story of one thing leading to another, this was it, and even today when I meet any of the women involved we talk of it with pleasure. The wonderful thing about it was the way everybody in the road co-operated. The idea spread to other sections of the town and by similar co-operation and self-help, the whole place was cleaned up.

☆ ☆ ☆

The first task Don had been given, when he arrived in September, was to implement the legislation of the 1949 Act, for a partly elected Legislative Council, scheduled for opening by the Governor General in November. Looking into it, he found there were just four days to get the writs out and the legal processes complied with in time. So it was a great scramble.

Pre-war, Papua and New Guinea each had a Legislative Council chaired by its Administrator. They consisted of a small group of Government Department heads and some nominated non-official members. Then in 1949, the Papua and New Guinea Act contained two new provisions. Firstly, three of the nine non-official members were to be elected, representing three regions, which were the electorates of Papua, New Guinea Mainland and New Guinea Islands and for which all Europeans had to enrol. Secondly, the Papua New Guineans were to be represented by a member appointed by the Administrator from each of the same three regions. Then, only four elected Local Government Councils had been set up; Hanuabada Village, Baluan Village in Manus, and Livuan and Vunamami Councils near Rabaul. As so few had experienced voting, the first priority was to introduce the idea of having their own representatives.

Planning the celebrations connected with the opening led to an amusing clash Don had with prejudice. There was to be a Parliamentary dinner at the Papua Hotel. Two days before, the manager rang saying he was awfully sorry, but if natives were there, they couldn't put it on.

Rachel leaving the butchers shop in Moresby 1952. An old army freezer barge.

Evan standing at the corner of Musgrave and Douglas Street,
Port Moresby 1951.

"Why?" said Don.

"Because the staff have refused to serve them."

Don said, "You'd better come and see me".

In the meantime, he rang Eddie Frame, general manager of Burns Philp, which owned the hotel, told him what happened, what he proposed to do, asked for his backing, and got it. The manager then arrived. Fortunately he was ex-Navy. So with his best Brigadier manner, Don said:

"There will be a Papuan and two New Guinean members of Council at the dinner. You have undertaken to hold it and it will go on. If your staff won't serve, that is no problem to us as we will just take over and run it with staff from our hostels".

The manager gasped and said, "Yes, Sir". He almost saluted.

And that was that. We did chuckle about it. Anyway, the dinner was a great success and so were the local members.

In Sydney we had heard that Colonel Murray was called 'Kanaka Jack' because he entertained 'natives', as everyone then spoke of the local population. But he had broken the ice, so we found no problem, especially after the dinner episode. Local people were invited to the 'dos' we had and over the years came freely to the house of their own accord and, as far as I know, it was accepted quite happily by expatriates. When we noticed that local people tended to stay together in a group and there wasn't very much mixing, it seemed to us that it was shyness on both sides as well as a language problem, so I would ring up one or two Australian guests and ask them to look after one or another Papua New Guinean. Matching interests if possible, we would introduce the two and leave them to it. We found this worked very well and was an easy and unobtrusive way of helping the mixing process.

By this time I was settling in better, but missed my family terribly and often felt in despair of ever liking the funny little town that Moresby then was. The dry season went on and on, and we worked very hard trying to make a garden. The £4,000,000 Australian grant had been cut to £3,750,000 and out went a new house for us; all very discouraging.

Don had never been an easy person to live with, for I was always trying to fit in. With a man of such strong character I could never get anywhere in an argument or any kind of tussle. It was no use trying persuasion or to 'influence' him, for his strength made him quite impervious. However, we had an extraordinary empathy of mind and the way we thought about things. Eventually I learnt that in any difference between us, it was better to think my way through whatever it was and let him know that I had something to discuss when he was free. Sometimes days would go by before he would say:

"Well now, what is it?"

If I then 'put up a case', he would listen attentively, probably ask me some questions and then chew it over while I would giggle inwardly, feeling like an advocate in court. If my 'case' was good enough, he might accept it either in whole or in part; but if not, well, that was that. If such a performance does sound rather priceless, it was the only way I had a chance.

We also had a big temperamental gap to bridge. Don found my enthusiasm and effervescence trying at times and would be irritated, while in those first few months his taciturnity and moodiness, when he became withdrawn, left me feeling very lonely and yearning for the liveliness of the boys and their young friends. Thus I felt more and more the need to find my own identification with the country.

None of the other wives seemed involved with the local village people but I felt sure that interesting things were happening and wanted to discover them. Then I met two outstanding women. Thelma Price, wife of the Government Pathologist, was the Girl Guide Commissioner, whom I met through Margery (now Lady) Beale, then staying with us; and Barbara McLachlan of the Education Department was in charge of the education of women and girls. Barbara had started Village Women's Clubs, where the women learnt to run their clubs and elect their own office-bearers. Devoted young women in her section, with Papuan girls in training as assistants, helped them to work out programmes and taught them whatever modern skills they wanted to learn.

Barbara took me for my first village visit, just before Christmas. Our landrover bumped over a terrible track through hills and bays, past the police barracks in an old army camp, and came to Vabakori in a coconut grove behind a sandy beach, where the people returning after the war had rebuilt their houses in traditional style with one huge room on stilts, but of old army black iron. They weren't exactly pretty.

We arrived to great rushing about as they formed a line from the car to the house steps, where the office-bearers placed sweet-smelling frangipani leis over our heads as we shook hands with club members in their white church dresses and with flowers in their hair. Then the tricky business of climbing the wide sapling ladder to the house verandah, to find the inside spotless, as are all village houses I've ever been in; the floor polished with coconut husk and the black iron walls decorated with coconut palm leaves and flowers.

Two chairs were set for us and mats for the club members. It was their Christmas party and I was enchanted. They gravely held a brief meeting with welcoming speeches and, putting grass skirts over their dresses, danced and sang, while others prepared and served morning tea of scones and cakes they'd learned to make in camp ovens on open fires. Afterwards everyone joined in the dancing. Little boys played small guitars and danced in the corners, burlesquing their elders, who tried to shush them out. When they saw we enjoyed the children —

for, though naughty, they really were very funny — they gave up and soon everyone lost self-consciousness and joined in the fun. It was so spontaneously natural and infectious that I found a wonderful sense of peace and ease.

The women were all ages, shapes and sizes but all showed equal zest. In fact the older the women, the better and more abandoned was their dancing. For me, this first village visit remains significant, for driving home round the now familiar Koki road, quite suddenly, as I saw the curve of Ela beach backed by its palms and casuarina trees and the little town beyond, it seemed beautiful. I had other days of homesickness and low spirits, but that day was the turning point and I began to find in the country and among its people something of what Don had found during the war.

☆ ☆ ☆

It was decided to add on to our tiny three-roomed house, and plans for extending the living room and adding a patio were completed by the end of the year and work began in January, 1952. During the building there were various traumas, especially after Don had gone to Rabaul and Evan, who had come up for the Christmas holidays, was away on a patrol in the Goilala, a district in the Owen Stanley mountains behind Moresby. So I was alone when they took the roof off to prepare for the extension and wakened in the night wondering whatever had happened. The 'dry' had ended with a cloudburst, the living room was awash and the ceiling fell in. The next day they put up a tarpaulin. I had got used to walking across the floor joists to get in and out of the house, but I had no experience of what rain did to the Moresby ground. So when the phone rang and I was in the garden, I did not realise that my shoes were coated with fine and very slippery clay. Stepping across the joists was a different matter — and down I went, breaking a rib. That night I woke up again to a terrible noise.

A 'Guba' — a violent wind and rain storm — had hit us, and I lay awake shuddering as the wind lifted the tarpaulin and smashed it down on the roof, spilling its collected water through the ceiling. Whatever kind of country was this?

Day dawned on my birthday, but no word of greeting from any of my family had reached me, so my spirits were at an all time low. At the end of the day I went up Tuaguba Hill for my evening walk and looked down on our house on its desolate, treeless, rock-strewn, dusty hillside, in utter despair and revolt. How could I ever endure it? Fortunately you can get so far down that there is only one other way to go, and that is, up. Don and Evan came back, the house was eventually finished, I made curtains, we put the carpets down, furniture from our Sydney house arrived, chairs were covered, pictures hung, other furniture locally made and installed and the result was a room that was large, cool and beautiful.

We had designed and planted a garden and with the rain, the growth was fabulous. It was all finished by March 1952, when Robert came up for his 21st birthday. We'd collected all the young folk we could find for a party and were all very happy together before the boys returned to Sydney, Robert to the university and Evan to begin as a jackaroo. At last I was beginning to feel settled and having had our sons home for the holidays helped a lot.

Don's visit to Rabaul, while I was coping with house alterations, had interesting consequences. It had once been a lovely tropical town, soundly built by the Germans, but then had twice been destroyed in seven years. In 1937, Vulcan, the volcano on the edge of the harbour, blew up causing appalling devastation and over 200 deaths. Then, of course, it was the first town to be bombed and taken by the Japanese in 1942 and suffered frightfully when our own planes, in their turn, bombed the Japanese. As Matupit, another volcano, had erupted during the war, there was a feeling that the town should be rebuilt somewhere else. About 1948, a report had been made by Mr. Holmes, the Secretary for Lands, and Alan Roberts, the Director of Native Affairs. This recommended rebuilding the town at Kokopo, about 10 miles down Simpson Harbour. That part of the bay was very exposed, so an artificial harbour would have had to be built, costing several millions.

But in 1952, six years after the war, nobody had made a decision on it. The people were restless and unhappy, still living in makeshift paper houses and even earth-floored shacks. Some had got tired of waiting and were building permanent houses and business premises and it was reported in Moresby that public opinion was changing.

While in Rabaul, Don received the following instruction from the Administrator:

"Feel sure Territories will desire your views regarding proposal concerning Rabaul township. You are aware of contents of Holmes-Roberts report. Would like you assess usefulness and alleged unanimity of local opinion which is said to favour retention and development present township and report. See Minutes Rabaul Advisory Town Council 7th December. Have informed Territories. Your visit would be appreciated by them."

In the next nine days he invited discussion on the question of moving Rabaul to Kokopo, from all sections and all races — Australian, Chinese and Tolai — and found a general attitude of "Even if the Government moves to Kokopo, we'll stay here". He did a thorough reconnaisance of Rabaul, of the possible escape routes, of safer residential areas nearby and of Kokopo as an alternative. He also closely studied vulcanological reports, especially that of Dr. Stehn, a leading vulcanologist, on setting up an observatory. He therefore wrote a report recommending that Rabaul be retained as a town, providing an observatory was built which, he was assured, could give from three days' to three months' warning of an eruption, that escape routes and facilities should be developed and maintained and an escape plan be kept always in readiness.

The result was interesting. He submitted it to Col. Murray early in February, who minuted that he could not accept any of its recommendations and would send it to Canberra with his advice against it. However, Murray first placed it before the Territory's Executive Council, which unanimously supported him. Afterwards a number of them said to Don:

"Sorry I didn't support you, old chap, but I wasn't going to stick my neck out," But when Cabinet considered it, they decided in favour of Don's view and plans were made immediately to rebuild Rabaul.

An argument was also still going on about Lae, as to whether it should be on the old site on the limited waterfront area or up on a low escarpment which, though heavily covered in jungle, had an unlimited hinterland. Most of the old residents and firms were fighting for the old one as they owned land there. When I first saw all these towns early in 1952, I must say I was pretty appalled as they were even worse than Moresby. They had been totally destroyed as towns and the mess of war was everywhere. We kept hearing stories of the scandals associated with the war scrap disposal sales and of the fortunes made. It seemed all wrong that either the money or the materials couldn't have been used to rebuild towns.

But in 1952, the District Commissioner for Lae was still living in a make-shift house with paper and woven bamboo walls, though some of his staff was moving into the newly built 'Bulolo' houses, very good, simple timber pre-fabs developed by the Bulolo Timber Company. The District Office and the hospital were incredible rabbit warrens of army black iron and Quanset huts. However, Don precipitated the decision to build Lae on the escarpment and it, too, then went ahead.

Chapter 2

Ivan Champion, Don and Rachel Cleland visiting Misima Island after the cyclone

Lost Opportunities—First Visit to Government House—Col and Mrs Murray—Public Service—Department of Education—Misima Cyclone

Konedobu, meaning deep or wide beach, is what the Motu people called the area from the edge of Moresby harbour up into the hills, on twin spurs of which Government House stands. The view is dramatic. About two miles away to the south and east are Tuaguba and Paga Hills, the town and port squeezing in between them, brimming with the liveliness always around wharves and shipping. Beyond is the open sea and the islands marking the entrance to the harbour. Grassy hills on the far side stretch away west where Tatana Island guards the huge deepwater inner Fairfax harbour, backed by a jumble of quite high hills, pale in the dry season and a wonderful purple in the wet.

A mile to the west the lines of houses in Hanuabada Village creep ever further into the sea as the Iduhu or Clans increase in numbers. It is always interesting and picturesque. On the northern side beyond Hanuabada, the range, on which Government House stands, drops the pinky-red cliffs of its headlands straight into the harbour, leaving little bays backed by pleasant valleys between them. Part of all this beauty is the changing colour of the sea. In the dry season the hills, pale brown, rise from water that is a brilliant turquoise, and the shallows of the reefs streak it with gleaming blue-greens. In the wet, the sea is softer and the hills — either vivid green or tree covered to the west are deep with changing blues and purples emphasised by great banks of clouds.

Below the house is a valley, where the original barracks of the Royal Papuan Constabulary had once stood, and where the American Army had built offices when Government House above had been General MacArthur's Headquarters. During the war Don had lived in the pre-war Government Secretary's house in the valley, used as Angau Mess with bush material offices put up behind it.

When MacArthur moved on to Hollandia — now Jayapura — Don took over not only Government House, as Angau mess, but the American army offices, as Angau headquarters. At war's end they continued to be used by the returning Civil Administration. As money could be spared, new extensions were built here and there until the whole valley, later extending across the bottom of Government House grounds, became covered with temporary buildings. This then was Konedobu, the unlovely seat of Government for Papua and New Guinea during its exciting and formative post-war and pre-independence years. No doubt much time was wasted there. But it was also the seat of great endeavour; of enthusiasm and heartbreak; of hope and frustration. It was where Don worked for nearly eighteen years in war and peace.

Returning in 1951 Don could see from his office the port, becoming crowded and inadequate, and then glance to the west and remember the huge naval repair depot built by the Americans on Tatana, the offshore island separating Moresby and Fairfax harbours. The sight shocked and distressed him, for neither his plan for the smooth handover from military to civil administration, nor the survey indicating which army installations could usefully be taken over by the civil administration, had been used, resulting in a heartbreaking waste of resources. Now he daily looked at one of the worst. Moresby is a bad anchorage, with reefs to negotiate coming in, water not deep enough for large ships nor protected from the strong north-west winds of the wet season; and, with hills rising straight from the sea, there is absolutely no room for the necessary cargo sheds and installations of a port.

On the other hand the deep Fairfax Harbour is without reefs and the steep drop on the western side of Tatana meant that the largest ships had safely come alongside the substantial American wharf. Moreover, the range of hills rising steeply from Moresby Harbour veer north, leaving a coastal plain behind Fairfax, with ample room for installations and industrial development. A five-kilometre army road through a gap in the range had connected the American depot with the Waigani and June valleys, where a hundred thousand men had been camped, and which was the obvious place for urban development. Instead the opportunity had been lost. The wharves had gone and roads were overgrown. The new urban area was being developed in the Boroko Valley, condemned by the army because the water table was too high for latrines and it was swampy in the wet season. However, there it was; he felt a sort of wry despair as the first batch of pre-fabricated aluminium houses had arrived from Hawksleys in England and were being erected. The dry season made the septic tanks installed for each house no particular problem, but when the wet season came, the people living there had a dreadful time. Hastily they had to devise an extensive system draining water into the Loloki River, 15 miles away, and substitute sewerage for septic tanks.

The irony is that now, with self-government, the new city centre has been planned and is fast growing up in the Waigani Valley, with forty thousand people already living there and high-rise buildings springing up. But the industrial area was already at the Boroko end of the valley, with the twelve-kilometre road making its tortuous way round and over the range of coastal hills to the wharves in Moresby Harbour, where necessary port installations had meant filling it in. Pleasant houses built on the hills now look down on acres of yellow containers marching in orderly rows on the reclaimed land which has replaced their view of the coastline and yacht anchorage.

Of the other areas which distressed him, the most glaring and expensive to rectify was Milne Bay. The pre-war centre of administration and commerce had been the tiny 50-acre island of Samarai, lying in deep water in the China Straits off the mountainous tip of the mainland. On instructions for a scorched earth policy in 1942, it was destroyed when the administration left — houses, shops and stores — everything was burnt, so there was nothing there to go back to. The huge indentation of Milne Bay is a few miles north and the fighting took place on the level north-western end. Here the U.S. Army had built an airstrip, wharves and storage sheds and, on a plateau a few miles to the east, a 1,500-bed hospital. The strip is not very large but is still the only possible place for a plane to land in a hundred square miles of mountains, sea and islands.

On our visit Don walked me up the mountain behind the plateau, where all you could see were blackened stumps and squares of cement from the hospital. Mystified, I trudged on till we came upon a truly enormous water tank holding thousands of gallons.

"I just wanted to see if it was still there," he muttered, kicking at a rusting pipeline. "Wasted, all wasted, the bloody fools."

In Don's plans he had proposed that, as Samarai was destroyed, was so small and without an airstrip, it should not be rebuilt. Instead, Australia should take over the going concern of the hospital and all the wharves and installations in Milne Bay, to be the nucleus of the new District Headquarters. Apparently under American Army rules a Commanding Officer must either get a signature from the returning power or destroy the installation. The story that drifted back to Australia told of the American doctor who had worked among village people in the bay, as well as with servicemen, pleading with the new Administrator to sign his document and let him leave the hospital for them, but lacking the authority, Murray felt he could not and the American doctor wept as he ordered its destruction.

It is certainly true that the big companies Burns Philp, Steamships and Buntings made such a fuss at the suggestion of a town in Milne Bay and were so set in rebuilding Samarai that they won the day. No one visualised the post-war growth, thinking that the sleepy even tenor of its pre-war days would go on for ever.

Samarai was already becoming overcrowded in 1951 and only had access by seaplane or boat. Using the strip in Milne Bay meant a four-hour launch trip to Samarai in fine weather and longer in bad, which was often. Returning from Samarai to Moresby was worse; you could battle back again and return next day, even perhaps once more the day after. With the country depending more and more on air transport and less on ships, it was an impossible situation, and it became increasingly obvious that Samarai was doomed.

Stories of scandals about war disposals of all sorts had been drifting back to Australia and we heard plenty more as we settled into Papua New Guinea life. Problems were inevitable, of course, but both the Australian Government and the PNG Administration should have got far more benefit than they did. Shady practice was rife, individuals made fortunes, and I often recalled Don's exclamation when he read that he'd missed out to Murray in 1945 — "He'll be no match for those wily old Bs in PNG. They'll run rings round him." It indeed had been the case.

'Ifs' are profitless words. But over this I can't help thinking them. Had Don accepted the offer to remain in New Guinea as the first Administrator, with the chance of putting his plans into action and carry out his vision, many of Moresby's present problems would not exist and development in many areas would have been further ahead. On the other hand, he had a wide experience of the whole of Australian political life, had been closely in touch with the leading parliamentary figures of the day, Labor as well as Liberal, knew many departmental personalities, and his knowledge of the 'corridors of power' in Canberra was an asset.

By this time a pattern was forming in our joint lives. People entertained in small pleasant dinners often with interesting visitors, where the talk was lively and stimulating. There were a certain number of official do's to attend, often given by the Murrays. Their house, rather grandly known as Government House but given great respect by the population, was built by Sir Hubert Murray in 1913 at the top of a small hill above Konedobu, then only accessible from the town by boat. On another knoll of the same hill was an earlier Government House used by the Official Secretary, then Des Sullivan, a colourful war-time bomber ace. In front of the old house is the flagpole where Robinson, when acting Lieutenant Governor, had shot himself after much criticism of the way he handled the massacre of the missionaries, James Chalmers and Oliver Thomkins, when they were also cooked and eaten at Goaribari Island in 1901.

Government House was constructed by a builder from Queensland — a typical north Queensland station homestead, with a central living room, bedrooms opening from it by french doors, and with other french doors from them onto a wide verandah, which completely encircled the house. The verandah was then enclosed by the old push-up shutters but now fitted with blue crinkle glass louvres, so you couldn't see out, and it too was painted ochre inside and out. The drive up the valley between the two knolls of the hill had originally gone to the back of the house but during the war Don had a branch bulldozed along the flank of the hill to a point below the front door, but it was still a rough track and crotalaria trees had grown along its lower side obscuring the view, while between the drive and the house, the Murrays had made a terrace edged by a high and colourful croton hedge.

On this terrace I attended my first party at Government House. It was a still, hot night, the mosquitoes were bad and I thought I would die with the damp and breathless heat, but a few days later at a dinner party for the Governor of then Dutch New Guinea and his wife, the house was even hotter inside. I looked about with interest. For most of Sir Hubert Murray's long reign of 34 years as Lieutenant Governor from 1906 to 1940, it had been a bachelor establishment. Sir Hubert had been an austere man, rather oblivious to his surroundings other than the contents of his bookcases. The original furniture was still there, including the same much painted and rather chipped glass-fronted bookcases, but without the books. The J.K. Murrays had introduced a beautiful natural hand-made Indian carpet, but heavy Tudor side tables, Parker Knoll chairs covered in beige and brown tapestry, screens of beige headcloth in front of the french doors leading to the bedrooms, made it terribly cluttered. It seemed shut in, breathlessly hot with no cool colour to rest the eye and no view from the house.

Mrs Murray was not an easy person and she and I approached each other amiably, but warily. She was a handsome woman but much troubled with rheumatism and walked with a stick. She had the reputation of being brainy and, probing her interests one day expecting to find a common taste in books, to my surprise she said she spent a lot of her time cooking. When my turn came I found this was only too necessary but I set about training my staff to cook so that the whole burden didn't fall on me as it obviously had with Mrs Murray.

Don's work, with the novelty of his problems and the sheer fascination of the country, caught my interest more and more. He was finding a happy working relationship with Col. Murray, a dedicated and conscientious man of high intelligence and integrity — all qualities Don much admired. Murray adored his wife, who was the stronger character. They had no children. Don's chief problem in their working relationship was Murray's reluctance to make decisions and a tendency to refer the tough ones to committees, which proliferated at headquarters, while men half-way down the line chafed that holdups prevented them from getting on with the job. Even decisions made one day, Murray would want to reconsider the next; however, Don became adept at acting immediately before this could happen. Also, with Don there to discuss matters, he became less dependent on committees.

In a scientific and academic training, a man studies all aspects of a problem and considers all the data before coming to a decision. But he is not necessarily experienced in the techniques for putting decisions into action or the know-how of the processes of administration. Colonel Murray had to cope with colossal tasks with a structure under him also lacking in administrative skills.

His office was the small original one close to the house with a wartime conference room beside it. It was obviously inadequate and Don felt cut off from the rest of the administration housed in the valley below. His worries at this time were compounded by the lack of training in administrative procedures and the general process of government by the public servants.

The outside men, that is the patrol officers, and personnel of 'District Services' were pretty good — in fact very good indeed in patrol work, opening up new country and running very capably the patrol posts and small government stations. Much, of necessity, was left to their own initiative, which they used fully and effectively. For them, mercifully, there was a minimum of paperwork at that time. Many of these men had been trained in the pre-war days and were still inspired by the ideals and influence of Sir Hubert Murray. In addition they all did a two year course at the Australian School of Pacific Administration, known as ASOPA and housed at Mosman, N.S.W. Its first Principal had been J.K. Murray when it opened at Duntroon in Canberra during the war, then John Kerr (of Governor General fame), later R.R. Conlon, followed by C.W. Rowley, who remained for many years. Many notable men and women with most modern and forward-looking ideas have been on its staff, so the 'outside men' had excellent training.

But the staff at headquarters were much as Sir John Gunther has described them in an article for 'Overland' No. 65, 1976:

"In the provisional administration's public service, we were a pretty mixed lot. There were the 'befores' from the Papua or New Guinea services; some had served with the Australian New Guinea Administrative Unit (ANGAU); some were recruited from Australia; and two kinds of persons from the armed services — those seeking a career and those who were promised accelerated release from the army if they volunteered to spend a year in Papua New Guinea. There were three separate public service associations: the Papuan, the New Guinean, and the Provisional administration. There were disagreements, misunderstandings and even dislikes between the two pre-war services, and yet a somewhat petulant ganging-up by the 'befores' as a whole against the newcomers. The public service was an ineffecient service from its beginnings. We were like untrained troops, with insufficient skills, suddenly thrown into battle ill-equipped and with poor logistic support, and its structure was ill designed."

These men had come in haphazardly and, being on the whole good blokes, did their best. They worked very hard, but being untrained, the whole set-up was inefficient, not only not giving good enough backing to the 'outside men' but slow to carry out instructions and give effect to policy.

The small pre-war scale meant that separate departments for many aspects of government just did not exist and had to be built up from scratch, which needed first class and really well-trained departmental heads, but in no case was this done. Several men with natural flair did remarkably well; notably Dr John Gunther of Health. He was a colourful man with tropical experience working for Lever Bros. in the British Solomons before earning a fine war record as a doctor in the Air Force. He had vision, immense drive and, what appeals to me, a good practical eye for the possible, thus making incredibly good use of the resources available, both human and material. He was also good at formulating his plans and putting up a properly constructed case for money. Therefore he got more than any other department.

The direct opposite to this was the Department of Education, which was indeed tragic. Before the war there was no such department in either Papua or New Guinea. Rabaul had small government schools at Nordup and Malaguna, all other education being conducted by the missions, in local languages and pidgin and directed to reading the Bible and training evangelists. In Papua the government gave a small subsidy to the missions. But they, being English and Australian, had a far more liberal view of education and, while early primary schooling was in local language or Motu, English was also taught. At war's end the obvious thing was to get a schools policy going quickly with a really good education administrator, experienced in practical teaching and teachers' needs, as director. But being an idealistic time they appointed W.C. Groves, a delightful anthropologist who had worked in New Ireland. But he had no administrative experience for setting up a school system or a formal education department and the administration set-up needed to support them.

As Don began to get a grip on things, the poor performance of the Department of Education began to worry him very much indeed. Shortly after my arrival we visited Sogeri, a boarding school opened during the war by Frank Boisen. Later he was District Education Officer at Rabaul and greeted Don as an old friend on a visit there, telling me with a sly chuckle and possibly some exaggeration how, during 1943 he, a Captain in the Army, had been sent for by 'The Brig.' of Angau, when the following took place:

Don — "Boisen, I believe you're a teacher."

Boisen — "Yessir."

Don — "The medics are moving out of the hospital at the end of the Kokoda trail at Sogeri. I want you to take it over, find the best educated natives in the army headquarters set-up, give them some more education and make them into clerks."

Boisen — "But I didn't join the army to teach, sir."

Don — "But you do have to obey your senior officers?"

Boisen — "Yessir."

Don — "Well, get cracking."

And get cracking he did, finding other teachers and setting up a first class school. As education officer for New Britain, he established a sound and extensive school system, remaining there till he retired, when the Boisen High School at Rabaul was named after him.

In 1951 Sogeri School was teaching grades 5, 6 and 7 — primary schools then teaching only grades 1 to 4. I was amazed to find that the pupils were grown men, anything from 17 to 25 years old. This of course was because all education had ceased during the war and the primary school children of 1941 had a five-year gap. At the end of grade 7 these men were given three months of teacher-training and sent off round the country to start schools. They did a fantastic job and it is on their work that the whole school system was founded. Now a Senior High School, Sogeri is still the most prestigious in the country and still a boarding school.

In 1951 the only government schools in Moresby were a small primary school for expatriate children at Ela Beach and another small one for Papuans in some rusting Quonset huts at Kila Kila. In addition there was a large L.M.S. and a small Catholic mission school at Hanuabada, a Catholic expatriate primary school in town, a Catholic primary school at Koki and a Catholic boarding school for mixed race children at Bomana. L.M.S. pastors also ran schools to about grade 2 or 3 in the nearby villages.

For this to be the situation of formal education in 1951 and 1952, six years after civil administration returned, was appalling. But the offices of the Department of Education in Konedobu were a hive of activity and enthusiasm. Bill Groves was interested in adults and in change in the villages, so most of his energy went in social development activities. All excellent, good and necessary in themselves, but not at the expense of formal education. After all, everything for the development of a country rests on that. Trained educationists on his staff were thoroughly frustrated but there was an excellent broadcasting section, run by an able and delightful man called Cochrane, which used about a quarter of the ABC broadcasting time. A publications department published a magazine called 'The Villager', a craft section, designed not for work in schools but in the villages, while village women's clubs (which I have already described), came under 'education of women and girls'.

When there is a close rapport between husband and wife I suppose most wives find what I did — that is, you hear far more about problems and trouble areas than successes and therefore must make conscious efforts to keep the whole in perspective. But for the rest of the fifties, I seemed to hear more about his problems of getting Bill Groves to make a proper, forward-looking education plan, with proposals for proper education budgets, than about any other single problem. Groves was a great hand-wringer, was jealous of Gunther's Health Department and blamed everyone but himself.

Don's worry was compounded when Hasluck also became concerned with the slow development of education and began peppering him with exasperated minutes. Who could blame him? But the problems of the department went on for almost a decade and through the years a strange misconception began to form, which grew into a myth.

The myth is that Hasluck impeded Bill Groves' work and held back the development of education with his policy of gradualism. Nothing could be further from the truth. There was no policy of gradualism. There was a policy of aiming for universal primary education so that as many as possible could at least be literate, making communication easier and giving a broad base from which candidates for higher education could be drawn. Hasluck rightly thought that an elite should emerge on their own merits and that every part of the country should have the right to participate in this emergence. That this policy has been successful, even with such a slow start, would be revealed by an examination of the geographical background of the university graduates and the top people in government in the 1970's.

From the early fifties children with some chance of coping with secondary education were sent to Australia. About seventy percent were able to get their intermediate certificate, but of these only about thirty percent could pass the full secondary education and a very few managed to go on to Australian universities. The critics don't seem to grasp that in 1946 there was no government education system from pre-war to build on. As soon as enough students had adequate sixth grade passes, secondary schools were opened, and by the sixties there were more than in Western Australia when I grew up. In addition to Teachers' Training Colleges, the Education Department had Technical and other tertiary training schools in many towns. The Health Department had its Nursing, Medical Assistant and other paramedical colleges and schools, as did Agriculture and Forestry. So it seems to me that in spite of everything the achievements were not too bad. And if the impression got about that 'gradualism' was indeed the policy, it was Groves' administrative inability that caused the impression and not Hasluck's policies, a restriction of money, or his lack of drive.

After Groves was finally retired in 1958, it was found that his assistant G.T. Roscoe, who succeeded him, had a plan all ready. Moreover he had been urging it on Groves for years. It was immediately funded and put into effect and a proper educational system very soon became a reality. Had an educationist, not an anthropologist, been appointed in 1946 to establish the Department of Education, this could have happened ten years earlier. On the other hand, Bill Groves did bring a very enlightened attitude to the social development of the villages and has left his mark in that way. Mrs Groves, too, was a leader among expatriate wives and pioneered the C.W.A., which played a notable part in the community.

In the six months since Don's arrival in September, Col. Murray and he had worked very happily and in harmony together, the one complementing the other. But Don had become increasingly concerned at the worsening of the tone in the letters and minutes passed from Hasluck to Murray and would come home really indignant on Murray's behalf.

At the end of March Col. and Mrs Murray went on leave and Don became Acting Administrator. We enjoyed being able to do the necessary entertaining in the enlarged house, in addition to doing the honours with a garden party for the Navy. I particularly remember Professor Spate, a keen-minded man with a quirky sense of humour, who was up on some sort of economic survey. Then an Air Force plane, instead of landing at Bena in the Eastern Highlands, accidentally came down on the disused Finentegu wartime airstrip amongst 6ft high kunai grass, and needless to say the crew had to be rescued. Since we expected their possibly unofficial passenger, Sir Wilfred Kent Hughes, Minister for Air, to be our dinner guest that night, the party was hastily postponed. The next night his adventure lost nothing in the telling and he took our ragging in wonderfully good part.

In April 1952, Hasluck came up for a visit and Don accompanied him on a tour of the Sepik and Madang districts. I met them at the airport on their return and Paul gave me a most cheerful greeting:

"Oh, Rachel, you should have been with us. We've had an awful time. Everywhere we went the women wanted to know where you were and why didn't we bring you. There's no doubt you'll have to go with Don when he travels."

I always felt that it was very lucky that the Minister did have this experience, for from thenceforth I always accompanied Don. Quite apart from my own enjoyment of many wonderful experiences, my presence certainly did bring the women and children of all races much more into the picture. The Administrator could hear of their problems through me in a way he never could have heard directly, and in consequence quite a lot of good came of it.

☆　☆　☆

Shortly after his return from the Sepik visit with Hasluck, a cyclone hit the islands of the Milne Bay District. Papua New Guinea is normally too far north for the cyclone belt in the Pacific. Though we got very rough weather from them when they hit Queensland, no one could remember having had a cyclone itself — not even in the oral traditions of the people. The government station on Misima Island was totally devastated, as were villages on other islands in its path, so it was decided that Don and the Assistant Director of Native Affairs, Ivan Champion, should go down, and I was taken along. It was my first visit from Moresby. We flew in an old Catalina and came down in Deboyne Lagoon near a coconut-palm-covered island named Nivani. A small launch shot out from the island and for the first of many times I manoeuvred myself out of the Catalina bubble into a bobbing boat (a feat I defy anyone to do gracefully) and sat aft in the cabin. The others remained on the roof. Presently a small, neat man, with quick birdlike movements, came down, gave me a panicky look, buried his head behind the engine and we shot off. As there was no one else there I took the tiller and headed for a waiting trawler.

"Is the trawler right," I asked, "or do we go to the island?"

He looked up, startled.

"The trawler. But can you round up?"

"Yes," I replied. "There was nobody here so I took it."

"The boy is on top, ready to steer with his toe," he said.

They were both most disconcerted. However, I rounded up alright and we clambered aboard, while Ivan Champion waited to thank old George Munt, a colourful recluse from way back, who lived on Nivani with his Papuan wife. Ivan came aboard chuckling.

"My, you gave him a shock. He wasn't expecting a VIP woman from Moresby and he was terrified. But you've really amazed him that you could handle a boat."

Anyway, the story has been told back to me from many places in the Milne Bay area ever since. On board Ivan told us more about him and that he had a son Albie serving in Malaya with the Australian Forces.

George Munt was my first introduction to that fascinating group of people, women as well as men, who had remained behind from the successive gold rushes that began in the eighties of the last century in Sudest Island at the end of the Calvados Chain, which stretched east from the lagoon we were leaving. Such gold rushes were to happen in many parts of Papua and New Guinea over the next thirty years; the last at Edie Creek, above Wau, high in the mountains behind Lae, was in the twenties.

On subsequent trips I got to know Albie, a good-looking young man who traded in the islands, with the Scots wife he brought back from Malaya. Recently, twenty-five years later, I sailed in a private yacht from Kieta on Bougainville to Moresby. When we called in to Misima, Albie and his second wife, from New Zealand, gave us a wonderful day and drove us up to the old gold workings there. Later, over-nighting off Nivani, we went ashore, but old George was dead and the plantation was owned by Dusty Miller, another character born on Samarai in the gold rush days. Next day, sheltering from a terrible storm behind an island called Tube Tube, we went ashore to a small village and most unexpectedly met Albie's mother, Mrs Munt, a woman of character who had chosen, when widowed, to go back and live in her old village.

But to return to Misima in 1952. The movement of the cyclone was weird. It took a narrow path, whose edges were as though cut by a knife. One side was as usual, while on the other trees were stark and stripped of leaves, coconuts like telephone poles, the ground stripped of grass. Small buildings on the government station and whole villages were blown clean away. Sheets of iron were folded round coconut trunks like iron flags, the radio mast was bent like a hairpin and a water tank on the second storey of the A.D.O. residence was blown through the house and landed 100 yards away. The cement lower storey of this house stood firm and here all the people on the station made their way through the screaming darkness. The A.D.O. lit a fire in the middle of the living room floor to give them warmth and dry out their clothes and here they all huddled through the night.

Don listened to all the stories and took stock of what they needed for rehabilitation. Our trawler had come loaded with fresh supplies and then we set out to visit all the devastated islands to make the necessary distribution. The people were still in a state of shock and it was incredible that there had only been one fatality. Again Don and Ivan talked to them all and listened and comforted them and, with the officers travelling with us, worked out ways to help them.

It took hours and days to go from island to island and we could only spend such a short time in each that I could not help wondering how effective it was. But at a New Year's Day party in 1978 I was talking to Jacob Lemeki, a Misima man and Member of Parliament for the area. He had just returned from a visit to his electorate and I was amazed when he said:

"The people always ask after you, and they still talk of the time you and Sir Donald came to see them after the cyclone".

Chapter 3

Don and Rachel working with the Garden Boys on Sunday morning.

Retirement of Col Murray—Move to Government House—House Staff and their Stories

One Saturday after our return, we had spent the day painting bamboo blinds; Don was hanging the last one and I was looking round with pleased and rather smug satisfaction when the seven o'clock news came on. Suddenly an announcement that Col. Murray was retiring as Administrator of Papua and New Guinea hit my ears and I cried out:

"Don, did you hear that?"

"Yes."

"Did you know about it?"

"Yes, a letter came from Paul this afternoon."

I looked around the room in a panic and asked if it would affect us, to which he said, "Yes". Thinking of that terrible old house on the hill, I asked if it would mean leaving this and when he said, "I'm afraid so," I felt like crying. While he had expected that in a couple of years Don would probably succeed Murray when he would be sixty-five, his early retirement was indeed a shock. Only some years later Don told me that Paul had informed him of the Government's intention while they were in Madang in April.

The announcement was very confusing to the public. Although Murray had his critics, he was so gentle and sincere and so upright in character that he was also held in great affection. Don had been warmly welcomed, not as a rival but as a man who could support him and supply the qualities he lacked. At that time there was certainly no rivalry and no pro-Murray or pro-Cleland camps. Although I contemplated the immediate future with some misgiving, and although we knew that the period of the Murrays' return would need tact and understanding to overcome the embarrassment of the situation, the difficulties which arose were considerable and needed all the composure and social diplomacy we both possessed.

A complication arose on the 9th of June, when everyone was going out to meet them. In those days and throughout our term, coming to New Guinea meant an overnight flight and 6 a.m. arrival. The week before, another torrential downpour of eleven inches in twenty-six hours, causing widespread flooding and damage to roads, scoured our beautiful new gravel drive with a foot-deep chasm. So Don and I spent all Saturday trying to repair the damage. He worked with mattock, hoe and rake pulling washed-out gravel back into place, exposing the back of his head and neck to the full glare of the sky all day.

He woke in the morning his usual self and had first go at the bathroom. Coming from my shower I stopped in my tracks to see him standing in shoes, socks, underpants and shirt, pulling on a second shirt and, as his head appeared, saying, "I forget. What is it we are doing?"

Feeling a mixture of alarm and sense of the ludicrous I said he had already put his shirt on and we were going to meet the Murrays.

"Yes, of course," said he and selected a tie, but repeated the question every few minutes till I got the giggles, but rather scared, rang the Official Secretary, Des Sullivan, who got John Gunther to come in on his way to the airport.

John told me to get him back into bed, keep him quiet and ring Dr Alex May, the Assistant Director of Health, to come because he was going on to Canberra. He said he would make our apologies to the Murrays.

Dr May examined Don and diagnosed a touch of the sun from his day's raking, brought out by the cold shower on his head. He just said to continue keeping him in bed and quiet. But Don would get up every few minutes calling out, "Hey, Rach, what am I doing here?" I would explain, get him back and soothe him down, but in no time the performance was repeated, so I rang Dr May, who came back and put him out with a shot of morphia.

About one o'clock he woke up completely rational and full of beans, spending the afternoon quite normally working on the files he always brought home, and we had a good laugh as I described his comical performance. The thing that did distress him was not to have been at the airport to welcome the Murrays back, and naturally it was a much noted absence.

To his even greater consternation, the ABC news that night made quite a feature of Brigadier Cleland being unable to meet them having suffered a suspected stroke. Even worse, it was picked up and repeated over the Australian news. Don was really angry, realising that such a thing getting round could affect not only his whole career, but matters such as insurance too. The next day he was back at work and requested Dr May to arrange a consultation with Dr Finlay, a private practitioner, to give him a thorough examination and make a written report. This pronounced no sign of any stroke and stated that the phenomenon was due to working with the back of his head in the sun. However, it's funny how an error, once published, keeps dodging up again.

Back in New Guinea, though hurt and disappointed, Col. Murray conducted himself with admirable composure and dignity, though Mrs Murray found her understandable bitterness hard to hide, and indeed gave the impression of shabby financial treatment by the Australian Government. But in actual fact, there being no provision for an Administrator's pension, the Government did make a financial settlement.

On his farewell visits to each district the people showed genuine affection and sadness at his going; similarly in Port Moresby all the organisations gave them farewells, as did many individuals and companies. Of course Don and I attended them and the social tact needed put us both under considerable strain.

This strain must have been hard on the Murrays too, and tension grew as the time for their departure on the old *Bulolo* came nearer, when feelings began to coalesce into a horrible atmosphere of pro-Murray and anti-Cleland, with the words 'political appointment' being bandied about. We both felt it best to ignore it completely and carry on as though all was well. Neither of us spoke of it or invited any comment to us personally and fortunately our reticence was respected.

At their departure I inadvertently witnessed an illuminating incident. The whole population went down to the Wharf to bid farewell, two queues forming for last goodbyes. Having said mine to Col. Murray it eventually became my turn for Mrs Murray, but before I stepped forward, Ted Glover, the young editor of the then South Pacific Post, dashed in with a beaming face saying, "It's all fixed up..."

Mrs Murray took him by both hands, and with more animation than I had ever seen said, "What are the arrangements?"

Glover said the Australian press would meet the boat, at which Mrs Murray, in a most uncharacteristic way, gave a delighted little jump, saying, "Oh, goody, goody."

Realising that my presence and unavoidable overhearing of this would be embarrassing to us all, I ducked back to the other end of the line before either of them saw me. But it was fair warning that something was in the wind, of which it was possible Col. Murray knew nothing. So we waited to see what would happen.

Sure enough, the next day the Australian papers carried a long attack on the Government and on Don as being a political appointee, and we found ourselves the centre of an unpleasant controversy. Many people who should have known better got on the bandwagon; again Don decided to keep silent and not add fuel to the flames, but as the catchcry 'political appointment' still dogs us to this day, even after his death, I sometimes think it might have been better to have made a statement then.

Quite recently I talked with Ted Glover, recounting to him the incident I witnessed on the wharf and asking him what was behind it. He told me unhesitatingly.

When J.K. Murray returned he showed Ted the letter he had received from Paul Hasluck, which had greatly hurt and distressed him by its brevity and ungracious baldness, because it seemed a deliberate climax to the harsh minutes and letters he had been receiving. But what hurt him more was the first notification; just a telegram delivered to him in Brisbane.

Ted was shocked and very indignant, and in his own words said, "I was young, brash and aggressive, and I urged Murray to fight it and not accept it quietly."

As Ted spoke I remembered Don also coming home distressed after Murray had shown him the letter — which, I note, Paul Hasluck did not quote in his book. It's sad, the little things that make a difference. More graciousness then could have saved much pain and misunderstanding to a number of people. Ted told me of accompanying Murray in a charter plane to all the airfields in Papua New Guinea on his farewell visits and continually urging him to make a fighting statement before he left. For a long time Murray resisted but Ted himself wrote a statement and eventually persuaded him to sign it. Ted then cabled it to Australian newspapers the day they left and it was reference to this I had so inadvertently overheard.

This is the first public reference by either Don or me. In private conversation Don always stoutly defended Col. Murray, saying it was not in his nature. But if, as it seems, it was planned by Ted Glover and Mrs Murray, it was equally not in his nature not to support her. Murray's reported comments were contrary to the working relationship they had developed, and certainly at complete variance to his inscription in a copy of his Macrossan Lecture on the Provisional Administration which he had presented to Don. This inscription reads:

"Brigadier D.M. Cleland, with compliments. May I say how greatly as D.A. & Q.M.G., A.N.G.A.U. and as Chairman of the P.C.B. you contributed to a healthy native administration and an economic situation facilitating the establishment of the Provisional Administration in October, 1945.   J.K. Murray."

This is the way we have liked to think of them as time has passed. In later years they have both visited Papua New Guinea as guests of the government and have stayed with us. I am delighted to say that all the traumas of the past have disappeared and we meet at ease and in friendship. Papua New Guineans have remembered his sympathy and understanding of them, and as independent people have had the last word when a knighthood was bestowed on him in 1978.

After their departure, the next thing for us was to take stock and see what we would do about Government House. We let a few days go by before going to see it. After a good look round I realised its possibilities and that some of its furniture would mix quite well with our things in Lawes Road. We then marked everything to be taken away and on moving day Don supervised the exodus from Government House, while I remained at Lawes Road to see to the packing.

When I arrived after the last load I could scarcely believe my eyes at the transformation. The old clutter had gone. As they arrived, Don placed our things in the rooms, rather than dumping them anywhere, so it looked better already and my spirits rose. Mrs Waterhouse, mother of Gwen, now Lady Cassidy, was staying with us and she and I fell to and made loose covers out of my lengths of dress material to cover the brown tapestry; my first such efforts, but they remained for years, for those were indeed 'do it yourself' days.

Margaret Jaye of Sydney still had a bolt of my white printed linen so I was able to add to my 10ft drop curtains and make them the 15ft necessary for the fanlighted french doors in the dining room and to cover a sofa and some chairs.

We thought about opening up the house a bit and making it generally more attractive and livable. Had it not just been re-roofed, rebuilding probably would have been best, for white ants were a problem then and went on being so for many years. But as so many public servants were still living in paper and native material houses, it was politically unwise to rebuild Government House. So good money went on being thrown after bad to keep it habitable.

The first consideration was lining. It's hard to imagine, but the walls were a single thickness of vertical tongue-and-groove boards, with the smooth side in the bedrooms and the joists all showing in the living rooms and verandahs. Can you imagine trying to hang pictures, for instance, or to bring any elegance to such a room?

We finally decided to remove the two french doors between living and dining rooms to make a wide archway. A small breakfast room opening from the dining room was enlarged by removing the wall to the verandah, so incorporating it into the room and using the old french doors for access to the rest of the verandah, making a large airy room. Don rescued Sir Hubert Murray's old desk from being a typist's table, an old cedar table was brought from the office for my desk, while

Sir Donald's swearing-in ceremony at the old Red Cross Hall, now Port Moresby District Court.

Justice Gore and Mr Justice Bignold with Rachel and Sir Donald at his swearing-in ceremony.

Sir Donald about to inspect police. Background building was formerly the American Officers Recreation Buildings which was given to the R.S.L. when the Americans left. One end houses the first lending library to be established after the war.

built-in sideboards were extended as bookcases. When the roof was being replaced, two beautiful Persian carpets had been found, evidently hidden at the beginning of the war. With these on the floor and books filling two walls, we had a warm and interesting study with a view down the harbour.

We took away the heavy wooden door and wall at the entrance porch, substituting folding glass doors, and had all the blue crinkle louvres changed for clear glass. The verandahs continued on from the living room without a break, so we made them more part of it by hanging curtains at each verandah post, making the effect a series of windows and so more livable.

Our new wrought-iron dining table and chairs went on the verandah at the end of the living room and we always had breakfast and lunch there. Some lovely old woven rattan chairs and a big sofa came to life painted white and with white and yellow striped cushions made a lovely sitting area at the corner of the verandah.

The crotalaria trees in the drive were cut down and the crotons on the terrace replanted in another place, revealing a fabulous view of the harbour. Its westward aspect meant that in the afternoons you literally sat in the sun even on the far side of the living room. So we had a wide pergola built all round outside, which was soon covered in creepers, giving us not only merciful shade, but a soft greenish light in the room. As in the Lawes Road house, my aim was to make a room that was as cool-looking and restful as possible, and the inside was painted a pale grey, so soft as to be almost off-white. This did wonderful things to the colours we put with it.

Outside, the walls supporting the terraces were of local stone found on our own hillsides and pinkish in colour. The house was built on large three-foot-high tree trunk posts, and coming up the steps you saw the accumulated debris of the years underneath. To hide this the garden boys and I built a double wall between the posts, filled it with soil and planted it with ferns and small shade plants. To carry on the colour of the stone, the outside was painted a sort of dusty pink. It sounds odd and at the time the 'Pink Government House' gave rise to much ribald comment, but the effect was good and the house began to look as though it belonged on its site.

We eventually gave up the Sydney house and brought up more old furniture, china, glass and silver. So the house gradually became home and we grew to love it as our beloved home for nearly sixteen years. It housed precious, intimate occasions of family life. Our eldest son was married from it, two grandchildren born and three christened. We saw our young people through various crises when wife or child was rushed in from the bush by 'mercy plane' to the hospital. But in the end I was glad to leave it, not because of the house, but because I longed to have an end to official life. Visiting since our retirement, under successive occupants, I always feel real warmth and affection for it.

We gave quite a bit of consideration to the 'style' we would develop. In the 1940's the Official Secretary, Des Sullivan, had been sent to Government House in Canberra to study the various formalities associated with its running, some of which had been adopted in Port Moresby. The impression of my first visit had an aroma of the ludicrous; for, though both Col. and Mrs Murray had all the dignity necessary within themselves, the house simply did not lend itself to these practices. In addition, both Don and I were by nature rather informal people and liked bogging in and doing things ourselves such as gardening and messing about with cement, and didn't see why we couldn't continue, combining a more relaxed style of living and entertaining with being perfectly correct and formal when a ceremonial occasion demanded it.

There were few hotels then in the whole country and the best of the two in Moresby was in such demand that there were never enough rooms and guests were expected to double up with complete strangers.

This situation not only put a strain on Government House, but on the District Commissioners and young 'outside men'. Even patrol officers in remote areas had to put up the many and varied VIPs who came to see the country. While Don himself received a small entertainment allowance of £800 per annum, which at least went toward the cost of house guests and all the dinners and cocktail parties, the burden on the public servants in the field was heavy. Not only did they have the overseas VIPs but also put up visiting judges and their staffs and travelling public servants. It was some years before Don managed to get acceptance of government responsibility to pay them at least out-of-pocket expenses.

I am sure that this situation was never realised and thus not sufficiently appreciated by their guests. Once the Secretary of the Department, who was travelling with us, said with a touch of contempt and not a little envy that these young people seemed to live very well. We had had chicken and ham lunches at various out-stations in a district, served on very nice china and silver. He did not realise that in those days of no local shops, chickens could be bought from village people, and the same ham had been travelling with us from hostess to hostess. These young people always put their very best foot forward on such occasions, lending each other things and pooling their best linen and tableware. When I explained we had a good laugh, but not nearly enough official credit has been given to young wives for their work and ingenuity to make a good showing on behalf of the government they represented, and at their own expense, too.

The many letters we had from visitors gave us much pleasure and made us feel that we had achieved our aim, both in doing up the house and in the style we set. I will quote from an early guest, Sir John McPherson, the leader of our second United Nations visiting mission:

"I have stayed in many Government Houses round the world, my own and other people's. But never have I found such a delightful mixture of charming informality and dignity as I have enjoyed with you."

Coming from Governor General of Nigeria this meant a lot to us, as it expressed precisely the atmosphere we had set out to create.

Other letters fascinated me, indicating that the grander the house (or mansion) our visitors lived in, the more they seemed to appreciate something about the simple old house in Port Moresby.

An amusing, yet touching one, came from Sir Hubert Murray's son Pat, then a Professor of Geology at New England University, who with other members of the Murray family stayed with us for the unveiling of a memorial to his father. Pat wrote:

"Dear Don and Mrs Cleland,

This seems a most disrespectful form of address; but since you called me 'Pat' and invited me to reciprocate, I do so. I wish to say 'Thank you' for your very great kindness to all of us while we were your guests, and in arranging for us the opportunity of visiting Port Moresby at all. I had often thought of going to Papua again; but I had been deterred by the risks involved when in later life one visits again a place where in boyhood one has been very happy, and everything seems different and sad. It is true that Port Moresby has changed, and Government House in particular is no longer the austere house of the spider and the wasp, nor are its bedrooms now invaded by thirsty goats or its lounge by errant horses, but not even the most determined palaeophil can lament these as losses. Even the houses of Hanuabada, though less picturesque, are doubtless more sanitary than those the Japs demolished. I thought the things that had not changed more important than those that had. Old men who were friends when I was a boy, are friends still. The enthusiasm and devotion of the many teachers of today matches that of the far fewer of thirty years ago. The National Police of yesterday were obviously the same force, and were in the same uniform, as the Royal Constabulary of today. And if my father's ghost was present when you, Sir, spoke at the opening of his Memorial, I do not doubt that he afterwards went back to wherever he now is, well content.

So, thank you both once more for giving us so happy an experience, and please allow us to send you all good wishes for yourselves, our newest friends, and for all our old friends still in Papua, and for the continual success of what is, by any measure, a great and noble work.   Yours sincerely,
Pat (P.D.L. Murray)"

The last words on the house I leave with old Lohia, a Hanuabadan who had been Sir Hubert Murray's personal servant for twenty years. One day one of the staff came and said that an old man wanted to see me. I went to the kitchen and there was indeed a very old man talking to Dosi the cook, who introduced him. We talked of this and that till I asked him if he would like to see the house and it was obvious that was just what he had come for. We entered the dining room through the open french doors and he stopped, looked around with amazement, slowly shaking his head saying:

"Ah-h tst tst tst, ah-h tst tst tst. Sinabada, you've made it cool."

The wartime cook Dosi, a Gosiago from the mountainous D'Entrecasteau Islands off the entrance to Milne Bay, and Mathaias the laundryman, also from Milne Bay, were still there, to Don's delight. Two of the four stewards from Rossell Island wanted to return home so we brought our two Rigo men, much aware that the situation might be tricky. However, Dosi and Mathaias were very welcoming, but some tension developed between the stewards. Dosi, a bright-eyed man under five feet tall, had been well trained in the essential elements of good cooking and was always eager to learn new things. Gradually he replaced the original stewards with his own young relations. Raw from the village, they were trained on the job and an excellent system developed with more trained men in the village than we needed, they themselves deciding who came back after leave, as long as Government House had its quota of four. This worked like a charm; for with the staff under control Dosi kept their standards high, while they could all have periods in their villages to court wives and carry out tribal obligations.

Moreover Dosi was a born organiser, a quality still not widespread among Papua New Guineans. The stewards did the housework, waited at table and were on roster for duty days, serving morning and afternoon teas, pre-dinner drinks etc. But Dosi taught them all to cook — and cook well, organising his job to be mainly supervision. He was with us for our whole time but after Don's retirement became chief cook at the University of Lae, where he still is.

Dosi came back from his first leave with a pretty, shy young wife wearing only an ankle-length grass skirt. We got him materials to extend his house and before long he had trained his wife in the ways of housekeeping western style as well as he had trained the stewards. Later she attended pregnancy clinics at Sister Camillus' little maternity hospital at Badili, while I anxiously asked Dosi to give me plenty of warning. But no. Dashing in one morning he gasped that the baby was nearly there. Only the Administrator's big car A.1 being in, we went off with Namoliani lying on the floor and me fearing I'd have to deliver, but luckily got her there just in time. Drawing away we heard the first cry and stopped. It was a boy whom they named Donald but spelt it phonetically Donol.

One day recently there was a knock on the door and when I opened it a nice young man was standing there but said nothing. So I asked if I could help him and he said:

"I am Donald."

"Donald who?"

"Donald Dosi."

Great excitement! Just that morning he enrolled at the university, having matriculated from Keravat Senior High School near Rabaul. I was touched that he had come straight to see me and the sound of his first cry came vividly back. He sometimes brought a friend and spent the weekend, but didn't work hard enough, so failed his examination and is now training in the Bank of New South Wales.

The last staff member was a dear little elderly Hanuabada woman called Keke, who looked after me and my clothes and those of our women guests. Keke had great dignity and was a woman of some consequence in Hanuabada. Through her I got to know many of the people there and her sister's children, who were of the mixed race community. She had no children of her own, but as 'auntie' mothered many, including our growing staff families. She helped the young village wives to adapt to town life and saw that they attended clinics and brought up their children properly. Her loving care extended also to our grandchildren and she played a very real part in their lives and is remembered by them still. In the 1960's she grew very frail and was given a government pension. We missed her sadly and felt no one could take her place.

Mathaias, like Dosi, was a man of considerable character. Ruling over the laundry, he also kept Don's clothes brushed and pressed, shoes bright and uniform medals impeccably shiny with possessive pride, as he had done during the war, so there was a strong bond between the two men. Each morning they would discuss the clothes needed according to Don's programme and for visitors, whom Mathaias looked after too. He used to tell me stories of the war, which usually began, "Me and the Brigadier".

One day in the later 1950's I went into the laundry to find Mathaias sitting on the table, hands gripping the edge, legs swinging and head sunk on his chest. He didn't even look up and was such a picture of gloom that I exclaimed:

"Mathaias, whatever is the matter?"

A most disconsolate voice said, "I'm tired of working at Government House. I've worked for twenty years. I'm tired of it. But I can't leave. It's him" — nodding towards the house — "I love him." And he went on gloomily sitting there.

I just didn't know what to say. I understood that he felt time was running on and he wasn't getting anywhere, and I was deeply touched that he was torn by his loyalty.

Don had a talk with him and he expressed a desire to drive, so Don arranged for lessons. But after several he gave it away. It terrified him. Then he began making strange and oblique suggestions involving a house in Hanuabada, having married a Hanuabadan widow. Distinctly bemused by the implications of what he expected of us, it was years before we understood his thinking. He eventually retired to run a trade store in Hanuabada and our modest gift towards it left us feeling that we had let him down, his expectations being far higher than we could possibly have met.

A few years later, when the Administrative College was started in a large private house, the first students being men with some years' experience in the administration on scholarships to upgrade their formal qualifications, their Principal, David Chenoweth, started monthly formal dinners. Asked to be their guest speaker one night I found that dear old Mathaias was presiding over the kitchen. On last enquiries he is still at the very large institution it has now become.

Government House had no garden, there being no piped water supply before the war. The hills below the house had been planted with coconuts, there were frangipani trees nearby, and the Murrays had begun making a garden by building a series of walls near the house forming two levels of garden and a grassed terrace at the top, but the hillsides were still burnt off every year.

Four labourers came every day, swept up leaves, slashed grass with sarifs and then, thinking the day's work was over, lay sleeping under the coconuts. Working in the garden ourselves, and planning their work more, naturally met with considerable resistance. They were all Keremas from the Gulf district and at that time Keremas were regarded by their fellows as uncivilised bushmen and responsible for all troubles. There was no fraternisation between them and the house staff. But Keremas are now men of considerable public esteem, represented by no other than the Governor General, Sir Tore Loko Loko and Sir Maori Kiki. Their place at the bottom of the ladder of esteem was taken over by Chimbus and now by Goilalas.

After about a year I discovered that the Labour Department was billing Government House for the Keremas' services and a suggestion taken up by the Secretary made all the difference. In MacArthur's day a number of cottages were built about the grounds for officers' quarters; those at the back were used by our house staff, one near the house became the guest bungalow and another below it was empty. So the labourers were put on permanent staff and became gardeners. Their prestige and personal pride went up, as did their willingness to work. Two, being Seventh Day Adventists, worked on Sunday mornings, the other two on Saturday, so both weekend mornings we each had a helper as we gardened and were able to teach them. Eventually each man had charge of and took great pride in his own part of the garden. We gradually re-designed and extended it, brought back plants from all our travels, planted new trees, cut out others and made a considerable collection of indigenous orchids.

The garden gave us both the greatest joy and was Don's release from pressures. He would come home tired and scratchy, get into his old gardening clothes and work away for an hour or so. By six o'clock drink time he would be relaxed and serene. Though he concentrated on his gardening, not his problems, he used to say that solutions often came to him then. It was the soil itself he loved — as well as the plants he grew.

One day I had an afternoon tea and later gossip was all round town that Government House now had a European gardener. Guests had seen Don without recognizing him and great were the chuckles when in turn the name of the new gardener went its rounds.

The four Keremas, Aihe, Oahu, Lerai and Maiva, remained with us but only Aihe married, bringing back from leave a pretty village girl who gardened with him, when they weren't looking at each other with lovesick eyes. It was a charming idyll. Eventually a child was born and at 3 a.m. that night a panic-stricken Sister Camillus rang to say that mother and baby had disappeared. I woke Don, who went up and woke a driver while I got Aihe and both went off to look for her. At dawn they came back for more searchers and at last found Halau huddled on a hill-top in pouring rain with the tiny, cold, wet baby in her arms. I wrapped her in blankets and hot water bottles while Aihe fed her hot soup, keeping them with me till I found out the trouble. Eventually it transpired that the taking of a blood sample made her sure she was going to die from 'puri puri' — sorcery.

Sister told me that her blood count was lower than a European could survive and she would need transfusions, but to do this would literally risk her dying of fright. So I left her with Keke and took Aihe down to the Red Cross to see slides and have the process explained to him, hoping he could then reassure her. Realising that she would run away again unless she returned to hospital of her own will, it was mid-afternoon before she agreed and Sister asked Aihe to stay with her but he came home before dark.

About nine o'clock I suddenly got worried and felt something was wrong, so getting Aihe, went to the hospital and I don't think I have ever seen such panic and terror on a human face. She'd had a transfusion and I knew she would either run away again or die, so I rang Dr Price, the Pathologist who knew so much about Papuans, to see if any of his staff came from her language group. By luck one did, and leaving Aihe with Halau, I set off to find him.

Fortunately he lived not far from the hospital, was at home and came and sat by her bed talking for a long while, till gradually she calmed down and some of the fear left her face. He was so patient, and being a trained laboratory assistant could explain in a way just not possible through Aihe, who was nearly as frightened as she was.

I asked the two men to get a woman 'one talk' to come and see her and found that not one other woman speaking her language was in Port Moresby, their village up the Vailala River was so remote.

About a year later I was wakened on another wet night by an urgent voice calling outside our window. It was Aihe saying, "Come quickly, the baby is here."

I put on shoes and a coat, found a torch and slithered down the steep path to their house. A rope tied across one corner of their room had a blanket draped over it. I looked over the top. The floor was spread with fresh banana leaves and Halau's little face looked up at me from her squatting position. There in a pool of blood was a baby girl with the cord still uncut. So we tied it in two places with banana fibre and cut it and sent Aihe up to wake a driver. This time she went quite happily to the hospital. They named the baby Keke and she has just graduated from the typing college.

Her father is the only one of the gardeners still at Government House and last year he was awarded the B.E.M. for long and faithful service. He and I both had tears in our eyes when I congratulated him. You remain feeling very close to people when you have gone through such human crises together.

Chapter 4

Visiting an Outstation. Don is greeted by a Patrol Officer, Rachel talks to the women.

Highlands Visit—Madang—Mt Lamington Eruption Memorial—Popondetta with Mr and Mrs Hasluck

A fortnight's visit to the Highlands in October filled me with excited anticipation as our DC.3 landed on a small strip on a wide, seemingly flat grassy valley, but which in fact was broken by gullies leading run off from the mountain spurs to the Asaro River, wandering down the valley's length.

The Downs, recently our neighbours in Lawes Road, had just moved to Goroka. Ian, as the new District Commissioner, had men of high reputation to follow; the work of Jim Taylor and George Greathead, the two post-war D.C.'s, was renowned. Jim, as government officer, travelled with the Leahy brothers' prospecting expedition in 1933 which discovered these great valleys. The first post-war D.C., he had resigned to marry a girl from the Wahgi Valley, settled near Goroka, pioneered coffee and involved the village people to do likewise. A man of personal distinction and charm, he was greatly respected and loved. His younger daughter Meg, then a baby, was one of the early university students and the first Papua New Guinean woman to graduate in Law and to be called to the Bar.

George Greathead, calm and slow-spoken, like Jim Taylor, had understanding and an empathy with the people. The increasing tide of visitors gave him and his wife Nell many problems trying to fit both them and their growing family into the small 'Bulolo' house, and on an earlier visit Don, shocked by what Nell was trying to cope with, authorised building a guest cottage. Greathead, known as 'farmer George' because of his slow ways and great love of everything that grows, designed and planted gardens wherever he was posted and the numbers of new plants he introduced soon spread about.

Brilliant cannas and poinsettias surrounded the airstrip, while along the bush roads cosmos gone wild were clouds of pink and white. The residency garden was a picture with gladioli, roses, stocks, iceland poppies and a host of spring flowers, but Nell Greathead had scarcely furnished her enlarged house before George, too, resigned to take up land and grow coffee.

Ian Downs was also a remarkable character. One of the most intense people I have ever known, he was the right man in the right place at the right time. Judy, his wife, balanced his intensity by her delicious sense of humour. She had a flair for making a house into a home and could do wonders with whatever was at hand. Ian was tackling his first job as D.C. with drive, imagination and enthusiasm.

At that time Goroka consisted of five Bulolo type houses, several others of pit-pit walls and kunai thatch, and a pit-pit and thatch building for the District Office. Across the strip was an agricultural experimental farm, the police depot on a nearby plateau and a sprawling hospital with long pit-pit and thatch wards filled the valley in between. There were some miles of dirt road east and west of the station and the bridges were of massive tree trunks felled high on the mountains and dragged into place by hundreds of villagers.

The air was like champagne and everyone we met was full of enthusiasm. Village people flocked to the airstrip in full regalia to meet us and made speeches of welcome with great dramatic effect in the peculiarly rolling tones of Highland voices. At five o'clock all the expatriates—missionaries, the half dozen planters, keen young patrol officers, and other governmental people with wives and children from the whole valley — came to meet us. There were ninety-three people and everyone marvelled at the rapid development, only thirty-seven having met Don in May.

I just couldn't tear my eyes away from the grandeur of the valley itself, 5,500 feet above sea level and brilliant green. Goroka nestled under the northern mountains and then, miles away to the south endless grassy spurs came down, throwing triangles of purple shadow from their tops rising another 5,000 feet above the valley. Behind them again even higher, tree-covered mountains reared up twelve to fifteen thousand feet. This magnificence went on and on for twenty miles east and west of Goroka.

One night, Judy and I were chatting, with the men engrossed in discussion across the room, when Ian's urgent voice penetrated our talk saying:

"Sir, give me 100 shovels and £2,000 and I know I can do it."

Judy and I stopped and listened. Ian was telling Don that rough roads stretched out from many villages and that it wouldn't be difficult to link them to go through to Kainantu — the first Highland station built at the eastern end of the valley. Don was listening and asking questions while Ian was enthusiastically selling his ideas for a road system on many grounds: better native administration, communications, village development and less reliance on the expensive air transport; for the landrovers, plumbing, roofing iron, timber — everything — had to be flown in.

With an interested listener, Ian went further and proposed cutting a road from the wartime airstrip at Dumpu, at the head of the Markham Valley, over the 9,000-feet range to Kainantu. This, he said, would be a bigger task. Gerry Toogood, when D.O. at Kainantu, had surveyed tracks both during the war and afterwards. Though several possibilities were known, a practicable route would have to be found but Ian was sure it could be done and, moreover, could be finished for Don to open on June 30th next year. Don promised to give the proposal serious thought.

On our last day we flew down to Aiyura Agricultural Station and then across the valley to Kainantu, where Gerry Toogood was District Officer. Here a group of 'hatmen' — village officials called luluais and tultuls, who proudly wore sort of Trammie's hats to mark their status — were assembled outside the District Office. While the 'big' men were making speeches with magnificent oratory I was dodging about taking pictures, and noticed a small, wizened old man, standing one foot on the other, with two brown paper parcels on the ground beside him. Finally it became his turn, for the most important man spoke last. Stooping down, he picked up the parcels and, fairly staggering with them, placed them at Don's feet, saying in ringing tones what translated as this

"Here I give you £2000 in silver money. You seal our airstrip so that planes can come in all weathers and take our vegetables to market."

There were murmurs from the government men: "It's old Anaroi."

Thinking quickly, Don thanked him very warmly, but said no government man could accept money: "So put that money in the bank. When we start building a road to Lae you can get all your people to help us make it. When the road is finished that £2000 will buy a truck and you yourself can take the vegetables to Lae."

The old man beamed and said he had a request to make.

"I am a big man, but I have no education. That is alright now, but my son will need education. I will give you my son. Take him to Moresby with you and educate him" — and he pushed forward a rather ungainly boy of 15. Even more of a poser than the £2000!

Don promised to talk with his officers, resulting in a younger son being chosen for an education in Moresby. Four years later schools came to Kainantu.

Back in Moresby Don's enquiries revealed that £2000 remained in the Eastern Highlands road maintenance grant, so he diverted it for use on Ian Downs's big idea.

As to the road, old Anaroi was as good as his word, rallying his people and taking it over a very difficult part of the divide. Moreover he lightened the patrol office's work by supervising his village groups himself. When our son Robert joined the service he was posted to Goroka and sent to help Rupe Haviland get the road finished. He said old Anaroi was magnificent, and still talks of him with affectionate admiration.

The next day we set off to the west in the old, wooden, single-engined Norseman with Helli Tschuschnigg, nephew of the 'Pocket Chancellor' whom Hitler overthrew in Austria. Helli, a much loved pilot, is still flying there. Looking down on rough mountainous country between the two huge valley systems of the Asaro and the Wahgi, we saw densely populated country with innumerable villages of round houses, looking like clusters of mushrooms, and intensely cultivated gardens everywhere. Flying over the Kundiawa airstrip and the spectacular Chimbu Gorge, the huge Wahgi Valley opened out ahead, strangely empty in contrast. Don explained that the beautiful grass below grew in swamps, and that dry parts were traditional fighting grounds, while the villages were strategically built on surrounding ridges.

Close to the rising foothills on the south we came down on a small strip bordered by gay plantings of cannas. It was Minj. Not a soul was in sight. We made our way to a footpath up a low, lightly timbered hill and, hearing men singing, quickened our pace. Over the brow dashed a young and very good-looking patrol officer, making profuse apologies with a broad smile of welcome; behind him the singers in a loping trot were all carrying several long poles on their shoulders.

"My house," he said by way of explanation.

Barry Griffiths had just built the airstrip, living in a tent, and using a pit-pit store cum office. Now building the first government patrol post at this end of the valley, he led us proudly explaining the layout. Meanwhile the men had dropped their poles and gone back for more.

Before us, nicely situated on the rise and looking down on the airstrip and across the valley to the northern rim, where the 15,000-foot bulk of Mt Wilhelm hid its head in the clouds, was a novel scene: construction of a house, Papua New Guinea style. Tree-trunk posts and joists supported a floor of rough pitsawn timber and an architrave sturdy enough for the steep roof. One group was scrambling about up there, erecting the gables and ridge poles, another group fastening lighter crosspieces to a wing of the house already gabled. Nails were not necessary, all being lashed with kunda or bush rope — long lengths of immensely strong lianas from the mountain jungles above. Some women were busily tying bundles of kunai grass ready to fasten to the crosspieces for the thatch, while another group emerged like walking haystacks, bringing freshly cut kunai for them. In a cleared space men bashed pit-pit stems with a club, making pieces three to four inches wide and six feet long. Another group squatting in a line was weaving them into sheets to form the walls, and with great speed and dexterity made beautiful patterns. Variety was achieved not only by different weaving designs, but by varying the textures, using some pit-pit with the hard, shiny outside uppermost, and some with the soft, whitish inside part.

Always interested in houses and building, I was fascinated and remained watching and studying the plan of the house; and when Don and Barry returned and told us he was bringing back a bride after leave I ventured a suggestion or two. Next time we came that way, a year or two later, it was a home indeed, with a pretty garden and a charming and pregnant young woman dispensing hospitality to us, after our inspection of the fully fledged station complete with hospital, police barracks and houses for the married Papua New Guineans.

But this day we flew across the valley to Kerowagi, where a jovial priest and crowd of adherents were waiting. Volubly telling us of his work and the mission, he drove us in an old wartime jeep a mile or so to Nondugl, the famed bird sanctuary and sheep project started and partly financed by Sir Edward Halstrom. We stood by a large attractive pit-pit house looking down a sweep of lawn to a man-made lake surrounded by beds of brilliant flowers and backed by a spectacular purple mountain. We were standing spellbound by the technicolour scene, when the door opened behind us and a handsome and astonished young woman came out, saying almost accusingly,

"Well — right on time. The letter said twelve and it is twelve. First time it's ever happened."

Olga Blood, who (we later found) was known both for her blunt outspokenness and for her kindness, had us thoroughly disconcerted, but her husband Nep (short for Neptune), tall, fair and relaxed, who managed the farm and sheep experiments, took us beyond the lake to the fifty-foot-long aviaries tenderly looked after by Fred Shawmeyer. Fred was a gentle elderly ornithologist, widely known and respected in the scientific world. Inside the aviaries he had planted the trees and shrubs from the birds' own environment to acclimatise and try to breed them in captivity.

You often hear birds of paradise calling in the forest but seldom see them, for the tree tops are hidden by the dense tangle of shrubs and creepers. So it was an experience indeed, seeing these wonderful birds flying and displaying their fantastic feathers, and it was hard to tear ourselves away to the delicious lunch Olga had prepared.

Showing us the sheep that afternoon, Nep was full of his problems. Footrot from the perennially damp ground, grass which grew too fast and became too coarse for sheep, intestinal worms of every sort and no dry season to break the cycle, caused a rapid increase, not of sheep, but of their pests. As another agricultural officer said despairingly on another occasion:

"It's perpetual spring. No frosts or droughts to kill off the wogs or slow down the grass growth. How can you grow sheep?" Certainly a novel viewpoint — Perpetual Spring.

We then flew to Mt Hagen — a little strip at the end of the valley. A large group of men, hair tucked into mob caps made of beaten bark tapa cloth, shiny as leather with pig grease, were in an excited frenzy, digging away a hill to widen the strip. They dropped everything and, yelling and laughing, surrounded our plane as we landed. The D.C., Bob Cole, his wife Kay, the D.O., Phil Robb, a Viennese doctor and their wives, the only married people on the station, met us. We climbed the half-demolished hill to speak to the people, the crowd by then having considerably enlarged.

These groups, large in the highlands and smaller on the less densely populated coast and lowlands, were a feature of our official life in PNG. Though they changed in aspect over the years, with growing sophistication, and though often there were surprises and unique variations, in essence the pattern remained the same. They came in varying numbers, often travelling long distances on foot in the mountains and by canoe on the coast and great rivers. They came 'to see the Namba Wan' or 'to look at your faces' as they so graphically expressed it. And 'look at his face' they did — literally. A crowd was usually flanked by a line of leading men, whether 'big men' or luluais and tultuls and later local government councillors, and we would walk down shaking hands. I soon found it wise to wait till Don had progressed about 30 feet before offering my hand. Each man would look intently at him when he shook hands, then keep his eyes on his face with the greatest concentration, often leaning forward till he could no longer see. It was useless for me to begin till the first of the line had looked his fill and straightened up again. Then he would usually shake my hand warmly and give me a beaming smile; thus I was a sort of light relief after a tense and important moment.

On this visit we were 'new boys', alert to see what happened, to ask the D.C.s, and just play it by ear. We eventually developed 'techniques', I suppose you could say, which allowed for the maximum use to be made of the occasion, making it worthwhile for the people and keeping the Administrator in touch with their thinking. It was usual for the leaders to have 'first turn' and for the Administrator to speak at the end, so that he could both answer any questions they raised, reassure them, if possible, on any worries and put across any message or policy matter occupying the mind of the field officers or the government itself.

Though these leaders were always welcoming and courteous I never found any backwardness in asking curly questions or saying exactly what they thought. At times it could be salutary to hear what they thought and at times I have noted with amused sympathy a young P.O., or even a senior officer, looking acutely embarrassed. Always, especially in the highlands, they looked you straight in the eye and spoke as man to man; a very likable quality.

Throughout this first highland visit, I was entranced by the sheer facination of observing the people; of this particular morning a vivid mental picture remains of the freshly dug earth and its smell, of the half-hill on which we stood and of the sea of intent, upturned male faces in their round turban-like caps, and the women and children fidgeting and rustling at the back.

The doctor, a rather plump and very courtly Viennese, then took us over the hospital, largely built by himself. His office and operating theatre, the only part made of sawn timber, was painted gleaming white, had an operating-table, a glass fronted cupboard with neatly displayed surgical instruments and a large overhead light powered by a small diesel generator outside, the only electric light in the Wahgi Valley.

The doctor was telling Don of trying to overcome the people's fears and being increasingly successful since he had built wards which more nearly approximated their own living conditions. By this time we were walking down a path bordered by red hibiscus. He suddenly stopped, picked a flower and with a courtly bow presented it to me, as we reached the first ward.

It was a long pit-pit and kunai building with an earth floor and a low, six-foot wide bench on each side. Right down the middle, on two rows of stones with packed earth between, were little fires, all smouldering away. The roof was glistening black from the smoke, which found its own way out. Peering into the gloom our eyes took some minutes to see the patients on woven mats, lying feet toward the fire or sitting crosslegged on the bench. We walked down, smiling and talking to them, and observed a white cardboard form on a clip hanging from a hook by each patient; I picked one up and read among the usual information of temperature, pulse etc. — Diagnosis — pneumonia. Treatment — penicillin. Recently having paid 17/- a dose for one of our sons I was impressed, and found similar records on the other cards.

Looking at the hibiscus still in my hand I was suddenly conscious that here in this remote place was the meeting of these people, so recently confronted by the outside world, with the very latest scientific treatment and the grace and culture of Europe. I was proud that the efforts of my own new country, Australia, had brought them together.

The Coles' house, one of the first pitsawn timber buildings in the highlands, exuded a sort of Edwardian flavour (and later became the local museum). Their two little boys ran out to meet us. The talk that night had a pioneering slant, as exploratory patrols were still probing into the country and finding more people. Bob and Kay Cole were loved and respected for their teamwork. Bob was a slight, well-knit man, whose twinkling blue eyes and calm efficiency gave everyone a feeling of confidence, while Kay mothered the young people of all races on the station.

The next day the dashing veteran flyer, Bobby Gibbs, flew us to various newly opened out-stations, the last stop being Wabag — a very small strip cut into a mountain in a narrow valley, with a gorge dropping away from the side and one end. By mid-afternoon the clouds were gathering and Bobby gaily didn't know whether he could get in, but, suddenly seeing a gap, dived under the clouds and landed. I must say that at least one of the passengers unclenched her teeth and let out a breath in relief.

This was still uncontrolled country, so there were no married officers. Besides the usual sergeants, interpreter and five police and some medical orderlies, the personnel were two, a Patrol Officer and an E.M.A. — European Medical Assistant. They lived in two earth-floored kunai houses. In the centre of the main room half a 44-gallon drum, partly filled with earth with draught holes in the sides, held a fire whose smoke found its way out through the thatch. It was really cold at 6,000 feet.

While we were still inspecting the station, it was obvious that we would not get out again, with the day drawing in and the clouds thicker than ever. We thought of poor Kay Cole, organising a buffet dinner for everyone to meet us, and wondered if they'd go ahead or hold it over till the next day; and the shy patrol officer looked shattered, as he realised that he'd have to put us up for the night. A roar from the strip told us that Bobby Gibbs, his plane lightened by three, evidently thought he could make it and as it disappeared into the clouds there was a general shaking of heads and a muttering, "Bobby'll do it once too often one day". So far, a quarter of a century later, miraculously he's still around.

The P.O. made us comfortable with drinks, advising us that by sitting down we would be out of the smoke, and rushed away to organise for the invasion. All out-station houses have a guest room, so Don and I stayed with the P.O. and Bob Cole with the E.M.A. All I remember of our sleeping arrangements was that his pyjamas fitted me but not Don, who had recourse to underpants and singlet, but the dinner and evening I remember well, especially being intrigued by the roast. It was delicious but I simply couldn't place what it was and kept asking, till Don kicked me under the table and afterwards was really cross:

"You embarrassed our host so much, when you should have known it was only goat."

I said, "How silly. I would have been thrilled and enjoyed our meal even more had I known I was eating goat for the first time, especially with biblical overtones of 'a young kid' being killed."

Round the fire after dinner the two young men were telling us of a recent patrol north-west into new country of rough mountains, where the Sau and other streams feed the Sepik River and others flow south to the Strickland and the Fly. They were questioned closely by Bob Cole and Don about the numbers of people, how they built their villages, health and nutrition standards, prevalent diseases, fighting and whether gardens were good and food plentiful. In the course of discussion they told of something never found in the Highlands before. One of the groups were cannibals. I then asked a question I'd often wondered about:

"Are the people cannibals because the lack of animals means a protein shortage in their diet?"

Both men answered at once, tumbling over each other in their eagerness.

"No. It's not like that at all. They don't think of human flesh as meat but eat it ritually, to partake of the virtue of the dead person. If he was a great bowman, they would eat his arm to gain his strength; if he was a great fight leader, they eat his liver, as that was the seat of bravery, as we say 'guts'. They eat it ceremoniously, saying little chants."

I was fascinated and probed further, asking lots of questions. They were talking, I realised, not only from this one experience, but in the case of the P.O. with knowledge of anthropology from the course at Asopa.

I had begun to feel rather peculiar as a sort of familiarity made itself felt and the Communion Service penetrated my consciousness. The parallels seemed so obvious as to be disturbing; beginning for me a long process of complete readjustment. I did a lot of reading and thinking, not only into this phenomenon, but into the whole field of the religious attitudes of the people and how their concept of their own relation to the universe, which we call animistic, really appears to them. I also read again *The Golden Bough* by Frazer and whatever books I could find about the early religions of the Middle East at the time of Jesus and St. Paul.

What I developed was a far greater appreciation of the content and quality of Papua New Guinea thought, the nature of their ritual and why, and the values it expressed. I also came to appreciate, in a different way, the magnitude of what Jesus did. Besides building on the Jewish development of monotheism, in the Last Supper, he took and used the most ancient ideas current in his day, spiritualised them and embodied in them, not only the central point of Christianity as it developed into a religion, but gave it a continuity that went deep back into man's earliest consciousness. It was a Sri Lankan Anglican Bishop, staying with us when I was going through this re-thinking process, who gave me this idea of the continuity with man's earliest history. But in the meantime it had some odd side effects, in that for some months I would feel faint, sometimes passing out, at the chancel as soon as I knelt to take communion and had to desist until I had sorted it all out.

That evening in Wabag is especially clear because of the effect it had in my own inner life. But it was also typical of many similar nights in all kinds of places and conditions when the formalities of the day were over, the inspections made, staff discussions in the office finished with and everyone relaxed over their drinks and dinner. At these times Don gleaned what made a young man enthuse, to what he was blind; could drop new ideas into the conversation, or draw men out on their thinking on this or that problem and generally feeling the pulse of the service. From his book I gather that Paul Hasluck found the same thing.

Next morning Bobby Gibbs came very early for us. The day's activities included visiting Father Ross, the pioneer missionary and the first person from the outside world to live in the valley, Ogelbeng Mission which the Lutherans pioneered some time later, and the nearby Korn Farm, the Government Agricultural Station. It was presided over by Jack Fox, one of the much liked twin brothers, Tom and Jack. They were both in the expeditionary force which captured Rabaul in 1914, and returned to New Guinea in the early twenties to try their luck at mining, but put their hands to many things. Now Tom was 'Roadmaster' at Madang and Jack was agriculture officer at Hagen.

We drove into a grassy, fenced courtyard, formed by several of the usual bush material houses separated by clumps of the lovely feathery bamboo which are such a feature of the Highland countryside. Jack Fox came out to greet us, followed by two delightful small boys of three and four, named Tom and John, who followed us while looking over the station. While their father discussed agriculture with the men I talked with the children. I see Tom quite a bit now and his wife Pauline, a journalist, told me that Tom remembered this visit largely because I had sent him a book about pussycats. He was one of the early graduates in economics from the university and is now Managing Director of the Investment Corporation, while his brother John was the pilot of a plane which was recently lost in a tragic air mystery

Sir Donald, Lady Hasluck, Syd Elliot-Smith and Sir Paul Hasluck.

Constructing the Mt Hagen air strip on which we had just landed (1952).

Walking the plank to the jeep.

The jeep being pushed across a river.

when a plane carrying Doctors Tom Gaunedi and Kila Wari, two of the first graduates from the Suva Medical School, disappeared without a trace in the Milne Bay District. These were all men of talent and experience who are so desperately needed now. John's death was such a shock to his father that he too died a few days later.

After lunch we drove over a slippery new road to see Danny Leahy at Kuta. Three of the famous Leahy brothers, prospectors and explorers who had discovered the Highlands and many of the other remote parts of New Guinea, now middle-aged men, had settled down as farmers. Mick, the eldest, with a wife and large family, pioneering in cattle on the Zenag plateau between Lae and Bulolo, was still fiery, still the true Irishman, outspokenly 'agin' the government whatever it might do, and however good his own personal relations might be with individuals in it. Jim, the middle one, calm and benign, had taken up land in the Goroka Valley, growing coffee and trying out sheep.

Danny was the youngest and perhaps the most loved. He still worked gold at Kuta, where he had built a house on a ridge with a fantastically lovely view and was trying out coffee and pigs. Danny never formally married but fathered and brought up a number of mixed-race children who, as Hagen grew into a town, were accepted and welcomed at the pre-school and primary schools and attended children's parties, because they were Danny's children.

Mendi, the first government station in the Southern Highlands, which was still uncontrolled territory, was our next visit. I felt a tremendous surge of excitement; for there were not many places in the world where you could be among people who had no knowledge of a world beyond their mountains and to whom people like our little group would be as strange as beings from Mars to us.

We flew over high open moorland before coming to a formidable mountain range, circled over it and dropped down sheer sides of jagged limestone cliffs turning as we did to reverse our direction, and landed on a tiny strip below the cliffs. Four men were waiting to receive us: Gerry Toogood, the new D.C., (whose wife and family having gone ahead to Adelaide from their last posting) would be returning with him after their leave, an A.D.O., a P.O. and an E.M.A. The small group of police stood stiffly to attention for Don to inspect them, pausing by one or another as he noted their war medals, to ask where they had served. On some of these early visits Don often wore his Army uniform, which gave the police and many of the village leaders who wore medals a sense of continuity and identity with the man they had served under during the war.

My most vivid memory was the way people crowded round us, touching our skins, examining every part of us, chattering and laughing among themselves. I began to appreciate how monkeys at the zoo must feel. Surrounded by all the women and children, I tailed after the men as they went round inspecting the station — a small hospital, police barracks, calaboose (prison) office and three houses — all of bush materials, and then we set out to visit the mission. On this walk I discovered a gimmick which served me in good stead as a communication bridge over many years.

One of the children had a ball, so I put out my hands in a catching pose and he threw it to me. I threw it several times to different children then, keeping it, turned and walked on, with the children following like a comet tail and the women and babies behind that. Every now and then I would suddenly turn, throwing it to a child, who needed quick reactions to catch it. There were always shouts of laughter and a wonderful sense of expectation and fun developing among the children, with the surrounding mothers proudly approving. On other tours I often carried a ball.

Soon we came to a deep ravine with a torrent rushing and foaming below. I had heard of kunda (bush rope) bridges and here was my first one. Three or four lengths of cane, loosely plaited together at the bottom, formed about a 6-inch footway, above it two single canes about 2 feet apart were surmounted by kunda handrails, connected every few feet by thin canes passing from one to the other under the footway, which gave a slight feeling of security. The bridge was cleverly slung from trees on one side and held by posts and stones at the other.

The men were far ahead. I looked at it dubiously, but didn't dare show fear, having already learnt that it's far worse with dozens of excited helpers than coping with a thing yourself. So I gingerly put out a foot, realised the need to go sideways like a crab, and picturing the swaying if they all came over with me, gestured to the children to wait. In any case the wretched thing swayed up and down and the river foamed far below. I tried to develop a rhythm to match the bridge and almost fell off the other side with relief as a shout went up from the children, who scrambled over with no trouble at all.

We walked up a long grassy slope with several kunai buildings, wondering where to find the men. The farthest and smallest had a cluster of people by every window, so, walking towards it, I found it was the first school in the Southern Highlands, opened only a fortnight before. The teacher, a delightful young woman, had made most ingenious teaching aids for the six-to eight-year-olds, selected as the first pupils. They were sitting on the pit-pit matting floor while fathers looking through the windows enthusiastically joined in the lessons.

One day in 1978 I heard over the news that Peter Paypool of Mendi, who graduated from the university in 1973, had been appointed assistant secretary of the Department of Foreign Affairs, and Roya Yaki was administrative secretary of his own Provincial Government. Could they have been among these children?

What other country had produced senior public servants from an unexplored, untouched stone-age people in 25 years? Again I am proud that, under Australia, Papua New Guinea has done it. What grounds have too many academics and journalists for their reiterated accusations against Paul Hasluck for what they call his 'policy of gradualism'? I repeat that there never was such a policy. Outsiders, stating it so often, have made it a myth, though its growth must have been given impetus by a Chifley lecture in Sydney by Murray Groves, son of William Groves, and himself an anthropologist.

We left the school for the mission house and a CWA like tea, to hear their eager tales of experiences in setting up the mission, not without a few dicey moments; but mostly the people had been helpful, co-operative and enthusiastic. The new little schoolteacher told us shyly that she lived near my cousins in Adelaide and was at college with their daughters.

Back at the station Gerry Toogood was rather in a spot with the domestic arrangements, as he'd only been there a week and was coming out in our plane for leave. Then it transpired that a new rule made it mandatory for officers to use local people as servants instead of bringing their 'old faithfuls' with them. Rules, unfortunately, don't fit everything, so here were these four bachelors, without time in their strenuous lives, to introduce the stone-age men they took on as servants to the mysteries presented by a rough bush house with little household equipment. The stories they told were hilarious and often heartrending. Don immediately exempted them and others facing a 'new contact' situation from the rule. Somehow a meal was produced and I found ingredients for a chocolate cake as a surprise for the young men on the station.

The next day Helli Tschuschnigg flew in early to take us to Tari, worrying that the clouds might be too low to get over the Doma Peaks. However, we went off to take a look; no chance whatever, so back to Mendi; sat on the strip for an hour or so and off again to look at the peaks. Weather even more murky, but might clear at midday. Another long wait and a third time we set off — again no good, so Helli turned in another direction down valleys to keep under the clouds and though I marvelled once again at the knowledge of the country and the weather by which these pilots flew, this was one of the few occasions when I felt that things could be a bit sticky and speculated on a forced landing. It would be cold, I thought, and put on my coat and examined the old Norseman for the exit — a sliding manhole in the roof, and worked out how to negotiate it quickly. Soon we emerged from the maze of valleys over lovely Lake Kutubu and eventually turned north between Mt Bosavi and the Doma Peaks, Helli miraculously finding the new strip.

Crowds of people were waiting for us, every man clutching bows and arrows, and among them was Ron Neville, a swashbuckling P.O.

with a strong, vibrant personality, jet black hair and a flashing smile. Only months before he had walked in from Mendi with a few police, built a hut which, packed with implements and stores, left hardly room for a bed, table and chair, and set about urging the local men to help build a strip. A straightforward job in that wide valley, the main thing had been clearing it of trees, kunai and pit-pit, levelling it, finally holding a celebrating sing-sing when several thousand dancing feet effectively compacted the earth ready for a plane to land.

Only a fortnight earlier an Unevangelised Field Mission and a Methodist couple had come in to establish their missions, so I was only the third white woman to land and was again the centre of interested, laughing curiosity by the women and children. Ron rustled up a much-needed cup of tea in his little hut and, though disconcerted by being watched by the crowd noting and commenting on our every move, we were swept up by the atmosphere of intense excitement. Again I could imagine a packed Sydney Domain out to watch the arrival of Martians.

Government business done, we walked to the UFM mission which Len and Eva Twyman were building. Here we struck a unique road system. The Tari people were great fighters, its essence being the surprise raid. So friendly villages were connected by trenched roads about 4 feet wide and 6 feet deep with nice straight sides and a well-formed footway — a ramp led us up to the mission in a pleasant clearing.

The Twymans had already built a simple fence which, being crowded by onlookers from dawn to dark, was more for protection from their curiosity than for safety, though only unstrung bows were allowed. The house was mainly a tent but a pleasant living room was completed, even with a fireplace and chimney. The Twymans were so enthusiastic and cheerful and full of information that it was late before we returned along the sunken road, where Helli met us saying the weather had closed in with no hope of getting out. Once more stranded on the wrong strip at the wrong time, we turned back to our lunchtime hosts, who cheerfully put us up, while Gerry Toogood and Helli walked the four miles to the Methodist Mission.

That evening again was unforgettable, with Ron Neville and our hosts telling us and discussing with each other the characters, customs and their experiences of the Huli people round Tari. On patrol, Ron had found fighting going on which he and his few police not only had to stop but get across the idea that now the government had come they must not fight any more but bring disputes to the government and hear 'the Law'; the law would settle their dispute. Ron's stories were picturesque and colourful, losing nothing in telling and I must say I thrilled to the immediacy of hearing this 'first contact' experience.

Ron Neville is still at Mendi. He married and left the government and was the first business man in the Southern Highlands. He and his wife have built up a wide-ranging business and reared a large family. An elected member of parliament for years, Ron has remained the cheerful buccaneer, giving many a headache to the authorities and to other business men, but has kept good relations with the southern highlanders and made a tremendous contribution.

When Ron finally wound up his tales and went off home, we were introduced to a novel bedstead. I knew that on patrol you carried a 'bedsheet', which was a 6 by 3 piece of canvas with a hem at each side wide enough to take a sapling. To make camp, four forked sticks were driven into the ground, the saplings rested in the forks and there was your bed. But this was an improvement — to start with it was a double bedsheet and boxed, with the saplings at the top of the boxed sides, to hold an innerspring mattress which would be flown in one day. In the meantime, box edges gave the contraption a good deal of play, to the great disadvantage of the smaller of the two sleeping persons. It was icy cold and, especially with dampness coming up through the pit-pit covered earth floor, canvas is not very warm. Whenever Don rolled over, all the blankets went with him and I would have to retrieve my share. Grateful as we were to the Twymans for giving us their room, it was a disturbed night. We didn't know where they slept and we only hoped they had enough blankets for themselves.

On a beautiful sunny morning flying over the Doma Peaks, which looked calm, lovely and very different from the lowering aspect of the day before, we touched down at Mendi to gather our luggage and for Gerry to give last minute instructions to the A.D.O. who would be responsible till he returned with his wife and family after leave. Then into Hagen once more, goodbyes to the Coles and off we flew for a brief visit to Madang, my first.

After a full afternoon's programme in the steamy heat, our strenuous activities of the last ten days caught up with me. I remember flopping onto the bed in utter exhaustion for an hour's rest before a buffet dinner at the Residency to meet sixty new people and of lying in the heat wondering despairingly however I could summon the strength to shake another hand and smile another smile. However, I pressed a frock, we showered, dressed and joined our hosts as the first guests were coming.

They were so warm and welcoming, so pleased to see us, that I experienced a phenomenon which has rescued me on many an occasion since. Something passes from the people to you and you respond. Tiredness seems to fall away and you find that their very niceness gives you the strength to carry on. For that I've been grateful so many times. The evening is my only clear recollection of that visit to Madang and after such a fortnight I remember the bliss it was to come home again.

* * *

A month later we accompanied the Minister and Mrs Hasluck to Popondetta for the Consecration by Bishop Hand of the cemetery where the expatriate victims of the Mt Lamington eruption were buried, the unveiling of a Memorial Plaque by Paul Hasluck and the Investiture of Honours for Bravery by Don, including the George Cross to George Taylor, the volcanologist who had daily risked his life. In January 1951 an extinct volcano near both the government station Higaturu and the Anglican Mission at Sangara in the Northern District had been puzzling people for a week or two because rumbling could be heard and the earth was getting hot. Suddenly it exploded and blew out sideways, totally destroying both mission and government stations and the villages in an eight-mile radius. Thirty-seven Europeans and nearly 3,000 Papuans lost their lives, with many others hideously burned among the 6,000 left homeless. It was an appalling disaster for an area which had already suffered horribly in the war.

Emergency headquarters were established at Popondetta, then an agricultural station near an airstrip, and an amazing work of relief was organised by Col. Murray and carried out by many devoted people. By January 1952, the homeless had all been re-established in new villages and the emergency camps closed. The village people were buried in their own cemeteries and the Europeans and remaining Papuans in this beautifully laid-out Memorial Cemetery.

In the plane were relatives from Moresby and Australia and the ceremonies were very moving. After lunch in an open-sided shelter from the emergency camp, the plane returned with the visitors, while we and the Haslucks remained for a longer visit.

Sid Elliot Smith was the D.C. following Cecil Crowley, who had been killed. A large man in every sense, he had lived in Papua since long before the war and had a tremendous 'way' with the people. His vitality, energy, twinkling blue eyes and rollicking laugh as well as his sympathy were just what was needed to rally the people after such a disaster. His wife was tiny and genteel — a complete contrast.

We all had to fit into a very small Bulolo house with no mod cons and Paul and I, both with a tummy wog, spent a hazardous night avoiding each other as we competed for a pit latrine at the bottom of the garden. The decencies being as they were, twenty-five years ago, neither of us blinked an eyelid about it next day.

Popondetta is on a plain with many incalculable rivers racing down from the mountains. They are subject to flash floods, changing their courses, leaving bridges high and dry and generally making movement as difficult as they can. On our first day we drove as far as possible towards the volcano, looking now so serene, but still with a plume from its top. We met many village people, vigorous as only Orokaivas can be where they had been untouched. But some were sad little groups, remnants of a larger village trying to rebuild their lives after the disaster and many had scars of terrible burns on their backs as they had fled before the lava flow.

The effect on the rivers rising on the slopes of Mt Lamington was extraordinary. The molten rocks and lava hurled out were carried away by the rivers, making the water itself boil, the heat killing the trees for some metres on each bank from the volcano to the sea, thirty miles away. The desolation of rock-strewn banks, huge grey trunks with whitened branches against the sky was indescribable.

Alix Hasluck and I felt we were really having adventures. The men were in one landrover and we followed in another. Once a flash flood caught us unawares in the middle of a river crossing, with boulders rolled down by the water crashing into the landrover, pushing it sideways — we held our breath and were relieved when we made it. For some reason we had to wade another river and, clutching our skirts up above our knees, were photographed from behind by our cheerful young patrol officer driver.

Visiting the Searles at Sangara Plantation, we heard tales of many miraculous escapes besides their own. They had heard a deafening roar and then it was almost as black as night and the overwhelming instinct was to get away. Mrs Searle and the servants ran out of the house and her husband came up in a vehicle and crammed everyone around aboard. Their description of just keeping ahead of the avalanche of lava made our flesh creep. The house was enveloped and a lot of rubber trees killed, but the extraordinary rain of dust which fell for days was so fertile that the regrowth was stupendous and the production of the unhurt rubber incredibly increased.

Another day we went through ten-foot kunai to Buna, near the mouth of the Girua River, and even here there were dead trees on its banks. In this area the war was horribly close — blasted coconuts, shell holes, rusting vehicles and weapons, bunk holes and gun emplacements. But above all was the kunai. It made me shudder to think of fighting in it. The heat was stifling enough on the road, but fighting through kunai eight feet high with the sun beating down and not a breath of air must have been awful, especially being unable to see a man only a few feet away through the thick grass but hearing him, not knowing if he were Jap or Aussie. No piece of country — not even the Kokoda Trail or Shaggy Ridge — has so stirred my imagination with the horrors as did the kunai round the fighting at Buna.

The Elliot Smiths came out of Popondetta with us to go on leave, taking quite a pile of luggage, which the pilot looked at rather dubiously. We came down at Kokoda for a quick look around and piled back on again. Now Kokoda, at the foot of twelve and a half thousand foot Mt Victoria, is only eleven hundred feet above the sea, so to get out and over the famous gap you have to circle round and round making height. The plane was an old Drover, having three bucket seats one side, a bench on the other, with me sitting at its end. There were scuddy sort of clouds but all seemed well until there was a frightful jerk and I was shot down into the back of the plane and trees passed by very close to our windows. There was a deadly tense silence and we circled some more. When it was obvious that we were over the top and the ground a safe distance below, everyone began talking at once and couldn't stop. Relief is a funny thing. Then it turned out that the pilot was new to the country and had never been into Kokoda before. I'm glad his reactions were quick and the old wooden plane answered in the nick of time.

Chapter 5

Highland women bringing in their kau kaus for sale.

Routines at Government House—Visitors—Don's Work and the Public Service—Christmas in Sydney—Robert Joins the Service—First United Nations Visit—Coronation Celebrations—Highlands Road

As we settled into Government House a sort of routine had begun to emerge, taking shape on three levels, as it were. The first was in our own personal lives, another was how we fitted the official life we had to live into our personal one, and the third was how Don coped with his enormous workload as Administrator. The most important way we preserved some privacy and personal life was to keep Sundays as free as possible. Though guests often arrived on the Sunday plane, we never held any function that day and only rarely involved ourselves in their itineraries. This gave us one day to be relaxed and be ourselves.

The official life was shaped by people and events quite outside our own control and any life we could shape for ourselves meant doing so around the official demands made upon us. For instance, we had only been in the house a couple of weeks, and had a huge contraption of scaffolding across the living room, under which we had to stoop to get from the bedrooms to the dining room or verandahs, with hammering and sawing going at full blast, when Don came home saying that Canberra had phoned that the Baileys were arriving to stay next week. Mr. (later Sir) Kenneth Bailey was then the Solicitor General and Iseult, his wife, was the president of the Australian Pre-School Association. Luckily, knowing them, we were confident that they would take the chaos in good part, and their visit was fun. With the construction finished but painters everywhere, we then had a New Zealand General and his wife to stay and the Canadian High Commissioner and Mrs Fraser Elliot, who remained friends for many years.

Actually this was good experience, for there was nothing we could do about Canberra's arrangments nor about the carpenters and painters. So hosts and guests alike had to make the best of it and we found how readily people enter into the spirit of whatever is happening — in a way those circumstances set the tone of how we looked after house guests.

Don liked order and a certain basic routine to his life, so running his household was predictable. Early morning tea, brought to the study at 6.30, meant we could hear the news and be dressed in time for 7.30 breakfast. Believing that breakfast is no time to be sociable, an attractive sitting and dining corner on the east verandah flanking three guest bedrooms allowed breakfast to be served to guests separately, thus giving us all more privacy. Habitually Don walked down to the office, enjoying meeting young folk walking to work across our grounds from their hostels.

The Official Secretary, living in the tumbledown original Government House until his new one was built, would first come to the house, discuss the day's itinerary with any guests, see to their needs, organise cars and introduce whoever was to accompany them. There were usually household problems and arrangements to discuss with me before his office day began. Then I tackled the usual household chores that fall to a woman's lot anywhere. Organising the day's meals with Dosi, doing the shopping, at first training the stewards into my ways, cooking for parties, doing the flowers, working with one or another of the gardeners if necessary, answering the telephone, becoming involved more and more in Red Cross and Girl Guides etc., seeing people on request for this or that. It was a full and demanding life and continually grew more so.

The 6 a.m. plane arrival set a note of informality for guests. Protocol demanded our meeting some and how I remember those 4.30 am alarms, rising in the dark and being mollified by the early freshness driving into the sunrise on the way to Jacksons Airport. The Official Secretary could meet others and we would simply greet them at the top of the steps in our dressing-gowns.

We inherited the custom for guests to have the morning of arrival for sleep and recovery with an afternoon itinerary, till I observed that their novel surroundings were so stimulating that people were restless and kept poking about and going for walks in the garden. So we reversed the order, sent them off after breakfast and home by 11.30 for much appreciated cool drinks, and left them to sleep soundly after lunch.

Don, of course, had to keep up an exacting office routine, but early began the habit of a half-hour 'shut-eye' in a long 'planter's chair' on the verandah before returning to the office at 1.30. Instead of moving the clocks as Australia does in 'summer time', PNG moves the office hours to take advantage of the cool early mornings, so the working day is from 7.45 till 4.05 p.m.

When Don came home he usually gardened till drink time. On the western side of the house we made a new terrace, furnished with a table and wrought iron chairs made by a clever craftsman from war scrap in Lae. Not only sheltered from the prevailing strong south-east trade winds, it had the loveliest view across the harbour and here the household foregathered for drinks at 5.45 p.m. This evening hour remains in my mind as the happiest and most relaxed of the day, yarning with the sun going down behind the purple hills the other side of the harbour and the soft and familiar sounds of retreat stealing out as a police detachment marched up the hill to lower the flag. We all came in the clothes we'd worn all day and then broke up at seven to shower and change for dinner.

On our own, Don would usually unburden the troubles of the day or turn round and round a problem that was worrying him, using me as a 'talking horse'. I was always intensely interested; but what I might say was quite irrelevant, for it wasn't my views he wanted, but just to have an interested and sometimes critical listener. With guests, we usually kept at least one night en famille and this is when I recall the most interesting discussions, talking of 'shoes and ships and sealing wax' and everything under the sun.

I have a vivid picture of Julian Amery, who had been Foreign Minister during the Cyprus crisis, describing how a Lebanese Ambassador had told him, "Your job is easy. Cyprus is like a valuable carpet. You have it and the Cypriots and the Turks want it. All you have to do is to sit on it and they'll have to come to your terms." I suddenly visualised this neat, bright-eyed man sitting cross-legged, arms folded and turban-topped, looking rather impudent on a Persian carpet.

One of our very early visitors was the German Ambassador. We'd told ourselves how careful we'd have to be to keep off any reference to the war. But on his first night it somehow transpired that before the war in Greece he was representing a tobacco firm in Athens but the British came in and took over his building. Life is strange. It had been Don, as an Australian officer attached to British Headquarters, who had been the man to commandeer that particular building. From then on they enthusiastically thrashed over the war from opposite sides filling in gaps for each other. It showed me a phenomenon I've noted since. There is more of a bond in after years between one-time enemies who have fought and thus shared an experience than there is between soldiers and civilians on the same side.

Later I can see Tom M'boya from Kenya, a quiet man with emanations of inner strength which made him very impressive, and his lovely wife Pamela. Tom was genuinely puzzled when asking about political awareness and political demand, and being unbelieving with Don saying what a problem we had to stimulate and develop it. After visiting other districts we met up again at the Goroka Show. Tom caught straight up to Don, and still puzzled said, "You're right. I've questioned people everywhere and find no demand for self-government. On the contrary, they say they don't want it yet." It was obviously beyond his understanding. But that was before the days of Warwick Smith as Secretary for Territories and the wage decision. Political awareness came very soon after that.

Tables must develop auras, for so much happens round them. Quite apart from the interesting and amusing times of exotic visitors, I have been present at so many off-the-record discussions with Canberra officials staying with us. I can't remember one who wasn't charming to me, tolerating and even egging me on when I joined in discussion, often in disagreement. I'm afraid at times I traded on a woman's privilege to be quite outrageous, with Don glaring to shut me up. But afterwards on our own he would sometimes grin and say, "I'm glad you said that to so-and-so." But I was always discreet, never bringing up such discussions anywhere else. They were always free and interesting and fun and I can never remember tension or anyone taking exception to what was said in discussion, though I kept quiet when it was strictly between active participants and was glad they trusted me as a listener.

We always wished it were possible to have similar discussions with Paul Hasluck. But he could not bear people to disagree with him in conversation, and if you did, you never knew when his face would suddenly suffuse and with clenched teeth he would put you down in a most shattering manner. It was such a pity, for he hurt so many people and his visits were not nearly so interesting as other people's. A front of light-hearted, though witty, chatter and banter, at home or when travelling with him, would prevent discussion of the interesting events of the day or the problems which had been revealed. It seemed such a waste. The wide range of his mind and intellect was only projected on paper, not in conversation.

In this first year Don was still technically Assistant Administrator and was only 'acting'. But even after January 1953, when he was sworn in as Administrator, he was still doing single-handed the job which two years earlier had been assessed to need two assistants or deputies, so the inevitable files were brought home, and if visitors were there he would excuse himself if matters were pressing and retire to his study and work. An assistant was sent up in '54 but he had a nervous breakdown and later that year Mr Rupert Wilson was appointed. He had a wide knowledge of agriculture and land matters and had served in Treasury in Canberra. However, he found it hard to adapt to the tough conditions after Canberra; to grasp just what governing a country really involved, and especially to produce good work himself without staff who were properly trained in administration, so he accepted another overseas appointment in 1956. It was not till 1957 that Dr John Gunther was appointed, and there began what grew into a long, close and remarkable association between two outstanding men, each complementing the other with a mutual respect which grew into affection. But that was five years ahead of the settling-in period of '52, and long, hard years they were.

Until we came to Moresby I had never had anything to do with a Public Service. During the war Don used to speak of Reg Halligan, secretary of that part of Ward's department which looked after Papua New Guinea. Lunching with us in Melbourne in 1944, I was surprised to find a man with an obviously limited outlook and narrow field of vision being in charge of a department responsible for a whole country. So I didn't know what to expect in Papua New Guinea. What I found were a lot of colourful characters, working cheerfully in terrible hot little buildings, many still the wartime huts put up first by the Americans for MacArthur's staff and added to by Angau, conveniently built below A Mess, erstwhile Government House. By the early 1950's there was still no money to do anything else and periodically sums were squeezed from here and there to put up more single-storey temporary buildings, making an awful rabbit warren. There was no air-conditioning so open louvres were essential and dust was blown in from the bare ground by the incessant south-east trade wind and covered files and desks. Similar conditions or worse were common to all towns in PNG.

Quite obviously the service was insufficiently trained in administration, and quite obviously was not as efficient as the Reg Halligans of Canberra. But conversely I couldn't see the Reg Halligans coping so cheerfully in a war-devastated country, living in paper houses and working in Konedobu, rather cynically dubbed 'Happy Valley'.

Someone who was both cheerful and efficient was Mr Ernie Head, a neat, compact and kindly man with an imperturbable countenance. He was seconded from Canberra as Public Service Commissioner to try and weld the incongruous group of a thousand or so men and women of varying standards of expertise and competence into a service able to carry out the functions demanded of it. I know Ernie Head did his best, but I'm less sure how successful he was.

One of the disturbing discoveries Don made when he first arrived was of the set-up which had been embodied in the Papua and New Guinea Act of 1949. Before the war, in each territory the Administrator had been responsible for the Public Service and in turn was responsible for it to the Minister. The 1949 Act made provision for a Public Service Commissioner who, instead of being responsible to the Minister through the Administrator, was given autonomy and responsibility directly to the Minister, standing in the same relationship to him as the Administrator did. So you had two men each responsible for different aspects of the work of the same group of men and women, each with separate and independent access to the Minister and his department in Canberra. That in itself was bad enough, but to make it even less workable there was no machinery for bilateral communication between the two.

As the Administrator was responsible for the 'law, order and good government' of the country, the onus was squarely on him, by his own efforts to develop the kind of working relationship between them whereby the Public Service Commissioner would work in harmony and consultation with him. In achieving this Don was more successful with some than with others. Ernie Head was co-operative; the next man, T.E. Huxley, was a loner, never really saw the need to work with the Administrator and remained antagonistic rather than co-operative. Therefore the weakness of the Act was very evident and made those years extremely difficult. Huxley himself had his own difficulties and took great exception to the Minister's minutes, finally resigning because of them. There were other problems and problem people at that time, to complicate matters even more.

It was a relief to have Mr R.E.P. Dwyer, who came up for a short time only, but it was not till 1957 (the year Dr John Gunther became Assistant Administrator) that the man who was truly 'right' came along. He was Mr Neil Thomson, who had been in the N.S.W. Public Service Commission. Neil's work experience therefore more nearly approximated that of a country such as PNG than one trained in the limited functions of the Commonwealth Service, and it was a breakthrough when Hasluck obtained his services.

With Gunther and Neil Thomson began the most productive and the happiest time of Don's years in office. I often wondered how he put up with this fundamentally unworkable set-up; in this respect it is worth quoting John Gunther once more:

"...to stir the murky potage and make it even stickier was the establishment of the Public Service Commission, with the Commissioner being responsible to nobody in Papua and New Guinea. Well after Hasluck's time it became ludicrous when the Administrator wrote to the Chairman of the Public Service Board in Port Moresby and received his reply from the Secretary, Department of Territories, Canberra."

Gunther was speaking of the situation in PNG as Hasluck found it and added this:

"Under the Papua and New Guinea Act 1949, His Honour the Administrator had certain clear gubernatorial functions. He could appoint times for the Legislative Council to meet and he could prorogue it; he could assent or withhold assent to ordinances or reserve them for the Governor-General; he could grant a pardon to any convicted person, except a person sentenced to death.

In the South Pacific Commission region there were six metropolitan powers: Australia, France, the Netherlands, New Zealand, the United Kingdom and the United States of America. All except Australia were represented by His Excellency the Governor, other than the New Zealander, who was His Excellency the High Commissioner. All lived in Government House (except in Netherlands New Guinea, where it was the Governor's Palace). The population of all the other South Pacific Commission territories put together was about half that of Papua New Guinea. All governors would take precedence over His Honour, and Sir Hubert Murray had been Lieutenant Governor of Papua for nearly thirty years.

These are the conditions that Colonel Murray and Donald Cleland had to suffer. Hasluck had also to suffer it. I think there were times in the Department of Territories when it suited them to have structural chaos in Papua and New Guinea with the Administrator sitting in limbo, neither vice regal head of the Territory nor head of the public service."

In reading Sir Paul's book I was struck with his very accurate assessment of what a bad Act this 'PNG Act of 1949' was, of his clear view of the options he had, which were few; and of his ultimate decision to make the best of a bad job and to get down to practical matters, doing what he could under its limitations.

It always made me cross that Don made no fight to try and have the impossible situation resolved, namely, of having overall responsibility especially when things went wrong but having no real authority, nor any responsibility for the Public Service. But no doubt he came to the same conclusions that Paul Hasluck had come to before him — namely to make the best of it. What I do find interesting is that in Sir Paul's book he made no mention anywhere of this most unworkable division of responsibilities, yet many of his own frustrations, which are the hallmark of his book, are due to it. From this I conclude two things; either Don did not seriously take the matter up with him or Hasluck himself did not consider it as a bad structural arrangement. Or perhaps, if he did see it so, he did not perceive it as the barrier it was to the efficiency, harmony and morale of the Papua New Guinea Public Service. There is of course a third possibility: he enjoyed holding the two strings in his own hand.

The Public Service Commissioner also had his problems, which in some respects paralleled the Administrator's. His basic functions were determined by ordinance, but with his usual attention to detail Hasluck himself enunciated the interpretation and stated for the Public Service Commissioner the way he wished them to be carried out. The effect was a restriction of his functions. In the same way reviews of staff establishment to meet development and changes all had to be approved by the Minister. But as they went to him through the department at Canberra, they were all 'mauled over' by the various experts and their staffs on the way, sometimes taking months. Nobody in PNG knew what requests for staff establishment actually reached him.

A further ludicrous and frustrating aspect concerned recruiting, which for some reason was entirely in the hands of the Department of Territories, who would advertise for and interview applicants. It later became the practice for retired District Commissioners or departmental heads to sit on the interviewing board, but these men had long left PNG and they could make no reference in their choice to the Administrator or his departmental heads or even to the Public Service Commissioner in PNG. Moreover, as much as six to nine months could go by between the job being advertised and the appointment being made. For when all the processing was done, the whole thing went to the Minister, who personally approved of each recruit, right down the line. As the best people seldom waited so long and applied for other jobs, many good men and women were lost.

I had personal experience when the Adamson Pre-School Report was being implemented. As the president of the Territory Pre-School Association, formed as part of the Report's recommendations to represent the community and the parents, I had definite responsibilities and was, moreover, the only person at that time in PNG with professional qualifications and considerable experience in pre-school work. We were entirely dependent on Canberra. Processing seemed to go through a long inflexible mill. They would advertise at the wrong time of the year for teachers. Applicants waited for months for an interview and further months before appointment. When pre-school teachers finally arrived they had been given unreal information about their conditions of housing and work, which made adapting and settling down doubly hard for them and for us. And the stories not only they but many of the new recruits for other departments told, of the fantastic process they had gone through, were both funny and tragic.

If this were not enough, Hasluck added the further complication of his insistence on studying and making personal decisions on every appointment, often writing long minutes on them.

☆　☆　☆

By December 1952, we had been in PNG for fifteen very exacting months, when Don went to Canberra for discussions with the Minister and the department and I joined the family in Sydney, planning a Christmas together. My sister Barbara went off to Perth and I settled down to housekeeping in Australia again. It was lovely to see friends and be with the boys. Evan came down from jackarooing at Wee Waa and we had a wonderful family Christmas.

Don returned before New Year and I remained in Sydney for a few weeks, Robert anxiously awaiting second year Engineering results. Though he wasn't too happy about his prospects, he was shattered the morning the results came out and he hadn't passed. We had vetoed repeating, so that was it and I was thankful to be there. We talked awhile and he went off to his room and presently tore out of the house, slamming the door. A long time later he returned, going straight to his room.

After a time he came back into the drawing room, where I'd remained reading, and I was amazed at the change. His face alight, he said:

"Do you know, Mum, when I got over all that, a tremendous feeling of relief came over me and I suddenly realised that all my life, ever since I was knee-high to a grasshopper, I, and everyone else, took it for granted that I was going to be an engineer and I'd never thought it out. Now I know absolutely that it's not what I want to do at all."

Don and I had always worried about his attitude to study. He spent so much time taking the car to bits and putting it together again, or making yet another radio set, to the detriment of the hard slog of maths or logic; and, of course, there had to be time for yachting and surfing and girls.

"Well, what do you want to be?", I asked.

"A Patrol Officer in New Guinea", he said.

I could see straight away that he'd be good at it, but saw problems ahead with his father as Administrator, so told him bluntly what would happen. Some of his seniors and colleagues would expect twice as much of him, to show they weren't favouring the Administrator's son. They would be the good ones. Others, if he wasn't careful, would smarm up to him because he *was* the Administrator's son. Either way, life wouldn't be easy. Don gave him much the same advice, but his mind was made up.

Enquiring from the PNG office, he was told that cadets were then being advertised, so he applied, went for an interview and found that his took far longer than anyone else's — the board giving him a real grilling.

However, he made it and came up with thirty-three other young men at the end of March. It was fun seeing these young cadets with Rob and through his eyes. They were a motley lot with varying backgrounds and from all over Australia. The majority were eighteen and straight from school. A few, like Robert, had either been at university or had other experience.

They were all living at House O'Malley, a hostel a few minutes away from Government House, while they did a quite tough and very concentrated six-week induction course, involving a lot of lectures and study. The older ones gravitated together and one or another would come up with Rob for a drink with us. They were bored with the rowdiness and skylarking of the younger ones, so we made a room available where five or six would come and study in peace. Eventually their results and postings came through. Much impressed by Charlie Bates, the D.C. who had addressed them, Robert had nominated for Madang, but so had others, so Rob was posted to Goroka instead.

We then started something we enjoyed and kept up for many years, with each new intake of cadets coming to a party at Government House on the night of their final exams. They had such young, round faces, and it always fascinated us to meet them again in the field, often in remote places, and note how their faces had firmed and matured, becoming men in a few months.

☆ ☆ ☆

In April '53, we had our first United Nations visit. Papua and New Guinea each had a different history. At Federation in 1901, Australia accepted responsibility for the Protectorate of British New Guinea and formally took over in 1906 renaming it Papua, that being a Malay word meaning 'frizzy-haired', given by early navigators to the people of the north coast and the western end of the island. This, in retrospect, was unfortunate. If 'Australian' had been substituted at that time for 'British', the step would have been easy after World War I when Germany lost control of her New Guinea colony and the old League of Nations mandated responsibility to Australia. By dropping both colonial names the whole country would simply have been New Guinea and at independence would have had a less complicated name and certainly a less complicated psychology.

The dual history is interesting. Australia's government recognised Papua as a Trust until it would be ready for self-government, though there was some confused thinking at times and some Australians saw its future as an Australian State. Even Sir Hubert Murray once wrote that he thought such was the Australian Government's aim for Papua. It was a relief when this impractical and disturbing idea was finally denied in the sixties. From the beginning native ownership of land was recognised and it never became 'crown land', as in other British countries. Its legal status was an Australian Territory and its people travelled with Australian passports.

New Guinea, on the other hand, was a German colony till 1914. Coming under Australian administration in 1921, business interests won against commonsense in a divided report by a Commission on Administrative Amalgamation, so the two halves retained separate governments and separate laws. It was invaded and overrun by the Japanese in 1942, who also overran parts of Papua. In 1943, when Don became Chief of Staff of Angau, he amalgamated the staffs in the military administration of the two territories. This was continued under the Provisional Administration of 1946 with the name Papua-New Guinea and incorporated in the Papua and New Guinea Act of 1949.

After the second World War, the United Nations assumed the responsibilities of the old League of Nations and Australia remained the administering power of New Guinea in trust to the U.N., the country having the complicated name 'The Territory of Papua and New Guinea'. Thus, though it was governed as one, the U.N. was only responsible for half of it.

This was a second misfortune, when Australia did not cut the legal umbilical cord after the war and voluntarily accept the U.N. Trust over Papua as well as New Guinea, ensuring more even development of the two territories and allowing the people to grow together as one, long before independence came. Such an act might also have softened the problems of the dual legal system with the Trust Territory laws and customs inherited from the German administration and the Papuan from the British-Australian.

Triennially four men, elected by the Trusteeship Council, came and spent about a month visiting every part of New Guinea, but not Papua. Though Port Moresby, the capital, is in Papua, they were almost unaware of its existence.

After these U.N. visits they made a report to the U.N. on what Australia was doing, criticising this and that, and recommending changes of policy. The report was then debated by the General Assembly, when everyone seemed to enjoy attacking Australia, especially countries like Russia or India, and throwing her on the defensive. This was ridiculous. Records of what other nations, not accountable to the U.N., have done in the third world should leave Australia holding her head high and proclaiming both the fantastically good job she actually did do in New Guinea and her financial generosity.

However, U.N. pressures on Australia for development in New Guinea did starve Papua of development funds. This was aggravated when Australia invited the World Bank to examine conditions and advise it on economic development. Their report of 1964, which recommended putting development money into resource-rich areas only, meant further neglect of Papua. Years of resentment by Papuans and old Australian residents later surfaced and were given expression by

Josephine Abaijah in her Papua Besena secession movement of the early seventies.

But back to 1953, when Besena was far in the future. The U.N. mission arrived in the middle of March, flying as usual by charter plane from Guam after inspecting the U.S. Trust Territories. Over the years they arrived at different airports in New Guinea, where Don would meet them. Accompanied by an administration officer, they would follow an itinerary enabling them to go wherever they wished and inviting comments and representations by the local populations. At the end they would stay three or four days with us, during which they could see and talk to heads of departments or their staffs and have discussions with the Administrator. On these visits nothing was hidden. They were shown the problems and what we were doing to cope, in the hope that they would get a realistic picture and make a fair report.

Returning from meeting the group in Lae, Don shook his head in some bewilderment, saying that they were a rum lot, especially the leader, one Dr Marchena, a relation of President Trujillo of the Dominican Republic. Then stories of their progress began to drift back; of Marchena's total uninterest in carrying out the programme; of how he would look at the small plane and then at the mountains and refuse to go; of the demands he then made to fill his day while the others were making the inspection; of his personal behaviour — some stories unprintable. So we awaited their arrival to stay with us with interest, to say the least, and I was glad Barbara Osborne, a Sydney friend, was there to help me cope.

In the middle of April they arrived. The three other mission members were Sir John MacPherson (from the Colonial Office in London), a Frenchman, Mr Pigniu (Governor General of Overseas France) and Majmuddin Rifai (Head of the Permanent Delegation of Syria to the U.N.). Rifai tended to be singled out by Marchena as his buddy, in which role he was sometimes uneasy and sometimes responsive. The other two had obviously given up the unequal struggle and could only appear dull — which they were not.

Marchena dominated everything. He was so overdrawn a character, larger than life, that he epitomised whatever you had heard or imagined about Spanish Central Americans. His flamboyance, self-aggrandisement, self esteem and attitudes to the poor of his own country and to the people of New Guinea were quite incredible. He treated Barbara and me with flattery and exaggerated courtesy; Don, as head of a country, was his equal. To others he could be rude, demanding, pleasant or ride roughshod; to the servants, police drivers and other more lowly people he was just plain impossible. He half amused Don, but the particular brand of wit he used when necessary, to put people down a bit, just rolled off Marchena unnoticed.

We had the usual largish reception for them and one or two to dinner on the other nights, but with Marchena's dominance, conversation in any real sense was difficult. On the last morning, with all talks concluded, bags packed and gone, the plane was delayed several hours, so Marchena went off in a car for some photographing while morning tea came in for the rest of us.

There was almost an explosion of highly intelligent talk and discussion, as though the lid had come off a compression box. Each of those men fairly scintillated and I remember it as one of those times when one's mind is really stretched in the intellectual exercise of the exchange of ideas and pitting mind against mind. Everybody blossomed and each was a surprise, especially the Syrian, Rifai. As an outcome of our discussion, he sent me a book which became a milestone in my thinking, and I have read it several times. The book was *The Meeting of East and West. An Enquiry Concerning World Understanding*, by F.S.C. Northrop, Professor of Philosophy at Yale University. One of the wonderful things in life is the surprises you find in people.

Soon stories of their visit to Canberra and their talks with the Australian Government began to drift back. Paul Hasluck was not amused. In fact the shadow of that visit hovered over PNG for a long time. The U.N. itself was greatly embarrassed, and all future missions were very carefully chosen, especially their leaders.

☆　☆　☆

The next excitement for the whole country were the preparations for celebrating the Queen's Coronation in June 1953. Each of the fifteen districts was planning its own, even down to small government stations, mission stations and villages. But Don, wanting some ceremony common to and linking them all, hit on tree-planting.

Most of Papua New Guinea is either thick jungle or treeless grassland and in most towns and government stations there were few planted trees. So he arranged with the Director of Forests for a programme of raising suitable trees at all forestry nurseries, setting up new ones where necessary. Committees were asked to include extensive tree-planting in their plans, culminating in a ceremony on Coronation Day with a tree being planted in a significant place by the D.C. or prominent citizen.

The zest shown everywhere resulted in the transformation of many a bare and uninteresting little town. In Moresby we planted all the streets of the new suburb of Boroko and the commemorative tree, a *Cassia fistula* planted in bare bulldozed earth, now showers its golden glory at the end of every dry season in what has become a lush little park next to the Catholic Cathedral.

99

In Moresby celebrations lasted a week and gave us a heavy programme. On Sunday attending special Coronation church services; Monday, Children's Day, meant visiting every school, opening a new one and naming it 'Coronation School', attending interschool sports and a State Coronation Dinner at night. Tuesday, THE DAY itself, began with a Communion Service and afterwards Ela Beach Oval, surrounded by trees with the bright blue of the Coral Sea gleaming through them, was the scene of a parade no one will ever forget.

Led by a naval contingent from *HMAS Macquarie,* the Papuan Infantry Regiment and the Police with their band marched past, followed by volunteer groups including Red Cross, Scouts and Guides, some in uniforms of grass skirts and neck scarves only, and many other youth groups and sporting bodies. They were upstaged by the surprise arrival of canoes from Hula cricket club, with about fifty men immaculately attired in spotless white worthy of Lords itself.

The civilians grouped on the far side of the oval, while the Pacific Islands Regiment formed up for the royal salute of twenty-one guns, followed by a 'feu de joie', and at that precise moment three RAF planes from Townsville swooped low over the oval in salute. Nothing could have been more dramatic, or have a more unexpected side effect. All the trees were bright with Papuans in gay lap-laps who had climbed up for a better view; as the planes swooped the trees were suddenly empty — and we all ducked our heads.

After Don addressed the parade, the Royal Standard was raised over the dais as everyone left it, to signify the presence of Her Majesty during two minutes of silent prayer for her. One could really see and sense her slight figure there by her standard. It was so simple that everyone could understand and partake, and therefore so telling. I was suddenly aware that things like this were happening, not only in hundreds of places in Papua New Guinea, but in thousands of places among millions of people all over the world. And I felt a rush of gratitude that I belonged to this wide and varied Commonwealth of Nations. I was to feel a similar gratitude, tinged with a sense of wonder, twenty-five years later, when this country in its turn became an independent nation within the Commonwealth.

The Chief Justice read the Act of Loyalty, the parade marched past once more and up the road to the little park for the tree-planting. The rest of that day and the following week were given over to a great variety of activities, in which all groups in the community took part in celebration. News of similar events all round PNG coming over the radio made us feel that, as far as this little outpost of Empire was concerned, Her Majesty was well and truly crowned.

☆　　☆　　☆

Shortly after this, Ian Downs's road was to be ready for the opening on the day he had named — end of June. We had, in actual fact, been hearing a great deal about it. After being posted to Goroka, Ian Downs sent Robert off to help Rupe Haviland get the road over the Kassam Pass finished in time. Rupe was then working on the most difficult stretch through uninhabited mountainous country. Therefore men had to be recruited. Getting them food was such a problem that it needed someone else to help, so Robert's first job was to go off to the nearest villages to buy food. Later, going farther and farther afield, he had to arrange its carriage, usually by a line of women with packed billums bringing enough to feed the hungry road-builders.

Going straight from an engineering course into the practical problems of road-building was interesting and instructive. These boys had to survey as they went, needing a good eye for country. They had to keep their grades reasonable for wheeled vehicles and decide whether the distance from A to B was long enough to be able to keep within this grade. They had to watch drainage of the run-off from the heavy rainfall.

The mountains, being geologically young and unstable, were really elevated clay without a rocky core, so what looked like rock was mudstone, needing a few more million years to compact it into rock. When exposed to the air, mudstone crumbled into shale or dissolved in the rain, so landslides were a daily fact of life, as were the innumerable small streams to cross at steep gullies between every spur.

The hundred shovels had mysteriously disappeared into the villages long ago, so tools were mainly digging sticks and mats with long poles lashed to each side. Placed on the ground, the earth from the hillside was levered down onto the mat, forming a hillock, when a number of men, yelling and singing, would seize each pole and tip the earth at the outer side of the bench they were working on.

The run-off would soon have washed loose earth downhill and was only one problem their resourcefulness and originality had to overcome. A deep drain against the mountain collected run-off from both mountain and road, the bench sloping from its outer edge inwards. Down at Gusap, the wartime airstrip where the road began, there were literally thousands of empty forty-four-gallon drums. There a group knocked off the ends with cold chisel and hammer, while pairs of men shouldering a pole slung with three or four drums carried them up the mountain to the workers, who laid about four end to end under the road, taking water from the drain and discharging it well below the level of the road edge. This was done every twenty yards along its whole length.

For the hundreds of culverts and bridges, large trees were felled and dragged down the mountain by groups of men, yodelling and chanting rhythmically. Such chants were an integral part of their work pattern, governing their style of organising themselves in a surprisingly economical and efficient way. Two large logs would be laid across from bank to bank of the stream or ravine. Closely packed across them, smaller logs from six to nine inches thick were firmly bound with kunda or bush creepers; lastly a mat of saplings, laid across, were bound and packed with fine river gravel brought up in baskets on the heads of the women and children. Nothing would have kept them away from so novel and exciting an activity. Scampering up and down, laughing and fooling, however perilously poised the basket looked, it never fell off.

Robert's letters were full of all this activity and what really came through was his enthusiasm, and also the heartbreak, as when several days' road bench would slide into the valley in an extra heavy thunderstorm, or several miles would have to be abandoned when they came to an insurmountable impasse.

Rupe had been born in New Guinea, his father being a senior officer in the service, and no young man could have been luckier in his first work-mate and companion. They would talk over the camp fire far into the night, arguing and discussing, Robert imbibing New Guinea lore all the time. From their main camp on what is now a lookout and stopping point, they set out on motor bikes every morning, supervising and organising the village work groups.

Don and I left at the end of June with some insight into what was involved. Staying overnight with the Nialls in their makeshift house in Lae, to be ready for an early charter to Gusap, where Ian Downs had a landrover waiting, we woke to a steady downpour from thick, low-ceilinged cloud. With no hope of getting out, we waited for a break, but three inches fell before lunch and, by night, seven.

Saying that bad weather sometimes lightened for a short period before dawn, the pilot told us to be ready at five to seize an opportunity. Just after dawn, his eyes discerned what we could not and we took off into the murk, which thinned as we flew up the Markham, trusting that Ian would hear the plane. Sure enough, though it was still drizzling, he was there.

Ian drove, I sat in the middle and Don on the left, with the windscreen wipers mesmerically keeping peep-holes clear in the mud-splattered windscreen and the canvas flaps successfully hiding our side view. Ian said that yesterday had begun fine. All the villagers who had helped on the road were out in their full glory of feathers to celebrate our coming and looking forward to the pigs waiting to be killed after we had passed. Instead we had not come, and with the rain they had all dejectedly gone home.

We easily climbed the foothills to the uninhabited, problem part of the road in the stickiest, worst part of the mountains, and here were the wild men, recruited from the hardly explored Okapa to the south.

Wearing G-strings only, their hair in hundreds of tiny plaits, they stood glumly with arms crossed over their chests, as is their fashion; the rain streaming off their well-greased skins.

We then noted that two tracks of twigs were giving our wheels some grip, the men grasping another bundle in each hand to rush and place underneath when our wheels spun. Dear Ian, nothing would defeat him, and my heart ached for him and even more for the wet and miserable tribesmen. This gala occasion was now so dreary.

I felt we must do something, so leant forward waving my hand madly back and forth, rivalling the windscreen wipers. But they didn't see. Don asked Ian to toot his horn and waved too. Suddenly they saw the waving hands and their bodies quickened. Waving even more madly we began beckoning until they caught on with a sort of explosion and fell in behind us, running and yelling, while those we'd passed heard the noise and joined in. When Don sat forward and they saw his red-banded army cap, a great shout went up and I could sit back and watch.

At campsite for morning tea, our comet tail of wet but happy and excited tribesmen swarmed round us and started a veritable orgy of handshaking as Rupe Haviland, the hero of the road, waited to welcome us. Looking for Rob, Ian told Don that he'd flown him back to Goroka, thinking the publicity would be inappropriate. Poor Robert, our warnings were coming true already.

Rupe, a good-looking, rather retiring young man, modest about his achievement, gave us a very welcome morning tea, took us to the lookout they'd cleared, showing a fabulous view of the Markham Valley through a gap in the mountains, and asked if I'd like to retire, to which I said — no thanks. Saying our goodbyes to the cheers of the builders we pressed on to Kainantu, while Rupe prepared the celebration pig-killing.

Harry West, the A.D.C. at Kainantu, gave us many tales of the road over lunch and on we drove to reach Goroka in daylight. Announcing our arrival with the horn, the road, now a tunnel through ten foot pit-pit, finally emerged by the cleared space in front of the first house we came to — that of Snow MacFarlane, the Qantas agent, busy also in planting up coffee and opening trade stores.

A white ribbon stretched between us and the detachment of police in charge of the ramrod-straight figure of Robbie Robertson, ex-guardsman and new police officer. A small group of Europeans, Robert amongst them, with highlanders and others running from every direction, came to watch. Les Williams, the D.O., handed Don the scissors to cut the ribbon and, with a short speech of eulogy, he declared the road open. He inspected the Guard, shook hands, had a few words with the groups of people and that was that — almost an anti-climax.

Robert came for a quiet hour with us at the Residency, and good it was to see him. Eagerly asking questions about the road and our adventures, he finally said:

"Mum, what did you think of the loo we made for you?" And when I said I didn't use it, he looked absolutely horrified.

"Mum, how *could* you? You've no idea the trouble we took. We even hand-carved a seat and got it finished just before I left."

Another lesson learned! From then on, when asked if I wished to retire, I always said "Yes".

The Gorokans of 1953 had made a sports ground and had just finished a clubhouse, measuring twenty feet by forty, and there everyone gathered that night, bringing dishes of food for a buffet. We ate and we drank, made speeches, danced to records and generally had a wonderful time, accented by the four young bachelors, who shared a Bulolo house, concocting verses about their elders and singing them to a folk tune. These youngsters, including Robert and Robbie Robertson, kept putting their heads together, coming up with others — each a bit more outrageous as the party went on, but so refreshing and funny.

Robertson, now Official Secretary to the PNG Governor General, reminded me that Don had spoken to this effect.

"I know you all think Goroka is it. I know you are all so enthusiastic and that development is going ahead here. But you mustn't forget that there are other parts of the country, where others are working just as hard, and developing too."

He was right. But even so there was something special about Goroka.

This night so well expressed the pioneering spirit, when everybody came and none were left out. The little building was stark. Cold and muddy outside, we were far too crowded inside. But everyone thought it was wonderful that they had a building at all. The road was a miracle and a constant toast. Ian glowed. True, the party was all European, but everyone had good and friendly relations with the Goroka highlanders, whose sights at that time were certainly not on coming to such a party. For one thing, all still wore traditional dress, their skins gleaming with a thick coating of pig grease. It kept them warm but did not go with a party of this sort and a pig-killing was far more to their taste.

There was no doubt about Ian. The new road was a fantastic achievement in any terms. True, the actual physical work was done by young patrol officers and the hundreds of village people, but his was the conception, his was the organising ability and the drive. Above all he had the incomparable gift of enthusing people and inspiring them to believe they could do the almost impossible. Robert's letters were full of Ian's sayings and of the way he would come to where they were working, stay for a meal or sit down and yarn with them, hear their problems, suggest solutions, and go away leaving them feeling they were not only men, but supermen. Robert did not actually say this, but the feel of it came through in his letters.

Anyway, Ian was never one to miss an opportunity, or even a chance of creating one opportunity out of another. So next day he drove us to the far western end of the valley, where the Asaro River takes a southern turn across it before winding south-east down its full length, eventually finding its way to the huge Purari, which drains into the Papuan Gulf. Here, right under a bluff behind which mountains rise up and up, supporting the great 16,000feet bulk of Mount Wilhelm (the highest in PNG), Ian had taken his road and built a bridge. Just completed, we were the first vehicle to cross and drive along the bluff on a muddy bench for a few hundred yards, from the end of which we could see along the flank of the mountain to our right and down the valley to our left.

Poor Don. Here was Ian trying to sell him another almost impossible idea. From this spot to the Wahgi Valley is the tumbled jumble of mountains of the Chimbu, making what had been considered an impassable barrier. Yet they held the heaviest population density in the whole country. Ian's case was that the dangerous little strip at Kundiawa gave totally inadequate access for pacification and development and that he was sure he could put a road through.

"Humph," said Don, with one of his pregnant silences. Ian fidgeted.

Roads, of course, need upkeep. You may be able to inspire the initial building, but they would deteriorate rapidly in that climate on the unstable mountains. Who was going to keep them repaired and in good order, and who was going to pay for that? The tight budget of PNG, utterly dependent on Australia, was always a problem.

The discussion went back and forth. Ian could see Don's problems and Don was sympathetic to Ian's enthusiasm and aware of his communication needs. And so the matter was left for the time being. Don made many enquiries, and chewed on it for some weeks, but finally Ian got his go-ahead.

Chapter 6

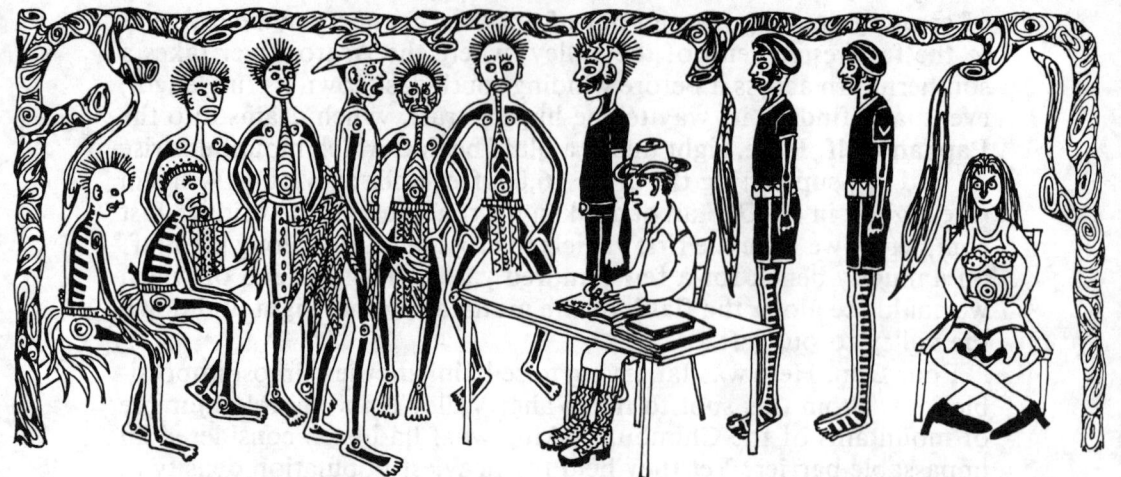

Village men came to ask Robert to make court at Daulo Camp.

Problems in the Office—House: Appointment of Daphne—Community Work and Visitors—Sir William Slim—War Cemeteries—Visit to Mekeo—Staying with Robert at Daulo Pass—Robert's Marriage

As the year 1953 wore on, the very complex problems directly arising from the personality of the Minister were pressing more heavily on Don. On the one hand, it was a joy to work with a person of wide vision, a quick clear grasp of a problem, an equally clear and lucid commitment to paper of his view of a situation, with the issuing of clear, concise instructions relating to it. He had a first-class intellect, sympathy for certain human problems and at times a poetic appreciation of beauty and atmosphere. But he had an exposed nerve and, if you unwittingly touched it, his reaction was immediate and savage. He not only hurt people, who were mostly his subordinates and thus could not answer back, but left them paralysed and shattered.

Fortunately it only happened to me once. He had made a comment about something and I put up a slightly different viewpoint, as one does normally in conversation, and the result was an explosion. I said nothing but decided that, as far as I was concerned, discussion with him was out; if he was ever so rude to me again, I would just quietly get up and excuse myself. Fortunately, through being careful, I never had to take that extreme step, though more than once I have comforted others in distress from their experience.

An odd thing was that Paul himself seemed quite unaware of the hurts he gave people, or that their effects were destructive to his own work and inhibited the success of what he was trying to do. The even stranger circumstance was his own hypersensitivity to criticism, which made him vulnerable, especially as far as the press was concerned.

Don had begun with an excellent relationship, feeling he had Paul's trust, while he admired and respected the Minister's capacity and gifts. The tone of minutes and communications received by J.K. Murray should have warned him, but, being aware also of Murray's administrative limitations, he was unprepared on finding himself gradually becoming the victim.

However, within the Administration, Don was getting somewhere with streamlining the administrative processes. He had gradually unearthed and examined the tangle of committees, which had proliferated until some men spent more time attending meetings than in getting on with the job of good administration, vital to producing results. Many were disbanded and he began the practice of reviewing regularly each committee's achievements, whether it had been disbanded when the work was done, or whether it had become a sort of 'too-hard basket'.

He was also bringing some order into procedures and setting up good clear lines of communication, so that information and decisions went more quickly up and down the ladders, and sideways too, so that matters of importance didn't get lost in someone's drawer. He was always a stickler for good, clear, quick communication, but used to come home groaning with trying to get efficiency from inadequate human material. Some of the good men were very good, but so many untrained people had been gathered in from here and there that the effort to make them into an organisation, with the ability to do what was required, was a pretty heart-breaking job.

For me, the rapid increase of responsibilities by the end of 1952 made evident the impossibility for one person to carry out increasing outside demands, organise the household, do party cooking and all the shopping, answer the telephone, as well as work in the garden and then appear to guests as though these things just got done by themselves. The staff establishment provided for a housekeeper; but the house was not large enough to take a person of an intermediate status, nor was I willing to risk the disturbance of the happy, easy relationship with our national staff if a person with bad attitudes was appointed.

The problems were compounded by the increase of community activities and consequent growth in correspondence. Those stalwart organisations of almost all countries, Red Cross and Girl Guides, existed in very rudimentary form. Although my position as President, resting, as it did, merely on my being the wife of the Administrator, was normally one of patronage only, I found myself being drawn more and more into things as a working member, largely because I had considerable organising experience and it seemed natural to help build them up as organisations.

Don was concerned with my plight and we suddenly realised the kind of person who would fit the bill — a girl who could help with entertaining, liked cooking and would be willing to help in the kitchen, do the flowers or answer the phone; who could organise and, most importantly, type. The Public Service Commissioner was most agreeable for us to find the right person to fill the housekeeper's position with a housekeeper's salary, but be called 'secretary' in an honorary way.

By that time, the needs of the Guides for a really knowledgeable person was becoming so evident that I had a brain-wave and wrote to Queensland Guide Headquarters, asking if they had a trained Guider who would like such a job. The happy outcome was that Daphne Carpenter, their State Secretary, who also ran a Guide Company, came up early in 1953. She became my second pair of hands and a cross between a daughter and a real friend for the next four years. With her knowledge and experience, guiding really took shape, while she trained me in guiding and gave me a thorough grounding in Guide organisation. When, in 1959, I was awarded the M.B.E. and the Citation said, "The recent development of Guiding in the Territory largely is due to the work of Mrs. Cleland," I always felt that it was in great part Daphne who had earned it. In her last year, she became the Chief Commissioner for Papua New Guinea.

So, in addition to the fairly frequent house guests and the consequent dinners or cocktail parties, the functions we had to attend and the various visits away to the districts, I was involved in an increasing number of meetings. We also had guiding house guests in Mrs. Lilian Gresham, the Girl Guide State Commissioner for Queensland, in May 1953, and Dame Lesley Whately, the Director of the World Bureau, in September. Each of these meant not only a programme of visiting Guides and Brownies in villages and a Guide-Scout Rally in Moresby to demonstrate sound development, but some hard talking to gain greater autonomy in running our own affairs.

Dame Lesley visited Pari Village, now fifteen minutes away, but in 1953 only a landrover could travel the track and needed an hour or more. The whole village turned it into a gala day and Dame Lesley had a wonderful time, not only with the Brownies and Guides, but Scouts and Cubs as well. Then the Women's Club and the Church Guild took over and, with the Papuan Pastor and his wife as hosts, gave us lunch in the big mission house. Freshly caught fish, cooked in coconut cream, along with yams, taro and bananas, made it a delicious and unusual meal for her.

When she was asked if she would like to retire, she refused, so I whispered, "I think you'd better". At her questioning look, I nodded and she rose nobly to the occasion to the beaming smiles of everybody. Way off at the edge of the village I'd noticed a brand new pit latrine, to which dear Dame Lesley, watched by the whole village, was proudly escorted along a path spread with clean white sand, decorated each side with festoons of flowers and ending with a floral archway before the latrine. It was obviously the 'piece de resistance' and I was glad I'd learned my lesson at Kassam Pass.

☆   ☆   ☆

In October 1953, we had a visit of some significance. Since the end of the war, the British War Grave's Commission had been searching for the remains of those killed, collecting the records and developing three cemeteries in Papua New Guinea — one at Bomana near Port Moresby, one at Lae and one at Bita Paka, near Rabaul. Each was designed to fit into its individual site, with an entirely different character and atmosphere, but having in common, with every War Cemetery in British Commonwealth countries, a most beautiful cross, known as the Cross of Sacrifice. In each cemetery the cross, situated for ceremonial occasions, brings to the whole an almost tangible presence of peace.

By October everything was ready, and that great soldier, Sir William Slim, then Governor General of Australia, was coming up to unveil the crosses. In addition, all the Australian Generals, Admirals, Air Vice Marshals, many Ministers, representatives of the services, both men and women, and other distinguished guests were invited — seventy or so in all. For the size and state of the towns in 1953, this was a major undertaking, but people offered hospitality and everybody was fitted in.

For us, and especially me, it was a time of some trepidation. Your first viceregal guests are quite an alarming prospect, and especially when the Governor General is a person with so formidable a reputation as the hero of Burma. Lady Slim was in England, so it was an all male party which was to arrive on Sunday in an Air Force plane, and included a staff of three and a valet, all staying in the house, while the Minister, arriving on Saturday, had the guest bungalow.

All week, Daphne and I had been drilling our staff, hoping they'd be adequate; the menus were worked out and everything possible planned. The flowers were done and the house really looked quite lovely. At that time we had our usual four stewards, while a new one, recently come in for training, had been mainly helping in the kitchen with Dosi and the stewards teaching him. A tall, attractive young man called Kila, he was shaping quite well, so had waited at table several times.

About mid-afternoon, a lad came to me looking awful and with a burning skin — temperature one hundred and four. So he was rushed down to the hospital. An hour later, another went down. By five the other two had raging temperatures. What, oh what a kettle of fish. An outsider can cook in your kitchen or wash in your laundry, but the house staff needs intimate knowledge. We cast around, trying to think whom we could borrow, but folks we knew with well trained staff were all putting up guests.

Then the doctor from the hospital rang up, saying, "Mrs. Cleland, this is terrible. Can I help with my houseboy?" My grateful acceptance. Finally, we borrowed two more, and by eight o'clock they were installed, with the new lad in charge and visibly swelling with pride. Daphne and I took them through the bedrooms, hoping they'd remember what to do. We sat at the dining room table while they practised serving from the left, taking from the right and holding a dish on the flat of their palms. They didn't do too badly at breakfast and lunch, so we hoped for the best.

Sir William touched down at 2 p.m. and at 2.30 I thrilled to see the Royal Standard flying from A.1., the long and elegant but rather ancient car, bringing them to the house. Sir William was reserved and strong, but relaxed and natural as we showed them all to their rooms.

Asking Don how everything had gone with the welcoming ceremonial, he chuckled and said, "Oh boy. He'll do me. Do you know what happened?"

Apparently the Minister and Don were to greet him at the gangway, Don then presenting to him the G.O.C. Northern Command, supposed to be standing behind him. Don turned round to do so, but no General. He was still chatting at the edge of the strip and a photo shows Don with a furious look beckoning him over. Meanwhile as they waited, they turned towards the Guard, who, by this time thoroughly confused, suddenly presented arms. Out of the corner of his mouth, Slim said, "The bastards. Half cock as usual." Don simply loved him for it, saying, "A man after my own heart".

The incident gave me an idea of easing the strange servant problem, and so at drink time, when everyone was relaxed after the busy afternoon, I turned to Sir William, saying:

"Sir, I do hope you have a sense of humour."

Startled, he said: "Well, I hope I have, but why?"

Then I recounted the staff calamity, saying:

"They're strangers, with our newest recruit in charge and they're sure to do extraordinary things; so anything could happen, but it won't matter as long as everyone thinks it's funny."

There was no doubt of the effect. His rather grim face had a delightful way of crinkling up when he smiled, and from then on the visit never looked back. He thoroughly entered into the spirit of it

110

all and during the next three days would come up to me, saying:

"Do you know what they've just done?" And out would come some funny little anecdote.

Daphne worked madly behind the scenes and they really managed very well. By the second night, with a dinner party before the large official garden reception, they had become really confident. The dining room was a long narrow room with three french doors opening onto a verandah — the study at one end and the servery at the other. Sir William was sitting on my right in the centre of the table with our backs to the verandah. The main dish, Chicken Maryland, was served on an enormous, century-old meat dish from the Spode service brought by grandfather Cleland to Australia in the 1840's.

The first two courses went off normally, then, sensing something unusual behind me, I looked round to see a procession of four pacing like something from the Arabian Nights, each with red hibiscus in his hair and bearing the dishes well out before them in a very grand manner. I tried to attract Kila's attention to our empty places, but he was far too concentrated, continuing down the verandah, sweeping magnificently into the far end of the room and, with a grand turning movement, bore down on Sir William, presenting the big dish with a flourish.

Sir William pointed to the empty place before him, saying, "Plates". A gasp of "Oh", from Kila; then he straightened up with perfect composure, the procession turned and went back the way they came, brought in the plates and then repeated the performance. By this time we were convulsed with laughter and our dear staff weren't the slightest bit discomposed. In after years Sir William used to remind me of that night.

The big ceremony took place on Monday morning. Port Moresby is situated in hilly savannah country between the Coral Sea and the main range of the Owen Stanley mountains. The hills are beautiful shapes, so everywhere has a lovely skyline. Fourteen miles from town, you enter Bomana Cemetery at the bottom of a gentle slope and see rows and rows — four thousand five hundred white headstones, set in beautifully kept lawn with colourful shrubs about and landscaped trees. On a rise behind the headstones is the Cross of Sacrifice and a steep hill beyond is crowned with a Greek Rotunda, bearing the names of the missing inside its columns, while a brass marker table shows the direction and the distances of the battlefields. Standing there, you look straight at the foothills of the Sogeri Plateau where, twenty miles away, blue and beautiful, is Imita Ridge, where the Australian 25th Brigade turned back the Japanese. The Japs nearly made it, but by then it was they who had to carry supplies over that awful track. Behind Imita the mighty Mt Victoria rears its bulk fifty miles away with Kokoda at its foot over 'the Gap' to the east. Bomana is wonderfully situated, with the young bodies lying in the shadow of the mountains they so heroically defended.

On this hot October morning, the ceremonial went off without a hitch and Sir William made one of the simplest, most moving and most inspiring speeches we had ever heard. During his speech he said something we had not realised before, using these words:

"This spot on which we stand is to Australians, indeed to all free people, especially hallowed and historic ground. For here, in this lovely garden, rest the men who, first of any, flung back and defeated a Japanese Army. Less than thirty miles from here, on the heartbreaking slopes of the Kokoda Trail at Imita Ridge, the great arc of Japanese conquest that swept across Asia and the Pacific was first halted. In the arduous campaign that follow- ed, the enemy, resisting grimly, was pushed back across the Owen Stanley range, and, on the beaches of Buna and Gona, was destroyed.

"It was Australian soldiers, airmen and sailors who broke the spell of Japanese invincibility on land, and inflicted on their ar- rogant army its first defeat. Let Australians never forget this. It is, like Anzac, part of their most noble tradition — and these men made it.

"The ripples of this first victory in the land war against Japan spread beyond these New Guinea shores. Far away a haggard army, battered and bitter with defeat, clung to the fringes of Burma. To it, the victory of these men brought a gleam of hope. If the Australians could do it, so, God willing, could they. I was one of them, and for that other army I would now pay our special tribute of admiration and gratitude to the men who fought here . . ."

As he finished, he unveiled the Cross and went forward to place a wreath; followed by all the visiting Generals and Admirals, represen- tatives of many local bodies and individuals, till the Cross rose from a mound of flowers, while a long pilgrimage went up to the little rotun- da on the hill. As we arrived, one name leapt out at me: David God- frey, the eldest son of dear friends of ours, whose plane was lost over the Pacific. I hadn't known his name was here.

Our dinner party that night was followed by an experiment. Previously, garden parties had been held in the late afternoons, just when the heat was most unbearable, and one could hardly call them enjoyable. This time we thought we would have it at 8.30 at night. Though handicapped by limited lawn space for the several hundred guests and having to use the drive, it was a great success. Later we built a wall on the hillside below the drive and, with excavating and filling, made a large flat lawn where evening garden parties have been given ever since.

Sir William Slim, Sir Donald (obscured), Rachel and two aides walking in the front garden.

Going aboard the Catalina at Samarai.

Sir William Slim talking to Kabua from Hanuabada, Supreme Court interpreter for 50 years,
Willie Gauera, Chairman Local Govt Council (back to camera), head of Taua Kapena can be
seen over Sir Donald's shoulder.

Sir William Slim, Rachel and Sir Donald on the side terrace.

On Wednesday the whole party went over to Lae and then to Rabaul for the ceremony and programme arranged in each place: each one had its own unique atmosphere. At Lae, one small incident remains vivid. During prayers and laying of the wreath, Sir William placed his cap on the ground, then back on his head for the march past. We were standing behind him and I could see a number of ants running around his neck and about his ears and yet he didn't flinch. Commiserating with him later, he said:

"Oh, but that wasn't the worst of it. My cap was full of the bloody things, all skating around my bald skull. It was almost intolerable."

And yet he stood for fifteen minutes without twitching and we were all lost in admiration at his iron self-control.

This was the first of many meetings with Sir William. Later, Lady Slim paid us a fortnight's visit on her own and I accompanied her and her party on an extended tour, when we really got to know one another. We always seemed to have unexpected drama on our Governor General's visits and hers was no exception.

The Slims came up several times and were always very good to us when we went to Canberra, and many years later, when Don had retired and Sir William was Governor of Windsor Castle, we had wonderful reunions with them in their suite in St. George's Tower. Sir William Slim was a really great human being, with more of the emanation and distinction of greatness than anybody I have ever known. And with it, the utmost directness and simplicity. Lady Slim was a fitting wife for him and they were a wonderful pair.

☆　☆　☆

Noticeable on the Moresby streets are men wearing long red or white ramis, carefully arranged with a wide black belt, neat close-fitting tucked-in T-shirt, a traditional throat necklace or red spotted neckerchief and a hibiscus or feather in their teased-up halo of hair. They are Mekeos, and stride along with great dignity and superb arrogance, exciting curiosity. So when Don announced a Mekeo visit, I was excited.

With Alan Timperley, the D.C., we flew to Bereina, the airstrip beside Epo, the government rice farm, looked over it and were regaled with the problems which were in part reason for our visit. Then we climbed aboard a wartime jeep without a hood, our transport for the next few days. Alan and Don, in front, had padded seats, while Bill Tomasetti (the A.D.O.) and I sat sideways on iron seats at the back. Luckily I had brought a parasol and wished also for a cushion.

The Mekeo, only about 80 miles away, is now linked by road, but then it was almost past the back of beyond. It is a flat plain of rich soil, good rainfall and plenty of jungle to cut down for shifting cultivation. French Fathers and Australian Sisters of the Sacred Heart, working there since the 1890's, had shown an enlightened attitude towards the people's culture, resulting in good blending of traditional ways and Christianity.

Research had pronounced the country suitable for dry rice growing, and time, energy and money were put into teaching the people to grow this crop on a large scale, the mission having introduced it early in the century among other plants for village gardens. Grain was unknown in Papua or New Guinea before contact, their staples being root and tree crops; their knowledge and skills were for these and they resisted those changes needed for grain. Moreover, none of their ideas and customs fitted in and they thought it foolish to work so hard when rice was easily bought in a trade store. Therefore, the Department of Agriculture really had a problem.

Leaving Bereina, our jeep trundled off across the plain in the burning sun to the Ungabunga, a problem river often shifting its course, thus causing great anxiety to the Fathers running Mainohana Boys' School, as it edged across their food gardens, even threatening the buildings. Staff and pupils gave us a warm welcome and lunch and then watched us sliding down the muddy banks to a waiting canoe which swept into the current, paddlers madly steering downstream across to the opposite bank. Rather heartstopping; I never thought we would land at the right place, but somehow always did.

The agriculture officer had a tractor and trailer with cane chairs for us — very grand, until mud flew everywhere, crossing a sago swamp to the agricultural station we inspected, where we spent the night.

Next morning's programme took us to a problem village, beautiful but empty, though they knew we were coming. Waiting to see what would happen, we relaxed on a log, just talking quietly. Finally, a house door opened and, with superb unhurried arrogance, a tall, slim, elderly man stepped down the house ladder and strolled towards us, halting a little distance away.

"The Sorcerer", said Bill.

The halt was not indecision, but done for pure effect before he approached with a wonderful contempt. Nothing was said for a while, then the D.C. offered him a cigarette. Regarding it a few moments, he took one, and slowly a conversation was begun in Motu. Periodically, either Bill or Alan would put Don in the picture, while gradually others drifted up and joined in. One got very heated and the heated talk spread as more men came. Alan and Bill heard them all out and then began the untangling of the problem, making sure it had all come to light, and then the long, patient discussion.

We must have sat two hours on the log and by then they were squatting on the ground around us and things were getting more relaxed, and from time to time, Alan and Bill would have short discussions with Don. Eventually, all the problems and antagonisms semed to have come to the surface and one or two solutions seemed to be emerging. Then Don spoke to them saying that he had heard their problems and could see their troubles. He made a tentative proposal and suggested they talk about it. They turned it over and over in Mekeo, and came back with a modification in Motu. The real discussion had now begun. Eventually, they worked something out to the satisfaction of both sides; and then from behind a house a gorgeous group of young men emerged, dancing. And when I say gorgeous, I mean it. Among all the fabulous plumes and headdresses of variety among the peoples of PNG, there is none with more exquisite artistry or perfection of workmanship and colour than the Mekeo. So these wily old men had had a dancing group ready, just in case we deserved it, and I'm glad we did. By then the hidden women and children came out and, though by no means expansive, at least the atmosphere had changed. We made our gifts of tobacco and said our goodbyes.

The tractor then trundled us back through the swamp to another village, which was a hive of activity, with the government-owned machinery going full blast, hulling, winnowing and bagging their rice crop. The whole village had a definite 'see what a good boy am I' sort of attitude, showing their great superiority to the Inawaia, where they knew we would have had a bad reception.

I must say, we really enjoyed the contrast, and went round looking with great interest at everything. They too, of course, had problems, but these were ironed out far more easily, and they were very proud to show us all their bags of rice piling up in their storage shed. We left with great handshaking and cordiality, and set off for Eboa, an equally enthusiastic village.

The interesting thing there was to meet the oldest-looking human being we had ever seen. He was squatting on the platform under the house, and had the most wonderful face. They were all so proud of old Auvo, and said that he was over 100 years old.

Off again to the canoe, waiting at another part of the river and, as we swirled into the current, we saw that a huge crowd had decorated our waiting jeep, laughing and cheering our arrival in such a wonderful welcome that I shook a few hands. These people had also decorated the road and were lined up along it from the landing to Aipiana village. Every hand was held out all the way for over a mile, so Don and Alan on their side, and Bill and I on ours, had to shake every single one — an exhausting, but highly popular performance. Finally, we drew up at the entrance to the village under an elaborate archway with a verse by the local poet, Alan Natachee, written in our honour and painted on a suspended board.

The Mekeo villages are well designed, with well-built houses surrounding a large open space with a church usually at one side. Aipiana had recently celebrated 'Corpus Christi' with other villages as visitors, and I was enchanted to find wayside chapels and altars built for the occasion, with altar appointments of local materials and their own symbolism turned to Christian uses and meanings. Studying their own myths, you find enough of relevance to be used and to my mind must give them more validity and understanding. The Catholics, especially the Sacred Heart Order, and the Anglicans are best at doing this.

By this time it was late afternoon, and we pressed on to spend the night at the bush material house of Geoff Angel, the agricultural extension officer, and his wife Vicki, passing through the large village of Beipa on the way. Officially visiting Beipa the next day, we just waved to people going about their business. Suddenly, two men rushed out, blocked our way and, with what sounded like angry shouting, threw something on the ground before us. I was quite alarmed, as it seemed hostile, but Bill said:

"Betel nut branches; a great honour and only done from one chief to another."

Stopping, the chief climbed up and sat beside Don while people rushed in from everywhere, throwing two-shilling pieces into the jeep, many hitting us. The good-humoured excitement mounted, more and more came pelting in till we felt we were, in fact, targets. Our laps and the floor of the jeep were gleaming with silver — all a present for us. More quick thinking for Don. The Queen's Coronation appeal for women and children still being open, he accepted it ceremoniously, once more explaining about government men not taking money, and said he would put it in the Queen's appeal from Beipa. When we counted it up, there was over eighty pounds and later the Mekeo got a mobile welfare clinic from the appeal.

After all this long and exciting day, it was bliss to flop on Vicki Angel's comfy bed for half an hour before coping with the bucket shower and changing. In the lamplight after dinner, as we sat enjoying the utter stillness of the bush, it was suddenly broken by a flurry of drums with a burst of singing and flaring of coconut torches. We rushed outside to see a typically dramatic Mekeo dancing group from Inawauni Village, four miles up the track and not on our itinerary. But they'd no intention of being left out. Gradually, the watchers swelled as Beipa people came to see what was happening, and an undercurrent developed with a few angry murmurs, increasing in intensity till a fight seemed likely to break out. Bill Tomasetti had been nosing around to discover the trouble, which gave us another insight.

The Mekeo make complicated headdresses which surround the face with a fanlike frame, inset with rows of tiny feathers forming patterns. Some people of a certain rank in certain clans have the right to wear, behind it huge frames up to six feet tall, supported by forks going over the shoulders and filled in with the mosaics of feathers framed by waving paradise plumes. Standing up from both types of headdress are separate uprights of white cockatoo feathers with notches clipped in their sides. Some are fixtures, but always one is on a hinge and swings back and forward with the dancer's movement.

Bill found that this dangerous-sounding, mounting anger, was over the notches in the white cockatoo feathers, which have special significance; certain notched patterns are only to be worn by certain clans or persons and the Beipas noted that the Inawauni had cut their cockatoo feathers in ways to which they were not entitled — rather like a MacDonald woman weaving a Campbell pattern into her husband's kilt.

It became necessary to stop the dancing and separate the groups, and both Bill and Geoff Angel said how much they quarrelled over the notches and how difficult it was to stop, so Don suggested the clans take out a patent which could be defended in court.

Thanking the Inawauni people for coming, and expressing our enjoyment, Don then raised the problem of the feathers, offered the suggestion of registering the rights to their clan patterns and explained about the court. Though they were impressed and it gave them something to talk about, I doubt if they ever did anything. Strangely, I've seen much Mekeo dancing, have often been personally involved, and have even taken a small group to a Moomba Festival in Melbourne, but I have never again seen anger like that which whipped up so suddenly that night.

Next morning we went off to see Geoff's extension work, inspected two more villages and had lunch at the mission with the Good Sisters who, with Frenchmen to look after, are celebrated cooks; and we did their efforts proud before going into Beipa for our official visit. Again an empty village, but, seeing a newly erected bough shelter over a table at the far end, we walked down. It was all set with a brand new cloth, trade store cutlery and plates showing price tags, and a gay candlewick bedspread slung under the coconut-frond roof. By then, women were coming down the ladders with bowls on their heads and placing them on the table, village elders appeared and made speeches inviting us to be seated for the food they'd cooked. As we sat, a plate of fried eggs was placed before each of us.

Belts already tight from the Sisters' spread, we tried to hide our dismay. Don, never good at eating strange food, toyed with the eggs, while the rest of us did our manful best to make up by sampling everything. By then, the entire village had gathered and our every move was watched and discussed — most disconcerting. We admired the cloth and the cutlery and enquired where they'd bought the bedspread. "David Jones catalogue," came the proud rejoinder. After lunch they escorted us round the village and, with happy farewells to the warm and generous Beipa, we went thankfully back to recover at the Angels'.

My main memory next day was of driving across a swamp on a perilous contraption of logs to a primitive jetty where the jeep was manhandled onto a barge — also primitive — and of its outboard engine chugging through the mangroves down the gloomy river and out to sea across Hall Sound to Yule Island, headquarters of both the Catholic Mission and the Government.

One of the worries of getting good district administration in Papua was that the number of district headquarters were situated on islands near the mainland, probably chosen originally for security and when all transport was by ship or on foot. But the advent of planes and the ubiquitous landrover had totally changed the picture, forcing a decision to move them. This visit had also been a reconnaissance for a new site on the mainland, resulting in the choice of the agricultural station at Bereina, which provided adequate land and the airstrip. The change was made by degrees and Bereina is now a thriving little town, with the new multi-million Hiritano Highway going through it to link Moresby with Kerema and eventually over the main range to New Guinea.

The Mission, originally a French foundation going back to 1885, still has many French priests and lay workers. Bishop Sorin, a well-loved and highly respected man, was French and he was followed by an Australian, but now a Mekeo is Bishop and a Tolai is Archbishop of the diocese. Apart from the network of mission stations in the Mekeo along the coast of the Gulf of Papua and in the Goilala Mountains, Yule Island had a boys' and a girls' secondary boarding school, missions then being far ahead of the government in providing secondary education. The older well-educated people went to these schools, and the first Papua New Guinean graduate, John Natera, with a Sydney degree in Agriculture, was educated at Yule Island and is now the Director of the Department of Agriculture.

In 1953, when Ian Downs got the go-ahead for the road from the Asaro over the mountains to link the Chimbu sub-district through the patrol post of Chuave, he gave the job of building it to Robert, who rode his motor bike to the end of the valley every day to organise the villagers, supervise their work, and keep his surveying and marking of the direction and grades ahead of the villagers. As the road went higher, he set up camp right on top of the pass at 8,000 feet. In 1954, I went up to spend a week with him in his hut of one room, about 15' by 20', with a screen hiding a bucket shower, a floor of pit-pit on earth, a 2' by 2' pane of plastic windowlite and a door 4' 6" by 2'. Going in and out needed agility — he is 6'3". Built for him by locals, the small door was their idea for the cold. And it was cold at 8,000 feet.

You climbed from the roadbench, up steps cut into the hillside to his house on a terrace bright with flowers. Some miniature chrysanthemums, which he told me were called pyrethrum, had been given him to try at that height — the first experiment in what is now an industry. Pyrethrum flowers contain the knockout element in insect spray.

I'd flown to Goroka in the morning and after lunch came by land-rover up the road, a tricky business with it far from finished. How good it was to see Robert in his domain! After greetings and saying rather mysteriously he had a surprise, he took me past the houses of his five policemen, the interpreter and Bai his houseboy, which straggled up the hill each on its own cutout terrace, to a path up the mountain. I kept protesting, but on and up we went, coming to a moss forest at 9,500 feet, quite the weirdest place I'd ever been in. There wasn't a sound, even our voices being curiously absorbed by the moss. The trees were gnarled and ancient, with wet black trunks supported on a tangle of twisting aerial roots, thickly padded with ghostly pale green lichens and mosses, which also hung like ragged banners from the branches. The mountain was steep and you climbed by using, as a ladder, tangled roots so slippery that you feared losing your grip and being smothered in the moss deep below; weird.

Half an hour's climb brought us out on a clearing, which was the surprise. Robert and his houseboy had cut down trees to make a lookout with an absolutely fantastic view; the whole Goroka Valley, a brilliant blue, lay below. The little town and airstrip, the few plantations, the villages, the road and the wandering Asaro River were all clearly visible, like an exquisite map. We just sat there, drinking it in, till quite suddenly it was gone, and we were enveloped in cotton-wool mist. The afternoon was drawing in and we had to hurry down, the mist making the moss forest spooky and harder to go down than up; it was a relief coming to the bottom.

At last we saw his little hut and he called Bai to make some tea. The Tilley lamp was lit and wood added to the half-drum fireplace. His furniture was only a camp table for his office, another for meals, packing-case shelves and wardrobe, two canvas stretchers and two canvas chairs. But it was snug and warm, the tea was good and I loved him for his enthusiasm and his surprise and for taking it for granted that I'd go scrambling up a mountain to 10,000 feet without resting from my journey from the coast.

Next morning, enjoying the crisp sunshine on his terrace, I heard Rob tinkering with his bike on the road below. Presently he called:

"Mum are you coming?"

"Coming where?"

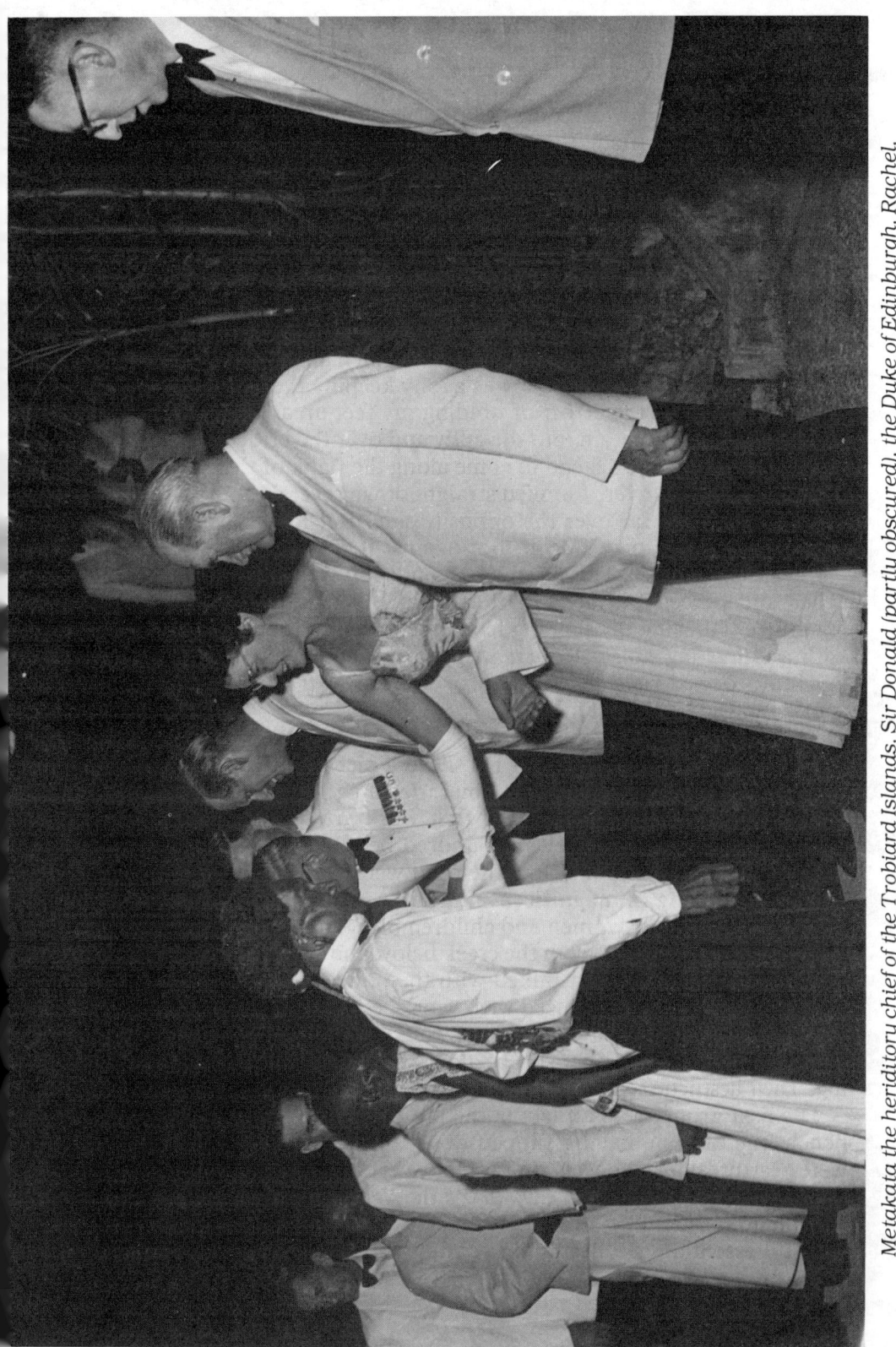

Metakata the heriditory chief of the Trobiard Islands, Sir Donald (partly obscured), the Duke of Edinburgh, Rachel. Sir William Slim, Mr Murray Tyrell. Far left in white jacket is Mr Harold Reeve the Treasurer.

"Down the road, I must get going."

"But what'll I go on?"

"Back of the bike, of course."

"But I'd be terrified. I've never been on a bike."

"Well, you'd better make up your mind. I'm out on the road every day and it'd be awfully lonely here on your own."

By this time I'd scrambled down the steps and was looking dubiously at a very small motor bike. I sat on the pillion with my feet on the ground.

"Where do I put my feet?"

"Sorry, there are no footrests, you'll have to use the hubcaps."

The rounded hubcaps stuck out about an inch and my rubber-soled golf shoes would not grip, so it was agony keeping them on the hubs, thighs aching with the effort of holding my feet up as we sped down the flank of the mountain into the gully and over the bridge. We made a right-hand turn at each end to come along the flank of the next spur. As the bike keeled over, I looked straight down several thousand feet, felt ill and leaned far over the opposite side. But Robert yelled out:

"Lean with the bike, Mum, not against it, or we'll capsize."

It was hair-raising. The sharp wind made my eyes water, my thighs ached and I steeled myself for the keeling over on the next bumpy log bridge. Hitching my slipping feet, my heel went through the spokes with a crunching noise. Robert stopped the bike and we extricated my foot, looked ruefully at the broken shoe, extracted the broken spokes and then Rob said:

"Golly, look at your heel."

It was pouring with blood — I'd sliced a piece neatly off the back — so we bound it with a handkerchief, deciding that bare feet would grip better, and we set off to the first work group.

It was really exciting. Several hundred people from a village you could see built on a spur below the road were working with tremendous zest, singing in magnificent unison. As the road was finished, some were paving it, women and children bringing baskets and bowls of stones on their heads from the creek below and the men laying them carefully by hand. Robert talked with the policeman supervisor and the village leaders and praised their work, especially the patterns of coloured stone in the paving. Others were planting brightly coloured tangets, begonias and other shrubs along the edges of the finished paving. Their aesthetic sense and pleasure in decoration always delights me.

The next group were attacking the mountain again, digging a new bench, the old one having slipped down the valley. These landslips were heartbreaking and went on for many years till most of the unstable ground had gone. Then in the 1970's the World Bank gave a multi-million dollar loan for a two-lane highway, rerouted in a few places, but still essentially Robert's old road.

We visited two more groups after lunching on thick dagwood sandwiches. Home by late afternoon, my fear of the bike had gone; later that night Robert made and attached six-inch spikes for my feet and pillion-riding became a pleasure.

One day Robert said:

"Oh, it's Wednesday. Clinic day at the Asaro Roundhouse. We'll go on down after seeing the working groups. You'll love it, Mum."

As roads went through, Ian Downs built roundhouses at strategic points. The same shape as a village house, only much larger with standing instead of crouching height, they were gathering points for activities, each roundhouse having a known programme. For instance, at Asaro, Wednesdays were clinic days and mothers from all about could bring their babies to the infant welfare sisters. On didiman (agricultural officer) day, those with garden, passionfruit, coffee, pig-growing or other problems would come, and on 'court day' people would bring in their disputes. Thus Downs used the roads to bring advantages of the government to more people, while having a roundhouse gathering point near them was an incentive to road-builders.

We arrived to a delightful scene. Groups of women chatting under the trees with babies and toddlers around them, older children running about whooping and playing, a landrover drawn up beside the roundhouse, with table and chairs set up, bearing the usual array of scales, bottles, first-aid things and record books. Mothers, holding their precious baby book, queued in a bunch by the scales, their babies squalling loudly as trained, blue-uniformed assistants weighed them before entering the weight in the mother's book, while the European sister sat at the dispensing table with another assistant as interpreter.

Most of the babies were simply gorgeous, rolling in fat with gleaming skins. The dangerous time came at weaning, when they were short of protein. Their small tummies can't contain, let alone digest, the large quantities of sweet potato, banana and sugarcane to give them the growth food they need. So toddlers tend to be skinny-legged and pot-bellied, consequently susceptible to colds, bronchitis and pneumonia and, on the coast, to malaria; so the death rate was heavy.

Dr Joan Refshauge, Director of Infant Welfare, did a remarkable job of training, organisation and propaganda till the whole country was covered by a web of welfare centres and trained local girls. The devotion and sense of responsibility conveyed to them by Dr Refshauge and Sister Bignold, her chief assistant, was higher than in any other field of work.

Even in the mid-fifties, their very success used to worry me and I tried to implore Dr Refshauge not to be too enthusiastic, for already I could see families, who would once have reared from two to four children, coping with eight to ten or even more. Dr Refshauge was devoted to saving babies and I would worriedly ask how their parents were going to feed and clothe them? Dr. Refshauge's success is demonstrated by the population explosion. It has doubled between 1950 and 1975 and the problems I posed are not only unsolved, but the solution seems out of reach.

Robert spent next day doing office work at home and it amazed me how much paper work was involved even in building a road. As the only man between Goroka and Chuave, with some 30,000 people around Daulo to whom he was 'the government', he had recently been sworn in as a magistrate of the Court of Native Matters to meet this situation. With five policemen under his control, he had also been granted police powers. With his office table near the door, Robert was surrounded with printed returns to be filled in — requisitions for tools, rations, the 101 things a small human community needs; he was also drafting reports and replying to correspondence.

Since it was a glorious day, I took a book outside and would read a few pages and then gaze on the shimmering blue of the Goroka Valley through the vee made by the two ranges of mountains, on whose connecting pass we were perched. The road snaked down the western range; from villages, just a double line of houses running along the tops of spurs, smoke drifted lazily up; parties of women and children were busily working in patches of garden, cleverly terraced and drained, on the steep slopes, each surrounded by a sturdy palisade to keep out the ever-foraging pigs. Groups of men were working here and there on the road. It was a peaceful scene.

Presently the sun moved and I shifted my chair. This time I was facing south, looking deep into the mountains, where, compared to the view the other way, it seemed all foreground; great trees with clamouring vines, clusters of orchids and ferns high in their branches, seemed to be marching up the slopes with dense undergrowth beneath them. The hills receded one behind the other, with gashes of red or yellow earth here and there where the road showed. Far in the distance a gap revealed the distinctive hump of Mount Elimbari, whose sheer drop dominates Chuave, the patrol post, thirty miles to the south-west.

Presently, up the steps appeared a line of ten or twelve women. The long strings of their 'dress' hanging back and front, swinging as they walked, bent over to balance the huge bilum or string bag of kau kau (sweet potatoes) and other vegetables. The bilum, resting on the back, its woven strap held by the forehead, is an ingenious way of carrying enormous loads. The women came on to the terrace, eyes looking up from their bent heads and smiling shyly.

Robert came out, calling the interpreter, who took them to the side, where with a delightful rolling motion they swung their loads to the ground. Each woman unpacked and arranged her goods, sitting behind them until the interpreter assessed their value. Money was just replacing salt as currency, so he ascertained which it was to be, then came over to Robert, collected the money and paid the women, who went off smiling happily.

I put away my camera and read a few more pages, then Bai came to remind me of my promise of a lesson in making rock buns. Rob had made an ingenious oven in the clay cutting behind his house. Biscuits then came in large tins about 12 by 12 by 15 inches. Inserted diagonally into the bank with space beneath for a fire, a length of water pipe took smoke to the top of the bank and a galvanised iron tray fitted inside from the corner to corner, it worked very well and he enjoyed the bliss of bread instead of damper.

Bai got the oven hot and I gave a careful lesson on the rustic bench of his bush kitchen, saw the buns safely in the oven and went back to my book. A luluai with his red-banded hat appeared up the steps, followed by a group of men, and I called to Robert again. After a short palaver with them and the interpreter, he came over to me, saying:

"They want to make Court, so you'll have to make yourself scarce for a while."

I went out of sight and watched with interest while Bai and the interpreter set things up. They took out the patrol table, carefully put it square-on near the flagpole, chair before it; then placed the court book, spare pad and biro very precisely. The interpreter, calling the litigants and their witnesses, who importantly came to stiff attention while he reported to Robert and escorted him to his seat, then stood smartly beside him.

It was remarkable. In a few moments on the sunny terrace, the dignified and formal atmosphere of a court was literally created before my eyes. I wouldn't have believed it possible. The court was unhurried, lasted over an hour, and the litigants went quietly away, seemingly satisfied, while Robert sat for some time, writing.

I came from my seclusion, saying:

"What was all that about?"

Robert looked up.

"I couldn't even tell you, Mum. It was the most horrible thing I've ever heard."

So that was that. It was probably sanguma, a horrible type of sorcery, which, not so long before, would probably have meant a life, or a long series of pay-backs. But they brought it to court and no doubt a settlement was reached and compensation agreed upon.

I've never forgotten that demonstration of the value of an 'instant' court, which could be called when and where needed, and of how the people treated it with respect and confidence.

This 'Kiap Court' was part of one of the three layers of the court system (of which the Supreme Court was the apex) known as the 'Non Interference System'. Kiaps, or the D.N.A. staff, were instructed not to deal unnecessarily with native matters, but to leave them to the traditional dispute-settling customs. Such courts were only used when these had failed, in which case the people, as they did that morning, came to a kiap and asked him to 'make Court'.

Kiap courts could also be used to reinforce the authority of native leaders, such as luluais, tultuls and medical orderlies, and could reinforce the government's administering of law and order in a local area by bringing certain defined criminal charges such as stealing, assaults, homosexual offences and indecent acts.

The penalties government officers could award were about one tenth as severe as in the ordinary system and appeal could be made to the Supreme Court. They were under strict supervision of a senior officer, while travelling judges reviewed all cases when on circuit. They were readily available, near the people and gave them their first lessons in 'the Law'. I was glad I had seen one in action.

Early next morning, we were both awakened by an extraordinary noise and Rob went down to investigate, soon calling to me. Reluctantly, I faced the bitter pre-dawn cold and, pulling on every warm thing I could and with a rug over my shoulders, went down to the road. And there, looming out of the mist, were those two old pioneers, Jim Taylor and Jim Leahy, driving for the first time to Mt Hagen and greeting us in a most jovial manner, quite excited at using the new road, where Jim Taylor had been in the party walking through this country in 1933 to discover the Wahgi. Later, Ian and Judy Downs, who had gone to Hagen earlier in the week, passed through on the way back, giving us quite a feeling of traffic.

On Monday morning I said goodbye to my lovely week of being a mere cadet patrol officer's mother, and returned once more to all the duties of being the Administrator's wife.

A year later Robert went on his first leave, driving to Perth with Evan, where both boys stayed with various relations, and Robert met Julie Kessell, also revisiting from Tasmania. Their parents and grandparents having been friends, they had known each other as children and now fell in love and got engaged amid great rejoicing, before Robert returned to New Guinea. The young people planned their wedding before Julie's parents, Kim and Barbara, went to England, which meant coming to New Guinea and, to our delight, being married from our house, Robert getting local leave. Evan came up from Australia to be best man.

It was a long weekend, packed with festivities for the Red Cross Appeal: an amateur race meeting, a ball and an army dinner, which we all joined in. On Tuesday morning the young people were married at St. John's Church with just the family present. Afterwards at home, cables, cake-cutting, chicken, champagne and much merriment. Then, after changing to catch a midday plane to Wau for their honeymoon, where the Hohnens of New Guinea Gold lent them their guest bungalow, we were all packing them in the car when the Official Secretary came rushing in with a horrified look, saying:

"The plane is grounded. It won't be going till tomorrow."

What an anti-climax, and how typical of Papua New Guinea! It was a ridiculous moment till Don saved the day by saying:

"Well, off you go for half an hour. The bungalow will be ready when you get back."

So we all continued the traditional send-off with old shoes, rice and confetti and away they went.

And then the scramble. We called the staff, turned out the guest bungalow, made the beds, did the flowers, put food and champagne in the fridge just in time for their return.

We sent down dinner, but they came up for coffee and a lovely hour with the added fun of the photos arriving, while next day they were able to see the Kessells off round the world, before their own plane at last left for Wau.

Evan was staying on for a few days, as it was the first time he'd been up since his school holidays in 1951, when he had not much liked New Guinea. Since then he'd done three years jackarooing on various properties in north-west New South Wales and had had further experience with pasture improvement in the Riverina. Now he was twenty and took a different view. Deciding to get some experience here, he approached Mr Fairfax Ross, General Manager of British New Guinea Development Company, for a job on one of their plantations. Taken on as a cadet plantation assistant, he was sent out to Aroa Plantation in the Hisiu District, a day's journey by trawler.

It was lovely having both our sons here — both cadets; one in the government and one in private enterprise. And they both made sure their father got the message from their respective angles at the bottom of the ladder and heard what he should hear for the country's good. So our family occasions were often lively, with father and sons, or just the two brothers, discussing and arguing issues of the day, each from their own point of view.

Robert returned to Australia to live, a year after Independence. Evan remained in New Guinea until 1981, having worked his way to the top and taken over as General Manager of the company when Fairfax Ross retired.

Chapter 7

Duk Duks dancing at the opening of Reimbu Council — Rabaul.

Visit to Rabaul—Nature of Land Problems—Christmas at Watabung—Susan—Evan's 21st Birthday—Don and Paul Hasluck's Relationship—Canberra and Government House Gates—Coronary—Leave and Adjustment—Return—Duke of Edinburgh's Visit

Looking through the Government House visitors book, Don's office appointment and memo book and both our engagement books makes my head whirl at the full programme we carried out singly and jointly. We did have time on our own, but reading these records now it's hard to see where, and also hard to see how Don, in addition, carried an enormous work load in the office. His other papers fully testify to that. We also spent a total of about three months of each year away from Moresby, either on visits to Canberra, on the many official visits to all parts of Papua New Guinea, or on leave.

My first visit to Rabaul was in 1953. I had heard so much about it, not only from Don on his previous visits, but since my early childhood, through the Wisdoms and my own young friends who stayed with them. Then there'd been news of the eruption, the war, Queen Emma and the planters, the beauty and the destruction. Now there was the colourful D.C., Keith McCarthy, and his wife Jean, and the new local government councils, cocoa growing and the siting of the town of Rabaul.

I flew up the lovely northern coastline from Lae with special anticipation as we dipped across a peninsular, circling the beautiful harbour, banked over Matupi Volcano's evil-looking sulphurous mouth, emitting puffs of smoke, and touched down on the small green strip at its foot.

Rabaul prides itself on doing things properly, never forgetting that it was once the capital, so leading citizens of the four racial groups had turned out to meet us and, while the McCarthys ushered us down the long receiving line making introductions, groups of school children sang. Then off we went along the dusty white coronus roads. Coronus is a raised coral reef, now part of the land, usually with an overlay of rich soil. Quarried, it very easily compacts into roads, giving no drainage problems, excellent in wet weather. But when it's dry I know nothing quite so gritty as the blinding white clouds of dust, giving your skin an eerie look and a feel like sandpaper. The sight of the town only a few minutes away made us salute the people who had lived for years in such makeshift conditions.

The street plan of the new town was just beginning to take shape, with the first permanent houses, shops and offices going up. We turned up a winding road through dense jungle to an open area at the top of a ridge, with a large tar-paper-walled hospital on one side and a rustic flight of steps on the other. Up the steps, crossing a footbridge over a gully richly overgrown with ferns, gingers, orchids and shaded by exotic trees, and out onto an open sloping lawn with a sprawling, temporary-looking house at the top and lower down an equally temporary little bungalow, both facing across sparkling St George's Channel, with the New Ireland mountains on the skyline.

The garden was lovely, the houses, though so temporary-looking, were charming inside and I didn't know which was the more colourful of our hosts — Jean or Keith. Keith was a reddish-fair Irishman, a born raconteur with an endless fund of stories. Don loved him, and got mad with him at the same time. He had told me after his first visit that ninety-five percent of the time he did an excellent job, efficient and capable; then, in the other five, he would do something darn silly and upset his earlier work. They were both larger-than-life characters. Jean adored him, created a myth of his considerable exploits, bossed him, and treated him like her naughty little boy at the same time.

Early next morning we left for the day's itinerary, going first along the north coast road to a meeting of Livuan Council in their new chambers — a fibro building, large enough for an office and a meeting room just holding a long table for twelve councillors. The Reimber Council members, whose new building we were to open the next day, were also there — two lines of middle-aged men, wearing lap-laps and spotless white shirts, sporting the two inch shield-shaped council badge, gravely welcomed us. Formally ushered to our chairs at the head of the table by the President, we all sat down. Dead silence, till it was obvious Don must break it. Saying what a pleasure it was to visit them, he suggested that they should speak about anything they wished to raise with him and he would address them last. The young, well-educated clerk translated. Smiles. One councillor after another spoke, paid compliments and said this and that.

Then an impressive gentleman rose and in the sudden tension I thought, "Hullo, what's this?" I knew that the nub of the matter was about to come out. He made a long and impassioned speech and every man was with him. My pidgin was not then good enough for me to follow but the translation fascinated me. The gist was this:

In the past, their fathers were quite happy to sell their land to the Germans but they did not know what they were doing. They were very pleased to get the axes and the red cloth and other presents and quite happy for the Germans to grow crops but they did not know their land was gone for ever. And now they and their sons and their grand-sons wanted the land back. Their families had grown, and the land was worth far more than the axes and red cloth the Germans had given their grandfathers.

What was Don going to do about it?

It gave me a strong 'gut feeling'. I knew they meant every word and that they would never let up, but felt an interested onlooker, noting that the councillors were probably trying out the 'new boy' — Don — and wondered how he'd handle such a sticky one. He handled it in the only way he could — thanked them for their welcome, replied to easier issues, said he understood their feelings over their land, stress-ed the difficulties and promised to study it. I thought he didn't do too badly but watched the faces as the translation came through. They were all blank.

Then we rose. With great courtesy the councillors smiled and shook hands but a fly on the wall after we left must have found it interesting.

That scene of the early fifties, the speech and question by the old Tolai is vivid yet and I can still feel the tension and get the nuance. The question hovered like a moth in the back of my mind for years. But although land, land problems, land titles lost in the war, claims to land the government thought it had title to, clan fights over land, exasperation over the slowness to get legal aspects clarified (only four government lawyers), Land Bills coming before Legislative Council, disagreement over the Bills, the Minister getting wild that this or that wasn't happening quickly enough — all these land questions continually came before Don and his officers and peppered my offical life, but it was all a puzzle I did not think out.

Over the years pennies dropped here and there. Without really think-ing about it, the pattern began to weave together, till a conversation with an old Koiari village leader who 'owned' the land 'bought' for the Rouna power station at Sogeri, brought back that day at Livuan

Council in a moment of sudden illumination. It was in 1966 when I was having a few days' rest alone in a weekender on Hombrom Bluff, with the nearby village charged (unknown to me) with looking after me. Old Wairiti came birdwatching and walked me many fascinating miles.

This particular day of my illumination, we came out on the cliff overlooking the work still being done on No. 2 Power Station at Rouna. Wairiti's eyes shone. With a magnificent gesture he proudly said:

"All my land."

I looked at him puzzled.

"Not all of it now; you've sold some to the government."

"But the land's still mine. I said the government could put the power station there and they paid me for it."

And he went on looking proudly and possessively at the workmen scurrying like ants far below and all the enormous engineering marvel.

"Goodness," I thought. "Your children and their children and their children's children will all know just where the old clan boundaries are; what trouble will come up in the future?"

Further talk with Wairiti confirmed what I had glimpsed and ignored that day in Rabaul: that there is a fundamental difference in the concept of land, what land is and what man can do about it. I wished I'd taken it more seriously then. All these years the two races have been using the same words but they mean quite different things to each side. Therefore, in every discussion and in every transaction they were unknowingly talking about and acting on two quite different concepts, without either side realising it. No wonder everything is so confused. No Papua New Guinean ever thinks of the land itself as a saleable commodity. It's not something that can be sold any more than the wind or the air. What is sold is the trees growing on the land, or the right to use the land for one purpose or another — for gardens, for building, for hunting. The land itself is part of the very soul of the clan. It is not the land itself that is sold.

But how I have wandered away from that first visit when we went bumping and jolting in a landrover through the Gazelle Peninsula and I was seeing for the first time land, scenery, people, gardens and villages which are completely different from anywhere else. The ground is deep volcanic earth, which the ring of volcanoes periodically refertilises. Although it appears hilly it is really a plateau, broken by steep gullies where soft volcanic earth has washed away, rising from a narrow coastal strip, and with the evenly spread rainfall the growth and regrowth is incredibly quick. There were no large villages; names apply to groups of hamlets, each of just two or three houses built in a garden. Coconut groves were everywhere with the new crop, cocoa, interplanted under the trees while the modern fermentaries of the Tolai Cocoa Project were being built.

The growth by the roadside hid all this as well as the large number of European-owned plantations, so we would go down side tracks visiting either a Methodist or Catholic Mission with its church, school and hospital, a government school, a fermentary, a plantation or an agricultural experimental station. Eventually we came to the far western end of the plateau at Vunadidir, where Max Orken, the A.D.O., gave us lunch in his little house, perched above a sheer drop into a huge valley with the Keravat area on the far side. Coming home on the Toma road along the southern edge of the plateau, where it drops to another valley from whose centre Varzin Mountain rises in stately solitude, we turned north on the eastern escarpment overlooking Rabaul Harbour and town. Here we had afternoon tea with another colourful character, Don Barrett, a Legislative Council member and probably the only really politically conscious man in Papua New Guinea at that time.

I remember getting back elated and filthy, just in time to bath and change for a dinner the Chinese community was giving jointly for their Consul from Sydney and for us. Several hundred people sat down to an elaborate Chinese dinner at the stark Kuomintang building.

The speeches began and finally, as Don rose to reply, a strange movement rippled on the cement floor underfoot and to our fascinated gaze four lines of people one side of the tables at right angles to ours bent forward and four on the other tipped back. Then they all went into reverse. We at our table had been thrown sideways and it took me a moment to recognise one of Rabaul's famous 'Gurias'. When the natural clamour was over and the ground and the tongues were still again, Don began his speech.

"I have never before been privileged to speak at such an earth-shattering moment..."

Next afternoon the Reimber Council House opening made a great impression. From the Tolai have come sophisticated and highly educated men and women; Tolai have also kept a vitality in their own culture and cultural institutions. An immigrant people from New Ireland, they drove the original inhabitants, the Makolkol and the Baining, into the mountains to the west, though there has been considerable merging of people and culture. This historic circumstance, plus their rich fertile ground, probably accounts for three things — their vigour, their adaptability and their holding to their culture with a gift for keeping old customs by merging them with the new, and using them as old means to new ends.

For this occasion the Council House, in a grassed area surrounded by jungle, was decorated with garlands and flowers, while birds and animals, made from folded coconut leaves attached to the springy midribs, literally danced in the air. Crowds of village people — men in white lap-laps and bare tops and the women in brilliantly coloured 'meri' blouses and lap-laps — stood around while two traditional representatives of a secret society and known as 'Duk Duks', only their legs visible beneath the leafy sphere totally hiding their bodies, each capped by its white cone with glaring red and black painted eyes, danced ahead of us to the door.

Don made a speech and cut the ribbon, then we went inside to a formal Council session, till drums and singing brought us out as groups of dancers were arriving. Two English-speaking Tolais, assigned to Don and to me, were very informative about each dance with its own dressing and headgear or dance wands, and Ismail Towalaka gave me vivid descriptions and answered my questions in beautiful fluent English. One dance was gaily delightful, the men carrying wands carved and painted with a man, a fish on his head and spikes from bamboo raying out from the fish, the theme being that the man who gets up before the sun catches the fish. He was intrigued when I told him our saying 'The early bird catches the worm', and rushed over to tell the dance leader, who was so pleased that he presented me with his wand. I have it still, decorating my patio.

Ismail then got secretive about the next group, saying women were not allowed to see it. I asked about those present, to hear they'd already hidden in the jungle while we had been talking; and sure enough, not a woman was to be seen.

"What about me and the others?" I asked.

"That's all right," he said smilingly, "you don't count."

I rather felt it really was true, we *didn't* count and they put up with us very nicely. The intricate head-dresses of wicker, cane and bamboo, cleverly fashioned into all sorts of representations, made me ask about them for the collection I was making for a future museum, but I found it would not be allowed as tradition required burning after the dance. But that night Nason, one of the big Tolai leaders, brought me two, carefully wrapped in banana leaves, when he came to the Residency reception — indeed a compliment.

Rabaul fascinated me by the number of its social strands; on the surface incompatible but in fact weaving together into a queer sort of harmony. Its four separate racial communities kept their separateness but seemed to respect each other. The two strong religious groups, Methodist and Catholics (or 'Popies'), were vigorous rivals but co-operated in a number of ways. The Tolai themselves had their own traditional differences and rivalries in addition to those brought about by introduced changes. Handling the crises erupting every few years in the Gazelle, have we taken their own traditions and enmities enough into account? I'm sure that some crises happened through trying to make one pie from too many different ingredients or in assuming all Tolai were the same.

The expatriate townspeople were the usual Australian transients, civil servants, bank and company people and the permanent business people, some great characters among them. The north coast and the Baining planters were of one kind, and different from the Kokopo planters, who were on their own, giving the impression that in their eyes they were far superior to other planters in PNG. Nice everyday people, their houses, though in beautiful gardens, less attractive and substantial than plantation houses elsewhere, they had this extraordinary superior attitude, puzzling me for years. The explanation must be the tradition and spirit of 'Queen Emma', the amazing part-Samoan, part-German woman who was the first settler in the Gazelle. The remnants of foundations of the great house at Ralum are close to the town of Kokopo and her influence must hover there still.

Plantation labour came mainly from the Sepik and lived rather uneasily among the Tolai, who were too busy creating their own plantations to work on anyone else's. At first the attitudes of the white community used to horrify me, but it's amazing how they have gradually adapted and modified and seem to fit very well into the new era of self-government, both the local, the provincial and the national.

☆ ☆ ☆

We returned from one of our many visits to Rabaul in time to fly up to Watabung, the patrol post Robert was still building some miles along the road from his old Daulo Pass camp, and had a particularly happy Christmas and New Year with them. Don then returned to Moresby while I waited with Julie for the arrival of their first child, staying in one of the bungalows that were then a feature of Mrs Pitt's Goroka Hotel, with its garden of spring flowers and fabulous view across the valley. We were in that curious state — a sort of suspended animation, living from day to day — waiting for the baby.

Robert came down from Watabung impatient to see how things were going, and the next afternoon we took Julie off to hospital. A newly erected bedroom, shower and doctor's office next to the sister's house, on the slope above the large pit-pit and thatch hospital, made it possible to remain in Goroka rather than the customary hospitalisation in Madang.

After dinner Rob and I went up to see how things were and were shushed away. So we just sat in the landrover talking quietly, mostly about Robert's own birth, which came back so vividly, sitting there with my big son about to become a father himself. Such moments are precious.

Soon we heard a sturdy cry and a head popped out of the window, saying:

"It's a girl. All's well."

Robert went in first and I followed soon after. For a woman I don't think there is anything quite like the moment when you first take in your arms the lovely, crumpled scrap of humanity that is your son's child. Julie was radiant and the two young things looked at each other ecstatically.

The next item on the family programme had been getting uncomfortably close — Evan's 21st birthday. He had been transferred from Aroa, one of three company coconut plantations on the coast, to Doa, a large rubber estate further inland, where the manager and his wife had offered their house for a party; so Evan had invited everyone in the district. We were to come out in a trawler, bring the food, etc., and afterwards make a district inspection. Little Susan was very considerate, arriving in time for me to get home to organise and cook the food for thirty people. We were to travel on *Laurabada II*, which had a deep freeze unit, sleeping on board and leaving before dawn. In the afternoon Don rang.

"We can't go," he said.

Aghast, I asked why.

"Because of the tides. High tide just now is not deep enogh for *Laurabada* to get over the Galley Reach sand bar."

"Well, we've got to get there somehow. What about *Leander*?"

"She has a shallow draught but no deep freeze, and the food won't keep."

However, they worked out that, by tying both ships alongside, food could be transferred to *Leander* at dawn and would keep for the eight hours of the trip. We stowed the grog, the presents, the flowers, cake, glasses, china and cutlery, and turned in about 10 p.m.

In the small hours there was a whang. The boat keeled over and we were nearly thrown from our bunks. A Guba — a sudden high wind storm — had hit us broadside on. Anxious shouts and running feet as they let the stern sheet go. The wind howled and we pitched and tossed and tried to sleep, while the poor crew had to get the food over *Laurabada's* swinging bows to the wharf high above us, then over our swinging bows. However, they managed, and before dawn we headed into the storm; and *what* a trip — the only time I've ever known Don to be seasick, and I felt horribly queasy. With relief we were over the sand bar into sheltered waters about midday, finally tying up in mid-afternoon at the wharf in a tidal creek, to be greeted by our cheerful, grinning Evan.

Our hostess gave me the run of her kitchen. I have memories yet of the heat, the wood stove, the strange kitchen and staff and me, headachy and squeamish still, getting the meal ready, table set up, candles on cake and flowers arranged. Evan and the young ones helped set everything up and mercifully we were all bathed, changed and ready at six for the guests. Everyone — the half-dozen planters and their wives, the young assistants, some oil drillers working for 'Papuan

137

Apinapi', a couple running a timber mill, even a mission father — all types, all ages, but only a half a dozen women, and they were not young. I realised we should also have brought down some young girls. But even without the girls it was some party and Evan was properly toasted into his twenty-second year.

☆　☆　☆

I have spoken from time to time of the various problems Don had to discover and cope with in those first years as 'Acting' and then as Administrator. They were years when he worked at a furious pace, beginning with what he felt was an exciting and good understanding between himself and Paul Hasluck. Then the minutes, which literally bombarded both the department in Canberra and the Administrator in PNG, began to take on a more acid and impatient tone. Often directed to senior officers, through the Administrator, they were on file available to others and caused tensions and problems in the service, not making day-to-day work any easier. However, at first the minutes did not particularly worry Don personally, because alongside the formal, official communications back and forth through the department, there took place also private correspondence going directly from Minister to Administrator and never seen either by the department in Canberra or the administration in Port Moresby. This correspondence was conducted by Hasluck with meticulous courtesy and freedom, letters being addressed "My dear Administrator", while replies conducted with similar freedom were addressed "My dear Minister". By this means views on policies were freely exchanged before they became public and tough battles could even take place, when Don could put his point of view forcibly, if necessary. It was one of the better aspects of their relationship and the one which he most treasured.

However, in spite of this, a situation began to emerge in 1954, '55 and '56 which became increasingly worrying and put Don under considerable stress. To put it in a nutshell, he was finding himself more and more in Murray's situation, realising that the problem side to Paul Hasluck's character was even more difficult to cope with than he had expected. In addition, during 1955 it was becoming apparent that personal tales of a very petty nature were being carried to Canberra. We had a shrewd idea where they came from but, though unpleasant and far from true, Don could only ignore them. However he worried about their effect on relationships between people in Canberra and Port Moresby as well as that between the Minister and himself. What hurt was that they were believed and because of their clandestine nature, were impossible to refute.

The day before we left on the visit to Rabaul in December 1955, the policeman on duty at Government House gates — then old cyclone ones in a three-strand wire fence — fell through the floor of the wooden sentry-box, and Don instructed that a new one be installed. When we returned we found a brick and cement archway over the drive entrance, one upright of which was for the sentry and the other for the visitor's book. It looked really nice and more fitting than the old cyclone gate and rickety wooden sentry-box. Everyone concerned with it was pleased with themselves in giving Don a nice surprise, but his comment was:

"Oh Gawd — what'll the Minister say to that?"

At the end of January 1956 he received word that the Minister wanted to see him in Canberra. Saying, "Thank God for that, there are a lot of things to take up with him," he made extensive preparation and went off happily to Canberra with miles of papers.

When he returned and I asked him how he got on, he laughed shortly.

"Do you know what the so-and-so wanted me for? He greeted me rather stiffly, sat me down at his table and proceeded to tick me off about the bloody gate. Then he gave me a real lecture, more or less saying I was getting too big for my boots and developing a 'house on the hill' complex, and more in the same vein."

I was horrified. "Whatever did you do?"

"I felt it was too petty to reply to. I leant my elbow on the table, with chin on my hand, and just looked at him and listened."

Knowing how penetrating Don's look could be I began to feel sorry for Paul. If Don said nothing it must have been quite hard for him to finish off his lecture satisfactorily.

Nevertheless, the incident did worry Don very much indeed and also troubled us both; neither of us in any way felt we had a 'house on the hill' complex, both being much more closely involved with the local people, officially and unofficially, than anybody else we knew. People came freely up the hill to see us if they wanted to, and as for Don's relationships in the Administration Departments, his very style was personal and relaxed. Actually I think that Don carried his forbearance too far. Though he listened quietly, the contempt he felt must have come through. It was probably best to have kept quiet that day, but I think he should have raised the matter later and cleared the air with the Minister. Had he done so at that time, I feel it would have helped their relations then and in the future.

In February, General Cariapa, High Commissioner to India, was with us and four other house guests during the month. From the first to the fourteenth of March was our first and very strenuous visit, entailing a lot of travelling, to the then 'Dutch New Guinea', and from Hollandia straight to Rabaul to welcome another U.N. visiting mission. By then it was over two years since we had had a holiday. More house guests came in March and April, including Eskie Lambert, head of the department in Canberra, and John Willoughby, assistant secretary, then Don did a quick trip to Nondugl for a Trust meeting with old Sir Edward Halstrom and back to Goroka for discussions with the U.N. mission, who were nearly at the end of their tour.

While in Goroka he had wakened in the night with a terrible pain in his chest; though it was better in the morning he felt very tired, in itself unusual, but neither of us realised its significance and he pooh-poohed the idea of seeing a doctor. Then the U.N. mission was with us again for several days and through it all his office diary seems extra full and the office work went on as usual.

One afternoon I was astonished to come home and find Don sitting on the verandah, having been taken ill in the office and brought home. The doctor arrived a few minutes later and ordered complete rest in bed with a cardiograph and other tests next day. He had never been ill before and was rather fuming about it. However, the cardiograph showed a recent coronary, which of course had been the pain in Goroka, and he was ordered out on sick leave.

The Assistant Administrator, Mr. Rupert Wilson, who had been appointed the previous year, became Acting Administrator. When Don and I left for Australia, he and Mrs Wilson took up residence at Government House and had to carry out quite a full official programme while we were away.

Sydney specialists confirmed the diagnosis but merely instructed Don to lose 1½ stone, take life more quietly and limit whisky and smoking, and referred him to a Perth specialist a month later. Don went to his brother's sheep station north of Kalgoorlie, while I spent a fortnight with my mother in Perth before joining him, and was concerned that he looked plumper, not slimmer; but on our return he saw Dr Bruce Hunt.

Dear Bruce, how grateful I am to him. When the other doctors had been reassuring Don not to worry, old man, they had frightened hell out of me, putting the onus on me to see that he didn't do this, that and the other thing. What wife can 'make' her husband do anything? It's enough to spoil their relationship anyway, and I had begged them to tell him the blunt truth, enabling him to understand his condition and deal with it himself. As they wouldn't, Don had kept asking:

"Why all the fuss, when the doctors keep telling me there's nothing to worry about?"

He came out of Bruce's surgery, after a long session, in the most furious temper, was unapproachable all next day and finally told me what happened. Bruce had been brutal in telling him how he'd been abusing his body and just what happens in a coronary.

"You hold your life in your own hands," was his message. "It's your choice. Go on overworking as you are now, and continue with your present smoking and whisky, and you will have another coronary or a stroke and die young; or you can lose two stone, accept that you have limitations, reorganise your life and live to a ripe old age."

It was the shock treatment that I knew a man like Don needed to make him take things seriously.

When he showed me the strict diet he'd been given we decided we'd have to be on our own to carry it out, so we borrowed a friend's cottage in the hills, with a glorious view, took piles of books and for a month didn't see anyone. We both followed the diet, went for long walks, read and yarned. It was a wonderful month. One needs a time like this now and then, to take stock of yourselves and your life and give life itself a chance to restore you in body and spirit. The most important thing was facing up to the problems arising from the strange personality of the Minister and accepting him just as he was. From then on, nothing Paul said or did could possibly hurt Don. The pettiness was just an oddity to be coped with and the new attitude left him free to enjoy the pleasure of working with a man of his integrity and quality of mind. He also accepted the fact which men find so hard to do — that in his fifties he just hadn't the physical capacity he'd had in his thirties. It's these mental changes in outlook and attitude which are always the hardest. He lost the two stone and listened to Bruce's advice.

So we returned, in August 1956, very much refreshed and restored in every way. Don reorganised his life and the way he worked. This became much easier when, in 1957, Dr Gunther became his Assistant Administrator and Neil Thomson the new Public Service Commissioner. With them Don had, for the first time, a really good and reliable team. A closer understanding began to develop also between Lambert, the Secretary for Territories, and himself, the fact of them both taking the brunt of the Minister's temperament vis-a-vis their respective staffs drew them together.

He continued regular medical checks, played golf in addition to gardening for exercise and seldom brought files home. For the first time I had a husband who would read a book or yarn to me after dinner. As barristers do their briefs at nights, working was a lifelong habit and I was glad it was broken. He ended by making a complete recovery and enjoying excellent health, so once again I say, "Thank you, Bruce Hunt".

Home again we got a more than usually warm welcome from Daphne, Peter Broman, the Official Secretary and especially from Dosi and the house staff. Letters from a steward I'd been helping with lessons to qualify for an apprenticeship, beginning "Dear My Mother Mrs Cleland", and ending, "Your loving son Stephen", had given me an inkling from the acid things he wrote about the state of affairs in the house, but now I found they had all had really a torrid time coping with a demanding and difficult person, who also had unfortunately been under the misapprehension that the government paid for the food. When all I had left in the pantry and deep freeze were used up, she refused to stock up again, only buying just enough for each day, leaving me with no stores at all and an enormous shopping list.

As the Governor General made a three-day visit and both the Thai and the U.S. Ambassadors came at different times, the food situation had been hilarious. Various ladies in the town were asked to contribute dishes for parties; even the gift of a weekly duck had seemed to be expected from the flock of an administration wife. To cope at all, both Daphne and Peter had put their hands in their own pockets when things were too lean. In the middle of one ambassadorial visit, the entire staff disappeared and Daphne was frantic — they had gone down in a body to the Official Secretary, stating they were all leaving and would come back when we returned. He ordered them back on duty, making play of the importance of being Government House staff whoever lived in the house, finally saying that anyone not returning at once would be shipped straight to his village. So ended the first and only Government House strike.

The Assistant Administrator left on leave a few days after our return and later took up an overseas appointment. He was an able man and made a valuable contribution to building up the efficiency of the service, though his short reign was not without its complications.

☆ ☆ ☆

Though 1956 was a full and worrying year it ended happily, with Papua and New Guinea's first Royal visit in November. The Duke of Edinburgh, coming to Melbourne to open the Olympic Games and travelling out in the *Britannia*, was to visit us on the way.

Months beforehand, a coming and going of letters and officials from the Australian Prime Minister's Department worked out the itinerary and then officials inspected the travel routes and evey house he was to visit. The Prince was to live on *Britannia* while in Moresby, so only came to us for dinner and a reception, but they officiously went into the menu and all details, inspecting my cutlery and table linen and appointments till I was torn between mirth and anger. But in Lae the D.C. moved into the guest wing and the house bedrooms were all refurnished and decorated, while in Rabaul the main bedroom was rebuilt as well as refurnished. But I suppose that is all part of the excitement of a Royal visit.

We were having a buffet dinner for thirty and a garden reception for about three hundred, giving us the usual traumas of guest lists for limited numbers which leave you feeling so badly about folk you cannot ask. However, at last I won a battle I'd waged on behalf of wives of Papua New Guinean guests. Traditionally women were considered too backward, but as I now knew many village women well, I thought they could easily hold their own. No one would agree, saying their clothes wouldn't be adequate and they'd never worn shoes and would be too shy and would only giggle. This time I dug my toes in, with the point that if we did not recognise them socially their husbands never would. Also, once asked, their husbands would buy them new dresses, each man wanting his wife to outshine other wives. People are people the world over and I was sure they would do us proud.

The invitations out, I talked with Mrs Ure of the London Missionary Society to let the word drift around Hanuabada and other villages that women curtseyed to Royalty, and arranged with the Local Government Council President for me to attend the chambers and show them how to curtsey. The President acted as the Duke, another councillor as Sir William Slim and I demonstrated, stepping sideways and bringing the other foot behind so that your knees lock as you go down, preventing a wobble. When you straighten again, another sideways step placed you before Sir William to repeat the curtsey, at the same time giving your hand, looking up and smiling. We had lots of fun and laughter and they all practised till they were perfect. They asked about shoes; so I said if they were used to wearing shoes to do so, if not, bare feet were quite alright. The most important thing was to curtsey properly. In the receiving line on the night I was standing next to Sir William and I must say I chuckled with pleasure when he commented on the beautiful Papuan curtsies.

Sir William Slim and Paul Hasluck arrived late afternoon the day before to welcome the Prince on behalf of Australia. By this time Sir William and his staff were becoming almost old friends, and we felt him to be a tower of strength. Welcoming radio messages were sent to *Britannia* coming through Torres Straits and thanks received. Discreet enquiries about dress brought word that Prince Philip would be wearing grey slacks and open shirt. Consternation among the men was comical. Everyone dressed more formally then than now and they also realised that thousands of people would be coming to see him, expecting glitter and uniform, as they knew him by his photographs. Sir William took over the effort to effect a change but the Prince would say only that he would think about it.

The *Britannia* was a lovely sight coming in early next morning, beautifully handled, we heard later, by the Prince himself. Sir William went down at once, well ahead of the official calls, to tackle him on the dress business and the best he could do was to persuade him to wear a simple white naval uniform, without any sword or accoutrements.

The calls were made, the band was playing on the wharf, the Pacific

Islands Regiment guard of honour inspected and the cavalcade came straight to Ela Beach oval, packed with excited people. Prince Philip changed from the car to a landrover, standing while the anthem was played and the Royal Standard beside the dais was broken. He drove round the oval rather negligently waving and the crowd waved back but was suddenly struck by uncertainty as to what to do. He then mounted the dais, leaned against the balustrade and began talking to the people in a most conversational way telling them how nice and clean they looked and he was sure they had washed behind their ears.

We were all dumbfounded and you could feel the excitement and high expectations of the crowd collapse like a pricked balloon. Evan, glued to the radio out on the plantation, later said he had never felt nearer to tears of sheer disappointment. The programme said the Prince was due to arrive at 8.37 a.m. and depart for Murray Barracks at 8.52, so the whole thing was over in fifteen minutes, and was a perfect example of how not to do it.

Don was with him for the day's itinerary, which took him to Bomana War Cemetery and Sogeri Plateau and its rubber plantations and the beginning of the Kokoda Trail, so I didn't see Don again till late afternoon, when he said the rest of the day went off much better. The Prince realised that the people expected more formality and ended by playing the part more.

For days hundreds of Mekeos had been arriving in Moresby Harbour from a number of villages, drawing up their canoes on the foreshore and installing themselves in the grounds and under the Girl Guide Headquarters building. Though this was quite unpremeditated, the guides thought it would be politic to give them formal permission to do so and to work out with them some rules as to what could and could not be done; so the 'invasion' ended by being a fascinating experience for both dancers and guides, who loved watching the immense care with which the Mekeos applied their face patterns. The whole face is first painted in yellow, with details put on afterwards in red, black and white in a great variety of designs, according to clan and status. The basic colour of the girls' skirts is also yellow, as is the tapa of the men's g-strings and their waist bands and streamers. I have described their headdresses in another chapter.

About twenty groups, each of thirty people, began dancing in a huge horseshoe shape on the grassy flat at the bottom of Government House grounds late afternoon, ready for Prince Philip to arrive in the last of the daylight. They were also provided with a number of Tilley lamps, which was just as well, as looking from *Britannia* across to the Hanuabada houses, all built in long double lines over the water, intrigued the Prince so much that he hopped in a speedboat to go and have a quick look. The reception there to his unexpected appearance was so overwhelming that there was no way it could be 'quick'. When he eventually got away, he was accompanied back to *Britannia* by every canoe in the village.

I thought our dinner guests would forgive me if I went down to see how the Prince responded to the dancers, so, leaving Don to receive them, Daphne and I went down. He came when it was nearly dark, the Tilley lamps were lit, giving an extra dimension to the colour and movement, and when we finally tore ourselves away to be ready to receive him we were in no doubt that he had been totally bowled over by the beauty and colour and magnificence of the feather headdresses. In fact, many years later after our retirement, when we were presented at Buckingham Palace, the Prince referred to them, saying that he had never seen anything to equal them.

In addition to the Mekeo, a number of other distinguished leaders were brought in from other parts of Papua. I remember the tall and dignified figure of the old Trobriand Chief, Metakata. A great man in every sense of the word, he was surrounded by a small group of young Kiriwina men and women working or studying in Moresby, who were beautifully dressed in their quite different fashion. Lepani Watson, ready for the Government House party afterwards, had his five-year-old daughter Julie looking enchanting in the tutu-like Kiriwina skirt. Julie is now a beautiful young woman, who after attending the university is now in a senior position in the government.

When Prince Philip finally came to the house he was so elated that our party was a huge success. It was arranged that I would take him in to the buffet, then on to the study and sit him down at the round coffee table, while Don would bring in interesting people from time to time. Don's and my desks had also been cleared so people could sit there too. The table had an underneath part where I kept my sewing basket, the magazines and books we were currently reading and all sorts of odds and ends. The last thing Don had said that morning was:

"Now don't forget to tidy up your mess under the table."

But I had forgotten, and the Prince kept diving under and bringing things up with pithy comments, especially on books; and before I knew where I was I found myself in a spirited argument about cannibalism. But as I said, "No, it's not like that at all," and proceeded to go into the matter, I suddenly realised I'd contradicted Royalty and tried to crawl back, but Sir William with a twinkle egged me on. The next thing he picked up was a WHO effort on food and population and on that he provocatively plunged us into discussing birth control, so it was a relief when Don brought someone else in to take my place.

By the time dinner was over, guests were arriving in the garden so we strolled down to the foot of the steps and formed a receiving line, where the Prince was marvellous, not only with bright words here and there but with a telling eye for an interesting face and popping appropriate questions. I was to accompany him as he walked among the guests. Michael Parker, the Private Secretary, whispered in my ear that he liked to feel free and not too organised, so while Michael strolled behind him I darted about, grabbed interesting people, bringing them to his path and he would stop and talk without any formal introduction and seemed to be enjoying it all in a most spontaneous way. I must confess I also headed a few others off by talking to them myself till he had moved on. It was all great fun and he was a wonderful guest.

Another interesting thing about that night was the enjoyment of the world's pressmen. All the big papers from many countries were converging on Melbourne and many were also covering this visit. It was extraordinary how many told us during the evening or when they said goodbye that they had seldom had so many interesting conversations or met so many interesting and colourful people on one night. We felt proud of our fellow citizens.

Don left early in the morning to accompany the Duke to Lae, Bulolo, Rabaul and Manus, while I stayed back and looked after Paul Hasluck and Sir William, who was returning to Australia in the *Britannia*.

When Don returned on the following Thursday, he was elated that everything had gone off without a hitch. Of course he had a few funny stories to tell, but Prince Philip entered more and more into the spirit of everything and seemed quite 'caught up' by New Guinea itself. There was not another sign of the strange attitude on his arrival and there was mutual response everywhere.

One funny incident was the visit to Gabensis Village, a particularly pretty one in the rich Markham Valley on the way to Bulolo. Don and I had called in only the week before, returning from the Wau Show and it looked lovely; well laid out, trim houses under trees, paths bordered with hedges of brilliant crotons and the village elders most elated about the honour. However, when they arrived Don couldn't believe his eyes, for in their enthusiasm — making it spick and span for the great occasion — they had cut back the five-foot crotons and the paths were bordered with little one-foot sprays of sticks.

Chapter 8

The usual crowd hangs around an Outstation District Office.

Don's Workstyle and Character—Work Problems: Papua New Guinea and Canberra—Personal Relationships—Notes by Stan Pearsall: Workstyle—Notes by David Chenoweth: Workstyle— Additional Redcurrent Duties

Though the problems and the way Don and others handled them emerge in the text, I will now draw some threads together to give a clearer picture, before introducing what two men have written at my request about their day-to-day experience. One worked in the Administrator's office over many years and the other in a closely associated outside capacity.

Don's primary aim was to forge an efficient administration with the capacity to carry out effective government. This was also the aim of the Minister. Hasluck saw clearly the constitutional relationships between Minister and Department of Territories in Canberra and the Administrator and his administration in Papua New Guinea. He respected these meticulously himself and saw that everyone else did so too. In his unfinished book Don quoted a letter of September 29th, 1952, written to Mr Lambert, Secretary for Territories, making the position clear in the following words:

"I have seen today, for the first time, copies of your two personal letters of 19th September addressed to Mr Cleland on the subjects of 'Staff Administration' and 'Functions and Efficiency of Departments'. While I appreciate the good intention behind these letters and the fact that they are written in a personal and helpful way to Mr Cleland, as to a colleague, I think that, to avoid any possible misunderstanding, I ought to make it clear at once that they do not accord exactly with the view I take of the position of the Territorial Administration.

"I do not regard the administration of the Territorial staff and the functions and efficiency of departments in the Territorial Administration as being the responsibility of the Department of Territories, or that either the Administrator or the Public Service Commissioner can be made subject to direction from the Department of Territories on these matters. It is my aim to develop more and more local responsibility in administration in the Territory itself."

After his signature he added that he 'enclosed a copy of a letter he had written to Mr Cleland'.

He was as good as his word and in anything to do with internal administration or the handling of problems the Minister never interfered, nor did he knowingly allow the department to do so. When a problem situation emerged, such as at Navuneram in 1958, he needed to be kept fully informed. This Don always did. But he was informing the Minister what was happening, not receiving advice from him.

Though Hasluck's observance of relationships was impeccable in general internal administration, it did not work out so well in areas where new policies were being introduced. His attention to detail led him to keep a close watch on progress. This tendency increased administration difficulties, especially as Hasluck did not have a good appreciation of the logistics of a situation or of what it was possible to do in a given time. More seriously, he had poor appreciation of what was wise. This was largely because he lacked a feeling for the time needed by a people being administered to develop a readiness to meet change and absorb it. His own sense of urgency blinded him to these aspects.

This same sense of urgency lay behind both the number of his minutes and their biting and exasperated tone. He was meticulous to see that they came to individuals through the right channels in the department, but they did give the men, who were coping with all the multitudinous everyday problems, the awful sense of being badgered, and so inhibited their drive. Thus the minutes often had the opposite effect from what Hasluck intended. He states in his book that early in his ministry he decided on this course of driving people hard. When it was not particularly successful, and he too suffered continual frustration, it is strange that he did not review it and try a different method or even try encouragement by occasional praise or recognition of the many achievements.

It was a very unusual circumstance that for twelve years Papua New

Guinea had the same three men, Paul Hasluck and Eskie Lambert in Canberra and Don Cleland in PNG, all outstanding, each in a different way, working together, tussling and battling together, complementing each other, balancing each other out, going through periods of distrust which grew into confidence. For the last six years the trio became a quartet, when John Gunther joined the team on becoming Assistant Administrator. Equally outstanding, he was also a most colourful personality. They were never easy associates and they were never easy years, but together they were immensely creative and Papua New Guinea was lucky indeed.

John Gunther had an intellectual affinity with Paul Hasluck and the two men enjoyed friendship. Don, on the other hand, was essentially a 'doer' and, in the literal sense, an administrator. He did not have the intellectual curiosity of following an idea or a subject for its own sake. He had the supreme gift of eliminating inessentials and keeping to the matter in hand. But he was in no way narrow in his approach and was very much aware of the many side issues which could affect the main one. His clarity of mind saw them clearly as side issues and, while taking them into account, never let them dominate or get entangled in the main objective or the subject under discussion.

I think his most outstanding gift was his uncanny sense of timing. This came from a highly developed political awareness and a very strong sense of the art of the possible. He also had a subtle awareness of the tides of thought and feeling among the people, Papua New Guineans and expatriates alike, and recognised that it could be highly dangerous to introduce new things before the population of either race was ready to accept them.

Don often held back John Gunther, whose drive sometimes made him impetuous and whose touch of ruthlessness made it easy to ride roughshod over people. He would say, in effect: "Hold it a bit longer, John," and John would chafe. Then, when he considered the time was ripe, he would say: "Go ahead now". In the end John came to respect and rely on his judgement, and many a time things which, if implemented at once, would have aroused opposition, were accepted quite happily when the people had been quietly prepared to receive them.

Don couldn't do this with the Minister but while reading Paul's book with its references to his exasperation when his instructions were not carried out immediately, I got the definite impression that Don could at times have been quite capable of deliberately sitting on them and enduring the Minister's anger, until he judged that they would be accepted without resistance. I don't know this, of course, but I strongly suspect it, knowing Don's political nous, good judgment and strength of character. As it was, Paul Hasluck did begin to perceive this gift in the last year or so and to seek his advice; but, had recognition and discussion of timing come earlier, both Hasluck himself and many other people would have been spared a lot of traumas and frustrations and the country a lot of problems.

Essentially the two men had the same broad outlook and approach to many problems. Had the 1949 Act been better they could have worked together more fruitfully. But even with all the problems the interaction of the four men was still creative.

Effectiveness was greatly complicated because of the independence of action and equal access to the Minister by the Public Service Commissioner and the Administrator. Unfortunately this constitutional circumstance had the effect of making the Minister in substance 'Head of State', as it were. That everyone in Papua New Guinea thought that the Administrator was Head of State, and treated him as such, was certainly not sought by the Administrator. But the respect in which the office itself was held and the way people looked up to it seemed to be a source of irritation to Hasluck and, reacting to such things as 'colonial', it became rather a phobia and complicated and distorted his judgment.

Another area which caused endless complications was that Hasluck did not study sufficiently the real nature of the legal system which had been developing in Papua New Guinea over a period of seventy years. His tendency in this, as in other fields too, was to note one or two incidents or conversations while travelling round, which, while certainly indicating attitudes or trends, did not warrant the conclusions he drew from them and which often bore no real relation to the actual situation.

Such conclusions, when drawn from wrong premises, tended to reinforce already-held prejudices and misconceptions. On legal questions there was little enough true dialogue anyway. When it did occur the Minister and the men on the spot could each be discussing a problem from different premises and points of view. The issues would become hopelessly confused, resulting in matters put up by men in Papua New Guinea being rubbished and the Minister's own ideas being issued as firm policy to be carried out regardless.

Carrying out his primary aim of forging an efficient administration with the capacity for effective government, Don found that, in addition to local problems affecting this aim, others stemmed from Canberra. Two complications stand out.

One was the Minister's propensity for calling for reports. From Don's angle it was maddening to have these constant demands on his understaffed public service. Away from Moresby there was always so much to be done on the ground; demanding work of a very practical nature claiming all their time, and it was the practical things these men were trained to do. Whether in the field or at headquarters, when people were fully extended planning, organising and carrying out a new development — and such was going on all the time — it was infuriating to have to drop everything and do a report for the Minister. As few were trained to write such reports, their efforts were not exactly pleasing to him and he always wanted them 'instantly'. Many in the service were multipurpose men, that is they handled a wide variety of different things, so it could happen that the person producing a report on, say, an aspect of courts, would suddenly find one required on land matters. Responding to these demands was time-consuming and responsible not only for holding up still further the day-to-day work of good administration, but the implementation of whatever it was the report itself was about.

The other problem was caused by the huge proliferation of the staff in the department at Canberra. When Don and I went there in 1951, before he took up his appointment they were housed in a few, simply furnished rooms in a temporary building near Parliament House. When he retired, many floors were sumptuously furnished in a multi-story building at Civic.

They kept appointing 'experts'; and every expert had his little army of secretaries and assistants, all jockeying for position and importance vis-a-vis other experts.

So that when reports did go down, or proposals for something new or estimates for the budget, they all had to run the gamut of the desks of the various experts in Canberra before they even got to the Minister.

As it grew, the department in Canberra tended to become a barrier between the Minister and the administration in Papua New Guinea, through things having to be processed twice, causing lengthy holdups.

It was not unusual for Don to put a phone call through from the house around 5.30 — this being a good time to catch a man before he went home — and I would hear this:

"Say, Bob," or "John" or one of the other secretaries, "What the hell's happened to that report on such and such we sent down in June?"...

"Well, it's now September and I've just had a stinker from the Minister, so for God's sake get it to him."

I don't think Hasluck appreciated the time element involved in the double processing or the fact that reports and information sent down from Papua New Guinea could take so long to reach him. Don often wished that half the staff down there had been recruited for Papua New Guinea and would add:

"It would be so much more effective if the Minister with a small personal staff could deal directly with us."

He may have been wrong about this, but it certainly expressed his irritation that, as time went on, more and more decisions and powers seemed to be assumed by 'some bloody clerk' in the department than either the departmental head or the Minister ever realised.

In addition much time was spent by administration people going to Canberra and departmental people coming up for talks and discussion. This meant full consultation between the two bureaucracies on forward matters, with plenty of opportunity for the Papua New Guinea administration to have its say in forward planning, in the preparation of estimates even on policy matters before they came up for ministerial decision. In this way Papua New Guinea was able to influence its own destiny up to a point. It was only up to a point because they were not involved in deciding in what form, or adorned with what comments, documents finally reached the Minister. And his decision was final.

However, once the Minister had made his decision, it was then the duty of the public service in Papua New Guinea to carry it out faithfully. Paul Hasluck always did try to see that the responsibility and freedom to carry out policy by the administration was respected by the department. And though contraventions did occur, by and large this freedom was respected while he was Minister. But his own propensity for keeping a constant personal watch on the carrying out of his policies did leave him open to being misunderstood, for it made the men doing the job in Papua New Guinea feel it was interference.

It was always obvious that Hasluck was the driving force. But the decision-making was always where it should be; that is, in his own hands. It was a very different story under his successor, who had quite a different idea of his ministerial duties. Under the new regime in 1964, the Secretary of the department was able to dominate, because the tools to do so had already been forged by Hasluck's attention to so much detail.

The first tool was the size and composition of the Department of Territories. The second was the very bad construction of the Papua New Guinea Act of 1949. However wise Hasluck's decision to put up with it may have been in 1951, the fact that there never was any later attempt to amend it, to get a better structure, seriously affected not only the relation of Minister-Administrator-Department, but also prevented the various reconstructions within the Papua New Guinea service from being effective enough, particularly that of the relations between the Administrator, the District Commissioners and the Department of District Services, vis-a-vis the other departments. The problem of these two sets of relationships was never solved.

Another tool was forged by the Miniser himself. He failed to see that any proper preparation for self-government must take into account that a country needs a Head of State. This is particularly vital in the field of law. He recoiled strongly and with emotion against relationships which had grown up as a matter of course over a long period to take care of this need. Thus he appeared to be out to destroy it;

what he denigrated or destroyed in Papua New Guinea he took over himself in Canberra.

In his book he spoke of separating the gubernatorial from the administrative aspects of the work of the Administrator and says it met with resistance in Papua New Guinea. But I never heard of any such proposal and would like to know if one was ever seriously made.

In Hasluck's time you had a strong Minister and a strong Administrator. Quite remarkably they balanced each other out. His successor, C.E. Barnes, had quite a different idea of his ministerial duties, and chose George Warwick Smith, an assistant secretary from the Department of Trade, as secretary for the Department of Territories. George was only too willing to assume complete responsibility, leaving the Minister as titular head.

With these two men the old balance was completely altered and Warwick Smith had all the necessary tools to hand to gain complete control over Papua New Guinea.

Don resisted this encroachment. But three months before his retirement he said:

"I think I can just last out the next three months, not giving an inch to George but without having a flaming row with him." He did, too.

Strangely, throughout and in spite of all the difficulties, Don and Paul Hasluck had worked through to a fruitful and enjoyable relationship. Don had accepted the problems, and missed him sadly when he left the office of Minister of Territories. For one thing, personal correspondence between Minister and Administrator ceased completely, and this was a loss indeed.

As far as the local scene in Papua New Guinea went, I was always aware of the extraordinarily relaxed relationship between Don and all ranks of the service as we moved about the country. His natural way of talking to people was man to man and friendly. He was essentially shy, with an inner reserve, and was better at drawing people out than talking himself. It used to fascinate me, the way so many people of all walks of life and all races used to feel that they had a special relationship with him and indeed still talk as though they had. At the same time he was always treated with respect and, if anyone did occasionally overstep the mark, they never did again.

Complementary to this relaxed relationship, Don possessed the valuable quality of forbearance, which was first pointed out to me by a man who had served in the Middle East with him. He could accept that each man has his limitations and would expect the utmost from him without driving him too far. He would use the phrase that so-and-so had been promoted 'beyond his ceiling'. When this happened he knew that the person in question would be under constant strain and in some cases a disintegration of personality could be anticipated. While he always expected a high standard, he was tolerant when people could not reach it, as long as they did their best.

I have asked two men who worked closely with him to write me something of their day-to-day experience of the way he worked in the office.

As appears below, Stan Pearsall was very closely connected over a long period — before, during and after Don's time — with the office of Administrator. He writes from a close inside view.

☆　　☆　　☆

Sir Donald Cleland In His Office
by Stan Pearsall

For fifteen years I worked in close, almost daily contact with Sir Donald Cleland — the 'old man', as he was affectionately known. I had served under Colonel Murray since May 1946 as his uniformed A.D.C. (on official occasions) and as his personal assistant. Although I left the Administrator's office in 1949 for the Government Secretary's Department, some of my duties continued. I found the new Administrator to be much less austere and formal than Colonel Murray had been. For example, whereas I had always been 'Pearsall' to Colonel Murray, from the start I was 'Stan' or quite often 'Laddie' to Sir Donald. I believe that Sir Donald's style was much more acceptable to subordinates and public alike. I remember a prominent citizen saying to me at Lae, "If he (Colonel Murray) addresses me again as J.... I will punch him in the nose".

Such a reaction was not helpful, although those of us who understood Colonel Murray's background understood that to him his mode of address was correct and even complimentary, to some extent.

One of my duties was secretary to the Port Moresby Building Board. Under the Ordinance, appeals or objections had to be decided by the Administrator. This resulted in my first interview with Sir Donald, in 1952. Fortunately I had sensed that he was a soldier in his attitude, and my approach to him was very much that of a junior subordinate to his commanding officer. As well, my documentation was complete to the last tag marking a reference to the Ordinance and Regulations. Sir Donald dealt very expeditiously with the papers and I felt he was pleased with my army-like presentation of the matters to him. My future relationship, which grew much closer as the years went by, was always maintained on this basis.

It was not long before I learned that one could disagree and argue

In the garden with the dog Candy 1956.

with the Administrator, provided that one was polite and did not continue the argument after a decision was made. I remember well a disagreement with him over the use of harbour foreshore land at Konedobu. The Public Service Commissioner (Huxley) desired to build a hostel on land where the Cultural Centre was later established. After listening to my arguments, Sir Donald said:

"If you can quickly find another site, the foreshore will be preserved."

Fortunately Alan Timperley, the District Commissioner, saved the day by persuading the native owners to sell land in Spring Garden Road, so I won that one. I was not the winner when the argument started about the Konedobu Club land. I had said to Sir Donald, with a smile on my face, that there wouldn't be enough land left to erect a memorial to him. He reminded me that no decision had yet been made. When it was, he called me into his office, handed me the papers and said:

"Well, laddie, you have lost this one."

In his dealings with subordinates, Sir Donald was always correct. He could be very firm and brusque if displeased, but never rude. He never 'cut people down to size', not even the only three officers I recall whom he just could not stand and with whom he preferred to have as few personal dealings as possible. His immediate subordinates were not always summoned to his office. He seldom used the intercom system with them and frequently came to their offices himself. His written directions, often done in his own handwriting (in red ink), were concise and clear. I recall only one officer who claimed that he did not know what was required of him.

From time to time Sir Donald would refer a file or document to me for comment or further information. This was always on a confidential basis and any written material I gave him was not placed on a file. This was awkward for me at times, particularly with Fenbury, who was my departmental head, but Sir Donald always protected me, except once. On that occasion he called me into his office straight after lunch and said:

"Stan, I have made a blue. I unintentionally left your notes pinned to the front of the file and sent it back to ..." (the departmental head concerned).

The fact that Sir Donald had told me of the error made a blistering phone call from the departmental head easier to take. I always felt that the Administrator was Number One, and he was entitled to seek information and advice from whomsoever he wished.

On those important matters which Sir Donald preferred to handle himself, he would seek advice and information from those who he thought could be helpful, whether they were public servants, missionaries, planters or whatever. He would then do a military-type appreciation, setting down all the aspects to be taken into account. Pros and cons were listed and all of this led up to a decision. Having done this he would call in his secretary and dictate. The girls liked taking dictation from him because he always knew what he wanted to say and seldom had to go back and change his mind.

Sometimes he would produce a draft, which he might show to others for their views on his presentation of the arguments. When preparing recommendations for appointments to senior statutory office or for appointment of members to the Legislative Council or later the House of Assembly, he would consider nominations, but always the final choice was his. In recommending people for honours and awards he again would consider nominations and with very strict confidence tender his recommendation which, as far as I know, was never divulged to anyone.

Naturally Sir Donald had many matters to be dealt with concerning the Public Service Association. He was always correct but that did not keep him from being helpful. I was Senior Vice President in 1956 and it seemed to me that the association had been on the wrong track in its dealings with the Minister and the Australian Government. There were far too many rude telegrams and press releases. I drafted, and had accepted by the Executive, a letter congratulating Mr Hasluck on his appointment to the inner Cabinet. The letter then asked for a new beginning in our relationship where we had gone wrong, and it was not in the best interests of either the Territory, the government or the Association that this should continue.

Fortunately we had told Sir Donald what we were trying to achieve and I showed him the draft. He was with the Minister when he received the letter. Sir Donald told me that he had taken great offence because he thought that we were blaming him for all the trouble. Sir Donald told him the full story and was able to convince him of our good intentions. This resulted in years of peace and co-operation, with frequent discussions between Minister and the Association. Without the good will of Sir Donald, and our feeling that we could confide in him, this would not have proved possible.

On another occasion, Sir Donald showed his scrupulous fairness and integrity. The first arbitrator was to hand down his decision in the first case before him on a Friday morning. It came to our knowledge that on Thursday he had handed the Administrator and Mr Huxley a copy of his findings. The Association was infuriated by what it regarded as partisanship. Sir Donald called me into his office, unlocked his safe and handed me a sealed envelope. He had not opened it and was not aware of what the arbitrator had ruled before we were informed. Typically he had nothing to say in criticism of the arbitrator but he wanted us to know that he had kept to the rules.

Sir Donald was always accessible to his staff and his subordinates.

Likewise his door was always open to missionaries, business people, planters, but most of all to native leaders and members of the Legislative Council and later of the House of Assembly. Generally speaking he was on good terms with the press, though he never gave them any sensational copy, which caused him to be criticised at times.

For many years I was Secretary/Executive Officer to the Administrator's staff conferences, the Central Policy and Planning Committee and many other ad hoc groups. Sir Donald was a good chairman. When he could, he gave decisions on the spot; otherwise he listened to the discussion and reserved his decision. He encouraged me to keep pretty full minutes of proceedings, because he felt that in the future people would want to know, not only the decisions, but how they were arrived at. He was always conscious of the need to build up and support the Government Archives. Consequently future researchers should find in the archives many useful records of his administration.

The office which Sir Donald used was not adequate. It was much too small, very hot and had no security. Unscrupulous people could stand in the corridor outside and hear conversations if they wished. On several occasions I spoke to him about the need to improve it, not from the comfort point of view, but to make it secure. I had visions of agitators bursting in through the single door as well as pressing the need for complete privacy. His answer was always the same. He could not spend money on his office when so many public servants in the field as well as in Port Moresby worked under shocking conditions.

I am reminded too of his reaction to another accommodation matter. A spec builder appealed against rulings by the Port Moresby Building Board, which required him to rectify many features of some accommodation he had built for rental, contrary to building regulations. I made some enquiries and suggested to Sir Donald that he should himself inspect the buildings, which were the worst I had ever seen. They were occupied in the main by Australian soldiers, who had brought their wives and families, when no army house was available. The rents they were paying were exorbitant. Sir Donald was appalled by what he saw and felt for the unfortunate occupants of these flats. He sent for the builder and, when he arrived, told him in no uncertain manner that his appeal was rejected and informed him that he would have him prosecuted to the limit of the law if he offended again.

By 1958 Sir Donald felt that the administration was failing to get sufficient feed-back from the native people about reaction to government problems, their aspirations and what they were thinking. The field officers were failing in an essential intelligence duty. He had me draft an instruction called 'Interpreting the People to the Government'. I followed this up with visits to every district to talk to District Commissioners about the Administrator's wishes. The situation improved somewhat, but generally neither headquarters nor field officers ever really understood what was required of them in this part of their duties.

During twenty-seven years I served four administrators on a personal basis. They were good years and one should be forgiven for retrospective thoughts about them. I believe Sir Donald's accomplishments as Administrator must be viewed against two backdrops.

Firstly, he had a very great love for Papua New Guinea and the people and felt impelled to do everything that he could to see that both people and country developed in the best possible way.

Secondly, he was always inhibited from doing much that he felt should be done by the ever-watching eye of one whom the late J.K. McCarthy depicted in a cartoon as the ever present, but unseen, all-knowing and all-wise God, sitting alone in Canberra. The Administrator was so hedged in by restrictions, even on the exercise of statutory powers, by controls on expenditure, by limitation of his room to manoeuvre or to initiate, that I am convinced that it was only his great love and devotion to Papua New Guinea that enabled him to carry on. His Minister on very few occasions thanked him or praised him for anything and frequently wrote churlish letters criticising and blaming him. It took a Prime Minister in the person of Sir Robert Menzies to show publicly the gratitude of the Australian Government for what was being done under the leadership of "My old friend, Don".

☆   ☆   ☆

After service under Don in Angau, during the war, David Chenoweth came back in 1956 to plan organisation and method in the public service; later he set up and was first principal of the Administrative College. It was in this latter position that he had the closest association with Don.

Notes on the Administrative style of Sir Donald Cleland by David Chenoweth

1. It was clearly military in origins; army staff work and command experience was evident.
2. A characteristic of this influence is apparent in the maintenance of a diary system; adherence to clear communication, in writing, on all matters of importance; the insistence on minutes of confirmation or verification of the action to be carried out; and a formal style of direction and communication of decisions.
3. Nevertheless, it would oversimplify his administrative practices to

say that they were purely military in character; in my experience he maintained a fairly flexible set of responses to different situations and to different persons and allowed the administrative arrangements to develop from them. He observed certain principles of administration but was pragmatic and adaptable to changes in administrative arrangements. For example, at different times he would use a consultation-and-discussion style of decision-making, at others a consensual style, that is, waiting for the feeling of the meeting to emerge and yet at other times could issue directions in the normal line of command.

4. It should be remembered that, as the Administrator of Papua New Guinea, his role was not a purely administrative one, but to a large extent was political, involving him in a fairly critical relationship with the Government of Australia, especially the Minister for Territories, who had full formal powers over the policies to be developed in Papua New Guinea; and also internally, as President of the Executive Council, then with the Legislative Council, local political relationships became increasingly important. The administrative style used to reach decisions, to arrive at opinions in common and to issue records of action, varied accordingly.

5. In the public service, or the administration of Papua New Guinea, as it was known, his most characteristic style was to call in departmental heads and other senior officers for discussion, reach agreement on the course of action to be taken, and then issue that agreement in the form of an administrative direction. A typical form would be "As discussed...", then the decision would be recorded and the course of action to be taken would be defined. The most favoured form of discussion was one-to-one confrontation. I formed the impression that he was not especially fond of committees, but used them when, clearly, a wide range of opinions had to be canvassed about an issue, or debate was needed before a decision was made.

I had a number of discussions about administration with him in the days leading up to the foundation of the Administrative College, with a view to ensuring that the basic elements of good administration were included in courses there. It was clear that he had been much influenced by his military experience of staff work and command; and on the other hand by writings of Urwick and Brech who during the thirties set down their experience as consultants in modern management under the title of *Principles of Modern Management*.

Colonel Urwick actually visited Papua New Guinea during Sir Donald's time as Administrator, and I recall that they got along famously, each drawing fairly extensively upon earlier management experience. The administrative styles developed in the Indian Administrative Services were quite clearly highly esteemed by both, and I recall that *The Men Who Ruled India*, the book by Phillip Woodruff (the pen-name of Phillip Mason), was well known to both of them.

Just for the formal records, the basic principles which Urwick and Brech set down, as a guide to management practice, were known to Sir Donald and probably served as a kind of guide to him. They were under the mnemonic *PODSCORB*, representing: planning, organising, directing, supervising, co-ordinating, originating, research, and budgeting.

It should be said, I think, that Sir Donald concentrated especially on the direction and co-ordination of his role, which he consciously saw as that of the intermediary between the Australian Government, whose policies were vested in the Minister for Territories, and the people of Papua New Guinea, who would be the beneficiaries (or victims) of those policies.

In conclusion, I don't think too much should be made of formal management principles or classificatory headings. The fact is that administration, even within established principles and along well-tried guidelines, is a highly intuitive art calling upon personal attributes of intelligence, perception and character — courage, determination, drive and so on — which are the most important in the development of a personal administrative style. In this respect, Sir Donald Cleland's instinctive gifts for choosing the right line of action at the right time were well known and in this he showed a highly developed political sense. It should be recalled that during his term of office there were relatively few political crises engendered by adminstrative dislocation, and none, to my knowledge, cause by mismangement as such. Personal leadership, with a strong emphasis on commitment and personal loyalty, were most characteristic of his administrative style.

There are some technical matters which Mr S. Pearsall, his secretary for a considerable time, would be able to list. For example, the careful maintenance of an action diary; the direct telephone network to all departmental heads and certain other senior officers; the formal manner of recording decisions and communicating it in red ink. Details of this kind should be used with discernment but they do need some statement because they indicate the concrete situation better than a discussion of general principles.

I am most grateful to both Stan Pearsall and David Chenoweth for this contribution and account of how Don handled his office work.

I had a general idea of how he went about things, but naturally I could not know from my own experience, yet I felt that some account was needed to round out this story.

☆ ☆ ☆

Over and above these daily needs of administration there was also a heavy load of recurrent duties.

Firstly, there was the Legislative Council, which later became the House of Assembly. It met three times a year, usually for a fortnight, and included four full-day sessions each week and two evening sessions. Don was Chairman of the Council, which, being the equivalent of the Speaker, was a totally demanding job in time and in responsibilities for many aspects, some of them conflicting, and called for a high degree of political judgment. Another component of this was the constant worry and the to-ing and fro-ing between Port Moresby and Canberra involved in the preparation of Bills.

As an extension of this aspect of his duties, he was also Chairman of the Executive Council, which met weekly, and among other duties was responsible for the regulations necessary to the ordinances passed by the Legislative Council.

Later a co-ordinating body was also formed from the departmental heads, called the Central Policy and Planning Committee, which also met weekly under his chairmanship.

Another recurrent responsibility was the annual Budget, which I remember as a sort of annual nightmare. First, quite early in the year, each departmental head had to prepare the estimates of the expenditure which would be needed for the following year, which ended on the 30th June. In some departments, making these estimates was very complicated and, especially at first, the knowledge and expertise on how to go about it were rather sketchy. Then the Treasury Department in Moresby had to put it all together and work it into a budget. Next, a team of senior men, led by the Treasurer or an Assistant Administrator, fought it through the gamut of the department in Canberra. Finally it became a document for Paul Hasluck to battle through Cabinet, where it could be cut and returned to Moresby for revision, before becoming a detailed entry in the Australian budget which was presented to the June Parliament.

Paul used to battle nobly and had a long, unpopular and lonely road to get it through Parliament. It was lucky he battled so hard, but even then it would usually be cut. Then the Administration departments would have to go through it again and adjust estimates to the grant the Australian Parliament had voted and have it ready to go to the Legislative Council in September.

Our Council members naturally wanted to have their say. I always remember a favourite ploy of the Highland members, led by Ian Downs, regularly voting to cut the expenditure on Port Moresby roads. So poor old Moresby, in spite of being the fastest growing town, was always behind everywhere else in getting its roads sealed — and then they complained about its being so dusty.

Because the budget had to run the gamut of two parliaments, Papua New Guinea had in effect a nine-month year only, with a sort of hiatus between June and September. This particularly affected building and construction. Each year the companies didn't have enough work at that time and had to lay off men. Then, after September, tenders were called and another month or so went by until they were put in and the winning contracts let. Any contract over $25,000 had a further delay: Hasluck insisted in making decisions on these himself, and though he handled them quickly, considerable time could be lost between Moresby and his desk via the department. Then the companies had to gear up and get their workmen and materials in place, often to very remote areas. By then the mid-year good weather would be over, with the wet season coming on again, and companies would be bogged down (by mud this time, not paper) and held up by bad weather.

Because of this nine-month year, the money could not all be spent and would go back into the Treasury. The three-to-five month hiatus would have to be endured again, while Paul Hasluck would be angry because the Administration was so inept that it couldn't spend the money he had worked so hard to get. To see this going on, year after year, always seemed to me such an appalling waste of money and time and in sheer human frustration. I hated to see all the worry it gave Don and it all seemed so stupid and such a man-made problem. But everyone seemed to be enmeshed in the system and unable to find a way out of it or around it.

There was always the need for regular district visits. In the early years, with slow and poor communications, it could mean being away for a fortnight or longer. To keep your finger on the pulse and keep a balance between fifteen districts took some planning to fit them into an already full and busy life. Yet these visits were vitally important to good administration.

My accounts only give the highlights and the travelling and inspections, which were strenuous enough; but at every place we went, there were usually a number of appointments made by people who wanted to see Don on a variety of subjects, and a considerable time was spent in conference with officers of the administration, during which a number of decisions would need to be given. Then on his return he would have a long list of matters to be taken up with various people at headquarters. In later years the Assistant Administrator could take over a lot of this responsibility, with the Administrator making shorter visits for a definite purpose.

Interspersed among all this work were the recurrent crises. Disasters could happen at a moment's notice, such as the Tzarka, Harris and police murders in 1954 at Telefomin, the May River massacre; the Raluana fuss in 1954 and Navuneram of 1958 in the Gazelle; the Anderson affair at Tapini and the long shadows it caused, the Pacific Islands Regiment riot of 1957, and the confrontation with the Hahalis movement on little Buka. These were among the most notable, and the list does not include the various cargo cult movements.

Such crises would explode without warning and would mean dropping everything to give them full attention, and would involve very careful handling and the exercise of fine judgment. Such crises also had a way of breaking at most inconvenient times, such as Navuneram the day after the Dutch Governor and his wife arrived for a ten-day visit, when I had to accompany them for their itinerary round the country alone.

In addition to all this long catalogue, there were the visiting ambassadors, ministers, professors, viceregal visits and many others who stayed with us and whose number increased over the years. All had to be given some time and attention and entertained with dinner or a reception. Lastly, there were the social needs of all races of the people of PNG. Shows, exhibitions and new developments to be opened, sports such as football and cricket shields to be presented; charity balls to attend, school prize days, army and police parades, village celebrations. The calls were endless.

The government ran the town, so there was no Lord Mayor and his wife. There was no fully elected parliament, so there was no Premier and his wife. There was no Governor or Governor's Lady. So the poor Administrator had to carry the lot. When John Gunther became Assistant Administrator, he and his wife Dot helped a great deal in sharing the load and made their own special contribution.

But PNG is quite a large country, whose inhabitants have just the same needs, resulting in just the same demands as any other country, yet the fact that such extensive demands even existed was not only neither recognised nor provided for, but was rather resented. Each in their own way, the two Administrators under Paul Hasluck did their best by their own efforts to meet these gubernatorial needs, but it always seemed as if what they did was, at best, incompatible with his ideas and sometimes distasteful, and you could feel his disapproval. What they and their wives contributed was never given any sign of appreciation, nor were the similar contributions of the District Commissioners and the out-station officers and their wives.

Chapter 9

Chief Metokata, attended by his officials, greets Sir Donald. Rachel and Nick Healy watch.

Missions: Pastors at Metoreia—Suau—Mainohana—Vunapope—Methodists—Dogura and Anglicans—Kiriwina and Metakata

I have often been asked questions about missions, usually in an anxious or slightly apologetic way. I can fully understand the questioner's concern as I myself came to New Guinea with the uneasy feeling that somehow we should not come in and change people's belief or destroy their culture.

However, seeing the people in their villages, meeting the missionaries of all nations and denominations, the village pastors and priests, the teachers and evangelists, I slowly began to see things rather differently. District visits included missions on our itinerary and we always seemed to enjoy them, mainly because we found missionaries to be such happy practical people, often full of fun, with nothing narrow or prudish about them. Any prudery would have gone after exposure to a Papua New Guinea society where 'the facts of life' are taken so naturally and are as everyday as eating and sleeping. They have their own reticences, of course, though not necessarily ours, and areas which must be respected.

Missionaries living close to them would constantly be faced with unexpected human crises, so inevitably they either become very human and understanding people or they can't take it and go home. They tend to stay in one place — as much as half a lifetime, some remaining in their retirement. Not always being moved around like govern-

165

ment people, they can usually speak several local languages and become much closer to the people. In addition to evangelistic work they bring enormous material and practical benefits, with schools, hospitals and many forms of practical training. I have noted repeatedly the open and happy look on the faces of children and mission workers and their clear eyes, as compared with the fear in the eyes of others.

Young Papua New Guinean intellectuals tend nowadays to idealise traditional life and forget that fear was never far away. To begin with, human enemies were not far away either, and you could never be sure when the next village would be planning a dawn raid. You could never be sure that someone would not need human blood or a human head to strengthen the main post of a new house. Additional hazards were spirits. Every person, living and dead, had a spirit; so had trees and animals. Spirits were very real, could be good or bad, and everything had to be done the 'right' way — with the necessary spells or chants or certain words said — to keep the good spirits on your side helping you, or warding off the bad ones and preventing them doing you harm. To a very large extent Christian teaching has rid the people of these fears.

Missionaries are often blamed for destroying the people's culture. And many did so. Others who have tried to preserve it have not been very successful; the sad truth being that exposure of a people to another group, with a more sophisticated technology, causes loss of faith and confidence in their own — a process going on since the world began. We can't blame it on the missionaries when it's the inevitable contact with the modern world which has disturbed their beliefs. It was amazing that the island of New Guinea was left so long in isolation, a situation which could never have lasted. But they were lucky that, when the modern world did come to them, their rights were respected.

The variety of human oddities, human virtues and failings is as great among missionaries as in any other groups. By and large they have made and are making a wonderful contribution. The government simply could not have acted alone. Just through their being there with all their technology, the people would have lost faith in their own beliefs and a vacuum would have been created. The missionaries have filled that vacuum and what they have done increasingly, in more modern times, is to encourage the people to adapt their own songs, dances and art forms for use in church services. This in itself is changing the culture radically but not destroying it.

Another point (often overlooked) is that, since all culture is subject to change, one has influenced another and made changes over the centuries. What was once slow development is now rapid, change, making a bigger gap between tribal and modern cultures; the very rapidity does not give time for absorption and adaption and much is therefore lost.

Luckily people themselves are now beginning to value their cultures. Schools and colleges are recording and cataloguing the old stories, songs, oral history and traditions, and producing them in printed form with fascinatingly drawn illustrations. In addition the Institute of Papua New Guinea Studies, initiated and brilliantly established by Professor Ulli Beier and funded from the special Australian Cultural Grant of $5,000,000, has an impressive record. The work of the Institute is largely carried out by young people trained at the university in archaeology, anthropology and the various necessary techniques to make and store these records. With the fine museum collection and the Institute's records, the people are now assured that enough will be preserved so that artists, writers and the people themselves can draw from and be inspired by their own sources in creating and developing an indigenous modern culture.

☆　　☆　　☆

In November 1952 the Rev D.E. Ure invited Don and me to the big mission house at Metoreia above Hanuabada Village, the London Missionary Society headquarters since 1873. It was their annual church assembly, when missionaries and pastors all come together to plan the year's work, and we came to meet and have tea with the Papuan pastors. We found about thirty middle-aged men, each elected by a group of villages to represent them at the church assembly. They were courteous, easy-mannered, loved to tell you about their work and I looked around thinking I had never seen so many faces filled with simple human goodness.

One evening, travelling by trawler down the coast, bad weather caused an unscheduled anchorage at Suau Island. Canoes came out, we were invited to the village for a sing-sing at eight o'clock and Don and I duly rowed ourselves ashore in the dinghy and walked over. No one was in sight, but a light drew us to the big mission house, dating back fifty years and built with two sets of rooms about eighteen feet apart and connected by a huge breezeway, acting as the living area for the pastor and family and the centre and general meeting place for the whole village.

We walked up the steps to see the people just quietly listening to the elderly pastor reading the Bible. He looked benignly over his steel-framed spectacles and went on reading, while people near us moved over and smilingly made room. We sat on the floor among them till the reading was finished and they said a prayer and sang a hymn. No one was fussed. They accepted us among them. Evening prayers over, they dispersed to the sing-sing ground, while the pastor gave us the warmest of welcomes and led us to a table by the kitchen, where his wife presented us with a cake she had just made. It was rather stodgy and it was iced with white sauce. But the gesture gave me a lump in my throat. The pastor said in answer to our question:

"Oh yes, the people all come every evening while I read the Bible."

One hot, dusty morning, we visited the recently opened Mainohana boys' secondary boarding school. Don spoke to the boys and visited the classrooms and dormitories, saw their excellent food gardens, admired the playing fields they were making themselves and finally repaired to the good Father's house, where he was offered a whisky. Now Don loved his whisky with the sun over the yardarm, but not on a hot morning. So he refused. Further talk, the whisky again offered and refused, causing such a disappointed look that Don said, "Well, . . . perhaps," and was rewarded with a beaming and much relieved smile.

"The Bishop gave us this bottle for you but said that, if you didn't have any, we'd have to give it back. Now it's broached we can keep it."

These men of the Sacred Heart Mission in the Mekeo district lived a very spartan life, so that bottle was a great treat.

On the shores of Simpson Harbour, the beautiful sunken crater at the eastern end of New Britain, is Vunapope — literally the place of the Pope — founded by Father Louis Couppe, a refugee from the ill-fated and bizarre Marquis de Ray's expedition to New Ireland. Arriving in 1882, he began work a few miles south of Queen Emma's large trading establishment and beautiful house at Ralum, near the present town of Kokopo.

With a romantic beginning, this mission has also had a dramatic history. Before the Japanese invasion in 1942, it had 78 buildings, being the headquarters of the Sacred Heart Mission, which extended over New Britain, New Ireland and Manus, where 58 mission stations with sixty priests looked after 60,000 adherents. Each station is quite substantial, with a school, hospital and house for the nuns, lay workers and trained local people who run them. A station would in its turn be responsible for churches, schools and aid posts in the surrounding villages. But in 1953, Bishop Scharmach, who showed us all they were doing, was having to rebuild after its total destruction in the war, with the loss of many of their workers during the four years they lived out their imprisonment in Ramali, a remote and inhospitable valley. Many stories recount Bishop Scharmach's courage and resourcefulness in looking after Methodist and Anglican mission people and civilians as well. We found him a cheerful and vigorous person of great character.

Vunapope, like a town in itself, had its cathedral, houses for priests and lay staff, its convents, boarding schools for both boys and girls, an excellent hospital and printing works, with school books, prayer books and the like, printed in nearly forty languages. There were carpenters and engineering shops, plumbers, painters, vehicle maintenance and repair shops, while on the waterfront were a shipyard with slipway and repair depot, wharves and storage sheds, with small ships anchored or loading. All the workshops, run by lay workers, gave young Papua New Guineans valuable practical training, and the hospital was a recognised training hospital for nurses. Over the years I got to know many sisters at Vunapope and some of their mission stations and found them wonderful women, who had given of themselves to hundreds of girls.

Later, a Seminary, opened a few miles inland, began training young men from the splendid high school they maintained at Vuvu on the north coast. Many seminarians eventually became priests in charge of village churches.

The Methodists came to the Gazelle even earlier and were, like the London Missionary Society (L.M.S.) in Papua, the first European residents in the area, when they set up a station in the Duke of York Islands in 1875. Their charming, rather 18th-century-looking churches are a feature of many villages and they too maintain first-class schools, a teachers' training college and a college for training pastors.

☆　☆　☆

Towards the end of a five-week trip in the small ship *Leander,* along the south-east coast of Papua and among the eleven hundred islands of the Milne Bay district, we steamed all day off the north east coast. Inhospitable because of a marked wet and dry season (like Port Moresby's), it has little forest, grassy mountains rising straight out of the sea, and dangerous reefs offshore.

At sundown we anchored in a cove with a jet-black stony beach, and looked in wonder at an enormous and beautiful cathedral silhouetted against the evening sky on a grassy plateau to our right. This was Dogura, headquarters of the Anglican mission established in 1891, where we were to spend two days. A jeep, followed by a stream of children, came dashing down the steep road and our old friend Bishop Strong came aboard in a canoe. Though appearing an other-worldly man with his head in the clouds, he produced a typed programme for our visit and gave us a more businesslike and specific rundown than anyone else on the trip. It's so much easier to be relaxed and respond adequately with businesslike hosts who tell you what's ahead.

That night a service in the cathedral was followed by a formal dinner at the mission house, for which we had been asked to bring evening clothes. A long taffeta dress hanging at the back of my tiny wardrobe all those weeks had fallen down during a bad overnight buffeting and was saturated, so I couldn't do them proud, only managing a fuchsia-coloured cotton cocktail dress to accompany Don in dinner jacket and black tie. The Bishop returned looking splendid in his purple and white and we climbed into the jeep. As we were trundling up to the plateau, rain suddenly came down in torrents, collected on the canvas hood and broke through above me, emptying into my lap just before we scrambled out and dashed into the porch.

The Cathedral of St Peter and St Paul is larger than St Andrews in Sydney. Of cement, with twin towers, Norman arches separate the nave from the side aisles, with clerestory windows above. Each supporting pillar has a piece of carved stone from one of the old English cathedrals on its face. Built in the nineteen thirties, it was done entirely by voluntary labour, whole villages rostering themselves to come and stay for a week or more and working under the direction of the Reverend Robert Jones; it was indeed a labour of love done joyously. The walls round the altar were richly painted with murals by Father James Benson; having been a prisoner of war with Bishop Scharmach in Ramali Valley he returned to Dogura after retirement and in thanksgiving painted hundreds of figures of Papua New Guineans and expatriates, many of known people, to represent the history of the church there. Above them the Hands of God are blessing an olive-skinned Christ with the Dove of the Holy Spirit coming to His people around Him.

The cathedral was full. People from schools, hospital, seminary and nearby villages were sitting on the floor, where rows of pandanus mats were placed instead of chairs. That evensong was an experience which will remain always in my memory. The lovely Papuan voices, so suited to the old settings of the Magnificat and Nunc Dimittis, soaring in the high roof of the cathedral, and the simple piety and faith which enveloped us, made us feel, like the pastor at Suau, part of something which our rushing world has largely lost.

The rain-washed air, stars in the dark sky and the sea splashing gently below the plateau were a further balm as we walked across to the big mission house afterwards. My fuchsia dress was deep purple fore and aft from the spill of water and I was distinctly chilly; so asking to be excused, I made for the kitchen to dry myself before meeting the guests, giving everyone a good laugh as I did so before a huge wood stove.

We have been warmly and graciously entertained by many missions over the years and the fare and way of living have varied enormously. By and large, the Methodists put on the best spread, largely because their workers serve a certain term only and keep their home country's standards. The American Lutherans have delicious and 'different' cooking as do the Seventh-Day Adventists. The Catholics vary enormously from very frugal to lavishly good fare — often the latter, because the clever French fathers grow their own vegetables and keep a cow or goats to make butter and cheese. The most self-denying are the L.M.S. and the Anglicans. Anglican missionaries, at the time of which I am speaking, had £30 pocket money a year and were kept by the mission in the basics of flour, tea and sugar. Meat and freezer were rarities; for the rest, they used local food, to give more feeling of common identity with the people they worked among.

The main reason for variation in material standards was and is quite controversial. The first German missions in German New Guinea were Lutherans and Catholics, who took the practical view that to do effective work they must be self-supporting. Therefore they applied for and got large areas of land for plantations which are well run, often with the help of their adherents, and have supported themselves ever since.

But another school of thought believes that mission work demands self-sacrifice and depends on money raised by their home churches and by the local people themselves.

Both have their advantages and disadvantages. The Anglican, L.M.S. and Methodists, though without the impressive material back-up of missions like Vunapope, do seem to have developed self reliant people able to run their own affairs, who have obviously been influenced by the high qualities of the missionaries.

Which brings us to the formal dinner of Dogura. In the big main room, tables, arranged in a large U, were beautifully decorated with flowers and ferns and places laid for about thirty people, who were still arriving as the Bishop, an expansive host, presented them to us. All the senior mission workers were there, expatriates and Papuans being equal in numbers. Among them were Sister Rawlings and her Papuan assistant Septimus Nimo, responsible for the teaching hospital, Father Cassidy of Newton Theological College with his senior student, now Bishop Ambo, Canon Brady with student teachers from St Aidan's Training College, and Canon Byam Roberts of the secondary school, with two senior teachers, Kingsford Dibela (now Speaker of the House of Assembly and recently awarded the C.M.G.) and Richard Sorewa, whose son-in-law Rhynold Samana is now Bishop of Dogura. The cathedral priest was Father Taralato; his Canon, John Chisholm, is now Bishop of the British Solomon Islands; while by far the most revered guest was that dear old man, Father Peter Rautamara, the first priest (ordained in 1917), who died only recently at the age of ninety-five. Altogether an interesting and distinguished group of people.

The cocktails were fresh lime juice; later the Bishop presided with great charm, giving the dinner such a sense of occasion that it has remained an 'occasion' indeed in my memory. Service by schoolgirls was impeccable, though the menu was only local vegetable soup, sausages and mash, followed by jelly and custard. All the correct toasts were drunk in ginger ale and lemonade, the speech to Don by the Bishop was quite notable and Don was in good form for his reply. The dignity, happiness and atmosphere, created with such simple fare, conveyed the very best of the English tradition and the Bishop's formal dinner was a great success — but I must say that back in *Leander* Don enjoyed a double nightcap.

Dogura is like nowhere else in PNG. As an Anglican I always feel sad that it is so inaccessible. The coast is dangerous and not on any sea route. The only possible place for an airstrip is small and subject to dangerous cross-winds and the country is too rough and far from any town or centre for roads to be a possibility. Anglicans could feel so proud of it but few ever see it.

Set between the sea and high grassy mountains, the plateau on which it is built is flat and quite large. Like an English close, the big playing-field was surrounded by buildings, the Cathedral between it and the cliff top with the hospital in sight, the Bishop's house and the big mission house on the two sides near the Cathedral with the primary school opposite. A mile eastwards is the Holy Name girls' secondary school, to the west St Aidans for boys and beyond that is the seminary for priests. The atmosphere is happy and devout, with a sort of direct simplicity, while the isolation insulates it from worldly pressures and distractions. A religious community in early Christian times may have been like this.

Behind the landing beach is Wedau Village, where John Guise was born, his mother being a Wedau woman, and a few miles further east is lovely Wamira, presided over by Miss Casswell, affectionately called Cassie. She lived in a large bush material house with handsawn timber floors, kept gleaming by schoolgirls, first rubbing with coconut meat and then gaily sliding about with woollen socks on their feet. Beautiful pieces of old furniture with her Georgian table and family silver made it a gracious house, while her culture and personality rubbed off on the boys and girls in her school and left its mark. Many of them, now holding very responsible positions, seem to have an extra dimension of 'quality'. She also ran clinics and Mothers' Union groups, teaching the women cooking and sewing. A wonderful person, as were so many others in remote places like this.

The Anglican mission has always had a good name for the soundness of its education programme, and, with the Kwato mission near Samarai, is distinguished because a number of older men and women from each of them are well educated. The Anglicans were also the first to consecrate a Papuan Bishop. George Ambo and his wife went to the Brisbane archdiocese in November 1960 for his consecration by Archbishop Sir Philip Strong, so long the Bishop of PNG.

☆ ☆ ☆

One of the many interesting visits we made on this long trip was to Kiriwina on the Trobriand Islands, making landfall early one wet and drizzly morning. The A.D.O. and police guard met us with a large jeep-type war relic, the only wheels on the island, lent by the famous 'Ma' Lumley who had traded there since the turn of the century. Many villages, some flooded under a foot of water, gave us an enthusiastic welcome and eventually we came to Omarakana, where Chief Metakata was to receive us. It was a large village, its many houses built in Trobriand fashion at ground level. Before each was the traditional store-house, with carved and painted gables, full of yams, but not a soul was to be seen. On a slight rise at one side was quite a different style of house, made of hand-adzed timber planks, finely carved gables and house posts, a raised verandah and central doorway with carved lintels. In a semicircle surrounding it were thirteen ordinary houses and thirteen yam houses, for each of his thirteen wives, explained Mick Healey, as we began walking towards them.

Just then the door opened and out came a very tall, slim old man wearing just a g-string. He slowly came towards us with the bearing and gait of an Edwardian gentleman from Bond Street. Mick and I stood still and watched, my camera ready. His timing was perfect. Not exactly keeping Don waiting, neither did he hurry, but greeted him as the King of England would have greeted the President of France. Even with all his formal clothes on, no king could have looked more dignified or conveyed more kingliness or presence than Metakata in his g-string. Behind him a high-ranking attendant, fully clothed in western style, bore his Chief's symbols of office — a large yellow lime gourd, with exquisite patterns in black, and an ebony staff.

"Good heavens," I thought, "the orb and sceptre."

By then the three men had strolled down from the little hill to the flat central green of the village.

"Look behind," said Mick. I turned to see several hundred people advancing on their knees.

"Now Metakata has come down from his hill they mustn't be higher than he is," explained Mick.

Strangely, I remember nothing more, though I must have shaken hands with Metakata. But that fascinating moment of the two men meeting — the head of the Trobriands and the head of the government — has remained so vivid that everything else is blotted out until we arrived at the Lumley establishment for lunch.

We drove through a gate and cow paddock to a small building, an immense woman with a strong face was waiting with hands on hips. Picking our way through the cow pats over the sodden ground, Don remembered that lack of official visits was a sore point.

"Well, Mrs. Lumley," he called out, "here we are at last."

"And so you bloody well ought to be," said she.

Don chuckled as we shook hands and she led us into her store, filled with the carvings she had encouraged into an industry. Bowls of all shapes and sizes with the elegant, traditional, curvilinear Massim designs, coffee tables made from whole tree trunks, human and animal figures supporting the solid round of the trunk at top and bottom, platters, ashtrays, carved animals. The store was packed.

Mrs. Lumley, a formidable character, had remained from the gold-rush days. A widow of many years, one son of her large family had remained to help in the trading. Her house was an epic of imagination, ingenuity and, good taste. We went into a huge, pillared living room with the gleaming pinky-brown walls of plaited sago bark or kipa, the dark polished pillars being whole tree trunks which supported bedrooms, reached by steep, ladder-like stairs. The furniture was home-made, from the cane chairs to the huge kwila dining table and massive carved sideboard and coffee tables. Kwila, so heavy that it sinks in water, is the best wood for carving, with its fine texture and grain, and everything glowed darkly from constant rubbing with coconut husks. Finely woven pandanus mats were scattered on the floor and the whole place, presided over by its impressive mistress, caused the phrase 'baronial halls' to hover in the back of one's mind.

Next afternoon a huge crowd gathered on the oval for a sing-sing and we, watching from raised earth banks, were enchanted with the sea of twirling circles. The Kiriwina dance in rings. Girls in their short bouffant tutu-like skirts keep up a graceful movement of their arms and hands, with long pleated strips of pandanus, and the men quiver in 'dancing bats', two flat rounded boards about a foot across and connected by a handpiece, each carved in a variety of curvilinear designs painted in ochre, red, black and white. With headbands and white cockatoo feathers in their hair, the sight below us was gay and happy and different. Suddenly they all dropped to their knees.

"Whatever's happening?"

"Look," said Mick Healy.

Across the oval was Metakata, moving with great dignity through the almost reverently respectful groups. When he had joined us on our elevation, everyone rose and went on dancing.

For the rest of our visit we'd been to all the missions, met village leaders, talked to school children, seen the hospital (a horror and Don promised immediate renewal). Don had had his conferences with staff and received deputations, everyone making the most of the opportunity to air their grievances. The visit ended with Blue and Rosemary Geelan's buffet dinner, which, we discovered later, was a unique occasion.

The two factions of the expatriate population had, after much persuasion, only agreed to come if they didn't meet each other and the party was well on the way before Don and I twigged that the Greek trader and his faction were in one room and 'Ma' Lumley and her followers in another, with the neutral people commuting between the two, we of course doing likewise. The party seemed a great success when we said our goodbyes about ten.

As we left the house, the garden path and road to the jetty almost exploded into light, to reveal hundreds of Kiriwinas lining each side with limbom torches. The coconut fibre of the torch makes reddish light, is slow burning but flares up and subsides, so is almost overwhelmingly spectacular. The originator and organiser of this dramatic farewell, a cadet patrol officer on his first posting, escorted us. We'd been impressed with Des Fitzer earlier on and he is now one of the few of his generation still in the central government in Port Moresby.

Along the way free hands were stretched out to shake ours as we exchanged farewell messages, then following and crowding the wharf and shore as we boarded *Leander*. They were all singing and calling "Aiyune" — the haunting farewell word of the Massim people — while reflections of the hundreds of torches stretched their fingers towards us on the still, black water waving from the ripples of our movement.

Later in 1954 we landed on the dazzling white coronus expanse of the wartime airstrip, Momote, on Manus Island. First visiting the Tarangau Naval Base and the District Headquarters at Lorengau, we went aboard *Laurabada 11* early one morning for a few days among islands off the south coast, which, with the coastal fringe, were the home of the 'sea people' or true Manus, intelligent and vigorous people, heavily involved in trade from time immemorial. Before 1940 they occasionally saw a white patrol officer, planter or missionary, a few had ventured to the mainland of New Guinea to work on plantations, a few had become policemen, but to most, Manus was the centre of the world. They had a vague notion of other people across the sea, but it was all rather mythical and of no importance to their intense and busy lives of trading and exchanges.

Into this haven suddenly came many ships and thousands of Japanese to make use of the huge sheltered Seeadler harbour in the north east. Later, bloody air and sea battles and even more ships brought thousands of Americans and with them vast quantities of stores and armaments as a huge supply and naval base was built up.

The shock to many people could have been destructive but to the Manus it had a galvanic effect as the Americans were materialists and traders like the Manus themselves. The immediate post-war effect was confusing to the returning Australians. Whether the seething ferment was just another cargo cult or a genuine political movement was eventually sorted out and found to be two cults. One, in central and south coast Manus, was a typical cult. The other, with strong political elements, was led by a man of some genius called Paliau, centred on Baluan Island.

When Don came on the scene they had begun damping down the cult and its attendant hysteria, and encouraging Paliau in his constructive political ideas and passionate desire to get his people moving into the great modern world the war had revealed. He was a great man and a true leader of vision.

So this bright sunny morning, full of expectation, we passed the eastern tip of Los Negros Island and on to Pak, a little jewel with white sand and waving coconuts, in its turquoise coral setting in the dark blue of the sea. The young manager, with plantation tractor and trailer, was waiting to take us to a group of villages on the southern side of the island. Above the din of the engine he tried to explain things to Don. Obviously wanting to co-operate, he wasn't at all sure where it was all leading. Coming through jungle on the far side of the plantation we were amazed to see not an ordinary village but a well-laid-out street, new style of houses with separate kitchens connected by covered walkways and paths leading to well-made latrines. Each was surrounded by a fence with a path bordered by flowers leading to a gate onto the street — nicely cut grass each side and a flower bed in the centre. American Ladies' Home Journals must have stimulated such a startling new concept.

The islanders were all waiting to greet us on a sports ground at the end of the village, not in the usual casual grouping, but under a large bush shelter. They were sitting in orderly rows, men one side of an aisle and women the other, facing a small decorated platform for us, while sitting on two chairs in the sun in front of the people's shelter were the leader and his wife, holding black umbrellas. Both were impeccably dressed in European clothes, she with shoes, stockings, bra and lipstick. They rose, escorted us to our seats on the platform and returned to make a speech of greeting in English. As he finished, a group dashed into the space between us with a dramatic enactment first of a trade exchange of traditional objects — beautiful bowls, lime gourds, beaded leg and arm ornaments — then, of an argument and horribly realistic fight, ending in a truce, with ceremonial breaking of spears and arrows. The traditional objects of the exchange were then presented to Don and the leader spoke again, saying they wanted to show us their old way and demonstrate that it was finished because they were coming into the modern world.

Don thanked them profusely, admired their village and the way they had organised the reception and said he had heard of their interest in local government councils and co-operatives. Telling them how a council worked and fitted in with the government as they knew it, he said they must understand clearly and talk it over well before they made their decision. The Co-operative Officer who had come with

Coming ashore. 'Lorabada' II in the background.

A typical village church built of native material. No nails were used.

him would now talk and he and the local government officer would come back later and help them.

Talking to the notables from the three Pak villages, we agreed to visit Mokra and Tandul, taking their leaders on the trailer with us, and admired their 'modernisation' too. Passing back through Hahai, the formality had gone and the people drifting home cheered, shouted and ran after us in a happy farewell. We went back on board with a feeling of humility and very thoughtful indeed.

Our next stop was also interesting. This group had bought the plantation on N'Drova Island and were running it by a form of share farming, which so far was working out quite well. Buying European plantations is 'the thing' of the seventies. But the Manus had done this in the fifties. And, moreover, it was their own idea.

Our next stop, M'Bunai, a big mainland village, had already formed their local government council and were expectantly waiting for Don to open the new council school and the first co-operative store in this area. Later we called at Lou, another lovely island, with the Seventh-Day Adventist Mission in the north. The Seventh-Day Adventists had, as always, an excellent set-up and training facilities, but also tended to be exclusive. This one was the centre of local government council opposition, so while Don embarked on a discussion with the missionary to try and sort things out, I went off with his wife and all the girls to see their boarding school. I can still see the lively, bright eyed and very nubile girls and the earnest face of the missionary telling me how they did try so hard to make little ladies and gentlemen out of their pupils.

A lighter touch was shown by Baum Village, where our ship was to pick us up, with an uninhibited farewell in a tiny, rocky jungle-hung cove where they crowded round the dinghy, shaking our hands, stroking our arms, laughing and singing and following us out into the water, clothes and all. They truly are 'sea people'.

On and off we had been arguing about what should be stocked in a co-operative store. The D.C. thought stock should be what was needed for their best development and the co-operative officer held that it should be what the people themselves wanted, even if the items seemed frivolous. The argument had been going back and forth, with Don and me amused and interested, putting in a word now and then. After leaving M'Bunai the co-op officer seemed to be losing, till he said, a little defiantly:

"Well, I like to ask the people for their own list. What do you think that Baluans headed theirs with? Brassieres."

We roared with laughter and he definitely won the day as we visualised the leader's wife at Pak that morning. Actually I think he was right. Too many of us are 'do-gooders' and think 'father knows best', when the only way any of us ever learns is by making our own choices and our own mistakes. We could help in the elucidation of what the choices are and make suggestions but should never usurp making the choice itself. That, of course, goes for everything.

We were nearing Baluan, where Paliau lived, by late afternoon. Suddenly round a heavily wooded point came a double line of twelve or fourteen canoes, each with about a dozen paddlers. Manus canoes have a tall, slender bow and stern post, a high outrigger and platform with a rather short mast, and can be sailed or paddled. This was most dramatic. Sails furled, the paddlers, standing in the Manus coconut skirt with leg and arm decorations and wielding carved and painted paddles, swept out to meet us in two lines, crossing behind our stern to travel alongside us. Chanting and executing a sort of canoe dance — three strokes in the water and paddles aloft, three more, then held abreast in perfect unison with a variety of movements — it was lovely to watch and spectacular and exciting. Coming into a channel past an offshore islet, we saw ahead people cramming a causeway jetty, waving and calling, as we were welcomed very warmly by Paliau and his wife, Theresia, who escorted us with Ted Hicks, the A.D.O., across the sports ground to his house on the hill. With all the excited people and hands to shake it took us half an hour. Paliau and Theresia, the head teacher (Paulus Arek) and the Tolai council clerk all came in for a short visit. It was very interesting 'getting the atmosphere' and observing Paliau, whom we then had met only once but were to know well with admiration and respect over the years.

At dinner Ted engrossed us with past and present stories of the 'Paliau Movement', as it was known, before we bade him an early goodnight.

Don was to open the budget session at the Council Chambers and we woke at dawn to the sound of canoes arriving, till the landing place was crowded with people from the whole council area, men in spotless white and women and children in gay colours. The councillors and VIPs crammed inside the little building, while everyone else listened outside. Paliau was a magnificent orator and his power of the voice had carried his people with him in developing his new idea. This day he was strong, understated and most impressive. One sentence has stuck in my mind. Translated from Pidgin it was:

"I and my generation have strong ideas but we have no education. We have to employ a Papuan to teach our children and a Tolai to be our Council Clerk. But you wait. All our children are going to be educated. Then see what we can do."

Paliau was prophetic. By the end of the fifties, ninety-seven per cent of Manus children were in school, more than double that of any other district. Fifteen per cent of the first university enrolments were from the Manus — the smallest district in the country. So now many senior positions in government and private industry are held by Manus men and women, including the first woman parliamentarian to be a minister, Nahau Rooney, well experienced and with a university degree.

The rest of the day we saw the co-op store, aid post, schools, Baluan Village, even more modern than Pak, and seven other villages on Baluan Island. The get-up-and-go atmosphere was extraordinary and Don promised them an agriculture extension officer to help them develop their land to the best advantage.

We also saw the church; itself an interesting phenomenon. At that time a great old to-do was going on between the Catholic mission, based at Vunapope, and the Paliau movement. The Manus people still thought of themselves as Christians, even as Catholics, though on their own terms of enough independence of action, as befitting the new way they thought of themselves. But Vunapope was then still far too paternalistic to be able to meet them half-way, and was forced to withdraw the priest. So the people faithfully went to the church, with Paliau or another leader conducting the services until, much later, times changed and both sides were able to accommodate each other.

They were an interesting and stimulating people. We had had a wonderful day with them, and at sundown walked back to the ship saying our goodbyes rather sadly. Near the wharf a line of women came from the village; the leader, taking my two hands, pulled my arms up and another placed banana leaves across them, to receive all sorts of little presents — bags, tapa, shells, baskets — till they were up to my nose and I could see just over the top. The last gift was a live turtle in a string harness and lead, wagging its head from side to side, its beady black eyes close to mine. My expression must have been startled, for giggles began and we all laughed and almost cried too, saying our goodbyes.

Dear Paliau and Theresia, dear Baluan. Remote little island standing on your own two feet, determined by your own efforts to come into the modern world. Quite recently I was talking to Paliau Lukas, the Commissioner for Housing, who was a young schoolboy that day. He remembered the turtle, telling me of its special significance as a magical animal because it lived on sea and land.

In 1958 the headquarters station of the Gulf District had been moved from Kikori to Kerema and permanent buildings were replacing plaited sago bark and thatch. One morning we rose at 4.30 and crossed Kerema Bay by canoe to a landrover waiting on the beach. The early start was necessary to catch low tide, for the only way to the out-station Ihu (on the Vailala River) was along the beach or by boat. It was fresh and quite romantic to be dashing along the beach in the sunrise. Presently we came to a river, where men and a double canoe were waiting to manhandle the landrover aboard, helping us and cheerfully poling us across a sandbar. With much handshaking and thanks we went on our way to a coconut plantation for breakfast.

By departure time it was getting hot, but on we went all morning, crossing several more rivers by several more waiting canoes and eventually coming to the great Vailala River, where oil exploration had left a rusting barge attached to wire ropes, which wound it across with a capstan. Ready to handle the contraption was the young A.D.O., Graham Lambsden, and his group of helpers. We inspected Ihu, on the far side, before going to the Lambsdens' house for lunch.

His young wife had an eight-month-old baby and an adorable toddler. As we chatted, I looked at the children and thought of our morning's journey and all the organising needed for the canoes and men who handled our landrover, thinking of the awful isolation in a medical crisis with the children. When the opportunity offered, I asked how she made out in such an isolated spot.

"Oh, but this is the best outstation in the Territory," she exclaimed. How often in isolated and seemingly desolate places had I asked that question. And how often had I received that sort of reply!

These young women were truly marvellous. Both on government stations and isolated plantations, they identified with their husband's work and with the local people living round them, and were so caught up in the spirit of drive and development which infused the fifties that they were able to take the problems, difficulties and hardships in their stride.

I asked her about communication with Kerema. There were occasional boats, they had a teleradio, and a policeman walked there every week for the mail and freezer, but meat carried on their heads was sometimes rather off when it arrived, so the community looked forward to having the airstrip Graham Lambsden and the local village people were building. The D.C.A. men due that afternoon to inspect it were to fly us back to Kerema and they hoped it could open soon.

Urgently beckoning Don and me to the window our hostess said to watch the jungle, as we heard a motor bike. Through an unnoticed gap shot a nun in a blue habit, who stopped the bike and jumped off. The back hem brought through and tucked into her belt in front gave her a King-of-Siam look. Competently kicking down the holder and adjusting the bike she pulled the hem from her belt, shook herself, patting things smooth, meekly folded her hands in front and walked to the front door. It was delightful.

On introductions being made, Don complimented her with a twinkle. She left straight after lunch to welcome us at her mission on the way to Orokolo, a large village where a station of the London Missionary Society had been established at the end of the last century. The Catholic mission was fairly new, well set up and seemed only a mile or two from Orokolo, where the L.M.S. house, a huge inconvenient building of dark pit-sawn and hand-adzed timber, had dominated the scene for sixty years.

Mr and Mrs Dewdney were an elderly couple who had been there all their married lives. They ran a school and a hospital but seemed to be pretty starved for money. During afternoon tea I asked rather anxiously if the new Catholic station made problems by being so near.

"Oh, no. It's wonderful," said Mrs Dewdney, with real enthusiasm. "We've never had neighbours before. If we're out of something we just run down the road and borrow from the sisters and they do the same with us. After all, there's so much to be done, there's plenty of work for everyone."

We've found this same spirit widespread. Though you do get individuals who are incompatible, just as you do anywhere, the spirit of ecumenicalism was common here long before Pope John.

Chapter 10

A village school.

1951: The Judges—Respect for the Law—Growth and Nature of the Legal System—Keeping the Law by Patrol Officers—Police—Calaboose—Luluais and Tultuls—The Flavour of the Fifties—The Queen and Symbolism

The day after my arrival in 1951 we had attended the opening of the first bulk oil installation, where I met the leading citizens. From the mental confusion of meeting so many new people at once, two very contrasting personalities stood out. Both were judges.

The Chief Justice, Monty Phillips, was a small man with a large head, spare and wiry. While not exactly aggressive, he never left you in any doubt that he was there. Always with a fund of excellent stories, he liked to be the centre of attention and enjoyed a dramatic situation. He expected a great deal of his rather shy wife Jean, who supported him in every way.

Mr Justice Gore (Ralph), on the other hand, was six feet four and built in proportion, and his height made his head look small. His personality, though strong, was understated. He was a gentle and tolerant person and had a way at a party of standing at the edge of the crowd, arms folded and a little aloof, but with a smile full of human understanding and amusement, just watching. He was held in great affection and young ones who knew him well called him Judgie. When people came up to talk with him, he responded immediately, giving them his full attention. His wife May was attractive and plump and a social leader in the town. He treated her with a devoted but amused consideration.

Both Phillips and Gore had immense experience of the people and their ways of thinking and acting, each going back over a quarter of a century. Phillips had been Chief Justice of New Guinea and Gore had been Chief Justice of Papua. When the civil administration return-ed after the war, the burning question was — which of the two would be Chief Justice of the amalgamated territories? It was decided to settle it by choosing the one appointed first, and Phillips won by a day. But they made a tremendous team, complementing each other and each holding the other in great respect. They were two mighty men. Two other judges of long experience in the country made up the Supreme Court of four.

As we moved around the country and got to know the people — District Services staff from Commissioners down to patrol officer, private enterprise people, village leaders and 'big men', missionaries, schoolboys, planters and even the pilots who flew our planes — it was increasingly borne in on me with what immense respect the judges were held. This was all the more remarkable as there was nothing outwardly to mark them off from other men. There were then no courthouses. So courts were held in whatever was available — a grass hut in the bush, a schoolroom or church hall, a spare room in the district office or just outside under a tree. Only Moresby had a courthouse, and that was an ancient pre-war building, tucked in behind the equally ancient district office. So the respect didn't rest on anything external. As I pondered on it I began to observe and learn more about 'the law', which was held in equal respect, about the whole way justice was ad-ministered and the way law and order was kept.

And it was an incredibly law-abiding community. For instance, I don't ever remember locking up our little Lawes Road house. Doors and windows were all open for coolness. We would even go away and leave the house open. Yet nothing was ever stolen. It was the same everywhere.

Only four judges (at that time), no stipendiary magistrates, five lawyers, about thirty police officers in the expatriate public service of a mere sixteen hundred persons, supported by about two thousand PNG policemen and about a hundred clerks and one hundred teachers, were a very small number of people to govern, and to keep law-abiding, a country of the geography and size of PNG, with its scattered two million population. How was it done?

Having spent half my life in a legal atmosphere and with legal forebears myself, I had absorbed a fair knowledge of the workings of 'the law', and so with that background the situation here totally fascinated me. Seeing it at work in all sorts of places; hearing the talk as we travelled around; asking questions to clarify my own observations; and the picture gradually began to fill in.

It had grown up from long traditions, begun in the nineties in Papua by Sir William McGregor and developed by Sir Hubert Murray. In New Guinea it was based on German traditions, begun also by two remarkable men — Bulominsky of New Ireland and Governor Albert Hahl in Rabaul. Here the tradition was harsher, based less on native tribal ways, but with a very exact concept of justice. In places where it was exercised, German justice is still respected.

From 1921 the two Territories, though governed under different laws and with separate Australian administrations, began to grow together through common practices; and during the war, under Angau, they were combined as one. T.P. Fry and John Kerr (later Governor General of Australia) then began the long task of correlating and amalgamating the laws of the two halves, with preparation of the necessary legislation to put it into effect. When we came in 1951, this was still only half done. But though there were differences of detail between Papua and New Guinea the effect was much the same.

At the base, a simple face-to-face dispute-settling custom was carried out by those patrol officers who were invested with magisterial powers, with which they could hear disputes and adjudicate between individuals and groups and send cases up to a higher court. As a patrol officer was often the only government man responsible for a large area, he would need other powers, particularly when it was necessary to make arrests. Therefore he would also be given police powers. But these two powers were only subsidiary, as it were, to his basic one of being 'the government'.

It often made me smile when I realised that in the end the Minister and the bureaucracy in Canberra, the Administrator and bureaucracy in Moresby with all their varying powers and responsibilities, were all finally represented in the person of one patrol officer in his twenties, on a remote outpost. He was Law, Order, the Lands Department, the Public Works Department, the Post Office, the Health Department, the Education Department or whatever other government function was needed by the people, both national and expatriate, in his district. The situation never ceased to delight me.

To a professor of law, a judge or barrister in an Australian city, this way of working could appear scandalous; they would think it couldn't possibly work — but, strangely enough, in practice it worked extremely well. It fitted in with the people's own notions of justice, with the simple face-to-face hearing of the dispute or the complaint, when either an acceptable compromise was reached between the parties or, when necessary, justice was meted out and the wrongdoer taken away. Though all done by the same person it was completely understood and approved by the village people, largely because these young men were scrupulously trained in their duties.

As I learned more I also became aware that a great deal of the credit for the respect must be given to the incredibly hard and devoted work done by Monty Phillips immediately after the war, as he travelled through and held Courts in the war-devastated areas of New Guinea, and also to Ralph Gore, who did the same in Papua.

Monty had joined the Air Force in 1940 and served in Europe. He came back in 1946 with the agonised feeling that in some way, by not being here when the Japanese came in, he had somehow let the people down. It was irrational, because there was nothing he could have done. But the haunting feeling drove him to do a superhuman task in 1946 and 1947. His great message was — 'The Law has come back'. Always, 'The Law has come back'.

He carried out unbelievably full schedules on circuits which took the court everywhere as quickly as possible, and very literally wore out his Crown prosecutors. But his message certainly did get through. He and Gore inspired all the new young patrol officers and they too carried on the message — 'The Law is back'.

To guard against injustice or malpractice, these Kiap Courts had to be properly convened and the crime or matter under dispute had to be recorded, together with the judgment, in triplicate. One was held by the officer concerned, to remain the record of the court; the others were forwarded to his district headquarters, where they were regularly inspected by the visiting judges and either confirmed or disallowed.

A few years ago the then Chief Justice, Mr Justice Minogue, told me that he had been looking through these old court papers (the system by then having long been changed) and said he was surprised that by and large the judgments had been sound and he noted that very few had needed to be disallowed. But then a District Officer had to be good and the justice he dispensed had to be sound. For they knew jolly well that the good order of their district, which rested on their young shoulders, depended on whether or not the people were satisfied with the justice they dispensed. If they were not satisfied, resentment smouldered and the trouble broke out again. So an officer learnt in a hard school to ferret out what had actually happened in a given situation and to see both that the offender accepted his punishment, as a fitting retribution for what he had done, and that the offended people were also satisfied that he had got his deserts.

Another advantage of these courts was that they could be held on the spot, in villages perhaps several weeks walk away from a patrol post, and the people did not have to wait long months for a hearing, as they do now, with the trouble growing and festering all the time.

The people themselves had always had their own dispute-settling apparatus, quite highly developed in some areas; less so in others. These 'kivungs' or village courts were known to exist and were quietly accepted and tacitly acknowledged by the Administration. In actual fact they played a considerable part in keeping order within the villages, disputes often being brought to the patrol officer only when the village courts had failed. Therefore it had been a deliberate administrative decision in the late forties not to take them over and institutionalise them at that time, because that would have brought them into the bottom of the hierarchical system, whose apex is the Supreme Court, which derives its power from the State. Whereas, leaving them as they were, their power remained with each group of people and rested on consensus. Moreover, as things were, so soon after the war, they were a far stronger influence for law and order left in the hands of the village elders, and being tacitly accepted and acknowledged by the Administration.

However, within Papua New Guinea, a lot of discussion and thought was being given to using these as a basis, developing them into a recognised system and so involving the people themselves with wider responsibilities. Naturally there were many problems which would have had to be overcome and a lot of research needed to find common denominators between the many varied, yet similar customs of different areas, on which a system acceptable all over the country could be developed.

Don was extremely interested not only in discussions about developing village courts but also in the practice of having native assessors who would sit beside a judge of the Supreme Court or a lower court magistrate and interpret native customs. These ideas were widely thought about and discussed at that time by district service personnel — from the patrol officer up to the District Commissioner with many and varied viewpoints as to how it could be carried out and many problems which would need to be resolved. But there had been no formal study made, no pooling of ideas to work something out.

The judges and the Law Department were also very much aware of the value of these traditional dispute-settling customs. But they were even more aware of the problems associated with bringing them into the system and of the care needed to preserve their essence, based as it was on the consensus of elders. Otherwise the people could end up by losing something of their own of great value without a sufficient corresponding gain. This in fact is what has finally happened.

Hundreds of village leaders came to hear a notable case in Buin because they had heard 'talk' of supposed intentions of the judge. Monty Phillips reassured them, saying that their traditional village courts were essential to law, order and good government, and that the government supported them. But he made it clear that they were quite separate from the courts of the 'Big Government', and that their council of elders was quite right to bring this case to court because it needed a big punishment, and only the government court could do that.

From earliest days the Queensland Criminal Code was adopted in Papua and it was extended to New Guinea after 1921. In addition each Territory had its own body of civil laws in the form of ordinances assented to by the Administrator's Executive Council. Cases were always judged with due recognition of seeing that justice in its true sense was done and, equally importantly, that it was seen to be done. Very early in the century, when burning of villages and similar punishments were common in the colonial world, such things were very much frowned on in Papua, and the ideal of finding the actual man who had committed a crime, particularly the crime of murder, was instilled into the service by Sir Hubert Murray, himself a lawyer who had originally come to Papua in 1904 as Chief Judicial Officer. This idea was particularly applicable to murders or tribal fighting in far-away places, when a patrol officer and a few police, or the police under a sergeant, could spend months in the bush till they found their man and brought him in for trial.

It was this long tradition, understood and approved by the people and faithfully carried out by the four judges of the Supreme Court of the fifties, which was responsible for the great respect for the law and the stability of the country which so impressed me in our first years.

There were other components of this respect, one being the Royal Papua and New Guinea constabulary. In the 1880's Sir William MacGregor brought over ten Fijian policemen to be the nucleus of the force and to train Papuans, who were recruited from that time on. Men were chosen for their strength of character and qualities such as resourcefulness, loyalty and the respect in which their own people held them. They were the backbone of the patrols which were the essence of 'Native Administration'. Few of these men had had any formal education but they were wise in the ways of the bush and the ways of men. Over the years they did a magnificent job, particularly in their essential contribution to the success with which the country was so peacefully brought under control. Nothing quite like it has been known anywhere else in the world.

Great care was taken to see that all parts of the country were represented in the force, and the problem of finding the right men from newly contacted areas was not infrequently solved by recruiting men who had served their term for murder. We called them murderers but, when the crime was a traditional payback, they were not murderers in our sense at all, though they had to learn that now the government had come they couldn't kill in revenge any more, but must rely on 'the law' to look after it. Some years spent in 'calaboose', as the old loosely guarded prisons were called, when prisoners were not really cut off from the community, were enough to teach them something of the new ways of living and to develop a respect for the law. The very fact that they had killed meant that they were often men of ability and consequence, and some of the finest members of the early force had been recruited from such prisoners.

So many incidents come to my mind, recalling our early days of travel, which illustrate not only the wonderful qualities of the police and their versatility but the relationship which often grew up between government men and policemen. Once on Wau strip, after Don had inspected the guard, a man with a strong and wonderful face came rushing over to Horrie Niall, seizing him by both hands. The two men looked at each other with tears in their eyes, both too moved to speak for several moments; then came reminiscences. Horrie turned to me.

"We were in a tight corner together in the war," he said, and while I joined Don, Horrie remained with his friend finding out what he'd been doing over the last few years.

There was Kaupa, the old corporal whom Robert left at the patrol post Watabung, to look after his wife while he went on a long patrol, six weeks after they were married; he would have guarded her with his life. I went to spend a week with her to break the long time alone. Julie thought she was running the station, but old Kaupa knew he was. She was living in a temporary two-room grass house with a separate 'haus cook' and bucket shower room. It had a very wobbly, unlockable door. Watabung was only in the process of being built, on the road a few miles beyond the Daulo Pass where Robert had had his camp, and it was on the edge of a barely controlled area. Yet never for a moment did we feel any sense of insecurity, thanks to the respect with which the three policemen on the station were regarded. Every week, when she wanted mail and supplies, she put her letters and a list for the one store in Goroka (thirty miles away) into a split stick, and a policeman trotted off without a qualm and brought back her mail and supplies the next day.

The police could turn their hands to anything; show village groups how to build the road, set up camp on patrol, build houses on a new station, set up a hospital for the 'doctor boy', handle boats and canoes, barter with the people for food and see that they got the right payment, as well as keep an ear to the ground and advise the patrol officer of what the people were thinking. They could also suggest to him an acceptable solution to a dispute, or even settle it themselves. The exercise of their natural psychology in finding out what really did happen, in a case where one side said one thing and the other said the opposite, was proverbial. Sometimes they overstepped their powers or were guilty of malpractice and had to be disciplined; but the majority earned respect by their own qualities.

In the towns the police were just as effective. In the early fifties towns were all small, both in area and population, and the police had a pretty good idea who should and who should not be there, who was dishonest and who was not. Quite a small number of men under a

European police inspector kept order. Part of their duties was to patrol the town roads at night, and it was mighty comforting to hear the clink-clink of the brass chain on his bayonet holder, which was part of the picturesque old uniform, as the duty policeman padded barefoot up the road. He knew by sight all the people who legitimately lived in his patrol area and was suspicious of any strangers. We also knew him and greeted him as a friend.

A further aspect of the respect for the law of the early fifties was the calaboose or prison. These were rather casual affairs and very much a part of the community. There was no tight security round them and on an out-station or even in a town they consisted of dormitories, usually of pit-pit and thatch, a cookhouse and a toilet block, surrounded by a fence with or without some barbed wire on top. Sometimes the gate was not even locked at night. If a prisoner was sentenced to a month in calaboose, well, that was his sentence — and so he stayed there for a month. The calaboose was usually near the police barracks and every day the prisoners, wearing khaki lap-laps stamped with a broad arrow, would set off, with a policeman in charge, to do some work for the day. They may have repaired a road, built a new ward for the hospital, a house for a newly married policeman, or even just had a tidy-up day on the station. They seemed to me to be always a cheerful bunch, with excellent relations with the policemen in charge, and often were known personally and were on passing-the-time-of-day terms with the station residents.

In the town of Moresby, the jail was at Bomana, on a considerable acreage of rich river flats, where the prisoners worked on the only market garden in the whole country. There they grew vegetables and fruit for the hospitals, government hostels and schools. This jail was not ramshackle, like most out-stations, but here too, for the most part, the prisoners accepted their confinement without need for tight security. This calaboose system also contributed to the confidence both nationals and expatriates had in the law. The fact that prisoners had to work in public near where they lived meant they had 'shame' before their wantoks (the people of their own community), and this contributed to the effectiveness of the punishment, so the calaboose too was held in respect.

Another very important component of the social fabric was the presence in each village of government representatives. When an area was being brought under control, one of the first acts was to appoint a man in each village — called a luluai in New Guinea and Village Constable in Papua. The village itself had a fair bit of say in this choice, but the man they chose had, of course, to be acceptable to the administration. If thought desirable, an assistant was also appointed and called a tultul, while in Papua he was called the village interpreter. This practice went back to the last century in both Territories. In New

Winching ourselves across the Vailala River near Ihu on a barge left behind by an oil company.

Mr Justice Kelly, Mr Justice Gore, Chief Justice Phillips, Mr Justice Bignold.

Guinea the custom was adopted by Judge Hahl, who had studied the Tolai Village set-up, and both luluai and tultul are Tolai words.

They were given a navy blue 'trammies' cap with a red band, and in Papua a plain navy serge jumper and rami, and they received a small sum of money each year as a retainer. Their job was to be the spokesman in the village for the government, and the spokesman to the government for the village. They took their duties seriously and were very proud to be 'hat men'. Mostly they were very fine men and some had held their hats for twenty or thirty years. Some were no good or just nonentities and had to be weeded out. If they abused their office they lost their hat.

On the whole this system worked extremely well. Every village had a government presence, which made them feel linked to the big government outside. Each village had a man who could if necessary adjudicate in disputes or bring a wrongdoer into the district office to 'make court'.

My first personal experience of this system was highly diverting. In our early days at Government House we were having a large buffet dinner for some occasion and, as the staff were not yet very well trained, it meant being in the kitchen till the last possible moment and giving myself about fifteen minutes to shower and dress. I had just checked everything and gone to my room when a voice called that a woman wanted to see me.

"Please come quick quickly,".

Mystified, I dashed back to the kitchen, and on the verandah was a tall, angular, very angry woman and a pretty young girl. Her English was voluble but difficult to understand, but with her daughter and my interested staff helping I eventually got the story.

"It was my wire and he said it was his and took it from my garden, so I took it back and he put the handcuffs on me. Now we've got a Queen he can't put the handcuffs on a woman. Now we've got a Queen I came to you because you're a woman." Her excitement and anger was mounting as she came to the crux of the story.

Apparently certain village policemen are given handcuffs but not a key. That is held at the district office, to guard against temptation to secretly abuse their position. So this very important and well-connected Dorrie Vere had to walk all the way to the district office from Tatana Village, four miles out of town, to have the handcuffs taken off. Everyone could see her and she had to endure the shame, though it was her wire.

I explained that I was only a wife and not the government, but that the D.C. and the Police Commissioner were coming to dinner that night. I would tell them her problem and ask them what she should do. If she rang me up or came to see me in the morning I would tell her what they said.

I was rather touched at her interpretation of the importance to women of the fact that we had a Queen. Dorrie must undoubtedly have been the first Women's Libber. They warned me too that it was strongly suspected that she was the 'Mama Dika' of the village — not that this would have lessened her importance. However, the D.C. and the Police Commissioner were concerned that the village policeman had exceeded his duties and would need to be disciplined; and that a court would have to determine the rights and wrongs of it. Dorrie Vere duly presented herself early next morning and I gave her a note to take to the D.C.

Later I got to know the Tatana people very well. Dorrie's brother Willie Vere also had a powerful personality, and their old mother Pokara was a wonderful woman. She gave Mrs. Thelma Price and me lessons (behind locked doors in the Guide hall) teaching us some of the old traditional dances. In the sixties Pokara's grandson, Bobby Gaigo, has been the driving force in claiming much of the land the administration headquarters are built on, and demanding half a million dollars for it. He took the case to the High Court of Australia.

These then were the components of the situation which more than anything else impressed me in those first few years. But towards the end of the fifties it began eroding. Why? Could such respect for the law have been maintained as the country developed and came into the modern world? It would certainly have lessened, but it need not have been thrown away almost overnight. Change had to come; but it could have come gradually. It could have been planned more carefully. It is always a pity to throw away the baby with the bathwater. But this is largely what happened. The reasons behind this tragedy are complex and varied and are worth looking at.

Papua New Guinea has always been an exciting and stimulating place to live in for those who are willing to give themselves to it and enjoy it as it is. To do so means always to be ready to take what comes and accept the unexpected, to forget that time in our sense is important, to appreciate the qualities of the PNG people and accept the meaning of a Motu word 'dohori' — tomorrow is another day.

You find that the country does its own sorting out. Some people hate it or can't adjust and they go. Others are naturals and love it at once, and some grow to love it. Don was the former and I was the latter. But although still exciting and stimulating, the whole atmosphere in the nineteen seventies was completely different from what it was during the nineteen fifties.

Then, the trauma of the war and the scandals, greed and self-seeking of the war disposals era were sufficiently in the past; the cleaning up and rebuilding process was well under way; the far greater post-war emphasis on development, specifically through the education and development of Papua New Guineans themselves, at first causing horrified resistance by some expatriates, was later widely accepted. In fact this type of development came to be recognised even by the conservatives as a contributing agent to the common good, which of course in a lot of eyes meant for their own good.

To achieve all this reflects enormous credit on Col. J.K. Murray and his vision. Moreover he achieved it when both he and most of his staff were lacking in the skills and practice of government. So Don took over not only when the country was poised and ready to go ahead, but when the Australian Government was gearing itself to undertake far greater responsibility, by appointing a Minister solely responsible for its dependent Territories and creating the new department to help him. In addition, the Minister chosen had vision, drive and very particular qualities of mind.

Around the towns there was a tremendous feeling that at last things were moving, and this in turn stimulated a great release of community energy. All the main world organisations, Red Cross, Scouts, Guides etc., became active and began to grow quickly. The service organisations — Rotary, Lions, Apex — were founded. Garden clubs were started and every town would hold an annual Flower Show, leading to a great impetus in town beautification.

And then came the idea of having annual district shows. Though the inspiration for these was the agricultural shows of Australia, Papua New Guineans were involved from the outset in showing their garden produce, cooking, handicrafts etc., and they very soon became largely cultural, with very big emphasis on local sing-sing and dancing groups and showing local styles of house-building and collections of cultural objects. The shows also became vehicles for community education, with most government departments putting on displays of their work, the technical ones in particular being immensely popular, while business firms large and small put on grand displays. These shows always drew huge crowds and have played a very real part in the long, slow process of encouraging the growing-up of a national feeling of country which would encompass, yet be bigger than, the primary loyalty of clan, village and tribe.

In the nineteen fifties the school system was developing and for the first time it was becoming possible for a Papua New Guinean to acquire a modern education, with which he or she could work or compete on equal terms with an expatriate. When we visited schools we were always struck by the bright eager faces, and the dedication of the teachers of both races. Talking to the pupils and asking what they wanted to do, we were constantly impressed and touched by their sense of dedication; of wanting to train to help their country. We would look at a classroom of young faces and wonder which of them would come up as the leaders of the future, for they were all there then in the schools. Don and I both used to talk to them and try to stimulate their ambitions and leave with them the feeling that, if they knew in their minds and hearts what they wanted to do and worked hard for it, anything was possible for them.

But then, of course, the time when Papua New Guineans would have the education and training to take full part in their own destiny was still in the future. In the fifties, adults were pretty well confined by the limitation of their education to rather basic tasks. Because of this, both government and business were very dependent on expatriates — and in those days expatriates meant Australians.

Twice a year, a group of twenty to thirty young men would be recruited as cadet patrol officers. Similar groups of young teachers and medical, agricultural and other trained officers came up. These were of the age group who would have been at school during the war, hearing tales of the Fuzzy Wuzzy Angels, whose heroic efforts made the defeat of the Japanese possible. Few would not have had father, uncles or brothers who had struggled somewhere in PNG. The Kokoda Trail, Milne Bay, Buna, Gona and Shaggy Ridge were household words and meant courage in tough conditions. They had also heard the incredible tales of the coast-watchers — pre-war field staff and planters who lived behind the Japanese lines, sending out vital information by teleradio, and the post-war tales of how exploration and discovery in the Highlands was filling in the blank spaces on the map.

This all contributed to stirring the imagination of young men, who came up with a sense of adventure and purpose. They knew they were in for hardships and tough conditions, and in fact it was in part these very conditions which gave them such elan and the drive and enthusiasm of out-station life in those days. Young men and the wives who supported them felt that nothing was impossible.

The new people they contacted and brought under government control were infected with the same enthusiasm and attacked the road-building, the airstrip-making, helping the setting up of patrol posts with the attendant schools and hospitals, with enormous zest and not a little rivalry. If the people of one valley had a road, then the next one wanted one too. They quite understood that if they wanted a road they would also have to maintain it. So Monday was road day nearly everywhere. People turned out to fill in potholes, open blocked drains, resurface with stones, and would make it both a gala occasion and a means of showing off their superiority over the next group, by the state in which they kept the length of road for which they were responsible.

Driving down towards Asaro from Goroka one day we saw an archway ahead of us with a garland across the road, and a small man standing in front of it stopped us with an imperious gesture. Behind the archway was about a quarter-mile of road, garlanded each side, and people working and singing away. He stated that they were from a valley to the north-west — pointing. They had no road, so they had arranged with the Asaro people to look after this piece of road. He wanted the government to know that from now on this piece was his responsibility. There are many ways of 'keeping up with the Jones'.

All this then led them to coffee-planting, setting up trade stores, saving money to buy trucks, demands for schools and hospitals. So development was spectacularly rapid. The coastal areas had a leeway to make up of apathy from long contact without development. But this new spirit began to inspire them too. I would think that what you found in Papua New Guinea in the eight to ten years of the fifties was something quite unique in the world. Those who took part in it will never forget it and will always be nostalgic about it.

It was all possible because of respect for the law, which the judges and the courts had built up over such a long period — the story with which I began this chapter. It gave people great confidence and a firm sense of security. It was this background of security and trust in the government which had an almost mystical quality. For it certainly needed a mystique for such a small handful of people to achieve what they did in Papua New Guinea.

Staying in Robert's hut on Daulo I saw that the flag was ceremonially raised by a policeman at sunrise every morning and lowered at dusk, when everyone stood to attention. Policemen carry out the movements of any drill or ceremonial superbly, with a slight exaggeration and flamboyance which they thoroughly enjoy and take very seriously, winning approval from their fellow Papua New Guineans. As we stood one evening at attention, watching the policeman advance towards the flag and salute it, coming to attention with a spectacular stamp of his bare feet, and then with infinite slowness and loving care lower and fold the flag, I had a sudden vision of this same scene at this same moment on hundreds of government stations, at schools and aid posts, at Government House and the D.C.'s residence in towns and even of a weary patrol officer and his line of carriers who would first raise the flag before setting up camp for the night. I looked down the new road and even the village people passing by had stopped and were standing smartly.

I was almost overwhelmed by the impact of this mixture of thoughts and feelings as I realized that this flag-raising and lowering ceremony was part of the mystique — that it was part of the bond which held the whole thing together. A symbolism can speak far deeper than words. Papua New Guineans are bred on the language of symbolism and this, our symbolism, they and Australians could easily share together on equal terms without the need for language.

I went inside, hushed and quite awed by my discovery, and began to think of another observation over the years. That was of the many times and places I had seen pictures of the Queen, torn from magazines or one of an old official issue, tucked into the bamboo plaiting of a village house, pasted on the wall of a trade store, nicely framed in the entrance to a village church. Of course she was also in district offices and other government buildings, but the touching thing was to realise the widespread spontaneity of feeling and understanding of the symbolism of the Queen, and of so many families wanting her picture in their own house. This was not the sentimentalism it would have been with us, but a deeper and more dignified comprehension of the mother figure, the Head, the Source, that all both looked up to and drew strength from.

Chapter 11

Newly elected councillors at Taskul Village watch old Luluais throw in their hats.

*Judge Phillip's Retirement—Judge Mann's Appointment—
Tapini and A.D.O. Anderson—Quinliven's Report and
Johnson's Commission—Anderson's Trial, Conviction and
Appeal—Section 10: Investigation—The "Watershed" Year—
Mann's Style Brings Changes—Local Government Councils and
Luluais*

In 1956 everyone was delighted when the Chief Justice, Monty
Phillips, was given recognition for his work by a knighthood. But as
the year wore on his health began to fail and he was forced to ask
leave to resign. The ceremony at the Supreme Court, when the Bar
and Bench farewelled him in February 1957, was moving indeed, with
an 'end of an era' feel about it. But the change was to be far greater,
involving more people, and to be more unhappy and far reaching than
could have been foreseen.

Everyone expected that Ralph Gore, once Chief Justice of Papua
and often (since the war) Acting Chief Justice, would naturally be appointed now. But he remained 'acting' for some months. Don was
aware that Gore was not held by Hasluck in the high esteem given
him by the people of Papua New Guinea, and that he underrated both
his abilities and standing as a lawyer and the distinction of his career.

Before coming to Papua as Crown Law Officer, Gore had been
associate to Australia's first really distinguished legal mind, Sir Samuel
Griffith of Queensland, who had left him his wig, traditionally considered a very great honour. He had also edited the Commonwealth

Law Reports for Queensland and Western Australia, while later Sir Hubert Murray, himself a legal man of stature, had entrusted him with compiling his *Exposition of the Law among Primitive Peoples*.

Don was also aware that all sections of the community had such confidence in Gore that, with Sir Beaumont Phillips gone, it would be wise to appoint him for the sake of maintaining stability and the confidence of the people in the law. To my firm recollection Don had written earlier to Hasluck informing him of Sir Beaumont's ill health, of the probability of his seeking leave to retire, and suggesting that stability and confidence would be maintained if Gore could be appointed for a year or so before being retired himself in favour of a younger man.

In past usage judges had been appointed from lawyers who had practised locally. So Don commented that, if it were his intention to continue this practice, the only possible resident lawyer at that time was Jim Cromie, in private practice before and after the war, during which he had served in the legal branch of Angau. I also remember the Minister interestedly and amicably discussing the whole matter with Don on his visit in April, and of interviewing Cromie, incidentally giving Jim the impression that he was in the running, and likely to get the appointment, for he began making tentative plans about his practice.

One evening, some weeks later, we heard on the seven o'clock news the Minister's announcement that Mr Alan Mann, Q.C., of Victoria, had been appointed Chief Justice of Papua New Guinea and would be taking up his duties immediately. To have made a public announcement of such an appointment, without the courtesy of informing the Administrator, shocked Don considerably, but for Acting Chief Justice Gore, on circuit at Madang, the shock was so great that he collapsed. The legal development which he and Monty Phillips had been threshing out was on the verge of fruition, and Gore could see that this backhander could jeopardise its chances of becoming a reality. How right he was.

However, except for that one reaction to inconsiderate and unwarranted discourtesy, he never showed his disappointment, nor in any way held it against Mann or his wife. In fact, some months after their arrival, Yvonne Mann told me that in Canberra they had been warned to expect hostility from May Gore and others, but that their experience had been just the opposite; for everybody had been most helpful and kind, especially both the Gores.

Alan Mann, an attractive and good-looking man in his early forties, arrived in Moresby in May 1957, spending his first week with us, when Don's elderly cousin, Sir John Cleland, the emeritus Professor of Pathology for Adelaide University and a distinguished natural scientist, was also a guest. Mann showed an almost boyish enthusiasm in discussing botany, entomology and anthropology with him; it was quite an insight, as he was that rare person in the modern world — a true dilettante, in the eighteenth-century sense. In fact I grew to think that he must have studied law mainly because he came from a noted legal family, but that his true interests and real talents were in natural science. At the weekend Alan moved up into Monty Phillip's old house on Paga Hill, and his wife and four young daughters joined him shortly afterwards.

A fortnight after Mann had taken up office, Monty Phillips died. So one of his first duties was the sad one of calling a special sitting of the Supreme Court on June 10th in memory of Sir Beaumont, whose death cast a shadow on us all. He had been a tremendous person who, with Judge Gore, had truly carried on the tradition begun by Sir William McGregor and Sir Hubert Murray in laying strong foundations based on the Common Law. Phillips had made his own valuable contribution to what were then seventy years of judgements which had taken into account the customs and ideas of the Papua New Guinean people themselves, thus contributing to the respect and trust in the law and constituting a body of precedent which was then well on the way to developing into Papua New Guinea's own Common Law.

☆　☆　☆

In April 1957, shortly before Mr Justice Mann had been appointed, a series of incidents came to light at an out-station called Tapini, demanding a thorough examination, which went ahead in the normal way. The beginning was simple enough, but since the events which flowed from it cast long shadows, seriously affecting the respect for the institutions I have just described, and undermining the confidence both of the people of Papua New Guinea and of those responsible for governing them, I will tell the story in detail.

One day Don came home very worried about trouble in Tapini. It appeared that the European medical assistant, who had been charged with burning a village house, had then retaliated by accusing the Assistant District Officer of chaining up prisoners and doing other unacceptable things.

Tapini is an out-station in the tangle of mountains about fifty miles north-west of Moresby — a claustrophobic place, wedged between a gloomy, towering mountainside and an airstrip which is the most hair-raising I've ever landed on. The district is known as the Goilala and the people were as wild and untamable as the Kuku Kukus living in similar mountains to the west. The fascinating book *Mitsinari* gives a French father's account of fifty years' work in trying, rather unsuccessfuly, to civilise them.

For several years, problems of patrol officers at Tapini breaking down, and showing other signs of instability, resulted in a rule against spending more than three months there without a break in Moresby. However, lack of staff not only made the rule impossible to carry out, but made the strain even more acute. Staff at a quarter-strength also meant that officers could not give police the necessary supervision to ensure against excesses in the way they carried out their duties.

After this outbreak of accusations, the Chief Crown Prosecutor had been sent up to check whether a man called Siwoi, serving a sentence in Moresby, had been improperly convicted the year before. He was also required to make a report for both the Director of Native Affairs and the Director of Health about the general conditions on the station.

Paul Quinliven was Chief Crown Prosecutor at that time. I rang him when writing this, to check my memory of the case, and was able to borrow a copy of his report which made fascinating reading.

After showing clear evidence that the Siwoi case should be re-examined, he then went on to deal with the general situation at Tapini. He found it a 'hate-filled' station. The doctor, a lazy man who never went on patrol as he should do, was a born schemer, who enjoyed playing off one person against another. His assistant, previously a lay teacher with the Catholic Mission, had been taken on by the Health Department as an E.M.A. (European Medical Assistant). Unfortunately he had been trained by the doctor in Tapini instead of doing his training in Moresby. Thus he had been there over three years without a break. The A.D.O. was away on leave by this time, so Quinliven stayed with the relieving officer, who made the station files available. In the A.D.O.'s absence Quinliven thought it proper not to see the Medical Assistant.

At that time the Department of Native Affairs had only two officers in the entire Goilala sub-district, although according to the establishment there should have been eight. Therefore the A.D.O. had been thoroughly overworked. The only patrol officer was building an airstrip three days' walk away at Woitape, so the A.D.O. had been on his own at Tapini. In addition there was a private enterprise couple on the station, growing coffee and trading. The husband was dying of cancer, though this was a closely guarded secret at that time. His wife was carrying on the business and, though very brave, was under great strain.

But behind all these present problems, the Chief Crown Prosecutor found that an A.D.O. there in 1949, who had allowed the police to use various forms of terror as a method of keeping order among this very difficult people, had been charged, found guilty and dismissed from the service in 1950. Foolishly, some of those police had been left in Goilala, and had secretly been passing on their methods to new police. This, together with the shortage of staff, Quinliven considered to have been the main cause of the problem, with the people then on the station being caught up in circumstances not of their own making.

He therefore recommended, for a variety of reasons, that the criminal law processes should not be used to further this unhappy situation; and that, being personality problems plus the legacy of an equally unhappy past, they were quite distinct from the Siwoi case, which should be treated separately. He further recommended that all the police should be removed, disciplined and retrained; and that the Native Affairs and medical staff should be transferred and disciplined by their own departments. Finally he recommended that the A.D.O. himself should be severely disciplined by and within his own department. The circumstances were such, he said, that 'Public Policy' did not require anything more, and he noted that none of the Goilala people who were allegedly hurt had complained; though he did not consider that any weight should be given to that fact. However, when the further fact of a personality clash between two Europeans reporting on each other was taken into account, it meant that public policy needs should be looked at mainly from the point of view of the Goilala people. He concluded that, under these circumstances, an assurance to them that staff would be increased, and that malpractices would not happen again, would be wise and sufficient.

At that stage, however, the trouble became public, with headline news first in Australia and then in Papua New Guinea. This entirely altered the situation. Canberra became involved and public policy thus became not only that of the people and district affected, or of the Territory administration. Political considerations, both in Papua New Guinea and Australia, were now uppermost, and pressures upon Canberra resulted in the setting-up of a special Commission of Enquiry. Don's diary records, on May 14th, 15th and 16th, conferences with the Secretary for Law and other departmental heads regarding the drawing up of terms of reference for the Commission. These were:

"Whether there has been, in the recent administration of the Goilala subdistrict of the Territory of Papua and New Guinea, any abuse of authority or office by any Administration Officer or servant or any other malpractice which would tend to reflect on the administration of justice."

Syd Johnson, the Crown Law Officer, was then sent to Tapini as Commissioner, and presented his report on July 12th. I have not seen that report with his recommendation, but I was lent a copy of the verbatim transcript of the evidence he took from over seventy people. It is wholly in question-and-answer form and shows Syd Johnson to have been an able, penetrating and completely fair questioner. All on the station and nearby were questioned — Europeans, police, labourers, the prisoners who had been victims of the questionable methods under investigation, medical orderlies, village people whose houses were allegedly burnt, missionaries, the civil aviation men who had walked for three days to see the new strip at Woitape.

The last to be interviewed were the A.D.O., F.D. Anderson, and the Patrol Officer, J.W. McGregor. After a lengthy questioning, Anderson asked the Commissioner for leave to make a statement which, in all the circumstances, I find strangely moving. Here it is:

"I might say that it has been suggested that I did not act promptly concerning certain administrative matters at Tapini, but I would like to point out that I was the only officer at Tapini for almost the full time of my appointment there, that is after Mr Galloway left the station, and there were other things that were quite pressing and claimed my attention for usually ten hours a day. During the time I was at Tapini I heard three hundred and thirty-six courts of Native Matters; five courts of Petty Sessions; there were eighteen Department of Native Affairs patrols, and approximately one hundred and fifty police patrols, twelve agricultural patrols, seven hundred and eighty natives recruited by the administration as labour. There were an average of eighty-seven prisoners in the jail during the period. There were 911 air movements, 68 visitors from Moresby, 25 land transfers were effected, 9000 coffee trees were planted, 50 miles of graded road was constructed, a school was built of European materials, four 1000-gallon water tanks assembled locally, three cement blocks laid for a police mess and kitchen, cow bails and so on. Medical Officer's house was lined and a bedroom built onto it. Five large buildings were constructed of native materials. If it appears that action was not taken promptly, I would like it to be known that there were other things going on at the same time."

To me that last sentence was a masterly understatement. It's hard to imagine one man coping with so much on his own, even if his wife was helping him in the office, as wives of field staff so often did.

The civil aviation men were outsiders. Their evidence is also worth quoting. It helps to put the whole thing in perspective. Here is the leader's answer to the questioning:

"I am the sectional Airport Engineer in the Department of Civil Aviation, stationed at Regional Office Port Moresby. I accompanied Mr A.D.O. Anderson on patrol from Tapini to Woitape from 14th July to 24th July 1956 ... Throughout the patrol the local natives generally appeared to be extremely friendly — presented oranges to the patrol on more than one occasion — tried to shake hands frequently. The road did not go through villages and they came specially down to see the patrol. On the way back also the local natives brought food to the patrol. The patrol was physically arduous but was a very happy one throughout. The welcome extended to the patrol by natives was continuous all the way right into Woitape airstrip.

"Patrol Officer McGregor was handling the construction of the airstrip. From D.C.A. point of view he had done his job in a most efficient manner. Daily, there were about 500 or 600 natives working on the airstrip. When we went down to where they were working a similar welcome was extended to us, grinning, nodding, shaking hands. I was there for a week. The labour on the strip appeared to be working enthusiastically and well. They achieved a remarkable amount with primitive tools. They were under police supervision but I heard no shouted orders or anything of that sort. One of the village constables seemed to be the principal foreman. At one end of the strip there was a camp for the labour. We toured the area. They had built huts. This camp seemed to be quite adequate. They usually knocked off about 5 o'clock. Their women would be up at the huts preparing food. They would all bring tools up to be checked into store at knock-off time. The labour appeared to be comfortably and happily engaged in the enterprise."

Purely judging from what everyone questioned had said, including those whom A.D.O. Anderson had punished, and before I had come to the transcript of his own questioning, I had begun to form a better opinion of him than that previously gained from the highly coloured news reports before and during the subsequent trial, and from the views generally held at the time, in addition to what I had heard from Don. I did not have a harsh view then, but from the picture in my mind which reading the document gradually built up, I just don't see how, taking all circumstances into account, anyone could have put Anderson on trial, let alone the young patrol officer McGregor. Indeed I feel a strong sense of shame that the administration, including both my husband and the Minister, saw fit to do so. However, no doubt the circumstances of the time made it necessary.

The people who really emerged in a bad light were the medical staff — the doctor and the rather unstable medical assistant, who were neither liked nor respected by the Goilala people, none of whom, not even those whose maltreatment the medicos had reported and which led to the trial, showed any antipathy to Anderson or McGregor.

It seemed to me, reading Syd Johnson's transcript, over twenty years later, that headquarters of the administration was far more at fault in leaving only two men to govern a large mountainous district with wild and difficult people, notorious for the highest record of payback murders in Papua New Guinea, than were these two men themselves who 'bent the law' in order to cope with their problems. Anderson, or in fact any officer, should not have been left to cope singlehanded where circumstances made the temptation to authoritarianism too great.

I know how troubled about it all both Don and the Minister were at the time. Balancing against the facts and their interpretation were legal considerations and growing political pressure, arising from the highly charged atmosphere of rumour and speculation, which had to be cleared.

Anyway, charges were brought against both officers, in the Supreme Court Port Moresby, in September. The case was heard by the new Chief Justice and, to everyone's consternation, Anderson was found guilty and sentenced to twenty-one months' imprisonment. Such unexpected severity was a distinct shock to the community; and when Anderson sought leave to appeal, a committee of private citizens opened a public fund to assist both him and his wife, who was expecting a baby. This was an unprecedented gesture from the public towards an Administration Officer. In addition a defence fund was set up by his fellow members of the public service to help him with the expenses of his defence at the trial and for his appeal. It also was well subscribed.

Anderson had already spent eight weeks in Long Bay jail, before coming out to attend the appeal sittings in Sydney, with Sir Jack Cassidy, Q.C., representing him. Though the High Court under Sir Owen Dixon upheld the conviction after reviewing the evidence, the Bench also left no doubt that it regarded the whole case as 'much ado about nothing', stating that Anderson had already served a longer sentence than all the charges put together had warranted. They ruled that the sentence be terminated as from the day he had come out on bail. They also considered that the Chief Justice had not sufficiently taken into account that Anderson was a trusted servant of the Crown, with a creditable record, who had been working in a dangerous area with little aid and great responsibility. Sir Owen Dixon aptly referred to it as the 'Extraordinary Anderson Case'.

Interestingly, Anderson went back to Tapini, to receive a tremendous welcome from the Goilalas. He set up in business, has lived quietly and successfully there ever since and in 1964, when he stood for the House of Assembly, he did well with 3186 votes.

☆　☆　☆

In the meantime, soon after Syd Johnson's report of his Commission of Enquiry had reached the Minister in July, Hasluck had written to the new Public Service Commissioner, Neil Thomson, instructing him to initiate an "enquiry under the provision of Section 10 of the Public Service Ordinance 1949-56, into the management and working of the Department of Native Affairs, with a view to determine a number of questions arising out of the Anderson case . . . and the extent to which the practices employed at Tapini might be followed in other parts of the Territory."

Influencing these events, one of those curious chances which so often shape history is now highlighted. Not only was the Chief Justice new, but so was the Public Service Commissioner, both arriving after the Tapini sequence had already begun. It is very obvious that their lack of experience or knowledge of the country, of the people, or the working conditions of field officers, meant that events such as those at Tapini were far outside the experience of either man. Therefore neither would have knowledge of any comparable circumstances by which to evaluate them, so both would be operating in a sort of vacuum. The trial and the Section 10 enquiry, taken together, seriously undermined the effectiveness of the field staff in a vital role — that of administering and upholding the rule of law at the grass roots level.

When the newly arrived Neil Thomson received the Minister's directive it may have worried him, judging from an entry in Don's office diary under the date of July 29th, which also poses interesting questions about administration concern and, in particular, about Don's concern. The note reads:

"Conference with P.S.C. in regard to his investigation under Section 10 of the ordinance and various actions that may be taken by myself which might cut across the investigation."

The next day, 30th July, shows another entry:

"Further conference with P.S.C. before he proceeds to Canberra to see the Minister."

Another on September 6th merely records:

"Conference with P.S.C. on his progress with the Section 10 investigations."

But on September 11th another reads:

"Conference with the Secretary for Law in reference to the subpoena which the P.S.C. had received, to produce documents in relation to the Section 10. Enquiry and discussing the legal situation."

This is indeed intriguing and leaves one wondering who had issued the subpoena and why? Who was demanding what documents in the Commissioner's charge and why did the three men need to go into the legal aspect? That was Don's last entry on Section 10.

The committee which conducted the enquiry consisted of three men. Neil Thomson was Chairman. Dudley McCarthy, an assistant secretary of the department in Canberra, was the second; a charming, rather sensitive man, a pre-war Patrol Officer in New Guinea and author of the Official War History of the New Guinea Campaign. However, now a senior man from Canberra, he did not command the unreserved confidence of the field staff. The third man, Jerry McLauchlan, had only recently transferred to the staff of the Public Service Commission, having previously been the district clerk at Wewak and Goroka. McLauchlan had a chip on his shoulder, was a well known hater of the field staff and, though executive officer, he made no secret of this dislike during the investigation. Thus prejudiced, he was a most unfortunate choice.

To my own recollections of Don's concern, I have added as much research as possible and have talked to those still resident in Papua New Guinea who were 'investigated' at the time. A curious story emerges.

The first instalment comes through the eyes of a man in the Department of Law, who arrived in Madang, and was puzzled and intrigued to find in the hotel little groups of men of the Department of Native Affairs, from A.D.O.s to D.C.s, either pacing up and down outside or sitting morosely in the lounge. They were unlike any group of Kiaps he had ever seen, behaving as though the unbelievable had happened to them. Some were outraged; some stunned. Later he joined them and got their story.

They were from the Southern and Western Highlands. A plane had come in unannounced, with Jerry McLauchlan aboard. Full of importance, he showed them a directive instructing them to take an overnight bag and board the plane for Madang, picking up similarly instructed men from sub-districts as they went. While they were taken off to Madang, Jerry remained behind. There he searched the records and asked loaded questions of the staff, their wives and Papua New Guinean administration servants.

The questioning by the Commissioner himself was strange. They were called one by one into a small office, where Neil Thomson sat behind a table. None had met him before and the first to come in did not know who he was. Following the provisions of the ordinance, he handed them a Bible, upon which they swore to 'speak the truth and nothing but the truth' etc. — rather dramatic and giving a touch of the unreal. Although they were all men who had given loyal and honourable service to Australia and to Papua New Guinea, some for decades, and many with awards and decorations earned as coast-watchers during the war, they were treated like convicted, delinquent schoolboys, as I was indignantly told. Although as District Commissioners they were top men and the Administrator's representative in their area, there was no courtesy shown by offering them a seat, but they were left to stand and answer a list of degrading questions. No one knows who had prepared them, but Canberra is suspected, for they were very clever tricky questions and quite different from the type asked by Syd Johnson at the Tapini enquiry.

The following, as reported by men still angry about them, were the most hateful. They were used uniformly throughout the country and went something like this:

| Q. | You have a Mr ..... on your staff? | A. | Yes |
| Q. | He is outside? | A. | Yes |

Q. You must undertake not to speak to him after I have finished because you must realise that I am required to ask of him questions about you which are similar to those I will now ask you. Do you understand that? *A.* Yes

Q. Now, remembering that you are on oath, has Mr ..... ever hit a native? *A.* .....

The questioning went on like this, up and down the heirarchy of the station. It continued:

Q. Do you know any officer of the field staff anywhere in PNG who, at any time, in any part of PNG, has hit a native? Remember, we have to compel everyone to answer this question. All the confidential files will be studied and people outside the service will be asked also. The various answers will then be compared, so there is no purpose in hiding anything. *A.* .....

Q. Others will be asked if they have ever heard that you have ever hit a native, and those answers will then be compared. I now ask you on oath: have you ever hit a native? *A.* .....

The men neither like nor respected this performance, though some said that Mr Thomson seemed rather embarrassed by the questionnaire. They got home to find wives and junior officers upset and worried by the activities and, as they put it, the prying of McLauchlan.

In the two Highland districts and Madang the effect on the morale of the staff was deplorable. But Bill Tomasetti told me that in Goroka, where he was then A.D.O., they were not caught so unaware, so he made an effort, not only to answer the questions, but to try and convey to Mr Thomson something of what they were trying to do in their work; and he says he found him responsive. Therefore Bill rather cleverly put Mr Thomson in the 'new boy' shoes, and so to him the investigation was not so traumatic. But to Des Fitzer, then a young patrol officer, who had been brought several days' sail from Misima into Samarai, it was more than traumatic. His eyes flashed blue fire when I asked him. For to him it violated a fundamental principle and he protested vehemently at being asked to discuss his senior officers. To his surprise and relief he was dismissed without questions being pressed.

In others I found varying experience and reaction. Two had been on leave and came back to find everyone gloomy and disillusioned. But all found the enquiry extremely distasteful, especially the manner in which McLauchlan poked around, not only looking at the files, but the doubtful probity of the way he quizzed people on a station. All spoke of the questionnaire with anger and contempt, and I was surprised at the strength of their reaction, over twenty years later.

Mr Thomson made his report of the Section 10 Enquiry direct to the Minister and nothing was ever heard of its contents. It can now be seen from the records that there was a complete vindication of the integrity and conduct of the service. But the finding was never conveyed to members of the field staff, who were left not knowing where they stood and in doubt about still holding the confidence and support of their superiors. The fact that the Section 10 investigation was conducted during the Anderson trial, conviction and appeal, added to its disturbing effect.

Looking back, all this contributed to making 1957 a 'Watershed Year'. The events making it so were begun when Monty Phillips retired and Gore was passed over. The new judges who were appointed discounted the value of past practice. Without enough appreciation of the legal foundations built up over the years, or of the significant role of the field staff in the operation of that system, they did not give officers the support they needed to carry out their duties. The total effect was to undermine the linchpin of Australia's highly successful efforts in bringing newly contacted people under control and then in keeping them lawabiding. This linchpin was the practice of selected field staff holding both magisterial and police powers on out-stations and in small towns, where there was no magistrate and no police officer.

Accompanying these events was an indefinable atmosphere and attitude coming from the quickly growing Department of Territories in Canberra. Condescending rather than contemptuous, it affected all departments. It too helped to sap the confidence and therefore the effectiveness of the service.

The sum of all this was to rob the field staff of its pride. Yet facing them all the time in their work was the need to deal with actual situations, often potentially dangerous. They followed a long and honourable tradition, were well trained and in their legal work had depended on the oversight and backing of the judiciary. Now all at once they felt they had lost the support both of the authorities in Canberra and the new Chief Justice. They had to cope, of course, but had the nagging feeling of doing so at their own risk; that, in A.D.O. Anderson, it was a case of 'There but for the Grace of God go I'.

Pride in themselves, as men working in the high traditions of their service, had enabled them to overcome the incredible physical difficulties, live in hard conditions, to work long hours seven days a week or be away from their wives and families patrolling for weeks on end; to drop everything at a moment's notice and set off on foot across mountains, rivers and swamps, when word came in of trouble. Pride gave them the integrity to handle their triple role of magistrate, policeman and administrator in such a manner as to earn them universal respect. There were exceptions, of course — there are always exceptions. But the fact of so few exceptions, among hundreds of men, stands tribute to the quality of the whole. The indignities they suffered in the conduct of the Section 10 investigation spelt the beginning of the end of the proud era of the 'outside men'.

After this, there was a tendency to say, in effect, "Alright, if that's the way it is, that's it. I can stay in the office and shuffle files as well as a b ... clerk in Canberra". Or, "If that's all they think of us, I'm damned if I'll bust myself getting up at all hours of the day or night to sort out people's problems or to set off on long patrols", or again, "If that's all they think of me and my work, I'm not going to stick my neck out and get my head chopped off". They did continue to do those things, of course, but the zest had gone out of it.

A man uncertain of himself and the attitude of his boss does not do such a good job as a man with pride and confidence in his work. Moreover, uncertainty conveys itself to other people, and no one is so quick to sense such a change as an unlettered people who, of necessity, are very subtle in their apprehensions. Judges of the calibre and experience of Phillips would have done their best to restore confidence, but as the Chief Justice went on circuit a completely new pattern began to emerge which had the opposite effect.

Its origins may possibly be found in the way he interpreted his briefing by Hasluck. He certainly came up well briefed. But he may also have taken a good deal upon himself, for from the beginning his attitudes were anti-administration.

His own personality and attitudes in general contributed to the new situation. He was young, enthusiastic in the pursuit of his hobbies and attractively boyish, but that led to him doing things not expected in a judge. Some people have within themselves so much natural dignity that, whatever they do, dignity is never lost either in their own eyes or anyone else's. Those who have it are usually quite unconscious of it. It is, however, instantly recognisable by others, so it was unfortunate this was not one of Mann's gifts. People always long to look up to their leaders and draw strength from so doing. And the people in Papua New Guinea had always been able to look up to the judges. Somehow, he did not naturally command the respect of the general population, and his own actions tended to embarrass people and erode it still further. People liked him, for he was a most likable person. But they could not respect him and look up to him.

This fact of personality complicated things for everyone. Without the gift of natural dignity, he needed trappings to support him, and trappings were in short supply in Papua New Guinea. To boost himself he belittled other people, the chief sufferers being the unfortunate D.C.s and their field officers, with the Administrator collecting a good deal himself.

In the light of these characteristics it is interesting to look at his career. Alan Mann had applied young for his silk. He had practised law in Patents, which is a very specialised branch and does not bring

Luluais, wearing their trammies hats, with the local Government Councillors behind them outside the district office on an outstation.

Sir Donald with Marie, Robert, Evan nursing David and Sally in front.

a man much into the courts. Therefore he had not had very much involvement in court work, or experience in criminal law. Paul Hasluck says on page 346 on his book that "Mann was one of the best appointments I ever made". To me it seems extraordinary that anyone could consider it a good idea to choose for a Chief Justice, where the bulk of the work is in the criminal sphere, a man whose previous career simply did not give him the requisite experience.

Small but significant problems away from Moresby were illustrated to us in the early sixties at Wewak, after travelling in the Sepik. Word came in one night that the Chief Justice had arrived by charter in Angoram, and the D.C. went into a flat spin, muttering:

"I only hope to God that he'll be OK. I wish someone had let me know he was coming, so I could have made sure things were alright and proper arrangements made." I remember that he looked at Don as if fearing he might be thought remiss in not knowing the Chief Justice's movements.

Later in Madang, Des Clifton-Bassett was in even more of a tizz to hear that the Chief Justice was somewhere in the district, though no one knew quite where. Clifton-Bassett was horrified that he hadn't been at the strip to pay his respects, for it had always been automatic on out-stations that everyone turned out to receive a judge, even for a ten minute stop-over, while at a major headquarters the D.C. and some of the senior staff did the honours. Don was glad to be able to reassure Des that, as the Chief Justice had arrived unannounced by charter at Angoram, he had probably gone straight from there without landing at Madang.

Clifton-Bassett, like the D.C. at Wewak, was worried about arrangements for court sittings on the out-stations. Des, who was a very particular sort of person, would never be lax in necessary organisation or doing the honours. He then opened his heart to Don of innumerable incidents when none of them knew where they stood; of finding it hard either to work in with the Chief Justice or to please him and of being subject to what seemed deliberate slights. It was indeed very worrying and Don knew from his own experience how the men felt. All he could do was to advise him to continue offering the assistance and showing the respect they had always shown the judges and just hope that the relationship would improve.

But over and above all these small hurts to persons, and far exceeding them in seriousness, was the fact that every one of them would be sharply noted by the Papua New Guineans, who would come to their own conclusions, which unfortunately would be that the law wasn't 'strong' any more; in other words, not to be given respect.

To make things more complicated, even the Bench was affected. Instead of drawing on the long experience of the other three judges as a source of information in his new job, it became a handicap to communication between them. The previous trust was lost, not only with each other, but between Administration and Bench. No one could speak frankly to anyone else without feeling disloyal to someone. The Chief Justice was very obviously in close contact with the Minister at all times and seemed to have been charged by him with the duty of examining the court and legal system and making his own recommendations directly to him, and Don was never actually in the picture about it.

The Chief Justice did pay calls on him to have discussions from time to time. But he would beat about the bush or make unreal requests, such as for a private plane to be put at the disposal of the judges. Such discussions left Don puzzled, uneasy and wondering what the Chief Justice really was thinking and planning — doubting too whether he really knew himself. With the obviously close contact between the Minister and the Chief Justice, a sort of silly situation came about of 'Two's company — three's none' atmosphere, with Don the odd man out.

With many years of legal practice behind him and considerable political experience, Don found the situation very exasperating, especially as he had always been interested in constitutional law and had closely followed Tom Fry's work during the war and afterwards, when he was correlating the laws of Papua with the laws of New Guinea. Tom would dine with us in Sydney from time to time to bring Don up to date. But with trust gone in this queer atmosphere, Don found it difficult to discuss his own views; indeed it even seemed as though Hasluck did not wish the Administrator to be a party to discussions on legal matters at all.

The relationship between members of the bench should have improved as the old judges retired and new appointments were made, but the Chief Justice did not seem able to develop a rapport with them either. Sniping campaigns used to go on among them, tending to undermine each other, thus further eroding public respect.

However, it was not always easy for Mann. In human affairs there are often ironies. Back in 1952 a Sydney barrister had been appointed as an acting judge for three months and was on circuit in Milne Bay, travelling on *MV Leander* with skipper Bill Johnson. Saying he did not drink on duty, Bill used to refuse the judge's offer of a whisky at night. Though nettled, the judge accepted it until, arriving back in Samarai, he decided to stay on *Leander* instead of at the residency. Returning in the evening to the ship he found a rip-roaring party in progress, with Bill and his friends making up for his abstention at sea. This made the judge mad and he flew into a towering rage, saying that he'd been insulted. Bill Johnson, a Glasgow Scot, stoutly defended the goings-on, maintaining that while in port the ship was his home. The D.C. hurried down, trying to smooth things over, but the intervention only made the judge angrier, the situation going from bad to worse. The episode was an acute embarrassment to everybody, for Bill Johnson had been within his rights, and the angry judge had been so unreasonable that Chief Justice Phillips put it on file that he was not to practise again in New Guinea in any capacity whatever.

One day, when the Chief Justice was away on leave, Don came home for lunch really put out.

"Those fools in Canberra have just notified me that a new judge is arriving next week and to have a house ready for him. How can you conjure a judge's house out of nothing?"

However, after lunch he looked at what was available but came back saying that none was suitable, and chafed that he had not even been warned of the possible appointment of a fifth judge. He was the more apprehensive in that this was the very man who had been involved in the Samarai incident. However, he had the best of the houses painted, and selected some reasonable ones where junior officers could be moved out.

The new judge arrived early in September and stayed with us. Don put the housing situation to him, explaining it by having only been informed of his appointment the week before, but naturally he was not amused. We gave him a welcome party and, as the Legislative Council was sitting and Don had to preside on two nights, he left me to entertain him. I found him a pleasant person, discussing various things in a perfectly natural way.

The house situation had no immediate solution, for predictably he turned down those available. So Don offered him our guest bungalow as a temporary refuge, with the arrangement for one of our servants to look after him there. He seemed pleased and we all happily moved his things over on Sunday morning, when I explained a shortage of crockery, promising to bring it over when the new stock arrived. It came on Wednesday, so I took it over in a basket, calling as I went up the steps, the way one does with a neighbour.

"Ooh ooh, ooh ooh. Here's your crockery."

Sudden dead silence. So I put down the basket and knocked on the door. After much unlocking, it opened a little bit and a furious face looked at me. I was certainly perplexed and explained that I had brought over the promised new crockery. He took the basket from me without a word and shut the door in my face. I had never seen such an extraordinary change in any human being and wondered whatever had happened.

When Don came home I said:

"There's something dreadfully wrong with the new judge. You'd better go over and see what's the matter."

So over he went full of concern, till I heard angry shouts, and after a while Don shouting back; the only time in forty-eight years I ever heard him shout in anger. It must have been some provocation. He came back to the house stupefied, saying that, as soon as he arrived, the most ludicrous accusations were shouted against him. Don simply couldn't calm him, so shouted back.

Next day the judge told Peter Broman that he was in danger, insisting on the door locks being changed, which Peter did. A few days later he asked for bolts as well. Peter thought it wise to warn all staff but the one assigned to him to keep away from the bungalow.

A week or so later we realised that the bungalow was empty. Don was worried and rang the Supreme Court. No one knew where he was. He was eventually found. He had broken into the Mann's house and was living there. Poor Alan and Yvonne came back to find their house had been commandeered. Sorting it out did not make the easiest beginning for Alan to the relationship with a colleague. This judge remained permanently angry with Don and me, making no secret of it yet no one could ever find out the source of the trouble. He ignored invitations to Government House and if we found ourselves at the same function he ostentatiously turned his back.

☆ ☆ ☆

During these years, changes of all kinds were affecting both urban and village people. One of these had quite an effect, though more or less inadvertently, on the structure of administration, and influenced the 'law and order' of the country.

The luluais and tultuls in New Guinea, and the councillors and village policemen in Papua, had been representatives of the government in the villages. They were now being superseded by local government councils. The first councils were fairly experimental and aroused a lot of discussion, some argument and a great deal of interest. Growing steadily in number, they became 'the thing' by the beginning of the sixties and then spread rapidly. It was thought that the new councils could take over the responsibilities of luluais, who then became redundant.

Somewhere about '58 or '59, travelling in New Ireland, we went over to New Hanover, a small island to the north, to open the new Taskul Local Government Council. After a trawler crossing and the usual bumpy landrover trip on a pretty awful road, we came to a pleasant cleared space with the new council chambers — a small asbestos hall with push-up shutters, furnished with a long table and chairs for about twelve councillors, a council clerk's office at the back and his house to one side. Our fellow guest was the manager of the Commonwealth Bank, which always presented each new council with a handsome gavel in a nice wooden case, for the chairman.

Everything was beautifully decorated with garlands of flowers and coconut fronds, and a large crowd of village people were all dressed up for the occasion. Our hosts, the newly elected councillors, with new metal badges pinned onto new white shirts, were lined up to greet us.

Before going inside we were shown where to stand for the first part of the ceremonial. A blanket was placed on the ground. Then forty or fifty elderly men, who had given many years of devoted service, wearing their sign of office, their 'hats', slowly filed past, and each in turn threw his hat onto the blanket. I was wholly unprepared for this, not having heard of the ceremony before. Though we were often to see it again, it never failed to affect me deeply. There was such variety in the ways a man could 'throw in his hat'. A few would put it down reverently and gently. Some would affect nonchalance. Others would hurl it with a defiant gesture. Some would give a contemptuous look towards the mostly younger councillors and toss it with an incomparable look of disdain. Some had tears running down their cheeks. And so, before it was done, had most of us.

This ceremony troubled me very much indeed. There were forty or fifty elderly men, their faces lined and wise, some full of character, many with a notable dignity. Their responsibilities were being taken over by the white-shirted twelve, who were different types altogether, and I felt uneasy. I didn't know why and thought it was sentiment and the sadness of all those government men who were government men no longer. Don and I talked it over afterwards and we both put our unease down to the sadness of it.

But of course we should have known better. And so should everyone else have known better. But we didn't. It's funny how blind you can sometimes be to the obvious. But the unhappy results of this change didn't really emerge until a few years later, when lawlessness in the villages was becoming a problem. A councillor can take over one aspect of a luluai's duties: he can speak for the people to the government. But there is no way he can or would take on the odium of speaking for the government to the people.

Thus at one stroke we helped to break down the system of communication between government and people.

This was particularly disastrous when it was also between the law system and the people. Where once there had been a luluai or village policeman in each village, now anything from five to ten villages had to share one councillor in a council area. And he, of course, would have his likes and dislikes between different villages. But the most impossible thing we asked of the councillor was to expect him to take over the dispute-settling role of the luluais. Whoever heard of an elected man hearing a dispute between two of his voters? Whichever way it went he would be sure to lose the vote of one of them. Whoever heard of an elected councillor taking one of his supporters into the district office to 'make court' against him? If he did, he would never be elected again.

How so many men both here and in Canberra did not see all this at the time is a complete mystery to me now. What we did was to make everybody confused between the political man who must get votes — the councillor — and the impartiality expected of a government man who settles disputes. The confusion is there still to bedevil the political scene. What we should have done was to find some way for the luluais or a new but similar office to have fitted into the council system. Our loose thinking on what we expected of the councillors also brought confusion where well-developed village kivungs or traditional dispute-settling systems were operating, with rivalry developing between kivung and council.

At first, several contiguous villages elected one member to a council which only covered a fairly small area and so gave the people a measure of the face-to-face situation which was traditional. Then in the mid-sixties there was a feverish movement of joining a number of councils together in even larger groups, to give greater financial strength. All this did was to make local government more remote and to compound the original problems, destroying even further the means of communicating between the ordinary villager and authority — whether that authority was council, government or courts.

On the other hand, councils have made an enormous contribution to political awareness and to familiarising the people with the machinery of democracy. This they now understand very well. The pity is that, with councils as with courts, not nearly enough study was made of the people themselves, their own attitudes, customs and way of thinking. In fact, no attempt seems to have been made at all to ascertain what the people themselves could contribute from their own knowledge of their customary law, nor to study what they already understood of the legal processes which had been introduced to them.

Changes built up from what they understood already would have been sounder and more effective, since a basic tenet of education is to build from the known to the unknown. Instead, as we shall now see, we did the opposite. We took away the known and familiar and then substituted the unknown. This process began in the mid-fifties and became an avalanche after the watershed year of 1957. The results are a major problem now, which the people of a newly independent country are trying with great distress and confusion of mind to find answers for and to correct.

Chapter 12

A Supreme Court Judge trying a case in a bush or village setting.

Need for Development of Legal System—Outline of Legal System—Prof Derham's Visit—Report Advising on Legal Change—Secrecy and its Effect—Minister's Restatement of Policy—It's Effect—Effectiveness of Cases Prepared Under Old and New Systems—Loss of Respect for Law and its Results

I have referred earlier to the mid-fifties, that is ten years after the war, as being marvellous times when it was thrilling to be in Papua New Guinea. On their out-stations the generation of patrol officers who had been inspired by the judges with their message 'the law is back' were now well experienced in dispensing justice. This made them aware of the need both for the relevance of the law to a situation, and for the people to have confidence and certainty in its application. Those graduating from the long course at Asopa brought back fresh ideas and the feeling that change was coming in many directions, particularly in the administration of justice. Since law had been one of the most intensive courses at the school, it was a time of lively discussion between field officers, legal men and judges on the type of development needed.

Such discussions would often take place over dinner when staying with the officer in charge of whatever district we were visiting. There was, of course, considerable unanimity of ideas, but I was more interested when there was rather basic disagreement. It was listening to discussions like these, when young officers gave instances and cases to illustrate their points, that gave me insights into and respect for the way the people organised their lives; and I saw how basic is the human dilemma. The same old human transgressions are common to us all and all people evolve methods of dealing with them. Disagreement was mostly over how Papua New Guinean dispute-settling arrangements could be meshed in with the legal system we had introduced.

When the Minister put his mind to the legal system, he began calling for reports from different people on various aspects. As these reports reflected the wide variety of views, their inconsistency irritated him and made him disenchanted with the men on the spot, including Don; for he too had not reached clear views on some of the complex features of problems involving legal development. The pity is that this very divergence and multiplicity did not warn Hasluck to look a little deeper or give him more awareness of the pitfalls. Instead it turned him away from the body of experience in Papua New Guinea, eventually causing his decision to seek advice only from academic and legal minds in Australia.

This decision appeared to bypass work already done, including that of Tom Fry, who, with the Chief Justice, had in 1949 or 1950 called the first of what had been planned as a series of conferences, stemming from Fry's work directed to the development of the legal system. A number of people had taken part and one of them lent me the minutes, which made instructive reading. From this conference, held before Hasluck's time, certain matters of a technical nature had been referred to Canberra for decision before further work could proceed. However, Tom had died before these decisions had come through and his work became shelved. That was that and no further conferences were held.

Looking back now, the sensible thing would have been to revive the idea towards the end of the fifties and to bring together representatives of the Judiciary, the Department of Law, the Department of District Services and perhaps some anthropologists, so that the many problems and possible alternatives could have been thrashed out properly. A forum such as this might have been able to formulate a body of opinion in Papua New Guinea which Hasluck could have respected and mated with the Australian academic contribution.

The exhilarating times were followed, towards the end of the fifties, by a period of unease over mounting problems after the 1957 watershed. The field staff, responsible for administering justice in their districts, were very much aware of the adverse effects emerging from the new Chief Justice's way of doing things, which made their job of keeping law and order more difficult. Administration men felt that he himself was prejudiced against past practice, without properly studying it or seeking to find out the true nature of the seventy years of legal development. They were distressed that he showed no interest in probing the knowledge and experience of district service men, either in their magisterial roles or when acting in defence of a prisoner. They would have welcomed a dialogue, but were disconcerted by being rubbished.

The sad thing was that, by the time of his untimely death in the seventies, Alan Mann did come to have an awareness of the significance of the legal and court roles of the field staff and to appreciate them, both as men and for their contribution to the maintenance of law and order. It was sad because, even if he had lived, this appreciation had come too late, when so much of value had already been lost.

☆   ☆   ☆

In 1959, the uneasy atmosphere of wondering what policies would govern legal change and how they would be arrived at was resolved when it was announced that Professor David Derham, of Melbourne University, had been appointed and was coming to Papua New Guinea to —

'Enquire into the existing system of the administration of justice in the Territory of Papua and New Guinea and make suggestions for improvement, having regard to both the present and future requirements of the Territory.'

The appointment was enthusiastically welcomed, with a feeling of relief, by everyone from the Administrator down. In a way he was looked upon as the saviour to resolve an increasingly worrying situation.

He arrived in September and visited us when in Moresby. For many years, my family and I had known his mother, an unusual, original and very interesting woman, so I had been looking forward to meeting her son. We found him a delightful person and the talk and discussion with him was refreshing and stimulating. Don felt that here, at any rate, was the right man to do this job.

Before I go on to discuss his work I will pull together my references throughout this book and summarise the system of courts he had to examine.

There were two systems of courts existing side by side. The Minimum Interference System was the Court of Native Affairs or native matters, to which newly contacted people were introduced; the one at Daulo that I described in chapter six was of this type. Besides hearing disputes brought by the people themselves, as on that day at Daulo, Courts of Native Matters could reinforce the authority of such native leaders as luluais, tultuls, medical orderlies, village policemen and interpreters; and could assist in the function of administering law and order in an area, while criminal charges e.g. stealing, assaults, indecent acts, could be brought before the court by a government officer. In a Court of Native Matters, the penalty was about a tenth of that given by the ordinary system of district courts.

Courts of Native Matters could be convened in far-away places when officers were on their ordinary patrols, settling disputes on the spot. And it was this provision which did so much to encourage the cessation of tribal fights. As the people and their district developed and more staff became available, Courts of Native Matters were gradually superseded by western style courts in towns and government stations, but were still used on patrol where they were considered indispensable.

The ordinary or western style district courts were, in procedure and standards, similar to magistrates' courts in Australia. The five largest towns had permanent magistrates, while in the smaller towns and government stations the role of magistrate was carried out by a senior member of the field staff.

Appeals from both courts could go to the Supreme Court, and, as in Australia, both types of court sent up certain cases for trial by the Supreme Court, whose judges went on almost continuous circuit to hear them. These cases were defended by experienced field staff, unless it was either inter-racial or involved in difficult questions of law, when the defence was conducted by a lawyer from the Crown Law Office, or one briefed by the government from a private firm.

In both systems, government officers hearing cases would be experienced men who had taken an oath to dispense justice without fear or favour. This officer was bound to investigate the matter from both sides, listen to all the witnesses which either side wished to call, and then, acting judicially and impartially, pronounce his verdict.

It can be seen that, then, the whole emphasis was on justice. The courts traditionally sought to find the truth of matters brought before them and to impose punishment or compensation in such a way that not only was justice done but, by all the people concerned, it was seen to be done.

Both systems could and sometimes did cut the people off from their own traditional system of solving disputes by agreement, perhaps cemented by exchanges or compensation. It was left to the people themselves to decide whether to use their own system, but they were forbidden to inflict punishment. If their traditional system failed, they could then bring the dispute to a government court. As indicated earlier, that part of the court system which was administered by the field staff of the Department of District Service was already under considerable stress caused through the different style of the new Chief Justice and the changes he introduced.

In addition to the whole legal system, Professor Derham was also to examine the ancillary aspects of the administration of justice, such as the legal services, interpreters, police prosecutors etc., and the penal system.

That he went about it very thoroughly was obvious both to the field officers and the legal men from the Department of Law. He had done his homework well, so had a good comprehension of the actual situation, and approached it with a fresh and understanding mind.

A careful itinerary had been made out to give him an insight into the many varieties of situation and people at all stages, from those at first contact to the educated and sophisticated, and all conditions, from the distant tribal village in the bush to the growing urban populations. The men from the Department of Law who accompanied him developed not only a great liking, firm and often lasting friendship, but admiration and respect for the way he approached his task.

Everywhere they travelled they were welcomed by the field staff, who fully co-operated, wholeheartedly answering questions and showing him whatever he wished to see. Feeling the need of help in the coming changes, they were particularly concerned to assist in every way possible, hoping that the changes would be a development from what existed already, in a steady process which could be easily understood and accepted by the local people. From their contact with Professor Derham they gained a feeling of confidence in him and his whole approach and eagerly looked forward to his report and recommendations.

Professor Derham presented his report to the Minister in December 1959. For some reason Hasluck decided against its circulation and it became a secret document. Under strictly limiting conditions, only a part of the report was issued even to the Administrator. Assistant Administrators, the Secretary for Law and the Chief Law Officers were also given access to the partial report.

That it was not made available to the field staff and law officers was a very great disappointment to them. This decision to maintain secrecy had accumulating detrimental results in Papua New Guinea, where, not knowing its recommendations or the overall picture, men carrying them out had to work in the dark. Its provisions were dissected in Canberra and issued from there or Port Moresby as arbitrary instructions on specific aspects directed either to a departmental head or to persons holding certain positions. Moreover they were often badly co-ordinated, so that no clear picture of what was happening ever became apparent.

As a result, the confidence of the administration people slumped and an atmosphere of uncertainty and confusion began to build up once more, giving Don a great deal of concern plus the frustration of being unable to alter the state of affairs. He was always worrying about the effects of the secrecy, saying how unnecessary it was. He was convinced that in carrying out changes to our institutions it was vitally necessary that the people involved should understand what was happening and know the reasons behind decisions. This situation was made worse and much harder to bear by the constant minutes directed to Don and others by the Minister, always on the theme that the recommendations were not being implemented quickly enough. Looking at it now, it was indeed a silly situation, when both sides were equally exasperated with the other, when they were both equally anxious to do the right thing.

☆　☆　☆

Finally in 1962 Hasluck issued what he termed in his book a 'restatement' of his policy. Here is the quotation:

"1.　There is to be a single system of courts administering a single body of law.
　2.　By a single system of courts I mean —
　　　a. there shall be equal access by all races to all courts.
　　　b. there shall be no court constituted to deal only with native offenders or litigants and there shall be no court in which in practice only native offenders or litigants appear or in which the law applied or the procedures followed are different from those followed or applied in other courts.
　　　c. all courts are to be equally independent of the legislature and the executive.
　　　d. all courts shall be part of a single pyamidal structure having its apex in the Supreme Court.
　3.　Courts of Native Affairs are to be abolished and nothing similar to them is to be substituted for them.
　4.　Appointments to the lower court or courts should be, so far as possible, 'professional' appointments in the sense that the person appointed is free of all other duties and is appointed because of his qualifications to occupy the Bench. There is no objection to associating honorary justices or assessors with the professional magistrates, particularly during a period when the indigenous people are being trained to discharge magisterial functions.
　5.　Whether there is a structure composed of Supreme Court, or alternatively a structure composed only of Supreme Court and District Court, is not a matter on which I have formed opinion. If there is to be a local court below the District Court it must strictly conform to the policy directions given above.
　6.　If the Local Courts Bill applies to the policy set out above it can proceed. If it does not it has to be amended.
　7.　If there remains any difference of opinion, I give the decision in favour of the Administrator's proposal for local courts as

well as district courts, it being understood of course that the local courts conform strictly to the policy set out above.

Minute of September, 1962."

Reading this now, items 2b and item 3 seem incredible. Carrying them out at that time, in the context of all the Minister's other statements, meant that overnight Papua New Guinea people would be limited to a foreign law, unaccustomed court arrangements, and would be losing the advantages they had had through the simplification and amelioration of the Queensland criminal code in a manner to suit their circumstances.

As for those laws brought in by ordinance, some governed matters very real in the lives of Papua New Guineans, but would not apply to expatriates. Others, of necessity, were similar to those operating in any modern western society, and thus expatriate-oriented, largely because at that time there were few Papua New Guineans to whose lifestyle they were applicable. Indeed, a society at such varied stages of development, and with such varied needs, certainly presented problems. But in many respects they were not soluble in the context of what Hasluck laid down, especially item 2b.

My comment is: if it was desirable at this stage to have one system of courts only, why should it be those courts easily accessible to all Papua New Guineans, and suiting their needs, which were to be abolished? After all, seeing they were by far in the majority and it was their country, it seems illogical for the local people to be the ones who had to cope with such a loss.

Anyway, the very noticeable deterioration in the 'law and order' situation of the next few years made the public of all races increasingly concerned. The Minister's 'restatement of Policy' in 1962 unfortunately gave the impression that it was a condensation of the Derham Report. The Report thus became a sort of scapegoat and the public was blaming it for the growing lawlessness and other problems. This was quite unfair to Professor Derham, who had stressed the need for gradual implementation, and who was himself anxious for its release. However, all requests were refused.

The secrecy of this Report was still a problem in 1965, when Mr Percy Chatterton asked a question about it in the House of Assembly. Don therefore wrote at length to the Department, bringing the problem to the attention of the new Minister, and saying in part:

"The question of the Derham Report has been raised in the Legislative Council and then in the House of Assembly on a number of occasions since it was made. In fact it seems to be mentioned almost every time any question of law, justice or police comes up. It has, of course, also been referred to officially in the Council and the House and elsewhere. Because of the fact that the Report, although in the course of implementation, has never been released, a great many misconceptions concerning it appear to exist. I think it fair to say that its non-release is becoming something of an embarrassment. In these circumstances, I recommend for the Minister's consideration that the report must be released. It is known privately that Professor Derham considers that this might be done, although perhaps some or all of the annexures might be withheld."

However, in face both of strong pressure to see the report and the information about the serious problems which its secrecy was causing, the new men in Canberra also continued to resist all requests, both for its release and even for its distribution to those who were carrying out its implementation.

In view of this history I find particularly strange the charge in Hasluck's book against officers of the administration that the Derham recommendations 'were not being analysed but resisted'. Officers cannot analyse a report they have never seen.

The view became quite widespread in Papua New Guinea that the report was being kept secret because it was anti-administration in content and feeling. How to scotch this was what had worried Don so much, the more so because the remarks of the Chief Justice himself added fuel to this belief. For he was constantly saying as he went on circuit that he 'had won' on this or that, or that Derham supported his view that the other thing 'was wrong' and would be changed, and other such comments. Don was convinced that only its distribution would dispel the idea that it was anti D.N.A. But this did not happen till 1973, after self-government.

I myself have now read that part of the report in the Law Department files and examined some of the very interesting annexures in the complete report, released in 1973. It seems to be a clear analysis of the legal practices and other services connected with them, together with Professor Derham's comments, sometimes critical — and rightly so — and his recommendations for change. Far from advise immediate implementation of all his proposals, he stressed the need for their implementation to be gradual. I could find nothing that would not have been of great value, had it been made public in 1960.

This was certainly Don's view. After reading it when released in 1973, he angrily slammed it down.

"I'm damned if I know why it was kept secret. There's nothing the public couldn't have seen with advantage."

In any case, many of Professor Derham's recommendations had already begun, as part of the normal process of evolutionary development. For instance, full-time magistrates had been appointed in some towns to take over from field officers, as were police powers by police officers. A separate prison system was developing as fast as prison orderlies were trained and qualified prison officers appointed, while the Public Solicitor's office had been set up in 1958.

Since so much had already begun the Derham Report should have been used in the nature of a blueprint, giving direction to a long, steady process of change which those taking part could understand, and helping them feel that their efforts were concerted as part of a plan. It was undoubtedly meant to be that by its author.

But because of the way it was handled it became the opposite. For, imposed from the top, the changes did not bear enough relation to the existing situation. In fact there seemed to be a desire to draw a line across the past and to make a completely new start. In the event it had results quite contrary to the intentions of Professor Derham.

Firstly, keeping it a secret document over so many years led to the dangerous misconceptions which grew up in the community.

Secondly, Hasluck's drive for immediate implementation of all its provisions meant, among other things, that 'on-the-spot' law, which Courts of Native Affairs had dispensed, was terminated, long before there could possibly be enough magistrates and other legal service people to take their place in manning the new courts needed. The gap left therefore became a factor in the later breakdown of law and order. On the one hand, the abolition facilitated the rise of serious well-planned crime in the seventies; and, on the other, it led to the early and increasing tendency of village groups to take the law into their own hands, in a return to payback fighting, to obtain the justice that the new system was quite unable to give them.

Discussing the problem of tribal fighting and paybacks with me, a young local police officer at Goroka (in the seventies) bewailed the fact that they could no longer go in and try to settle disputes, but had to wait till fighting actually broke out before the law would allow them to do anything. Then they could only arrest people whom they actually caught fighting. It all seems so silly and a tragic legacy for us to have left them.

Thirdly, legal redress became almost inaccessible to people in villages and tribal circumstances.

Fourthly, it worked to the disadvantage of Papua New Guineans facing charges in courts, though this would have been quite contrary to Hasluck's intention (as stated in item 2c).

The move away from field staff to trained solicitors of the Law Department had, of course, begun years earlier and was a much-needed development for an urban population. The Public Solicitor and his staff were an asset in the towns, where communication through the language variation was not such a problem. But its expansion had not gone far enough to cope with the whole country. In practice it worked out badly on the government stations in the districts, for reasons which are part of related problems recounted earlier. To make it clear I give another picture of existing practices.

Suppose the Supreme Court on circuit was scheduled to sit at Wewak in the Sepik district. Prisoners from out-stations would have been sent on remand to the gaol in Wewak to await trial. In preparation for the sittings, the D.C. would examine all cases. He would find, say, that a man from Angoram was up for murder, and a man from Aitape for rape or adultery. He would then radio each place, ask the A.D.O. to appoint an officer to make an investigation and to attend the Supreme Court sitting, to defend the prisoner.

District officers not only had their law training at Asopa, but had also to follow their department's standing instructions, which laid down their duties very strictly, not only as guidelines in administration, but in carrying out the law. Under different headings such as health, land, labour, patrolling, census etc., the relevant ordinances are quoted and also the legal restrictions on their powers.

With this background a man would be detailed to gather information for the defence of the prisoner. Living in the area where the crime was committed, and thus knowing something of the customs of those particular people, he would be in a position to get the right information to help the man he was defending. He would also have to satisfy the standard then expected by the judge.

When this was to be discontinued according to the 'restatement of policy' in 1962, it meant that all defence would have to be carried out by lawyers from the Public Solicitor's office. So the Chief Crown Prosecutor made a submission that two lawyers should accompany each circuit. One, going ahead to get information and prepare his defence, could then remain with the court to defend the prisoners, while the other went on to the next place to do likewise. This leapfrog progress would have improved the likelihood that available information could be collected and used, giving a good chance of justice for the prisoner.

However, there were not enough solicitors, so only one could travel on circuits. He would be a well-qualified young man from an Australian university, but would know nothing about the man he was defending or his background. He would have poor means of communicating with the prisoner to elicit the proper information for the defence. Arriving with the judge he would have too little time to gather his information and, with a number of prisoners to defend, time just would not allow him to prepare his cases properly.

So it became almost inevitable that public solicitors began to rely on legal technicalities to defend prisoners and not worry too much if they could not get the facts of the case. The easiest technicalities to find would be holes in the way the police had made the charge.

Before the early sixties the police had little formal education, and even then, with at least a primary education and the training given at the Police Training Depots and the new Colleges, it was pretty basic compared to that of an expatriate lawyer. So you had, and for that matter still have, what looked to the general public like a tussle in court, which was uneven to the point of unfairness, between a sophisticated lawyer and a partly trained, bewildered Papua New Guinean policeman.

Another point of difference between the Murray-Gore-Phillips era and the Mann-Hasluck era is that, in the first, cases were well prepared, as the prosecuting authorities did their job well. They did not present cases which could be tossed out of court. Cases were properly investigated, for the natural qualities and gifts of the uneducated policeman had not been lost through school's having taken him away from customary life. So, if the 'Policemasta' or Patrol Officer said, "Go out there and investigate", it did not occur to him that it 'was impossible', as is the present tendency. He just went out, and did so, showing great skill in getting to the bottom of a matter and collecting the evidence.

After that way of doing things was terminated, many cases were being thrown out of court. This meant an increase in dissatisfied village people taking the law into their own hands and administering their own paybacks.

In the new era, with the police role of field staff being progressively superseded by newly recruited expatriate police officers, many unfortunately from African colonies, and by graduates from the new Police Training College, this careful collecting of evidence changed. They simply did not go out to collect evidence and see what they could see. Clerkism crept in. Working from within police stations, filling in endless forms, they began to rely on short cuts such as getting confessions using dubious means, often unwittingly destroying evidence in so doing.

Magistrates are on oath to decide according to the evidence, and it is no wonder they had to throw out so many badly prepared cases. The new system, introduced holus bolus, made it inevitable. The result, however, was the demoralisation of the police force, a bewildered public and a sudden proliferation of crime. Justice was no longer seen to be done.

Chapter 13

Three candidates of the electoral conference from which a member is elected to parliament.

Legislative Development—Council Proposals Rejected—Third Council and Tax Issue—1958: Evan's Wedding and Christmas in Sydney—Minister's Tour on New Legislature—Dunrossil Opens Council in New Chambers—Domestic Crisis with Marie's Baby and Julie with Sick Children—

When Papua New Guinea first flowered into self-government in 1972, and then to Independence in 1975, few people realised what a long, slow growth had made this possible.

The rule of law and the processes of law-making go hand in hand, the one dependent on the other. From 1885, when criminal cases in the British Protectorate were judged under the Queensland Criminal Code, a body of civil laws was built up by the process of ordinances, drafted by the Department of Law, covering the needs of the country, and passed by an Executive Council before gaining assent by the Lieutenant Governor.

In 1901, the new Federal Parliament of Australia assumed responsibility for British New Guinea, actual power being transferred in 1906, when its name was changed to Papua. As before, the Lieutenant Governor was President of the Executive Council, with six to eight senior civil servants, and some nominated private people as members. A similar arrangement operated in New Guinea after 1921 and continued when the two territories were amalgamated after the last war.

Then in 1951, the first true legislature, with elected, appointed, and official members, was opened. The sixteen official members from the Administration were 'the Government', while the three elected members and the nine appointed to represent business interests, the Christian missions and the Papua New Guinean people, became 'the Opposition'. Operating under parliamentary rules, this body initiated and passed all legislation, assent being given by the Administrator in Council, otherwise the Executive Council.

'Leg Co' sat three times a year in the Red Cross Hall, organised as in a Parliament: each member sat at a small table, an impressive ecclesiastical chair was borrowed from the Hanuabada Church for the President, while the clerks of the House and the Hansard girls sat at long tables between the President and members. A roped-off area at the back, accessible by its own door, was the Public Gallery.

Dropping in to hear debates became a popular pastime, not only for such interested persons as wives of members, but for all sections of the public. People liked to be around during tea break, when they could talk to the members and discuss debates. Council always had an atmosphere of excitement attractive also to Papua New Guineans, who came hoping to hear one of their own people, especially Simogun. This popularity gave birth to the idea of two night sittings a week.

Parliament was a completely new experience for everyone, so that first session in 1952 meant a lot of learning and shaking down. Some members stood out quite quickly as good debaters or as characters and eloquent speakers. On the government side, John Gunther, Keith McCarthy and Sid Elliot-Smith were forceful and colourful in debate, while Father Dwyer and Don Barrett batted hard for the opposition. Doris Booth and Fairfax Ross always talked sense, while Simogun was a natural orator. Speaking always in Pidgin, the point he wanted to make was never lost, even on non-Pidgin speakers, and no one could equal him in style. He extracted drama from his new glasses by sweeping them off his handsome Roman nose with a gesture, thrusting them towards the Chair or another member to make a point and pausing, with the distinction of a Disraeli, just long enough for effect. A policeman from near Wewak, Simogun had a distinguished war record with the army and was awarded the B.E.M. for single-handedly annihilating a Japanese machine-gun post, killing all seventeen. He retired to his village after the war, giving vigorous and notable leadership in the modernising and development of his people.

In that first three-year session, thirty eight ordinances were passed, many hotly debated, and some important opposition amendments were accepted by the government. All sittings were well covered by press and radio, while colourful reporting gave rise to political discussion in the clubs and social gatherings, and everyone felt this parliamentary institution had added a new dimension to public life.

This interest and the considerable discussion about the 1949 Act, which had determined the composition of Council, led Don to toss in an idea for a Select Committee to consider improvements to the Act and report on them for the information of the Minister and himself. He was anxious that the Council should feel that it really had a vitality of its own and was pleased when, a few days later, elected members Don Barrett and Jimmy James proposed and seconded a resolution that a Select Committee be set up to investigate and report on the composition of the Council and to examine its standing orders.

Members discussed it with enthusiasm, and a committee of six, with equal numbers from Government and Opposition, was appointed, with Don Barrett as Chairman. Help was requested from Canberra and Mr Tregear, a clerk from the House of Representatives, came up to assist.

But — there always seems to be a 'but' — Hasluck doubted the Council's power to appoint a committee to make recommendations going beyond its own competence, and referred it to the Attorney General's Department. In December 1953 a long legal opinion said, in effect, that the answer to whether Council was competent to appoint a Select Committee 'was probably yes', but it was without power to compel persons to attend or give evidence. It conceded that the Legislative Council should have power to debate any matter affecting the welfare or development of the Territory.

The committee went ahead, a little dashed by the cold water thrown on it, but with plenty of ideas to work on. Their Report, after being submitted to the Minister and the Administrator, was tabled in 1954 at the May sitting. There were a number of recommendations. The most important, also the most rational and progressive, meant making the electorates smaller and more workable, and giving more representation by increasing them from three to nine. Two others related to a system of Standing Committees and a proposal for Native Observers to attend council meetings for their political education.

The recommendations in the Report created a lot of public interest when it was debated and passed by the House in May 1954. But Don was chagrined when at the end of the session he had to announce that the Minister had not yet considered it. However, members felt that it was so practical and constructive that he would accept some of it, particularly increasing the elected members and the proposal for native observers, and that the Australian Parliament could amend the 1949 Act in time for the August elections.

This did not happen. The candidates in each of the three, over-large electorates found electioneering difficult, while the scattered voters had problems recording their votes. The combination meant a poor turnout of voters.

For this reason, paradoxically, Hasluck would make no decision on the report. Though discussions continued between the Administrator and Canberra, they remained fixed in the idea that the poor turnout indicated apathy, and decided that there was insufficient advance for any political development. The argument that the limited representation of the 1949 Act was inadequate and responsible for the apathy, or that such huge electorates were unworkable, would not be accepted by Canberra, and matters drifted on. The only decision made, was a rejection of the proposals for Standing Committees and Native Observers. The situation was depressing and frustrating for Council members and Mr Barrett, the Committee chairman, referred in a speech to "the deadly silence from Canberra on the Report".

Before the end of the second Council, John Gunther became Assistant Administrator and thus Leader of the House. In this role he made a notable contribution with his lively mind and the influence he exercised.

The 1957 elections for the third Council were again conducted without constitutional change, which meant still no elected Papua New Guineans. However, it had a number of changes in membership. Ian Downs, who has resigned as D.C. Goroka to plant coffee, was making a far-sighted contribution, organising the local village people who had planted coffee and other crops, by forming and nurturing a multiracial Planters' Association. Ian was elected for the mainland and Dudley Jones (a Rabaul lawyer) for the Islands; John Hohnen replaced Doris Booth, and Mahuru Rarua (of Hanuabada) replaced Merari Dickson, as appointed members. Later on, Roma Bates, the widow of the D.C. Madang, replaced Hohnen, and eventually Alice Wedega of Milne Bay replaced Roma. There were also a number of changes in the official members.

By this time Papua New Guinea was under considerable pressure from the Commonwealth Treasury to raise more of its own revenue, and had to recast its budget with this aim. Therefore the first sitting of the third Council provided for more customs duties, higher charges for public utilities, and a Bill was passed providing for a personal tax of 2 pounds for all male inhabitants. Not, of course, very popular.

The financial needs were rising as unexplored areas were brought under control and the new patrol posts to govern them called for more field staff. In addition the departments were building up in size and quality. All these additional public servants needed houses and schools. The larger government stations and, in the towns, the new suburbs for the houses, needed servicing with roads, sewerage and power. Institutions to train Papua New Guineans in the skills to replace expatriates became more pressing. Don used to say that, with everything expanding in every direction, growth — and expenditure to meet it — was not in arithmetical but in geometrical progression.

Commonwealth Treasury reacted by making it harder for the Minister to get the expanded estimates through cabinet. Thus pressured, he sent men from Canberra to work with the Administration on a complete review of Territory finances. This review was tabled in the Legislative Council on September 16th, 1958, with a special Ministerial message that it was a review only for their information and discussion; that the government was not committed, nor any decisions made.

If ever a bomb was dropped, this was it. No one then paid any income tax. Most revenue was raised by an export tax on primary produce, thus unfairly hitting the planters of all races, while indirect taxation also affected them more heavily than the rest of the community: as the largest employers of labour, import duty on all items of the compulsory ration scale added to their costs.

However, both the Minister's statement and the review of the unfair export duty went unnoticed and ignored. Not only the Council, but the whole community exploded into action on the assumption that the review was a prelude to income tax, and angry debate continued for days. Taxpayers' Associations sprang up in several towns. Taxation experts and Q.C.s were brought up from Australia. Speeches were made all over the country and a petition with over four thousand signatures from all districts was presented to the March 1959 sitting, 'praying that any introduction of income tax be proceeded by an independent public enquiry'.

At this sitting, too, debate was fiery and the Treasurer, Mr Reeve, tried in vain to get members to discuss the other methods for raising revenue suggested in the report. He found it extraordinary that members had concerned themselves only with income tax, which was not the subject of the report at all, and had not considered other possible ways for PNG to raise its own budget. Council was then adjourned till 20th April, to allow the Minister to consider the petition and the Hansard record of the debate.

On the 14th, Hasluck thanked Don for his prompt report, saying it had been carefully considered by Cabinet. However, he announced its decision to abolish export duties, substantially reduce import duty and introduce income tax. Thus it seemed plain to the public that its instinct had been right about the review being only a softening-up.

This view was confirmed when, at the adjourned Council in April, Don, as President, announced two Bills. Mr Reeve, moving leave to introduce them, declared them to be urgent and a division was called. Leave was granted by fifteen votes to twelve, but the three elected members walked out of the Council before Mr Reeve gave his second reading speech. On adjournment, Don invited members to submit amendments, assuring them that the Bills and amendments would be fully debated in the June sitting.

However, the unofficial members were so stirred up that they wrote to the Governor General, asking him to examine proceedings to see whether they contravened the principles on which British legislation was founded. An official member, Mr Carter, Director of Posts and Telegraphs, also wrote, asking whether he was bound by his position to vote for the government. Sir William Slim instructed his private secretary, Murray Tyrell, who replied in detail to the members that the proceedings did not contravene them. But he wrote rather trenchantly to Mr Carter, affirming his duty to support the Government.

When the next sitting opened on June 22nd, 1959, the three elected members handed Don their written resignations. Immediately afterwards, Bob Bunting presented a petition from the New South Wales Taxpayers' Association, praying that Mr McKellar, secretary of the association, have leave to appear at the Bar of the House. Mr Watkins, Secretary for Law, dealt with the legal position and leave was refused. Debate was then resumed and Don announced that the Government would favourably view variations of the original proposals.

Next morning, all members of Council were served with a writ by Mr Bunting, asking for an injunction restraining:—

a) The Defendant, Cleland, from presiding over any meeting of the Legislative Council in respect of or assenting to an ordinance to be passed thereby, entitled 'Income Tax Ordinance 1959', or making any regulations under the said ordinance.

b) All of the Defendants from holding any meeting of the Legislative Council in respect of, or passing the said ordinance.

The case was heard in the Supreme Court at the end of June by the Chief Justice and Justices Gore and Kelly. The plaintiff argued that, as there were vacancies on the Council (the three who had resigned), it could not act. He also challenged the Act itself. On July 6th, the Supreme Court found in favour of the defendants on all counts. The members then took the matter to the High Court of Australia, challenging the validity of the Papua New Guinea Act itself. Bunting, however, withdrew, refusing to endanger the government of Papua New Guinea, but the Taxpayers' Association went ahead, with Mr Fishwick of Rabaul as plaintiff.

The full court of the High Court of Australia heard the case on 10th August, 1959. Judgement was given in favour of the defendants; the validity of the Papua New Guinea Act was fully and firmly established.

With that judgement, it was almost as if a sigh passed gently over Papua New Guinea and everybody settled down. People had argued and talked for over a year. Quantities of hot air had gushed out, every conceivable argument had been used and all those clever ploys had been thought up, but it was all negative. They resisted accepting the need for Papua New Guinea to be more self-supporting and no one put their mind to working out more attractive ways than income tax. However, it wasn't quite finished yet.

New elections brought in Messrs Chipper, Barker and Sanders, who were sworn in and took their seats in the September 1959 sitting. During the adjournment debate that day, Mr Chipper rose.

"Mr President, this is my first and last speech. As the nominee of the Taxpayers' Association I am pledged to resign." He then made a most vitriolic speech attacking the official members, the administration and other individuals.

The other two did the same, though Vince Sanders spoke with more dignity and reason than the others. The three then formally handed in their resignations. This performance sickened everyone, and both Mr Fairfax Ross and Bishop Strong stoutly defended the administration, deploring the actions of the new members.

By this time everyone was heartily sick of histrionics and settled down at last to debate the Bills with good sense, and finally passed them with a great number of amendments. Although there were many battles in the house over the years, there were none so long drawn out, or with that touch of madness this third Council had developed. The hip-pocket nerve is very sensitive.

However, nothing could better demonstrate the working of democracy, and it showed good statesmanship on the part of Hasluck. All the ferment and drama must have shaken his nerve considerably, but an enormous amount of good came out of it, both as a safety valve, with a huge build-up of steam being let off, and in the final recognition and acceptance of responsibility, both by members of the House and by the public. Income tax was actually accepted with a far better grace because of the to-do than it would have been without it.

This account demonstrates the political judgment needed by the President: how long to let a matter be debated; when to make an adjournment; what discussions to have with people between sittings; how far to take the press into his confidence; what to say and what not to say in press conferences, and when to make things public.

Before and during each Legislative Council meeting, there were also Executive Council meetings, when bills were discussed and strategy planned. Later, further meetings discussed and passed regulations required by the bills. In addition, of course, to handling the House and the various departments and their heads in Moresby, Don also had to handle the department in Canberra, or to cope with finding himself being handled by them. It was really funny hearing the telephone tussles that used to go on at night.

The third Council still sat in the old Red Cross Hall on Ela Beach, but during its life the new hospital at Taurama was opened, and it was decided to turn the upstairs of the old hospital building into a

Council Chamber, with the Government Archives housed in the basement and the downstairs part made into a museum. This was to house the collection originally made by me, with later assistance and additions by the Government Anthropologist, and still kept in the old office and original house in Government House garden.

The hospital was a pre-war building, the outer walls of cement, inner partitions of timber, with a verandah all round. Removing partitions left a large chamber of pleasing proportions, which a young architect, using parquet flooring, attractive timber panelling, muted colours and good lighting, made into a dignified and workable chamber, with one-way glass in the press gallery and translator's box. Three-language earphones were installed for both the public and Speaker's galleries and to the members' desks. Offices and extensions were added and its opening was planned for when the fourth Council met in October, 1960.

☆ ☆ ☆

November 1959, with all the income tax drama behind us, found us in Australia for Evan's wedding. By now he was managing Aroa Plantation, where he had been a cadet in 1955. We had spent 1958 Christmas with him and he had also invited Marie Reid, a girl he had recently met. Once more Evan had invited the district for dinner and told me that he would be providing the essentials, duck, ham, etc., if I would bring the trimmings, which I took literally to mean the trimmings: cake, pudding, holly, chocolates, nuts and so on. But I hadn't bargained for the incredible bareness of a bachelor's pantry and the fact that the oven had rusted and sported a large hole in the back. He literally had the bare essentials and none of the bits and pieces you take for granted when cooking. Producing a festive meal with so many gaps took all our ingenuity, and Marie and I had rather a hilarious time coping. But, being bachelors, the guests thought it was wonderful.

After a happy few days we went on to Balimo for New Year with Robert and Julie. Balimo was a raw, new station which once more Robert, now an A.D.O., had to build on the Aramia River to the east of the huge River Fly. The station was beside a large shallow lagoon, covered with wild rice and lovely pink lotus.

Their second daughter, Kathryn, had been born there, though unintentionally, of course. The station having no vehicle, Julie had walked the two miles to the strip one Friday for the plane to bring her to wait three weeks with us for the baby's arrival. The pilot flew low, waggling his wings, and they saw that the landing wheels had stuck. The next plane was Monday. But Kathy didn't wait and arrived three weeks early, on Sunday. She was now ten months old, and

Sue nearly four years. The head station of the Unevangelised Field Mission, or U.F.M., was also at Balimo and Mr and Mrs Deasey were marvellous to the family.

On New Year's Eve, to herald 1959, Robert had a twenty-foot trench dug, a foot deep, eighteen inches wide, where a fire was built. The station clerks, police, orderlies, teachers and all their wives and families, plus mission people and nearby Balimo Village, had been invited to bring their own food and cook and eat it together. It was a marvellous night, everybody sharing food and then singing and dancing and seeing in the New Year. Someone brought me something on a banana leaf and when I asked what it was they just said, "Taste it". So I picked up a little roasted thing, like a cashew nut, delicious, with a nutty flavour but softer and with a crisp skin. I kept on eating them, trying to figure out what they were, till the last was gone and they told me they were sago grubs.

It was lovely having all the family on the same side of the Range and, with Moresby the nearest town, we saw them more often.

Marie and Evan had become engaged early in 1959, so here we all were at Macksville on the New South Wales coast for their wedding. The Reids were a large family of brothers and sisters, cousins and aunts, and two delightful grandmothers. Don and I were in the Reid family beach house at lovely Nambucca Heads and Rob and Julie had an aunt's beach house nearby. So in addition to the wedding and getting to know the family, we had a lovely holiday. Macksville has a dear little church and the reception was in the large old Reid home that had seen several generations of weddings, so it was all very happy.

☆ ☆ ☆

We went down to Sydney for leave and were back early in January to a full programme, including a fortnight's visit to the Western and Southern Highlands and a succession of V.I.P.'s staying with us in February — twelve in three weeks.

There seemed to be a great deal of planning and development and all sorts of activity in 1960, including the short last sitting in May of the turbulent third Council. However, it brought up again the suggestion for the political education of selected native leaders to attend Council sittings as observers, and carried it unanimously. This time it was not vetoed in Canberra. Preparations were put in hand immediately and it proved a very successful innovation.

The third Council was followed by another election to replace the three resignations. Don Barrett was again returned for Rabaul, A.L. Hurrell of Wau for the Mainland, and C.P.W. Kirke, a lawyer, for Papua. On the official side, a vacancy brought in Dr. Reuben Taureka of the Health Department.

While all this was going on, the Minister at last became interested in the need for constitutional development. Since 1954, when the Select Committee of the first Council had presented its Report, it had not again raised the question of its own development. I find this strange, but possibly they regarded the knock-back then as a shut door. However, it seems a pity that Council did not request a reconsideration of those proposals a few years later.

Looking back, it is astonishing that the very embryonic House of 1951 remained unchanged for nine years and four sessions without even a provision for more than three Papua New Guinean members or for those already there be elected instead of appointed. Had the 1954 proposals been re-submitted later, Hasluck might have viewed them differently and have been prepared to accept a more representative body while at the same time keeping a government majority. Standing committees could have been valuable political experience too, while the proposals themselves would have given a steadier and more gradual development.

When change did come, it is difficult to point to the precipitating agent, though it was the time when Macmillan's 'Winds of Change' speech in Africa was ringing through the world and the first British colonies had gained independence.

However, in view of Hasluck's early stated policy of throwing responsibility onto the Papua New Guinea Administration, it is interesting to see that he brought about the change without any suggestion of getting reports or proposals from the Legislative Assembly. Hasluck himself made an extensive tour on his own account in July, 1960, making arrangements to meet all sections of the community, seeking their views on the composition of the Council and what alterations they thought necessary or desirable.

We ourselves were then on a fortnight's tour of Bougainville. Landing at Sohano, we were besieged by anxious people, who had heard on the radio Menzies' reply to questions by journalists after the first Commonwealth Conference in London, with delegates from newly independent African and Asian countries. Not having heard the broadcast ourselves, we gathered that, being asked his views on independence, Menzies had said that his experience in London had convinced him that it was better for independence to come too soon, rather than too late. It was comical that everyone worried that Australia would withdraw from New Guinea, while the councillors and village leaders asked anxiously, "Is Australia leaving us?" The scene was repeated wherever we went in Bougainville and later in Rabaul and Lae.

Repeatedly Don assured them that, knowing Menzies, he would be speaking in general terms and not about Papua New Guinea.

But Don would add that his words were true, for it was not good to hang on beyond the time people themselves wanted their own in-

Lord Dunrossil leaving the chamber after opening the newly renovated hospital building for Legislative Council Chambers, Oct. 1961.

Sir Donald (chairman) with newly elected P.N.G. members of the enlarged Council, April 1961.

dependence. He had constantly to reassure all races that Australia was there and would help as long as she was needed and wanted.

But there was no doubt that Macmillan's 'Winds of Change' and Menzies' 'Better too soon than too late' gave an enormous impetus to people's thinking. For the first time, folk of all races began thinking positively of the whole question of political development, and the constitutional changes which would be needed. So Hasluck's tour came at a providential time.

We were home when he returned and Don spent two days with him, discussing and battling about the amendments he was considering as the result of the views he had heard. Don and others in PNG were certainly concerned at the direction the Minister's thoughts were taking. In Canberra drafting began for the Papua and New Guinea Bill (No. 2) 1960, to be ready in time for presentation to the September sitting of the Australian parliament.

I remember well the discussions and arguments between Moresby and the Department over proposals for the Bill, which went from one extreme to the other. The main change was to increase the numbers, as had been suggested in 1954; that is, from twenty-nine to thirty-seven, including the Administrator. But Hasluck's proposals reduced the number of official members to fourteen and increased the unofficial to twenty-two, thus creating a minority government.

"How could you conduct a government with a minority of eight?"

"That's your worry, old man, not ours." It seemed quite obvious that, acting under instructions, there was no way the Department was going to battle for a more sensible arrangement.

To try and work as a government with such a minority was not even following the usual practices of parliamentary democracy. From that point of view, it was the majority of unofficial members who should act as 'the government' and handle the Bills, not 'The Government' itself. But there it was. The Australian Parliament passed it in September 1960, and the House of Assembly was then presented with a fait accompli; and it rankled with members that their views were never sought.

Summarised, the provisions were:—
a) The membership of the Council to be increased from 29 members to 37, including the Administrator.
b) The official members to be reduced to 15, including the Administrator, and the unofficial members increased to 22.
c) These were to be 6 native elected members and 6 non-native elected members.
d) Provision for 10 appointed members, of whom at least 5 would be natives.
e) The Executive Council to be abolished and an Administrator's Council established in its place.

There were to be six electorates, with the native members elected by electoral conferences and the non-native members using normal electoral rolls.

Nothing could illustrate better the authoritarian streak in Hasluck's make-up than the refusal to accept Legislative Council proposals for their own development in 1953, and the bypassing of the Council in 1960 by his own direct discussions with individuals and groups in Papua New Guinea, forming his own conclusions from what he gathered from them. Then to prepare plans in Canberra and impose them once more from the top.

This action of the Australian Government, embodied in the new Papua New Guinea Bill 1960, thus placing an unreal political situation on the administration, was quite incomprehensible to people in Papua New Guinea.

On my observation, and to my concern for a loss in the high standards of integrity, trying to govern with a minority of eight led to unwise and even dangerous practices. The official members, that is, departmental heads, were forced to obtain the votes of at least eight people who regarded themselves as the opposition. To do this meant a great deal of lobbying, the use of various forms of persuasion, including blandishment and 'leaning' if they couldn't win them over by arguing the case. The need to do this set a precedent of political manipulation and squaring off, which was soon picked up by budding PNG politicians and which bedevils both the parliament and the public service today.

☆　☆　☆

The last elections under the old system were held in time for the Fourth Council to sit in the new Council Chambers, to be opened on October 11th by the Governor General, Lord Dunrossil, in the presence of a parliamentary delegation. As this date drew nearer, life on the domestic scene became really complicated.

To start with, a lot of thought and work went into the planning and preparation, as Lord and Lady Dunrossil, a staff of four and two personal servants were to be with us a week. A new guest bungalow was being built and, as money for such things was still scarce, I had to buy materials for Keke and me to make into curtains and bedspreads, and to refurbish the old furniture with loose covers and paint, so it was a great old scramble to get it finished.

Marie had been staying with us for some weeks, waiting for her first baby, due in September, and Mary Ritson, my youngest sister, was recuperating after an illness. October, and no baby, got Evan worried and he arrived to cheer up Marie. As the weekend passed, we all began visualising the simultaneous arrival of the Governor General and the baby, with Marie the butt of family speculation and chaffing. Evan went back on Monday morning to issue rations and check on his new young assistant, arranging a return charter early on Tuesday. But later that morning the baby made itself felt and I was told to bring Marie to hospital about four.

Then Robert rang on the teleradio. Despite my confusion with the 'Over and Roger' bit, I finally gathered that a mercy plane was coming with Julie and the children. He'd taken Sue, aged five, with him on a river patrol in the workboat, but had had to get her back as fast as he could when she began screaming and doubling up with tummy pain. He said the plane would be in about five.

I was able to sit a while with Marie before leaving her in the hospital and going to the strip. The plane came in with a rather woebegone little family and a worried mother, who thankfully went straight to Dr. Syme, the physician at Moresby Hospital. We all came home after peeping in at Marie and sympathising on the irony of the baby's coming the one day Evan was away. The phone rang at 3 a.m.

"It's a girl — all's well."

I went straight out, to find Marie looking serene and calm, and the loveliest wee mite with enormous dark eyes. Evan's face was a study when I told him at the plane early next morning that he was a father.

The next problem was to fit everyone into the household. Luckily, the old bungalow had not yet been pulled down, and Peter borrowed beds, table, chairs and a fridge from government stores for Julie and the children. So here we were, the day before Lord and Lady Dunrossil arrived, with the house full of family, all needing attention, all needing to be fed, the hospital visited, nappies and nighties brought home to be washed and returned. The one lucky circumstance was having Mary, who tucked the whole family under her motherly wing, organised them all and helped them through their problems. They, in their turn, helped me by producing all sorts of extra dishes in the kitchen, especially sweets.

Sue's trouble was an enormous roundworm, fairly easily extricated. Balimo was a notoriously unhealthy place, so Bill Syme tested them for other likely problems, and throughout the visit these tests were coming back, with most upsetting news. He found that Kathy, aged two, had TB and Sue had trachoma. We all thanked Bill and that roundworm for enabling the maladies to be discovered early enough for treatment and cure.

This, then, was the background of our longest and most complicated viceregal visit. But miraculously problems were finally worked out and we were ready on time. An Air Force VIP plane always brought a Governor General, and the arrival was made quite glamorous with the police band and a guard of honour from the Pacific Islands Regiment. Don and I would greet them as they alighted and, waiting for the inspection, escort the party to a line of invited citizens of all races. After introduction and short chats, we would drive away in the cars waiting at the end of the line.

Lord Dunrossil was a dramatic-looking man — a tall and angular Scot with a craggy face and mane of white hair. She was small and neat, not easy to know, and it took several days to get her wavelength. Much later, we became very good friends and still are. With them were our old friends Jean Lester, Secretary to Her Excellency, and Murray Tyrell, Official Secretary for a succession of Governors General, both of whom knew the house and the servants and were always the greatest help and pleasure to us.

Arrangements for the next day's programmes went smoothly enough and at home, Dosi and the staff coped with the luncheons and dinners and did a magnificent job looking after such a complicated household. Our personal worry was not being with our two daughters-in-law in their troubles, but Mary was a wonderful substitute.

On Saturday, we all went to Lae in the Governor General's plane, where he opened a splendid and interesting Show; my most vivid picture is of the knowledgeable way he looked over the cattle. A local catering firm had put on an elaborate buffet lunch, but with the honour of doing it for the Governor General, they had panicked and forgotten cutlery. So we wandered around, shooing flies from our plates, till knives and forks arrived.

The weather kept fine for all the day's activities, till that night, as we were leaving the Show Ball, one of Lae's drenching tropical showers came down. While we were measuring the distance between the door and the cars with some dismay, two trim and burly young P.I.R. officers appeared and, without a word, one swept up Lady Dunrossil and most gracefully and expertly carried her to the car, while the other held an umbrella. I caught my breath, afraid she might be annoyed, but luckily she was quite enchanted and laughed as they dashed back and carried me.

A leisurely morning, a flight back in time for lunch, with everything beautifully organised at home, thank goodness, in spite of more domestic complications. Dosi's son was sick, which meant mother and child both going to hospital, Dosi cooking them food and going with Mary when she took Julie and the children for their daily treatment, visited Marie and returned the baby's laundry.

Before going to Lae, I had noticed that Loana, the steward looking after Lord Dunrossil, had a bandage on his arm. It looked rather nasty, so Mary had another patient to squeeze into the car on her daily hospital trek. Returning from Lae, we were horrified to hear that Loana had leprosy and was in the leprosy hospital at Gemo Island. Everyone was sworn to secrecy and we managed somehow without him.

During the night, I wakened with a tummy wog, took

sulphaguanidine and just hoped others in the party were OK. But an aide came across from the bungalow quite early for medicine, as two of them had it. Commiserating with him, we urged him to see how the Dunrosssils were, and were horrified to find that Lord Dunrossil had had a really bad night — Don went in and found him looking awful.

"Cleland, I've had a very busy night," he said with a wry smile.

We sent at once for a doctor and nurse and he was kept in bed as long as possible. But we were deeply concerned, thinking of that lunch in Lae and worrying that his programme had been too strenuous.

On Monday morning, the first of several ceremonies was a simple one, in the presence of Council members and the Australian Parliamentary Delegation only. First the Minister unveiled a plaque in the entrance hall with a speech, supported by Mr Whitlam, Leader of the Opposition. Next, the Director of Works handed the key to Don, who passed it to the Minister. He opened the door to the Chamber, committing it to the care and use of the Legislative Council, and everyone went in for inspection and admiration.

They waited in the Chamber for the arrival of Lord Dunrossil to play his part as Governor General in Council, and assent to the Australian Legislation embodying the Constitutional Amendments providing for the new, enlarged Papua New Guinea Legislative Council.

The big event was in the afternoon. Planning it had problems, as the handsome cedar doors opened on to a narrow road cut into the hillside and flanked by a high stone wall. So a parking area at the side was used, its considerable slope being overcome rather cleverly. A false facade with 'Legislative Assembly' in large moulded letters, overlooking the car park, gave an external appearance of dignity. Under it a large dais which was erected, and handsomely carpeted in red, left plenty of room for arrivals and the ceremonial guard.

Guests had to be seated in the Chamber, while Councillors, the Parliamentary Delegation, Mr Whitlam, Col. and Mrs Murray, the Army Commander and ourselves were ready on the dais. Bands were playing, flags flying, and a huge crowd of the local population had come to watch it all. Every vantage point, including trees, was full of people for whom loudspeakers were erected to relay the ceremony and its description from inside the Chamber.

In a mounting atmosphere of excitement, first the outriders, then the car flying the Royal Standard, appeared. Their Excellencies stepped out and, mounting the dais, turned to receive the Royal Salute before being greeted by Don and me. It must be remembered that at all these ceremonies their Excellencies were accompanied by his staff of four, either in morning suit or uniform with lots of gold, giving the arrival glamour, while Jean Lester, attending Her Excellency, always looked lovely.

Preceded by the Clerk of the House, we then entered the members' door, walking in procession to the President's room, until all Council members arrived, were presented, and moved to their seats in the Chamber. The Clerk then escorted Lady Dunrossil and me to our seats, returned and preceded His Excellency, the Minister and Don to the Chamber, where Lord Dunrossil sat in the President's Chair (still borrowed from the L.M.S. pastor) with the Minister and Don on each side. Don then welcomed them in a brief address, followed by one welcoming the Minister, the Leader of the Federal Opposition, Col. J.K. Murray and the Parliamentary Delegation. Then he invited His Excellency to deliver an address inaugurating the Fourth Session of the Council. At the conclusion, a twenty-one gun salute boomed out.

The slow dignity and precision of a ceremonial occasion always has its effect on people. But this particular afternoon, looking around at all the familiar faces I knew so well, in the old hospital with its new dignity, John Gunther leading the government on one side and Fairfax Ross, the opposition across the aisle, Don sitting one side of the Chair and the Minister the other, I thought of all the human effort and the tussles that had culminated in this moment. It gave an extra intensity to what Lord Dunrossil was saying in his strong Scottish voice, with its soft cadences. His presence, too, dominated and almost illumined the Chamber.

I thought: "Here, in the newest country in our little part of the world, sits the man who for so long, was Speaker of the House of Commons, mother of all Parliaments." It was a tremendous feeling and I touched Lady Dunrossil, looking first at her and then at him, to convey without words something of what I felt.

Having opened the Council, Don and I, the Minister and the Parliamentary Delegation escorted the Dunrossils to the dais outside for the Royal Salute, and, to the cheers of the crowds, they drove away with outriders and escorts. The Minister and I then returned for the next part of the ceremonial, while Don went to his Chamber and the Parliamentary Delegation waited outside. The bells rang, the Clerk escorted Don to the Chair, where he read prayers and swore in the new members, who took their oaths of allegiance and office. He then announced the presence of the Minister, the Leader of the Opposition and Col. Murray in the Council and, with the concurrence of members, invited them to seats on the floor of the House, before moving a resolution thanking Lord Dunrossil for his speech to this first meeting in the new building and expressing the pleasure of the people for their Excellencies' visit. Dr Gunther spoke as seconder, the motion was put and passed as the doors were thrown open. The Clerk announced:

"Mr President, I have to report a delegation which has come from the Parliament of the Commonwealth to present a President's Chair to the Council.''

Don asked members to receive them at the table and we all rose as they came in and sat down, their leader asking our President to accept the Chair. Don acknowledged acceptance and, after John Gunther had moved and Fairfax Ross seconded a resolution of thanks, Don read messages of congratulation and it was all over.

I have no recollection whatever of our gala buffet dinner for the Parliamentary Delegation that night, so it must have gone without undue hitch and the only thing distinguishing it from dozens of other such dinners is my recollection of the children in their best clothes watching the arrival of the guests. Sue, entranced by it all, greeted people getting out of their cars.

''Are you going to see my grandfather? He's up there.''

Lord Dunrossil had returned to bed after the opening, but with the doctor's permission got up to receive guests and retired again before dinner. We were all very concerned for him and even more so when he entered hospital a few weeks later. Even though we were assured after his death that the illness was an entirely different condition, we always felt that the Lae wog must have weakened him. I like to think his spirit still hovers over PNG Parliament.

This last session had to pass ordinances implementing the provisions of the Papua New Guinea Act (No. 2) 1960, which gave the unofficial members a majority. Needless to say, they all voted with the government this time, relishing the thought of being able to outvote it in future.

With the legislation passed, the fourth, last and shortest of the original legislatures was prorogued, and the date for the opening of the new Council was set for April 1961.

☆　☆　☆

The next thing was a flurry of discussions and conferences with a great number of people on how best to organise the first elections for Papua New Guineans. By now a substantial proportion of the population was quite familiar with the processes of elections, through the spread of local government councils. But to hold a national election was quite a different matter. It was to be on the electoral conference system, so there was also a flurry about working out the boundaries of the six electorates where the Europeans were to be elected directly and the native people indirectly. For some reason, the Minister insisted in taking part in working out the boundaries of the electorates and Don had to go to Canberra to discuss them with him.

A call went out for candidates to stand for each electorate. The European rolls were brought up to date and their votes recorded on polling day. Native voting was new and more complicated. I don't remember exactly how many people made up an electoral conference, but I seem to recall that it was about twenty or thirty. So each electorate was divided into the requisite number of divisions and candidates for electoral conferences were called for. All this needed continuous propaganda over the ABC, while diagrammatic leaflets were printed and an awful lot of patrolling, talking and planning was carried out by the patrol officers. When polling day came, all the candidates in each division came to a central point and those who wanted to vote came too. Women had a vote as well as men and there were one or two women candidates.

After another explanation and some solemn ceremonial, all candidates stood in a line about four feet apart and the people were all asked to go and stand behind the candidate they favoured. It really was splendidly effective and graphic and everyone could see and work out for themselves what was happening and all could count the numbers. At this time there were lots of pictures of this process in the papers and everyone was enchanted with such a novelty.

When the different divisions in an electorate had chosen their members, the next step was to gather them together in the most central town for the electoral conference. There was much discussion about these conferences and they were used to the full in getting across as many of the new ideas as possible, not only so that the members fully understood their own role, but so that they, being leaders, would understand enough about the whole process of voting for a parliament, and the work of a parliament, to take it back and teach their people. When it was felt they had sufficient understanding of proceedings, each Legislative Council candidate could address the conference and be available to answer questions. This done, a secret ballot was held and the new member announced. The process might take several days in each electorate and in the meantime Don was busy choosing the expatriate and the Papua New Guinean appointed members.

For this enlarged Council, there was another grand opening in April 1961 by Sir Dallas Brooks, Governor of Victoria, who was Administrator of the Commonwealth following Lord Dunrossil's death. They were both exceptionally charming, easy and informal sort of people — in fact rather disconcertingly so. You never knew when Sir Dallas would suddenly appear for a yarn, wandering out into the garden or the study looking for Don, or into the kitchen looking for me. Lady Brooks adored the house and literally ran around, exclaiming:

"What a fascinating house. Oh, I do love it. I've never seen a house like this before."

I explained that it was a typical north Queensland or central Australian station homestead, which had been built in 1913 by a Townsville builder.

Again the Minister and a Parliamentary Delegation were present, plus the Governor of Dutch New Guinea and representatives of their newly opened parliament, which the Minister, Don, John Guise and other representatives had just attended in Hollandia (now Jayapura). Again we had a full house, with Jean Lester and Murray Tyrell and two aides, and again small dinners and a large parliamentary buffet. This time it was good to have more Papua New Guinean members as guests, some with wives, in addition to other local dignitaries.

The Council was extremely interesting in any number of ways, and the substitution of the Administrator's Council for the Executive Council was equally so. After the opening, Don announced its composition as — Dr Gunther, Assistant Administrator — H.W. Reeve, Treasurer and Director of Finance — Mr J.K. McCarthy, Director of Native Affairs — with Mr B. Fairfax Ross a nominated member, Mr Ian Downs elected for the Highlands and Mr John Guise elected for Eastern Papua.

The Minister planned this so that it could develop into a cabinet, and wrote very definite minutes about it. This has always been confusing to me; for, without the separation of the executive powers of the Administrator from the gubernatorial powers he also possessed, it meant that, whether you called it the Executive Council or the Administrator's Council, the same body had to exercise the executive as well as the assentive powers, both of which were held by the Administrator. Therefore it could not really develop as a cabinet in the true sense, especially as both the government and the opposition components of the House were represented in it.

The natural dichotomy of this body has really puzzled me, nor could I see how a body separate from the House could develop as a cabinet. I often wished the Minister was the sort of person with whom you could ask questions and discuss things. It always seemed to us that because, in the Westminster system, a cabinet consists of ministers, who in their turn are each in charge of a department, there is no way a dependent country could have a true cabinet. However, since some heads of departments were members of the Council, they acted in a legislative as well as an executive capacity.

An interesting body called the Central Policy and Planning Committee was set up about this time and became a very useful co-ordinating group, where a great deal of cross-fertilisation went on. This, chaired by Don and advising him, more nearly resembled a cabinet advising a Prime Minister.

The Administrator himself had to play two roles: the policy-making governmental head role (as far as the House of Assembly and the Administration was concerned), and the assentive and regulation-passing one imposed by the gubernatorial-type powers his office also imposed on him (which the Executive Council had always carried out).

When Hasluck changed it, enlarged its powers and membership under the title of Administrator's Council and instructed that it should develop as a cabinet, he seems to have brought a great deal of confusion into the political thinking of Papua New Guinea. The perception was blurred between the respective and separate roles of the legislative and executive powers of a government, which has its cabinet, and of a Governor or Governor General, whose office is above party and partisanship, and who presides over a body that assents to legislation before he affixes his signature on behalf of the State itself.

In Australia, this body is called the 'Executive Council', and can be 'Governor General in Council'. It seemed a pity that the old 'Executive Council' in PNG could not continue operating in the assentive role only, with the Cabinet-type duties being given to the new body.

Chapter 14

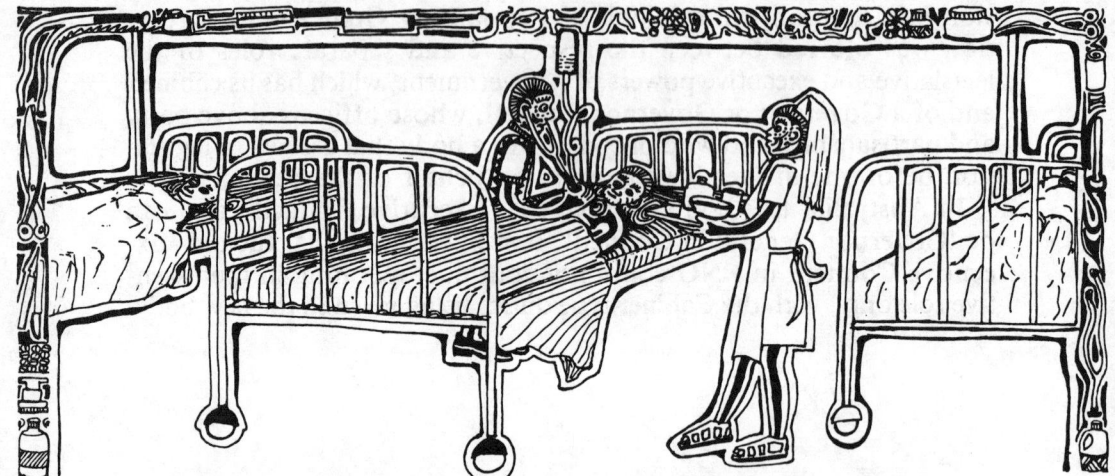

The Haus Sik, or hospital, with newly trained local doctor and nurse.

*Accelerating Development—Trade Unions—Target Dates—
Cleland — Gunther: A Good Team—Fifth Council Meeting:
Select Committee on Political Development—Five Year and
Three Year Plans—Morobe and Siassi Islands—U.N. Mission
and Foot Report—First Election from Common Roll—Elected
House of Assembly Elects Speaker—Opening by Lord de Lisle*

Nineteen sixty reflects the increasing complexities of government
due to the very rapid development of this period. In that year we had
eighty-eight house guests, several Ambassadors and High Commissioners, Margaret and Gough Whitlam on their first visit and a number
of other parliamentarians — the Wentworths, the Mackinnons, Arthur
Caldwell, Lance Barnard, C.K. Jones and John Gorton, the Minister
of the Navy; General Daly, the G.O.C. Northern Command, came
with his wife, Heather, and General Pollard from Victoria Barracks,
Sydney. Quite a number of our Australian High Commissioners and
Ambassadors visited PNG before their new postings, reflecting the
increasing interest of the outside world in what was happening.

Our engagement books reflect development — roads, bridges and
airstrips, schools and hospitals being opened everywhere. Towns expanding and the problems of being able to buy enough land from the
people living in nearby villages for this expansion to take place.

Rapid change was reflected in Don's office diary by the subjects
being discussed with increasing frequency. There were more references
to discussions regarding employment and wages, industrial organisa-

tion and similar matters, while an Industrial Relations Bill was brought in.

A few years previously, concerned people had started welfare associations to help their less educated wantoks (people from their own language community) living in Moresby. I have spoken of Maori Kiki and his wife Elizabeth, an Infant Welfare nurse, who started the Kerema Welfare Association, while Lepani Watson of the Trobriands had gathered Milne Bay people together to help youth from their areas, and was later joined by Tolai and other Methodists as the Methodist Welfare Association. Such groups were now developing into embryo trade unions, while the Public Service Association, in a way the first big union, was increasingly making itself felt.

There was rapid development of the apprenticeship scheme, largely run by an enthusiastic board of private enterprise men, among whom John Hohnen and Bert Stubbs did notable work. Standards of nursing and teacher training schools were being lifted to diploma level, as were technical and agricultural colleges. The Forestry College was opened at Bulolo, the first school for training Papua New Guinean patrol officers at Finchhafen and the first Magistrate training course in Moresby developed into the Administrative Training College. Two other most important new institutions were the Police Training Centre at Bomana, followed by the Police College for the first national police officers. Semi-government bodies such as Posts and Telegraphs and the Electricity Commission were set up and opened their own very impressive training institutions, while private enterprise was beginning to do the same, the first being the Shell Oil Company.

All this was becoming possible because enough young people were coming out of the schools with enough education to tackle this higher training. When you are interested in young people it is rewarding indeed to see their keenness and dedication.

One day about this time, whether in '59 or '60 I do not remember, Don came home for lunch covered in dust and grass seeds.

"Goodness," I said, "Where have you been?"

"John Gunther and I have spent the morning tramping over a valley we've just bought from the Baruni people. It's over the hills," nodding at the hills behind the house. "We're setting aside 1500 acres for a university."

"A university," I exclaimed incredulously. "You're looking a long way ahead, aren't you?"

"Oh," said Don, "You need a lot of land for a university and, if we don't put it aside now, it won't be there when the time comes."

The time came much earlier than either of them visualised, and the country was lucky about the quiet foresight of these two men.

Don's geometrical progression was becoming more apparent. The public service was changing to recruit the educated Papua New Guineans graduating from the new institutions. Change became so rapid that legislation or budget provision for new buildings or development proposals, laboriously battled through the two public services and the two parliaments, was often out of date or insufficient by the time it came out the other end of the pipeline.

For some years the United Nations had been putting considerable pressure on Australia to announce a target date for independence; Australia very properly and quite rightly refused to do so. Indeed as things then were, without Papua New Guineans with the education and training to man the public service, the proposition seemed ludicrous. Responding to the pressure, Australia clearly enunciated her policy of proceeding as quickly as possible in the development of people, institutions and country, stating that the decision for independence lay with the people themselves. When they wished for it and asked for it, then Australia would grant it.

At that time Don was entirely behind the stand Australia had taken. But in the early sixties the situation began to change quite considerably when two internal aspects were beginning to show.

The speed-up in the Department of Education, when Mr L. W. Johnson (Les) became Director, with the rapid development of tertiary training institutions and recruitment of qualified young people into the public service, was demonstrating that you could calculate when they would have had enough experience to give them some chance of running the country efficiently.

At the other end of the scale, the reluctance of village people to look forward to, or to be vocal about, wanting independence was becoming an embarrassment. Indeed, as we travelled round, a sort of resistance to change could be felt and Don found himself exhorting the people in the villages of the districts to take more advantage of the development opportunities the administration was offering. In other words the message in his speeches could now be translated as:

"For God's sake, get off your backsides, develop your land and get yourselves ready to govern yourselves."

It was exasperating when leaders assured him that they were quite happy with what Australia was doing — with a sort of 'why should we worry' implication.

To combat this attitude he began wishing that he had a deadline to refer to and use as a sort of goad. Around '62 and '63 he talked about it a lot, naming 1980 as a practicable target date, which would give enough time to develop a localised public service and reasonably experienced politicians, and he became very irritated when Australia doggedly stuck to her original policy stand, instead of moving with the times. He also felt that naming 1980 would take U.N. pressure off and allow Australia to move from the defensive stance it forced her into, to a positive one of pride in her achievement.

Though he talked about this to me and others, I do not know whether he formally raised it with Canberra as a proposition. Don always said that 1980 would give the time, but if the localising process went well and the country was ready before then, you could always bring the date nearer.

In the event, internal pressure, beginning with the iniquitous and politically inept wages decision of 1964, rapidly built up during and after the Mataungan confrontation of 1970, brought self-government in 1973 and independence in 1975. Had a date to work towards been set in the early sixties it might have given just that two or three years longer for more experience, spelling a better start for an independent country.

☆　☆　☆

The weekend mail was always the largest, as the Department of Territories would post its week's work on Friday. Without an Assistant Administrator, the official secretary used to bring it down to Don on Sunday mornings, so that he could look through it and study anything important. After John Gunther's appointment as Assistant Administrator the mail was taken to him and one of my vivid mental pictures is of John arriving in his gardening clothes, to find Don and me gardening in *our* old clothes on Saturday or Sunday mornings, either bringing some of the mail or coming to inform Don of some happening.

You could watch the relationship developing. To say the least, John was an irreverent man and no respecter of persons. At first he would come up, certainly without any disrespect, but with a businesslike and impersonal approach. As time went on this changed completely into one of a deep unspoken friendship and mutual trust. To see them talking there in the garden, both in their grubby old clothes, used to fill me with a profound sense of gratitude. The relationship continually ripened and went on long into Don's retirement. By then John was Vice-Chancellor of the university and Don was first Pro-Chancellor and then Chancellor. In these roles their close association continued until John's retirement in 1972.

In fact I think John Gunther made the most notable, varied and certainly the longest contribution in the post-war period. He literally created the health service; it was certainly the first department to get organised and be really effective. He had foresight and the practical originality to seize on whatever was at hand in human and material resources and make the fullest possible use of them. By the time we came, health care of the simplest and most basic kind was within reach of everyone in the areas under control.

To overcome a shortage of doctors he looked among the 'displaced persons' and recruited medical men from Europe, who were not allowed to practise in Australia. These doctors went to the remotest places and laid the foundations of the health service. He set up simple training centres in old army buildings where men, selected by each village in contact, came in and were trained to go back and set up simple aid posts, knowing how to treat the most widespread of tropical diseases and to bring others into a central hospital.

The hospitals were not all in the charge of doctors; many were built and run by E.M.A.s — European Medical Assistants — mostly men who would have liked to be doctors, and so took the opportunity to do six months' training, again in the simple tropical diseases most often encountered. They also went out into even lonelier places, built their own hospitals of native materials with village help and skills, trained their own orderlies and nurses — *dokta bois* and *dokta meris* — and ran them effectively and with devotion. We saw and admired their work wherever we went. John Gunther thought out, inspired and created all this.

These were the qualities he brought to the job of Assistant Administrator. He came at a time when they were most needed at the top level and could be given full scope. In the fifth and enlarged Legislative Council he was, of course, leader of the minority group of government men who had to get the numbers to pass every bill, needing all his personal influence with people and considerable political skill. Australia and Papua New Guinea have a great deal to thank him for.

An elected Council meant that the tussles between Don and the department became ever more frequent over the drafting of bills. The department never seemed to grasp that they could no longer get a bill passed as a matter of course, and seemed extraordinarily lacking in a sense of political reality. It took them a long time to recognise that they really did have to take full notice of the thinking of the majority members.

After the tussles over the drafting of the bills came the fun and games of getting them through the House. Sessions were more interesting than ever and, at night, getting a seat in the public gallery meant going early. Debates now became deadly serious tussles and the standard rose accordingly, while in the members' rooms the fourteen government men had to lobby hard to win over enough members to get a bill through.

Sometimes a complete deadlock would force those lobbying to probe and find out what amendments would make the bill acceptable. During these sessions Don would be on the phone to Canberra almost every night.

"That's the bill," was the department's attitude. "It's your job to get it through."

"That's the amendment they will accept," Don would say. "You agree to it or they will chuck the bill out."

Politics being the art of the possible, of course the department had to learn flexibility, and it was good experience for everybody.

This Fifth Council did not take long to find its feet and to begin flexing its muscles and it was never again going to let planning its own political development go out of its own hands.

Therefore at the end of the second sitting in September 1961, Lloyd Hurrell, ex A.D.O., then coffee-planting at Wau, gave notice of a motion he intended to move in the February sitting, saying:

"The reason for this decision is the policy statement by the Minister for Territories as reported in Hansard — Hasluck second reading — on the 22nd September, 1960. To date, changes in the Legislative Council have originated from Canberra. It seems to me that a committee within the Council should be formed so that we keep the people in constant contact with our problems, so that we may advise and recommend developments rather than squabble about it after it has been decided."

It provided for a Select Committee on Political Development, empowered to review and report to the Council on the political development of the Territory and its requirements, particularly the implementation of the Commonwealth's declared policies. It could do necessary research into any matters considered necessary or desirable to the above and into any related matters.

The committee was immediately elected, being two government members, Dr Gunther and Mr Carter, two elected Papua New Guineans, Mr John Guise and Mr Somu Sigob, and two elected expatriates, Mr Hurrell and Mr Downs. This was a really good committee. Dr Gunther was elected chairman and later another Papua New Guinean was added. I do not remember any fuss, so presumably it was accepted and supported by Canberra, and it worked hard and well, travelling widely, seeking views and sounding out proposals.

Mr Harold Reeve, formerly Treasurer, had been appointed as a second Assistant Administrator, so it was easier for John Gunther to be given time for the arduous work the chairmanship entailed. It operated in a very co-operative manner, aiming to keep informed everyone concerned, so that gaps in thinking would not develop and proposals would be kept in the realm of the possible. To do this, Gunther, as chairman, made frequent trips back to Moresby to keep Don in the picture, going also to Canberra to inform both the department and the Minister of the lines on which the committee was proceeding, making sure there was nothing diametrically opposed to government thinking. This was indeed an admirable and constructive way to work, with a valuable educative side effect as well. And, incidentally, it is an illustration of what could have happened much earlier if Hasluck had been prepared to trust the talent existing in Papua New Guinea and to delegate to them, thus putting into practice his own declared policies, to which Hurrell had referred in the speech proposing the select committee.

In many ways the early sixties developed into the most creative of Don's term of fifteen years, though the comment may seem inconsistent with my account of legal and other problems. It may be noted that legal matters were always complicated by the control kept by Hasluck himself, through the Chief Justice, vis-a-vis the Administrator; so that it was possible to accept the legal worries as a fact of life, because they were beyond his influence, and yet feel the sense of working constructively and in harmony in other areas.

The four leading personalities — Hasluck and Lambert in Canberra and Don and John Gunther in Moresby — had got each other's measure, accepted each other's oddities and appreciated and made better use of each other's strong points, so that there was far more a sense of pulling together. This was good, but a pity that the climate in which their natural gifts could flourish was so long in coming.

Both Don and John Gunther were creative and innovative people. Don was able to give John scope for using his natural energies and gifts within Papua New Guinea, but his own creative gifts were stifled. He was clamped by the restrictions on some of his functions, imposed possibly unwittingly, by the Minister; also by his situation in between the demands and stress from the Canberra hierarchy on one side and the effects they had on his public service on the other.

What did give him pleasure and satisfaction, as indeed it gave to all in Papua New Guinea, was the speed of development of those years. He or the Minister was always opening new roads, bridges, schools, the big modern hospitals, the first harnessing of hydro-electric power and new factories and buildings in the business world. The expansion of both primary and secondary industry brought, at last, good money into the hands of Papua New Guinea people. Perhaps most importantly, it gave Don pleasure and fulfilment to see so many young men and women being well trained in tertiary schools and colleges, with all its promise for the future.

Don rather dwelt on these material advances, probably in a compensatory way, to make up for his frustrations. He had so much strength that he seemed able to absorb the latter within himself without rancour. I have been surprised since his death at the people in all walks of life who have voiced their appreciation. They seemed to have sensed this and felt that he was a buffer and gave them protection. Once long ago, when we returned from leave, a missionary wife greeted me warmly:

"I'm so glad you're back. I always feel safer when your husband is here."

Typical housing immediately after World War II when people lived either in paper houses or houses built like this one of native material. Picturesque but uncomfortable!!

Sir Donald, Horrie Niall (now Sir Horrie) and Rachel riding 'rescue' horses after their jeep had broken down.

Lord de Lisle opening the first House of Assembly April 1962.

Local Government Councillors attending session of House of Assembly.

In these years, also, the general public in the country, which had often been highly critical of the Minister and the department, was beginning to perceive not only what Hasluck was trying to do but just what great efforts he made, particularly within the Australian Government and the Australian scene generally, to further the interests of the country. In fact people began to feel proud of him. I have always felt sorry that he himself was not able to sense this quite marked change before he left office to take over the Department of Defence; for he left feeling hurt and rather resentful of New Guinea. Many people of both races were distressed that he would not accept the invitation to the Independence celebrations, to which his own mighty efforts had so largely contributed. He was very much missed and his absence noted.

But back to the second sitting of the enlarged Legislative Council, which appointed the Constitutional Committee. All in all, Don thought they had got through creditably. He was particularly pleased with Hurrell's successful initiative, ensuring political and constitutional development as an on-going process.

In the meantime he had been mulling over electoral problems. Though picturesque and useful educationally, the electoral college method was only a temporary expedient; a common roll was becoming a sheer necessity. But how, oh how, to compile and use it? The wild nature of the country, the isolation of villages, illiteracy and 700 languages made the mind boggle; but he quietly set Gerry Toogood, a former D.C. and now a senior man in his department, onto the job of getting together a small team to study how it could be done.

Another problem growing bothersome was the question of liquor. From the first declaration as a British Protectorate, supplying liquor to natives was prohibited, with legal sanctions against the supplier. For eighty years this had worked well and protected the people from the destructive effects seen earlier in the central Pacific, but with education and development, bringing social mingling in the new society now emerging, prohibition was becoming an embarrassment. Don had tossed the problem to the last two government-sponsored mission conferences for them to worry over. The recent conference had rather reluctantly come to the conclusion that it was time for a change, as did a D.C.s' conference, to which he also tossed the liquor question. With this backing he proposed to the Minister that an independent Commission be set up to make recommendations.

In the early sixties, developments taking place were thought through to a longer-term projection than previously, with much discussion and hard work, first on a five-year and then a three-year plan. For the Minister and his department, the Administrator and his staff and departmental heads, it was a time of striving and hope, with a great deal of argument, discussion, analysis and planning. There was considerable coming and going between Moresby and Canberra, with members of the two civil services working together.

The hope was that, with the forward planning on a five-year basis, longer-term budgeting would be possible; in particular, Don hoped that the annual hiatus between June and September, with the works programme being held up so long, could be overcome. But once again it mostly came to nothing, because costing the plans made them prohibitive. One I remember, among many other costly projects, was the Minister's targets for building and setting up the new corrective institutions and courthouses. They were so astronomical that they simply couldn't be funded. As far as I remember, the old budget and works programme problems remained an annual headache; though there was some breakthrough on matters such as carrying over money without re-voting, and allowing alternative spending within departments. So I suppose that was something.

It is sad to reflect that the elan and high hopes for everyone working on the five-year plans ended in disappointment and intense frustration, though the exercise did clear people's minds as to where we were going, and gave them perspective.

☆　☆　☆

Towards the end of 1961 we had a particularly enjoyable fortnight's visiting, with several days in Rabaul, New Ireland and Morobe, where we inspected a number of newly opened patrol posts in the spectacularly wild mountains between the Markham Valley and the north coast, usually visiting about two or three posts in a day. Flying in and out of valleys in our little plane, I don't think I had ever imagined, even for New Guinea, such steep and narrow ridges. Coming down from the mountain range, with a valley or gorge on each side, they seemed only a few yards across, fifty feet or so from the crest. Shaggy Ridge was such a one. We looked at it in wonder, trying to imagine how men ever fought a battle on it. No wonder its name conjures up bravery.

This same day we went into Wantoat, perched beside a gorge in the mountains where the Leron River rises. We landed and climbed out of the plane to the usual welcoming party of the patrol officer and his wife, a small police guard to inspect, then a line of councillors and important village people to meet, before going over to a jumbled crowd of the men, women and children who had come to see us and to 'look at your face' and hear the 'No. 1 Government speak'.

This particular morning Don had just inspected the guard and was about to meet the councillors, when out from the crowd came striding the trim, angular figure of Pandana, our laundryman, who was on leave. Immaculate in stiffly starched and superbly ironed khaki shorts and shirt, a tie, shoes and socks — easily the most sartorially magnificent person on the strip — without a smile but with a very proprietory manner, he strode up to Don, shook hands and chatted a minute or two, shook hands with me and returned to the crowd. Even his retreating back said quite plainly to the people of Wantoat:

"See. I know the Namba Wan. You can see for yourselves the easy way we greet each other." It was one of those superb little incidents that Don and I so hugely enjoyed.

The next day on the same visit we flew to Pindiu in the mountains, where we lunched, and then to Wasu on the north coast. Here, after our inspection, we found the Lutheran mission had lent us an old jeep which took us on an incredible road along the crest of one of those ridges, so narrow that there was only just room for it.

A new patrol post had been opened at Kalalo, near the Lutheran mission. My chief recollection is of the ingenuity in finding and adapting places to put buildings on such mountain slopes. The young P.O.'s house had just enough room beside it for him to erect a jumping bar. He was a pole-vaulter, practising in the hope of making it for the Commonwealth Games. It looked so precarious that an extra good jump would surely take him over the edge and launch him into space.

Chatting to everybody at afternoon tea, I suddenly became aware of a wave of consternation sweeping through the room. Obviously some bad news. Just then it began to pour with rain and Don came over and said the jeep had broken down and there was nothing for it but to walk the twelve miles back. So amid laughter and commiserations we said our goodbyes and the four of us plunged off down the road — Horrie Niall (the D.C. in Lae), Eskie Lambert (the Secretary of the Department), Don and me. In two minutes my nylon dress, usually standing up well to days like this, had become horribly transparent and was plastered to my body; but there was nothing to do but laugh about it.

The road was so steep and narrow, and by now so slippery with water rushing down it, that I was really nervous that if any of us slipped we'd go over the side. We kept up a good swinging pace for about half an hour, with Horrie chanting 'The Man from Snowy River'. Then a diffident cough behind us indicated someone was there and we turned to see three horses led by a young man, who shyly asked us if they would help.

Joyously, three of us mounted our horses. I am afraid Don and I rode all the way, while Horrie and Eskie took it in turns. When it became dark Horrie switched from 'The Man from Snowy River' to 'Twinkle, Twinkle Little Star' in pidgin. We were glad of our mounts, feeling they could follow the road better than we.

Back at Wasu a trawler was anchored for us with a bottle of whisky and a hot dinner waiting, and were they both good. At the beach we found some elderly men waiting for Horrie, who promised to come ashore later and talk with them. About nine, fed and dry and all the rain gone, he and I rowed ashore.

There was something about that evening that made it a precious memory. Just sitting on the warm sand in the still night, with the rustle of coconut leaves and water lapping the shore, with five wrinkled village men. Two were ex-policemen and the rest were luluais. They yarned and gossiped about the past, and when I lost the pidgin Horrie would give me a rundown. Both in the war and after, they had from time to time shared danger, or just the hardship of a patrol. Somehow I found the obvious relationship of mutual friendship between them very moving. They were all so happy to be in each other's company and I felt privileged to be there.

About eleven we rowed back and turned in, the trawler leaving our anchorage at midnight to make the six-hour crossing to Umboi Island in the Siassi Group, between the mainland and New Britain. We woke to the slowing of engines and the sound of canoe paddles and soft voices, and looked out. A very tall island reared up before us, with grass and coconuts climbing the hillside, but with heavy jungly growth at the foot. The eastern sky was glowing behind it and the water was so still that the island and the canoes coming out to meet us were doubled in the dark green-black water reflecting the jungle. It was breathtaking.

We anchored, dressed and rowed ashore, where waiting children led us about fifteen minutes' walk up a steep hill to where a delicious American breakfast with smiling, cheerful hosts was waiting for us.

This was the head station of the Methodist mission of the area and they had much to show and tell us.

When we went aboard again, later in the morning, I felt a rising excitement. The Siassi Islands had long called me as with a magic spell. They are tiny and beautiful and are the centre of a huge trading circle, which goes far east up the coast of New Britain and west long past Madang. It is as large and as important as the Kula ring which, based on the Trobriand Islands, included all the Milne Bay district. The Siassi didn't have a Malinowsky to write a book and make them famous, but I am glad to say that at last in 1967 their world was studied by Thomas Harding and written up in the book *Voyagers of the Vitias Strait*. I had seen the lovely oval Siassi bowls traded as far as Talasea in New Britain and at Bogia, west of Madang, and now we were going to the islands where they were made.

It was a beautiful day and we lunched on board, arriving at Aramot soon after, seeing the village and talking to the people. I had never seen better built houses; obviously they were very skilled craftsmen, which showed also in the canoes. In basic construction they were like the Kula canoes, with a hollowed log base, built-up plank sides, fore and aft splash board, an out-rigger and a matting sail. But in all cultural decoration and finish they were entirely different.

However it was Mundok Island which totally fascinated me. It is only about three quarters of an acre, with huge and beautiful shade trees, coconuts, small beaches here and there where the surrounding reef allows. Three hundred and fifty people live there, so it's like Kings Cross; but beautifully organised and without squalor. The same finely built, quite sophisticated-looking houses, set close together in orderly rows, leaving narrow streets, all opening on a pleasant park-like open space. Every time a canoe goes over to Umboi they must bring back some soil to fill behind the retaining walls they build of coral broken from the reef. Thus they are constantly extending their island. They live in association with the Umboi people, trading bowls and fish for food, timber to make the bowls, and gaining rights to make gardens there.

Different little beaches were given over to different activities. I sat down on one with a group of old men making bowls. These were in every stage of manufacture, from chipping the shape with quite a long-handled adze in a relaxed, almost nonchalant motion (the adze is uncannily accurate and the blade never fails to land in exactly the right spot) to the finer points of both raised and incised decoration, the polishing of the wood with a boar's tusk, staining it black with a concoction of boiled tree root and finally rubbing lime into the incisions.

The canoe builders were on another beach, so I joined them too. Canoes and canoe-building have always fascinated me and I had barely time to study the likenesses and the differences between them and the Kula canoes and note that, instead of being carved and then painted, they were painted only, in the most beautiful formal designs. In fact they seemed more to be stained into the wood than painted on and were lovely muted colours of black, brown and reds, meticulously executed.

Everybody then assembled in the open space for speeches and presentations. Don was given a traditional bowl and mine was in the form of a fish. They both still adorn our study. We were sad as we left; this place had something special about it. The late afternoon sea was up in a stiff breeze as we sailed to the southernmost island, Tuam, where we made another lovely visit in the setting sun and gathering dusk. Dear Siassi people. I've always found a quality of independence and quietude about island people. They have to depend so much on themselves.

We anchored overnight at Tuam and left at first light for Finschhafen, which was becoming an important education centre and developing fast as a government and mission station, in fact beginning to grow into a town. Our most important visit there was to see the young men training as the first local patrol officers, and Don was well satisfied with their calibre.

After visiting a number of stations and towns in the southern mountains of Morobe District, Wau and Bulolo among them, we arrived home again, only to set off for Australia. The Queen's Birthday Honours had brought Don a knighthood, and thus we went down to Canberra for the investiture. It was our first meeting with Lord and Lady de Lisle. Among other Australians to receive knighthoods were several of our old friends, which made both the investiture itself and the knights' dinner afterwards especially enjoyable.

☆ ☆ ☆

Before we knew where we were it was well into 1962, with our fourth U.N. visiting mission about to arrive in April, the celebrated one led by Sir Hugh Foot. This time they flew from Guam to Sohano and Don went over to receive them. He came back chuckling and described Sir Hugh as a small, quick-minded man, brimming with self-confidence. His first words of greeting had been:

"Well, Cleland, we've come to put you chaps into a gallop." Don was highly amused, even though a bit miffed, and was looking forward to his views and reactions after he had travelled around and seen what we had actually accomplished in the face of the intrinsic difficulties of the country itself. It was no Nigeria, where Sir Hugh had been Chief Secretary, nor Jamaica, where he was the last colonial Governor.

In due course they came to Moresby for their last few days and we found them a lively minded group and their stay thoroughly enjoyable. On their last day they did what no mission had ever done before: they returned hospitality by giving a luncheon to the administration heads at the Papua Hotel, with speeches and toasts. It was marked by two things.

While Sir Hugh was making a witty and telling speech, a large lump of plaster from the ceiling (a bedroom tap having been left on) crashed onto his plate. Even though we hadn't reached the bomb-throwing era, it startled us all and Sir Hugh turned it to good account in his speech.

As he sat down he turned to me.

"And now I've got to try and achieve the impossible".

I asked him what that was.

"Do our report," he said "and try and bridge the inseparable gap between what the U.N. expects and how far the Australian Government is prepared to go"

"Oh, that's easy," I replied.

He looked at me in surprise. "How?"

"Just nose round and you'll find that a number of things are in the offing here. I don't know whether Canberra knows about them

264

yet. But they are on the way, though not public, and will happen whatever the U.N. says or does. So if you take them over for your report, the U.N. will be happy and get the credit, and the Australian Government will go along, as they are already in the pipeline.''

Sir Hugh was really interested and asked how he could find out and I said that I could give him four. When he pressed me I said:

"One — Fifteen hundred acres over the hill behind Government House have been set aside for a university.

Two — The Legislative Council voted unanimously to set up a constitutional committee. They have been travelling round the country getting people's views, visiting also several newly independent countries in the Pacific. You may find that the report they are working on has some interesting ideas.

Three — There is already a team under a senior man making preparations for a Common Roll.

Four — A Royal Commission is about to be appointed to investigate the question of liquor for natives...''

I didn't dare confess to Don what I'd done; but I was highly diverted, when the report came out and caused such a furore, to find that those were among the main recommendations. Eventually I confessed, of course, but the stir it made with the general public really did surprise me.

Another odd thing, to which Paul Hasluck drew my attention, was that, whereas all others were known as U.N. Reports and were rather stodgy, this was and is always known as the 'Foot Report' — probably because of the propensity of the Foot family for getting in the news.

Because of this propensity it took its place with two other events which both marked and caused a distinct change in the thinking of the people living in PNG and those involved in Australia. The first was Menzies' speech — ''Better too soon than too late'' — in 1960, and the last was Whitlam's sheer tour de force when, as leader of the opposition, he gave his 'Self-Government' speech to a huge, very peaceful gathering in the then much torn Rabaul of the Mataungan era of 1970. Don and I happened to be visiting Robert and his family in Kokopo at that time and it was fascinating to be observers. A very few months later, Prime Minister Gorton was forced to match it with a promise of self government at a public dinner in Port Moresby.

☆ ☆ ☆

Meanwhile, the Select Committee on Constitutional Change had been continuing their work and investigations, presenting an interim report to the Legislative Council in September. It indicated that a constitutional change should come in 1964, with a council enlarged to sixty-four, including ten official members and forty-four others with a basic educational qualification, elected from a common roll. In response to an overwhelming volume of requests from Papua New Guineans, there would also be ten expatriates (called Special Members) elected from the common roll, with the provision that it be reviewed before the 1967 election. Voting was to be voluntary and preferential, and all adults, regardless of educational or property qualifications, were to be listed on the common roll.

The final report, tabled during the sitting of February 1963, recommended also that the name should be the House of Assembly and that the presiding officer should be elected from the members of the House and be named 'The Speaker'.

This report was adopted unanimously, and ancillary legislation for its establishment was prepared and passed at the November sitting. At the same time the Papua New Guinea Act was suitably amended by the Australian Parliament and Don announced the proclamation, signed by the Governor General, before proroguing the old Legislative Council and announcing that nominations for the new House of Assembly would close on January 6th, 1964. The elections would be held over the period of 15th February to 18th March, so that the new House of Assembly could be ready to meet at the end of May or early June.

As the country was developing so rapidly, Don had increasingly been conscious of the anomaly of his position in presiding over the body passing legislation, which was later submitted to him for his consideration. Under this other hat, he made a decision whether to give it his assent, refuse assent or submit it to the Governor General. Therefore he was very ready to relinquish the Presidency and welcomed the idea of an elected Speaker. Nevertheless it was a sad moment when he was farewelled from the House, at the end of the session by many touching valedictory speeches. In thanking them he said:

"Dr Gunther and Honourable Members, this is a sad occasion for me. It will be the last time I shall preside in this chair. For twelve years it has been my joy and my pride to preside over the various members who have constituted this Council from its inception. Together we have achieved something which I think stands to the credit of everybody and the Council itself . . . and now we enter a new era. I am perfectly certain that those who follow on in their various capacities in the new House will still render to the Territory the unselfish service which you all have given me and this country, over the past twelve years."

One of the things which had greatly exercised the minds of the committee was how to compile the roll and how to collect the votes. For the roll, the work which Gerry Toogood had already done was of great assistance. It meant a concentrated programme of propaganda by every available means and long patrols by every possible man in the service. An electoral commission was set up, with Bob Bryant as Commissioner, who organised it all and did a magnificent job by having the roll ready for printing on time.

The commission also had to plan and organise the elections. Each district had to work out the most central of a group of villages to be the polling place, and to work out a six-week programme for each polling patrol, so that they could put a date when they would arrive at each polling village. They then had to let each candidate have the list of dates for his electorate, so that they as well as the polling patrol could get the word around.

And what a six weeks it was. It was bad luck that it was the wet season, in most places anyway. But that year it was extra wet and the news was full of the drama of the patrols, crossing flooded rivers, being constantly in drenching rain as they climbed mountains on foot, went up rivers in canoes, crossed the seas to hundreds of islands by trawler and workboat. Even the lucky ones in landrovers were bogged down in mud and had to dig away landslides.

But the dominant theme was that they all got through; a large proportion of the voters walked to their polling village and very proudly recorded their votes for the first time. Special light fibreglass polling boxes, which were waterproof and coloured red, had been designed. And just as well, as more than one was rescued from a river or the sea and nearly all were wet from the rain. I don't think I will ever forget the feeling of drama which gripped us all or the pride we felt when we had accomplished what most people had thought impossible.

Don and I were proud, too, to give a dinner for all the new members when they assembled, a week before the new House met. It was school holidays, so a seminar was held at Sogeri High School, for them to meet and get to know each other and have the workings of parliament fully explained. They also had mock sessions and elected the Speaker. There had been a strong move in favour of Keith McCarthy, then Director of Native Affairs, but Don ruled that an official member was not eligible. So Horrie Niall, who had retired as D.C. but lived still in Lae, and had been elected as a special member, became the first speaker.

The new House of Assembly was opened on the 8th June, 1964, by Lord de Lisle; the third grand opening in four years, when much the same ceremonial was carried out.

For months Don had been mulling over the idea of the Commonwealth Parliament's giving the Assembly a mace for its gift. All I knew about a mace was that it was carried into the House by the Usher of the Black Rod, one of the sergeants at arms, indicating that the House was in session; but Don seemed to know something of its history, so we both looked up more. Indeed it's quite fascinating and goes back to the dim ages, being essentially just a stone fighting club, as they so recently used in PNG. Of course a great many symbolic additions have accrued to the British mace, and it has become the traditional symbol of authority of a parliament.

Don let the idea drift in Paul Hasluck's way and he took it up with enthusiasm, as did the Australian Parliament. A great deal of thought went into its design, which incorporates symbols traditional in PNG. It was made of silver, plated in gold, encasing the club head of stone on a handle of timber, both timber and stone coming from PNG. With a speech recounting its history, it was presented by Sir Alastair McMullen, President of the Senate, who headed the Australian delegation. Its use indeed adds dignity to the PNG parliament.

It had also been decided that parliamentary under-secretaries would be appointed from the new elected members — men who could work with departmental heads and learn for themselves what was involved in running a department. These men and a new Administrator's Council were announced at this sitting.

Although Don's role had completely changed, now that he was not a member of the House, in some respects his responsibility had increased. John Gunther's role as government leader had also increased in responsibility, and there was very close consultation and liaison between the two men, while Don's almost nightly reporting to Canberra on the day's happenings during a sitting and the arguments seemed to go on as before.

This House also kept in mind its own constitutional development and it too appointed a select committee. However, by now there was a new Minister and a new departmental head, and the relationship became quite different.

Chapter 15

Raluana Village — an angry Tuvi the teacher, cracks Keith McCarthy on the head.

Various Crises—Raluana—Szarka and Harris Murders—Navuneram—Hahalis

It could never be said that in Papua New Guinea 'life went the even tenor of its way'. In pre-contact times all work connected with the tasks of gardening, house or canoe building, hunting and fishing had a rhythm of planning, of work rising to a crescendo of activity, a climax (often celebrated with feasts and dancing) and an aftermath of inactivity. Across this went the family and clan rituals connected with birth, puberty, marriage and death. This all sounds idyllic until you remember that everyone always lived under threat: the threat of a payback killing, a dawn raid on the village or open tribal warfare. There was also fear of the more subtle threat of malevlant spirits, the activities of sorcerers and the need for constant vigilance and protective activities to ward off the disasters they could cause.

For the expatriate, living beside a people with a totally different way of thinking and of seeing the world, life was always full of surprises, both for individuals in their everyday lives and on a national scale, when crises of various sorts were liable to errupt suddenly. I will recount some of these.

The Raluana Incident

The Raluana incident occurred in May, 1953, and had about it a touch of the ludicrous. Keith McCarthy was then D.C. of Rabaul, while David Fenbury was the man responsible for developing local government councils. David was a man with a brilliant intellect, who always knew he was right. Moreover, if he thought a course of action should be taken, he would try and force it through, thus inevitably causing any opposition to harden against him. This trait gave him endless frustration and led him into all sorts of one-upmanship. Keith, though D.C., was much under his influence.

When the Livuan and Vunamani councils were so effective, David, as Senior Native Authorities Officer, decided to bring the whole of the Tolai people of the Gazelle into the council system, twenty-seven thousand were quite happy to do so, but three small groups in different areas refused. Don and the Director had been counselling patience to the D.C., to wait till they were ready to come in. But the rest of the Tolai complained:

"We have to pay council taxes and do a lot of things for ourselves while those Raluanas stay out and the government gives them everything free." Since this really was a problem, Keith and David set out one day for Raluana, a coastal village near Kokopo, determined to bring them into the system.

Knowing both men, I would think that the combination of David's intensity and Keith's bluster made the Raluanas mad. A fracas developed when the Raluanas attacked the head of the Vunamani Council, which they did not wish to join, and during it a leader called Tuvi, who was lame, hit Keith over the head with his crutch, splitting the skin. Since the D.C. was the most senior man in the district and represented the Administrator, this assault was recognised by everybody, including the Tolai, as pretty serious.

The news went round like wildfire, was well highlighted on the news and the papers and was treated with a mixture of concern and merriment. I don't know how the two men extricated themselves or how much dignity they managed to preserve. Annoyed that they had been such asses, Don realised that there must be something else underneath the Raluanas' attitude, which should be brought out.

Tuvi, of course, was charged with assault and in the circumstances the case was heard by Chief Judge Phillips instead of the District Court. He summed up thus:

"I do not think this is a case where I can treat this as a mere first offence. It was an assault on a man who happens to be the chief authority around here, as everybody well knows. I do think, though, that I should not exaggerate the events of the 21st May; for had it not been for the dramatis personae involved, I suppose it would have been settled in the District Court in something like half an hour. It seems that, because of the dramatis personae and possibly other influences, the events that led to this case have been boosted up."

So much publicity could have brought political embarrassment to the Minister, so on his next visit he and Don, while in Rabaul, invited the people of the three villages to meet them, so that they could hear their views and their reasons for not joining the councils. Both men, incidentally, were very good at just sitting down and listening. About fifteen hundred came; each group had its spokesman and advanced the same story, namely that councils were good but they did not think they were sufficiently educated yet, and joining would take them out of the administration.

Paul and Don, after reassuring them that councils were still the administration, replied that twenty-seven thousand other Tolais, with their same standard of education or less, ran councils very well. The Raluanas themselves ran the most successful co-operative store in PNG. If they could do that, they had enough education for councils. The groups were invited to select ten leaders for a meeting with the D.C. to discuss and settle terms.

In the meantime, with the court case finished, Don had appointed the Director of Native Affairs as a Commissioner to examine the situation under the Commission of Enquiry Act. His report, handed to Don at the end of July, elicited a few more points, after examining thirty-seven witnesses. The people of the three villages were guided by the advice of educationally advanced fellow villagers who had not understood that councils did not mean severance from the administration. In addition there were bad feelings with neighbouring groups and reluctance to be linked with them. An incorrect and undefined official relationship between the D.C. and the Senior Native Authorities Officer caused confusion in their minds. This last interested Don as he had found the same confusion in the Mekeo with native rural progress societies. It was strongly suggested, but not proved that council opposition was provoked by certain missionaries, and this aspect was also dealt with quietly.

The ten leaders duly met and discussed terms for their entry; and out of it all, two changes emerged. Firstly, Don made it quite clear, through the public service, that specialised services were part and parcel of normal native administration. But, to clarify things, the cumbersome term S.N.A.O. was changed to District Officer (Local Government); and he emphasised that where all specialised services and other departments were concerned, the D.C. was his representative, captain of the team, and responsible for co-ordination and co-operation. Secondly, the Raluanas won the right to make their own decision and to come into councils if and when they wished to do so.

That right of all groups in PNG was henceforth respected. The Raluanas remained aloof. When they felt they'd made their point, they quietly came in without any publicity. David Fenbury was brought into headquarters and, when Keith McCarthy went on leave, John

Foldi, an immense, genial and very balanced man, took over from the volatile Keith and remained there till his retirement in the sixties.

The Szarka and Harris Murders

From his return in 1951, Don had been anxious about a station called Telefomin, because there the government had departed from its policy of spreading gradually outwards, and opening stations only when the people had been in contact with neighbours already under administration. Forty miles from the then Dutch (now Indonesian) border, Telefomin was opened because of the need to define the border by a string of patrol posts. Though in very mountainous country, between the headwaters of the Fly and the Sepik rivers, it was chosen because there was already an emergency wartime airstrip there, built by the U.S. for their planes flying between Australia and Hollandia.

As the crow flies, it was a hundred miles south of Ambunti on the Sepik and south-east of Green River Station — distances almost trebled for a walking patrol — while Mt Hagen was two hundred miles east and Lake Murray a hundred and twenty south. These were Telefomin's nearest neighbours, with unexplored country and innumerable unknown tribes, with no hearsay knowledge of a world outside their valley, in between. Don's concern about this kind of isolation was not made any less by the fact that only two out of five flights were able to make a landing, because of sudden clouding over the nine-thousand-foot pass above it.

One day in November 1953 he came home grave and anxious, because two patrol officers and two policemen had been brutally murdered while out on patrol. The news had been brought in to the Baptist mission at Telefomin by a third policeman and a medical orderly, who had escaped the massacre. Naturally, the evening news took it right across Australia, with headlines, comments and speculation in the papers. It was a terrible shock for everyone in PNG and all felt anguish for the parents and relatives of the young men. Nothing like it had ever happened before.

Alan Timperley, the D.C., flew in with a patrol to gather details as soon as the missionary radioed him the news in Wewak. The two patrol officers, with a small party of police, had been doing a census patrol in Eliptimin, the next big valley, twenty miles north east. For some unknown reason, possibly because they found it hard to get on together, they separated, thus disobeying a standing order that, in newly controlled country, patrols must be conducted in pairs. Harris left the base camp with two police on the 29th October for the lower end of the valley, and on the 3rd November Szarka set out for the upper end. That same night both parties were attacked, and Szarka and a policeman were brutally killed. Harris was badly wounded, while one of his police was killed. The other and the medical orderly, showing great heroism, tried to save his life and get him back; but he died. They escaped and made their way back to the Baptist mission at Telefomin.

Strong patrols were sent in, and finally one hundred and thirty seven men were flown down to Wewak, some being suspects and some witnesses. After an immediate lower court hearing, a number were committed for trial in the Supreme Court. The case began on the 7th July before Mr Justice Gore, the accused being defended by Mr. Peter Lalor, and it ended on August 14th.

This sort of crisis and tragedy always meant, for Don, handling them on two fronts at once. He had to see that everything possible was done, making what were often hairline judgments on the action to be taken, which could make all the difference between success and failure. At the same time, he had a lot of very anxious politicians in Canberra, hoping that events in PNG weren't going to give their opponents any opportunities to make political capital. Between these two fronts were the media. If the press were not kept informed they would start guessing, and the guess would be sure to be unfavourable to the administration; at the same time he had to be careful not to say too much. So it was most important that he should maintain good relations with the press, which he did on a carefully calculated basis of mutual trust. It worked well and was seldom, if ever, abused.

In the middle of this particular tragedy, Don had a worried letter from the Minister. Gerald Szarka had been barely two months on the station when he was killed. But in his letters home he had been highly critical of the manner in which his predecessor and other officers had conducted the station. Mrs Szarka, his mother, had handed all these letters to Mr Luchetti, a prominent member of the opposition, insisting that some form of public inquiry be made into earlier administration of Telefomin. The allegations had been used to discredit the administration and the government at question time on 6th April and during the adjournment debate on April 13th. Don records in his book that, writing about them to him, Hasluck went on to say:

"In such circumstances it is essential that the Minister should know with exactness and in detail what substance, if any, there may be in such allegations. Furthermore, when serious allegations are made in parliament, it is necessary to assure the House that the truth of them will be investigated, and I have given such an assurance."

An inquiry was set up under the Director of District Services and Native Affairs, whose report Don sent to the Minister on the 8th May, saying in a covering letter that the report "indicated that the Government shouldn't give a categorical and public denial to some of the allegations". Indeed the public feeling in Australia was such that Mr R.G. Menzies, the Prime Minister, had given an important Australia-wide broadcast, in which he drew a moving picture of the nature of the task of patrolling new country, and paid a great tribute to the skill and courage of the young men who did it.

Mrs Szarka was very persistent and began writing to Don. His diary makes several references to her letters and it must have taken all his tact, kindness and political sense to answer them.

As always, every effort was made by the Administration, in its arrangements, to assure a fair trial. Therefore all Szarka's letters to his mother, the report of the Inquiry and its relevant papers were given to Mr Lalor, who, as public solicitor, defended the accused. He was a man who never spared himself at such times.

After the trial, Don wrote to the Minister, giving him his review and quoting the end of Mr Justice Gore's summing up:

"This series of killings was not a new idea, and has no particular reference to the administration processes which were complained of. I really believe the desire to get rid of the government was conceived long before there was any aggravating incident, and only the opportunity was awaited. It was cunningly planned. The complaints were, to my mind, subsequent excuses, and not collectively the prior and actual motive."

He also quoted the similar conclusion reached by Mr Lalor, the defending counsel:

"I think the history of the attacks may be summarised as follows. Firstly, the plan to attack was no new matter arising out of injustices. It had originated, or at least been co-ordinated and directed, by the men of the Telefomin Valley, who allege no grievance, save the presence of the administration. It was largely carried out by the men of the Eliptimin, many of whom did have a sense of grievance against the administration; but this sense of grievance cannot be considered as more than an aggravating cause of the attack."

The result of the trial was that nineteen men were sentenced to death for the murder of Szarka, seven for the murder of Harris, seven for the murder of policeman Duritori and eight for Purari. Judge Gore spoke of the actions of the policemen and the medical orderly Bonat, "Thus began a story of heroism, resolution and loyalty which, in the cold marshalling of the facts in a judgement, must appear sublime."

After sentencing the accused, Judge Gore recommended that they all be treated alike and that their sentences be commuted to ten years hard labour. Don accepted his recommendations and advised the Minister accordingly. In view of the seriousness of the whole matter and the general reaction of the public, Hasluck took the unusual step of submitting all the evidence to the Federal Cabinet. They too accepted Don's recommendations.

During 1954 Don and I visited Telefomin. It was unlike anything I had seen before in PNG, though we were to see plenty of the same sort of country and the same sort of people in West Irian. The ground was putty-coloured and looked unbelievably poor and miserable, the vegetation was stunted and of a curious blackish green. It would be hard country to grow good food and the people were small and stunted too, with dry and scaly skins, so different from the vigour and gleaming good health of the rich valleys to the east. The people were cheerful and friendly, but the place gave me the willies; and I thought Mr and Mrs Green, the Baptist missionaries, very brave — in other ways than a possible fear of another attack — to be living and working there with their two little girls.

Visiting a Lutheran mission near Madang a few years later, we talked informally to students of a boarding school, and were asked afterwards if we noticed anything about one of the groups. We said they seemed a bright lot but no different from the others. They were some of the Telefomin murderers. The authorities had selected the youngest and brightest, to try the experiment of what education could do. We couldn't believe they had even an ethnic relationship with the miserable specimens of humanity we had seen at Telefomin. They had filled out and grown as much as three inches; there was intelligence, not fear, in their eyes; and the whole physical shape and appearance of their faces was different. I had noticed this before and began to realise the effect of face muscles on appearance, the effect of thinking and emotions on muscles, that therefore govern the type of face as much as bone structure. If ever I saw an illustration of this, I saw it that day. Don then asked to see the group and they spoke to him in good English.

In addition to the trial, it was necessary to educate the Telefomins about the outside world and the strength of the government, so leaders from different groups were taken to Wewak on visits so that they could 'take back the talk', while a school was built and staffed and an agricultural officer stationed there to back up the patrol officers.

Navuneram

Just before the Dutch governor and his wife came on an official visit, in August 1958, Don had been increasingly concerned with another build-up in the Gazelle. It will be remembered that in 1954 the Raluanas won freedom of choice about joining a council and, having won it, they and one of the other groups came into the system. But the Navuneram group, living up on the plateau, regarded it as a victory against the government, to be exploited, and by argument, threat and force, gained adherents as an openly anti-government group. They enjoyed nothing more than a clash with patrol officers, which they could claim as another victory, and became more and more arrogant accordingly. This was not only an unhealthy and unpleasant situation for Mr Foldi and his officers to handle, but was a source of irritation, giving a sense of gross injustice to the council Tolai,

275

because they paid taxes while the anti-council did not.

In January the Personal Tax Bill of £2 for males of all races had come into force. The Navuneram, furious, and claiming the government was tricking them into councils, refused to pay this tax. Field staff tried many times to reach a reasonable understanding with them. Don and Mr Foldi together made a personal effort to persuade the leaders to accept the situation, finally asking them to think it over well. They then made it perfectly clear to them that anyone who did not pay his tax, like everyone else, would have to be charged in court.

When time to think this over had still had no results by June, civil proceedings were started against individuals to recover tax. On 29th July, district office staff, accompanied by ten police, went to the Navuneram villages with warrants to serve in consequence of judgments against three individual men in the Magistrate's Court.

They were unable to serve the warrants, so took the next step and, looking for property to seize under the warrant, wheeled away a bicycle. They hadn't gone far when they were confronted by a well-organised group of people intent on getting the bicycle back, and violent fighting broke out. Being heavily outnumbered, the District Officer let the bicycle go and withdrew his party, faced by jubilant Navunerams.

When the party returned to Rabaul, Mr Foldi immediately rang Don, who discussed the whole situation with his senior officers. Quite obviously this was it: they had come to the point of no return, and would have to take strong action to enforce the law. After this conference, Don sent the following telegram to Mr Foldi:

"A677 following actions will be taken ensure collection tax from people of Navuneram (1) Officers will continue act on warrant execution and use required force prevent riotous behaviour and interference with course of justice (2) Persons involved in riotous behaviour or interference will be arrested and charged accordingly in this regard see secretary law signal (3) Persons against whom no proceedings as yet taken but who owe tax will now be charged under section 16 personal tax ordinance stop All officers have full support this headquarters to carry out duties."

He also sent over Mr Normoyle, the Commissioner of Police, who had served a total of seventeen years in Rabaul and knew the Tolai well, to give them his advice and support. In Rabaul a conference took place, when all the senior officers made careful plans.

On the 4th August a patrol of district service personnel, in charge of Jack Emmanuel, who had a particularly good rapport with the people, went to the school grounds, set up tables ready to receive tax money and prepared to hold court if necessary. Two hundred police, brought in from other areas, were smartly paraded with rifles and bayonets. They were drawn up in two rows on the edge of the playing-field, facing the road, while parked further down were the vehicles which brought them all, together with enough empty trucks for any who still would not pay their tax and so had to be arrested. It was hoped that such a show of organisation, with strength to back it, would discourage further resistance and enable people to pay their tax without loss of face.

Across the road, opposite the school, was a typical Gazelle solid bank of secondary growth. Unseen behind it a rough grove of coconut palms, underplanted with cocoa, and one or two houses straggled up a hill. Here the men had gathered and Emmanuel called out an invitation to come over and pay tax. The reply was a shower of large slingshot stones — the very effective traditional Tolai weapon. This was defiance indeed, and the police were ordered to fire a warning shot into the air. Some did not hold their rifles high enough to allow for the unseen slope, and so came tragedy. One shot ricocheted off a coconut tree and killed a man, while another caught someone standing on the verandah of a house on the unseen high ground.

While the patrol remained on the spot to handle this calamity, news of it was sent to Rabaul at once. John Foldi telephoned Don, who immediately informed the Minister and kept him in constant touch over the following days. Although these crises were very real political problems for the Australian Government as well as for the Administrator, the Minister's support for Don, and the confidence he showed in the way he handled them, was one of the things Don always appreciated.

On Wednesday the 6th, Don went over to Rabaul to assess the situation for himself, taking with him a solicitor-at-large to make sure that everything was being done correctly. When they visited the scene of the trouble he was shown large piles of slingshot stones heaped behind every coconut tree; so the men evidently had had their own intelligence of the government plans and had made full preparation to resist with violence.

It was decided that a few days later the patrol, reduced to Emmanuel and about fifteen police, which had remained camped in the area, should proceed through the hamlets in the normal way of tax patrols, but with instructions that any village which showed signs of opposition should be bypassed. However, there were no further incidents and all villages paid their tax.

Looking back now, what I remember of crises such as these is Don's deep concern and the way he talked, not to get my reaction, but to get things off his chest and to sort out his own solutions. In fact, quite often, I doubt if he even registered any comment I might make. What he needed was a patient and willing ear. But now, reading his office diary and the engagement books, I am amazed at how many other different kinds of things he was handling at the same time.

The Navuneram story opened with the visit of the Dutch Governor.

Protocol demanded that Don accompany him on much of his Port Moresby programme, which he did. But as we were about to leave on ten days of district visiting, he realised that even protocol could not demand that he be absent from Moresby at such a critical time. So I had to go with them and do the honours for us both. Fortunately Dr Plateel was most understanding, having had such problems to handle himself.

Once more a Commission of Inquiry was instituted. Don recommended Mr Justice Gore, with his long experience, and once more the Minister required Mr Justice Mann. Don handed him his commission a fortnight later and at the end of August hearings began at Navuneram. They were held in a small, open-sided resthouse from which a large crowd of onlookers could see and hear the proceedings. To invest the scene with due pomp and ceremony, Mr Justice Mann came attired in a black windsor coat with braid frogs across the front and wore his Judge's wig. Syd Johnson was his counsel assistant and a respected and educated Tolai the interpreter.

When the heat and the crowded bodies made the atmosphere too stifling, the judge took off his wig and put it on the floor beside him. His long solemn address about the proceedings was suddenly interrupted by jubilant cackling and a roar of laughter from the crowd. Startled, Judge Mann looked down, to see a village hen flutter off his wig — and there inside it was a nice fresh egg. It tickled Mann's sense of humour too, and he dined out on the story for years.

When the Commission rose at the end of that first day's questioning, the solicitor-at-large went to see the A.D.O. at Vunadadir and found that Colin Liddle had already been visited by some of the men from the hearing, telling him what the judge had said. He was quick-witted enough to switch on the tape recorder. Later he played the comments back to the judge, whose face was a study till he exclaimed:

"But I was saying just the opposite."

He was appalled to think what versions would be relayed around the cooking fires that night. In such ways was his experience of the law in PNG enlarged and he went to a great deal of trouble next day to give a short, more succinct address, to correct the misunderstandings of the day before.

The Chief Justice returned his commission and the report on November 5th, 1958. It was a good report, though long, being fifteen hundred pages. He had examined in detail events of previous years, with the attitudes of the different groups, together with their reactions to various government policies, among which he stated the following:

"I have dwelt at considerable length upon actions on the part of the administration and its officers, which in my view have shown weaknesses which have contributed towards the events that

Telefomin men.

Don (centre) and party outside Telefomin Hospital.

occurred at Navuneram. I have done this to give the administration the benefit which can only be derived from close attention to the causes of the trouble. All of the officers who gave evidence did so frankly, truthfully and without reserve. They are all men of outstanding ability and integrity, and of wide experience in the Territory, and they faced the very difficult problems with which they were confronted with great courage, and application to duty. The events at Navuneram were the culmination of many years' difficulty, during which important and indeed essential policies, being implemented for the benefit of the natives themselves, were being held up and frustrated by small groups of natives, and the particular situation which arose was something that had not previously been encountered in Territorial experience and was never properly understood.''

The report was tabled in the Federal Parliament and in the Legislative Council of March 1959. In parliament the Minister was generous to the officers of the administration when speaking to the report, when he said:

"We do have to satisfy ourselves whether any officer or officers of the territorial administration either did what they should not have done or failed to do what they should have done. Now, while it may be possible for various persons to reach various opinions on what was the best way to handle the situation which arose at Navuneram, and while some persons who were not there on the fatal day may freely express their own confidence that they themselves would have done better, I find nothing in the Commissioner's report which would justify any assertion that any officer of the administration concerned in this affair acted other than in accordance with his honest judgment of what it was best to do, and I find nothing to justify any charge that any officer either exceeded or fell short of what might reasonably be regarded as the demands of his duty...''

The report clearly revealed the tensions among the Tolai people. To discover more about them, Don proposed to the Minister that an exceptionally gifted and understanding retired officer, Ted Taylor, who had worked long years among the Tolai, should be invited to join the administration again for six months, to live and work amongst these people and see if he could find the underlying causes of their dissatisfaction.

In Taylor's review he detailed some administrative steps which should be taken to improve the situation. The two most important were:—
(a) Closer and frequent contact at village level with the administration, through experienced field staff with continuity of service; and
(b) the appointment of a senior field officer, constantly moving among the people in an advisory capacity.

Ted Taylor also said that, though there were individuals who were anti-government and showed signs of unrest, their attitudes did not reflect the general population's.

Ted's recommendations were carefully followed while Don was in the chair. But after his retirement, through a set of circumstances resulting from the style and the temperaments of key persons, all this went into reverse. The result blew up into the Mataungan Association, expressing the Tolai determination not to be pushed around. Were I a Tolai, I would most certainly have been a Mataungan.

The Hahalis Society

The island of Bougainville is different; or rather the two islands known locally as Big Buka and Little Buka. All over PNG, black cats are invariably called 'Buka'. The Buka people feel themselves to be different, and from a lofty height call all other people in PNG 'red skins'. For they are the blackest people in the world — a marvellous, gleaming, almost blue black. Their faces are square-jawed and their noses regular and well-shaped. They are a comely, very intelligent and independent people.

Don always used to worry about them. He used to say: "It's so difficult, when they are at the end of the line." The only way to travel there was by the weekly Catalina seaplane and then by boat. It was hard to bring development when there was so little money and travelling was so hard. Yet the soil was rich, with splendid volcanoes steaming away in the centre, and the plantations running down the narrow coastal plain, and dating back to German times, gave rich yields. Yet little of this potential went to the people.

The war had scarred the people, too, as Bougainville had been a big Japanese base. Australian coast-watchers, notably Paul Mason and Jack Read, well known to the village people, lived in the bush behind the the base for three years. They were fed, helped and protected by the villagers, at their own considerable risk. These men sent information of Japanese air and ship movement on their little teleradios, giving American fighters, further south at Guadalcanal, time to get off the ground and attack Japanese bombers as they flew down 'the slot' from Rabaul. Later the coast-watchers' warning of increased naval activity gave the allies an advantage which contributed to winning the Battle of the Coral Sea, so vital to Papua New Guinea and Australia.

On our first visit, the old Catalina landed us in Tonolei Harbour in the south, strewn with Japanese wrecks. A trawler took us to Buin, where war scrap was everywhere. One enterprising man had a sort of blacksmith's forge down by the beach, smelting aluminium from planes found in the jungle, and was surrounded by neat silver piles of aluminium bars. If only the so-called forward-looking Labor

Government, in power in the vital years at war's end, had thought to involve the people in bettering themselves by doing the smelting and collecting the war scrap, instead of letting the whole lot go outside the country by the War Disposals Commission they set up! Instead this opportunity was wasted.

And now here were we, seeing for the first time the wonderfully rich and beautiful island and meeting its people, with their dark, intelligent faces and their sense of waiting. They looked at you not with hostility, but certainly with a touch of cynicism and a question in their eyes. As though to say:

"And when is some development coming our way? We've waited a long time. We've waited eighty years. Why is all the money going to the Tolai?"

An unanswerable question. There was so little of it, too few trained men, and you couldn't start everywhere at once. But that didn't help the Bougainvilleans.

However, there were some very good schools on the island, particularly those run by the Marist Brothers of the Catholic Church. Visiting these schools, they always seemed to have an atmosphere of purpose and from them have now come some outstanding people, who were still schoolboys in the late fifties.

With this background, news of odd activities began to drift from Little Buka in 1960. This is the island to the north, where the people have intermarried with the New Irelanders, but are still marked with the typical Buka independence.

I have spoken already of the introduction of personal tax to increase the local contribution to the budget. For two years the people had paid it quite happily, but still the much-needed road system had not begun, nor had they an agricultural officer to show them how to grow the cash crops which were making the Tolai rich.

By this time a number of young people with a certain amount of more advanced education, gained at either Catholic or Government secondary schools, decided that, if the government was so slow, it was time they helped themselves. In February 1960, about seven hundred people from three villages — Hahalis, Hanahan and Telelina — formed themselves into the Hahalis Welfare Society, led by three young men: John Teosin, a skilled carpenter trained in Rabaul, Francis Hagai and Sawa. They worked out a programme and told the administration that their aims were to improve living standards by helping the people to establish copra and cocoa plantations, improve housing and organise road work. This seemed an excellent programme, in which the administration was ready to co-operate fully. Then, gradually, not only some problems, but some very odd things began to emerge.

One thing the administration had done for Buka was to help them organise a co-operative society, for trading in copra and to run stores.

By November it had become clear that Teosin was in total control of the finances of the Hahalis Welfare Society, and that they were boycotting the co-operative and marketing as a rival. This was serious for the co-operative's viability.

Then the anxieties within the Catholic mission grew, as news drifted in of strange cultist overtones developing, the most spectacular being what came to be called the 'baby farm'. They built a large house in the bush, which they called the stable of Bethlehem, with Joseph of Nazareth, the carpenter, as its patron saint. In this they installed about twenty young women, selected from the society villages, who were shared in common by all the young men. The idea was that the babies would be born without sin and would grow up to lead the people into the Promised Land. To understand the logic of this kind of thinking, one needs to read Peter Lawrence's fascinating book *Road Bilong Cargo.*

Early in the formation of the Hahalis Welfare Society the government had established extra district service staff in the area, showing its willingness to help people who were ready to help themselves, while John Teosin was appointed to the District Advisory Council. Later, Bougainvillean members objected to the government working with John Teosin, when his movement went in for such practices as the baby farm. Then other bizarre things began to emerge. So everybody was getting into a fix with everybody, and no one quite knew what to do.

When the 1961 tax patrol went into Little Buka, all the Hahalis people said they had already paid tax to the society, and refused to pay any to the government. A month later, the district officer went to Hahalis with a small party of police on another tax patrol. Seven hundred people assembled and refused to pay. An attempt to arrest some defaulters resulted in a determined show of force, so the patrol withdrew, leaving a patrol officer and twelve police to watch developments. In the next two months special efforts of explanation were made, to try and persuade both leaders and people — by personal discussion, distribution of leaflets in pidgin and dialect and by radio messages also in pidgin and dialect, from Rabaul radio. However, at the same time, Teosin was conducting a lecture tour outside the Hahalis area to persuade others to join him in resisting tax.

At this stage the District Officer, Des Clancy, came to Port Moresby to discuss with Don and his advisers the whole situation, which by now was reaching tragicomic proportions. A careful plan was made.

In February 1962 Clancy, two senior police officers and eighty police, augmented from New Britain and New Ireland came and camped near Hahalis. A few hours later over two thousand people moved onto the police camp. The police inspector invited Teosin and other defaulters to accompany them to Sohano and appear before a magistrate. On his refusal they arrested him, upon which the inspector was literally set upon by a crowd of howling women, who rescued Teosin. Very perplexing for the poor police.

Once more it meant withdrawal, but they remained encamped in the area. Teosin, Sawa and other Hahalis leaders then wrote to the District Commissioner, inviting him to Hahalis for talks on 8th February. The D.C. complied, and after some discussion Teosin and Sawa agreed that all tax defaulters would come and pay their tax at Sohano, the headquarters, on February 12th. But a meeting that night vetoed Teosin's agreement.

Hahalis is on an escarpment near the east coast with a protected beach below. For several days people from other villages had been moving to an encampment on the beach, food being brought by canoe and stored there, while men were carrying baton-type clubs.

The police were increased to one hundred and fifty, ten with rifles and the rest with batons, a senior inspector carrying all the ammunition. On the 19th they moved down to the beach and arrested a man. Immediately the party was rushed by over a thousand, behind a row of women and children who were placed in front, all throwing stones and using clubs, with a few knives and axes. A number of police were injured, so the party had to withdraw again. Firing two shots to seaward halted the Hahalis party, and the police withdrew to the cliff top. This tactic of women and children making the front-line troops really created a problem.

At this stage John Gunther went to Buka, to discuss matters with those on the spot and assess the situation, returning on the 21st. Don immediately called a conference with John, the Commissioner of Police and other senior officers. It was becoming ever more glaringly necessary for the government to get control of the situation — and to do so without risk of bloodshed.

From that meeting a new plan was formed. Its execution by Chris Normoyle, the Police Commissioner, using his radio network and with the full co-operation of the airlines was brilliantly done in complete secrecy. Overnight, four hundred police, collected by charter planes from all over PNG, were flown in and were in place at Hahalis by daylight on the 22nd. With them was a fully equipped medical team of a doctor, a nurse and a laboratory assistant. The laboratory assistant was Albert Maori Kiki, now Sir Maori. They were in such force, and it was such a surprise, that it caused the Hahalis people to stop and think.

Later that day John Teosin and two hundred of his followers, including fifty women and children, voluntarily came to the police camp. The women and children were sent back to the villages and the men were placed under arrest. The police were able then to move quietly through the villages and arrest four hundred and seventeen defaulters, with some others on other charges; and a total of four hundred and sixty-one people appeared in Court, to face six hundred and thirty-five charges. However, the result of the way the Court was handled is another story.

There was a lot of public speculation and publicity over 'The Hahalis Affair', especially about the 'baby garden', but it was not unfavourable to the government. Paul Hasluck, more as a matter of interest, asked Don why he had done such a dramatic thing as move so many police overnight. When Don gave the story and his reasons, Hasluck said that in any political repercussions he would back him to the hilt, and once again Don appreciated his trust.

Chapter 16

Jimi Valley tribesmen celebrate opening of airstrip they had built at Kagamuga.

School Children to Australian Schools—Josephine Abaijah—
L.G. Councillor Momei Pangiel—Jimi Valley—Thomas
Kavali—Koroba - Andirabi—First Doctors from Fiji Medical
School—John Guise—Maoir and Elizabeth Kiki—Ted Diro

Over the years, visiting schools, colleges and other training institutions, seeing the bright young faces and talking to students of all sorts from all tribal groups, Don and I often used to wonder which of these young people would be the leaders of the future and the outstanding and creative people to leave their mark on their country.

Now I can look back, in this chapter, to a series of incidents I remember where one or other of the participants is now a well-known person and a leader.

In January of the mid-fifties, someone in the Department of Education rang to say that the first group of Grade VI children had been selected to go to secondary schools in Australia, and would I like to see them? They came up to have cakes and lolly water (lemonade) with me and I found them a delightful group of young teenagers. They were all going to good schools and would be fitted with their uniforms when they arrived.

I had a sudden vision of these nice kids being accepted and made a big fuss of in Australia and then of coming back for the holidays. What would happen then? They could be treated with polite condescension or some rough Australian would insult them. I could see them coming down the gangway in a college uniform, when an Aussie, supervising the labourers unloading the luggage, could mutter "Black bastard", jealous that they had privileges that he had never known. It was sure to happen somewhere, some time. How could I help them? To make them aware and arm them.

So I brought up the subject, which they then talked about, before I spoke again myself:

"We have a saying, 'as miserable as a wet hen'. Well, what happens when a hen gets wet?"

We were all laughing, as everyone could picture what it looked like.

"We have another saying," I went on: " 'she took no notice. It was just like water falling off a duck's back'."

And we all talked about why water rolled off a duck's back; and all had seen that. Then I said:

"Some Australians are kind and some will be rude. Now when the rude one comes along, which are you going to be — like a hen or a duck?"

By this time they were all relaxed and laughing and talking.

"What's the best thing to help you be like a duck when someone is rude?" I asked, and helped and suggested they think of an Australian who had helped them sometime and set that memory against the rude Australian. I don't know whether it did help anyone, but I was much aware of this problem and used the two sayings many times over the years.

One thing was very striking about that first group — four of the six girls had been Girl Guides. Since they had been selected for poise, confidence and the ability to adapt, as well as on their academic capacity, I felt the significance, and this encouraged me in persevering with the sound establishment of Girl Guiding.

One girl came from Misima Island, where in 1952 an outstanding headmaster had impressed us with the quality of his school, while the Methodist mission ran a splendid Guide company. Her name was Josephine Abaijah. She trained as a nurse, later doing courses in tropical health, first in the Philippines, then at London University; now she is a member of parliament and leader of the Papua Besena secession movement. Another was Wassi Basinauro, now married to Evertius Romney, the former High Commissioner for Fiji, and herself a highly trained laboratory technician who has done an advanced course at London University.

After this, most groups of students came up to see me before going to Australia for the first time. Other departments would ring me, too, and I saw many groups of adults either going down or returning. I remember a good-looking man, in a group of local government councillors, who wore his dark suit with ease and grace. Speaking good pidgin, he made most acute observations, so I asked where he came from. When he said Mendi, I could hardly believe it, as it was barely ten years since the first patrol post had been opened there. His name was Momei Pangial. In the first elected House of Assembly he became a member, and we got to know him well. On our farewell visit to Mendi in late 1966, walking among lines of magnificently attired dancers, one gave a brilliant smile and, saying, "Hullo, Sir Donald," shook Don's hand. We both peered at his face, painted in intricate patterns. It was Momei. He came to the reception that night, very much a well-dressed man of the world, speaking quite good English and bringing a shy and very nice wife.

☆　　☆　　☆

In the early fifties the Jimi Valley was a problem. Lying parallel to and north of the Wahgi, it was steep, wild and inaccessible. Roads and airstrips seemed impossible; yet somehow the people had to be contacted more easily. An experienced old police sergeant took a patrol in and returned, saying he'd found a hillside which wasn't too steep to dig a shelf long enough and wide enough to get a plane in. A patrol officer set up a patrol post there, with a small hospital and a school. The people had already walked over the range and seen the Wahgi strips at Banz and Kerowagi, so they quickly decided they would have a strip themselves, and organised a succession of groups to come in and do the work.

After a check by the Department of Civil Aviation, Don and I were now to come in on the first charter plane and open the strip. We flew along this wild, forested, gorge-like valley, and ahead was a tiny red-brown scar on the mountain. We approached the strip with a 2,000ft drop beneath us to the floor of the valley, while along its length the drop from the edge ranged from 2,000 to about 200ft, the other side and far end cutting into the mountain and making a 50ft cliff. Qantas flew us, and we held our breath as we landed. Bobby Gibbs, with some more visitors, came after.

A welcoming party of a beaming patrol officer, a squad of police and village leaders were there to meet us with welcoming speeches and a dramatic account and demonstration of how they had made it — the usual mat between poles for the men to carry soil from the cliff face to the gorge side of the strip. Everyone assembled, while Don made his congratulatory speech, trying also to inspire them to go on and use the strip to develop their area. The school children sang and several magnificent dancing groups were advancing and retreating up and down the strip with such zest that I asked the interpreter for the words. They were:

"We are the men who built this strip. We are the men who built this strip. Qantas has been in, Bobby Gibbs has been in. We are the men who built this strip."

A zigzag path led up another 500 feet to the patrol post, so out of consideration for Don and me a line of women could now be seen threading their way down, carrying the morning tea on their heads, to set it all up on a table. Don talked with the leaders and I with the school children, and through them to the women. It was a lovely and exciting morning.

Not so many years later, but after Don's retirement, we were talking to some new members of the House of Assembly. One was the member for Jimi Open Electorate. We spoke of that morning and he told me that he was one of the schoolboys I had talked with. His name was Thomas Kavali and we had a grand old gossip about 'old times'. In the next House he became Minister for Lands, and we got to know him well.

☆　☆　☆

In 1963, on a visit to the Southern Highlands with the D.C., David Marsh, we went into Koroba, a station recently set up in a valley discovered only nine years earlier by a patrol led by Des Clancy, in 1954. The idea of discovering a large new valley with a large new population in the 1950's caught the imagination of the media and the patrol received world-wide publicity as a Shangri La valley.

We came down on a still unfinished strip, then walked half a mile to a pretty, rather scattered station, proudly sporting the first timber building in the A.D.O.'s house, the rest being pit-pit and thatch. We were taken to the new L.G.C. building of pit-pit and iron roof, where the newly elected councillors most expertly served us morning tea. Most were the usual run of councillors, in shirts and lap-laps, but the president, very young, very poised, was wearing shoes and socks, well-cut shorts and shirt, and spoke excellent pidgin. He was good-looking, with well-shaped head and regular features, and I was fascinated.

I asked if he had seen Clancy's patrol, and he said that he and his father had followed it for three days when he was a young boy. Had they talked to Clancy? No, they were much too frightened and kept hidden. Where did he get such good clothes? From Wewak. Had he been to Wewak? No, the mission sent for them. Had he been to Moresby? No, but he'd been to Hagen — very proudly — the big metropolis. (Hagen then boasted about sixty families.) Had he been to school? No, but he could read and write a little.

He so caught my interest that I asked the A.D.O. about him. When they sent a patrol in and later opened the station he had been the teenager who was always around — taking everything in, jumping in to help, earning bits of money and really clued up. At lunch he was a guest at the A.D.O.'s house, so I sat next to him to find out more. He couldn't be any more than twenty two or three, but he had a real vision of what he wanted to do for his people. So Don arranged that he and some of his councillors should visit Moresby and be shown around. I never forgot him and recognised his name in the list of candidates for the 1968 House of Assembly — Andagari Wabiria. He got in as a United Party candidate and, in the last self-government, sitting before was a Ministerial Member for Forests. By this time he spoke good English and was a sober and painstaking man.

☆　☆　☆

Early in the 1950's the Department of Health rang to say that the first four graduates from Suva had just returned. Would I like to see them? Four very nice and rather shy young men came up for afternoon tea. They were Reuben Taureka, Wilfred Moi, Frank Aisi and Tom Gaunedi.

We got to know all of them over the years, as we saw them on different out-stations, slowly climbing up the administration ladder, especially Reuben and his Fijian wife, Agnes. For wherever they were posted, Agnes started a Girl Guide Company and worked among the women, which brought me in close touch with her, and she made a significant contribution in many parts of the country. Eventually Reuben rose to be District Medical Officer at Mendi, Madang and Wewak, and while at Wewak Don appointed him to the Legislative Council, where he got his taste for politics. The first medical officer to rise to a senior administrative post in the Health Department headquarters, he then stood in 1972 as a Pangu candidate for Hula, his home area. When self-government came in 1973 Reuben Taureka became the first Papua New Guinea Minister for Health. Wilfred Moi specialised in mental health and is head of that section in the Health Department. Frank Aisi married Hani from Hanuabada, one of the first welfare workers. Posted to Balimo when Robert was there, their children, being the same age, became inseparable playmates. Frank died tragically in Kieta a few years ago and Tom was lost in the plane which disappeared in Milne Bay in 1978.

One day in the early fifties we flew into Kokoda, only 1,100 feet above sea level and right at the foot of the highest mountain in Papua, Mt Victoria. The rubber plantations of the two Kienzle brothers were close by the government station, then mainly an open grassy space used as parade ground cum football field, with a building on each of its four sides. The largest was the A.D.O.'s house, made almost entirely of native materials. Raised 10 feet from the ground with whole tree trunk posts, it had a wide verandah, breezeway living room with bedrooms opening each side, and a very steeply pitched roof with sago

John Guise leading the P.N.G. contingent to the Coronation 1953, at Fulham Palace, the home if William Wand, Bishop of London, who, when archbishop of Brisbane, had consecrated the Cathedral at Dogura.

thatch a foot thick. But instead of the bouncy limbom (the midrib of the sago leaf) floor, it had pit-sawn timber — a great comfort. It was a really beautiful house from every aspect, and built by Allan Champion.

The usual police quarters were on another side of the grassy space, the hospital at the end and the district office and clerk's house on the side nearest the Yeomans'. All were of sago-plaited walls and thatch roof — a typical government station of those days.

But the thing which fascinated me was what was going on under the house. Mrs Yeomans had been a teacher. She had gathered up all the station children and some from the nearby village and started a school. The Kienzle brothers and their wives had helped the Yeomans buy materials and books and they had scrounged what they could. The station carpenter had made long desks and forms and a blackboard. It was a lovely school. Mrs Yeomans had recruited Mrs Mary Kekedo, the wife of the district clerk, and was training her to teach. At that stage it was a purely voluntary effort, greatly helped by the Kienzle family and had no government assistance at all.

Mary Kekedo had been born on Yule Island, granddaughter of a Philippine lay missionary, and was one of the Natera family. She was educated at the school there before the war. Walter Kekedo was from Milne Bay and during the war had run the Angau radio station at Daru. In 1946, with the return of civil administration and the need to rehabilitate the war-devastated areas, he walked over the Kokoda Trail and set up a patrol post. Mary joined him from Popondetta when roads and tracks were made, two years later. By this time Walter had patrolled all the villages and got to know the people well. When we met him he had the reputation of being a walking encyclopaedia on his district and able to produce any file instantly. Such men, working as district clerks throughout the country, were its backbone and, with the police sergeant and the district officer, were the team which made everything tick.

Next time we went to Kokoda there was a well-built native material school on the station, with Mrs Yeomans the headmistress and Mary Kekedo her assistant, with two government-trained teachers. It was now a government school.

By our third visit, Mary Kekedo was headmistress, and remained so till her retirement. In addition she ran women's clubs, a Guide company, did a lot of work in the villages and brought up a family as well. Rose, the eldest, is an outstanding person, with considerable experience as a teacher, and before the days of the university she won a three-year scholarship to an American university. She became the first Papua New Guinean Principal of the Teachers' Training College, is now Director of Teacher Training for PNG in the education headquarters and has held many other posts, such as President of the

Teachers' Federation and Acting Chairman of the University Council, in addition to making a notable contribution to women's sport. Roland went to school in Australia, was in one of the early groups of Papua New Guinean cadet patrol officers and rose to a senior government post, until he resigned recently and went onto the management side in a public company. Jean, the youngest, took a degree in Social Science at Adelaide University and is making a unique contribution to the rural improvement programme. She was in charge of the village development office, developing teams of what she calls catalyst workers. These are people, if possible from the same language groups, who will live and work in a village and help the people to uplift their own material conditions, especially in such simple things as water supply, and introducing simple technology for gardening and other activities.

☆　☆　☆

One day in August 1965 I was called to the phone and a young man said:

"I'm the president of the Territory Students Federation. We've got a problem. Could I bring some of my committee up to talk to you?"

Saying that I'd be delighted, we arranged for them to have afternoon tea the next day. Four exceptionally nice young men arrived. The leader introduced himself and his committee, none of whom I had met before. They were from the Teachers' Training College, the Administrative College and the Medical College. When tea was poured I said:

"Now, what's the problem?"

The leader explained that N.U.A.U.S. (National Union of Australian University Students) was organising a project along with T.S.F. for Australian and Papua New Guinean students to work together in projects in selected villages in Papua New Guinea. The N.U.A.U.S. had written to say, more or less, "We have raised £2000, but what are you chaps going to do?" Obviously thinking of their slender resources they said:

"Could you help us?"

I considered for a few minutes and made a rapid calculation.

"The first thing to do is for you all to decide on a sum of money that won't be either too large for you to raise or so small you'd be ashamed. When you've worked that out we could see how it could be raised. Talk about it among yourselves."

I then excused myself, ostensibly to make a phone call. When I came back they had come up with a sum of £300, which — interestingly enough — had been my own assessment.

I then said that I would help them in any way I could, by coming to their meetings etc., but they would have to do the work. We discussed various ideas on raising money and the most sensible and popular was a 'sing-sing' by the students, but to do it as a performance on a stage.

I had long wanted to see a group do this; and here they had the same idea. The next thing was where. In Port Moresby then, there was no large hall or arena with a grandstand. They could have fixed up lights at either the Teachers' or the Administrative College, but both were then right out in the bush, far off the beaten track and bus routes. The only suitable place seemed the lighted basketball court at Murray Barracks, and again four pairs of eyes looked at me.

"Now two of you will have to make an appointment with the Brigadier and ask his permission."

They looked appalled. I explained that, if they told the secretary who they were and asked in the right way, I was sure he would see them. But I said they must think out their case very clearly and work out just what they were going to ask him. We discussed all sorts of practical things and off they went, planning to meet again the next week.

In the meanwhile I saw the Brigadier at a party and told him that a group of young men were going to ask for an interview with him.

"Now you jolly well be nice to them," I added, but wouldn't give him any clues.

They got their interview, the Brigadier granted his permission and even arranged for a young officer to liaise with them. Things proceeded in an orderly and very organised way. I was most impressed for, of the many groups I had worked with, they were the first who did exactly what they said they would do and always came to a meeting at the time arranged. The army and their own institutions co-operated fully, the army even lending chairs and a movable platform. The ABC helped with a sound system and Burns Philp and Steamships gave hessian to close off the area. We had a full house, a magnificent display and collected nearly £500 door money.

Throughout I had been emphasising the responsibility we had and the care needed to prevent damage to property the army and others had lent us.

"Will you return everything on Saturday night or wait till Sunday?"
Sunday was the answer.

"All right, who will guard them?"
They decided that they themselves would all sleep there.

On the night itself, as people were filing out, I was standing in a lovely warm glow of success, when suddenly I became aware of that ugly undercurrent and growl which can come from a crowd when trouble is about to erupt. And to my horror I saw an army chair being swung in the air. With visions of army chairs and heads being smashed I leaped to the loudspeaker. Not for nothing had I taught in a boys' boarding school!

"Everybody stand still," I said, in a controlled, slow, rather low voice, repeating *"stand still,"* and injecting as much personality as I possibly could. "Nobody move".

Eventually there was a queer, deathly quiet.

"Everybody take your hands off any chairs and put them in your pockets. Now please go out quietly. — Go quietly," I went on saying, till they were all safely outside. It was a narrow squeak.

When I had rushed to the mike, one of the committee had dashed up too, and stood with legs astride and arms outstretched, facing the crowd and protecting me. When it was over and the opening in the hessian closed, the committee all rushed over and we weakly sat down and then began to laugh.

Now the interesting thing is this. The chairman, who had rung me, was Ebia Olewale, who topped his year and was one of the first four secondary school teachers. He later went into politics, has been Minister for Education, Minister for Justice and is now Foreign Minister. The student who protected me was Michael Somare. He had been a teacher, then went into radio and had gained a scholarship to the Administrative College, where his passion for politics was canalised at the time of the pay decision. Later he and others from the college founded the Pangu Pati. He was its first leader in the House and his drive led the country to independence, when he became the first Prime Minister. The secretary, Joe Nombri, who had been a patrol officer, was then doing an advanced course at the Administrative College and became an outstanding D.C. He is now on the Public Service Commission. The treasurer was Hans Danomera, then a medical student, and is now a senior doctor at the Moresby General Hospital.

The year before I got to know them, Ebia and his friends had thought that all the tertiary institutions in Papua New Guinea should join together into an association. They talked about it a lot and later on Ebia, who had asked for and obtained an appointment with Don, had told him what they had in mind and asked his help to visit other institutions. Don had given him a travel warrant to visit the Catholic Seminary at Madang, the Forestry College at Bulolo and the Popondetta Agricultural College. The result was the formation of the T.S.F. with Ebia as president, Joe Nombri of the Administrative College as secretary and Hans Damonera of the Medical College as treasurer.

Warrants were also given to John Momis and Leo Hannet, from the seminary, and other representatives from Bulolo and Popondetta, to come to Moresby for a meeting to form the federation. John Momis became a priest, then involved himself in Bougainville politics and became a member of parliament and a Minister. Leo Hannet graduated from the university and won a postgraduate scholarship to the university of Hawaii, and was always a charismatic political leader.

Soon after we moved to Government House, a five-pound note I had popped under the inkstand disappeared from my writing-table. Having taken a stand against petty thieving (such as food from the pantry), feeling that I must have complete trust in the people around me and beginning to make my point, I was concerned that staff all denied seeing it. I felt I must establish myself as a person who meant what I said, so sent for the police.

Later in the day I heard a pleasant English voice and looked out to see who it was. The only one in sight was a police sergeant, questioning the gardeners. He was wearing the khaki uniform of police officers, then entirely expatriate. The voice went on and I looked out again and saw that it came from the Papuan sergeant and noted that he had a distinguished face. I was most intrigued, so later made enquiries.

His name was John Guise and he was in charge of the Konedobu Police Station, in the valley below the house, where all the departments of the administration were clustered. He was a man in his late thirties, obviously way ahead of any other Papuan I'd met, and had been educated at the Anglican Mission. Many of the Kwato-trained men also spoke good English, a striking exception at that time. The Kwato men were all courteous, thoughtful and rather gentle, people but none had the vibrancy and strong personality that radiated from this man, who had, I learned later, grown up in Wedau Village, close to the Anglican Cathedral at Dogura, responsibility for bringing up his father, son of a well-born Frenchman, having been assumed by the Anglican mission.

The next year John Guise was the sergeant major of the contingent of police who took part in the Queen's coronation in London and it was then that I met him for the first time. When they returned from London I invited him up to morning tea so that I could hear from him all about it. From then on a firm friendship developed. He often came up around ten o'clock on his days off duty, when he knew a cup of tea would be on, and we discussed everything under the sun. He was a highly intelligent man, whose sense of humour enlivened his talk, so we had many laughs about things.

One memory I treasure is his description of the Anglican Synod which he attended in 1955, with Bishop Strong and the Bishop's personal assistant, Laurence Modedula, now a priest. These men represented their diocese. It was the Synod where they had to decide on a separate constitution for Australia, as apart from the English Anglican church. On his return John came up one morning especially to tell me about it. They had been arguing this constitution for years and people felt strongly about it. But this Synod was 'it' and they had to decide. But the heat in the arguments really shocked John, so after a time he caught the Chairman's eye to speak and had to go to the rostrum. His eyes sparkling as he talked, and with a lovely impish grin, he said:

"The Bishop didn't know what I was going to say, and as I squeezed past him he tugged my coat to make me sit down, but I didn't take any notice."

"And what did you say, John?" I asked.

"Gentlemen, when discussing this constitution, couldn't we remember that after all we are all Anglicans and all Christians?"

"And what happened after that?" I prompted.

"There was dead silence for a minute, and then everybody clapped and I went back to my seat."

I was delighted, picturing hundreds of earnest white clergy and laity being reminded of this fundamental by a brown Anglican. Apparently it had its effect, from what I could gather.

Long before this, John had asked if he could bring his family up to wish us Happy Christmas, and came at five on Christmas Eve. This was the first time I met Anuba, his wife, a comely Hula woman from Lalaura Village on Cape Rodney, with the high cheekbones and particular kind of smooth beauty and set of the eyes that you see in pictures of some of the Andean people and north Canadian Indians. It is quite striking. They had a young family of beautiful children and this Christmas visit continued while they lived at Konedobu. Anuba is a woman of character and great dignity. Last time I travelled to New Guinea from Australia I looked up into the face of a trim and attractive air hostess. It was Anuba's face as I remembered it then, so involuntarily asked if she were any relation of Anuba Guise.

"Yes, she's my mother," came the reply.

John transferred from the police force to the Department of Native Affairs, as it then was, and worked as a patrol officer based at the Port Moresby district office, working in the villages of the Port Moresby area. He was particularly good at hearing disputes and finding mutually agreeable settlements, and in investigating that perennial problem, land matters. Now that they were living at Hohola I saw less of him, and missed the great interest of his talk and his point of view.

I was also anxious about him, as he had more brains and ability than many of his superior officers; and, knowing by then the Guise pride, I also knew that he wouldn't have an easy time and that sparks would probably fly. They did, too, on occasion. One night at a party I was sitting between two men in D.N.A., one I think a Land Commissioner. One leaned across me and asked the other:

"Did you see that report on such-and-such village by John Guise?"

"Yes," said the other. "It's quite brilliant."

I purred with pleasure, because about that time and later I had many arguments about him. Most people couldn't believe that he was as able and clever as he was, and they weren't geared to accept the fact and give him due recognition as their equal.

I think his experiences around this time caused him to develop, as a sort of protective mechanism, what has become a characteristic — the art of sitting on the fence. This was a pity. Although it has served him well in some aspects of political life, it has also brought him a burden: his own people have a certain fear of trusting him.

In 1960, when the old Executive Council was abolished and the Administrator's Council formed, John Guise was one of the three Papua New Guinean members. This gave Don an official assocation with him, as well as the long personal one. I often wondered how he felt about things as far as Don was concerned. As elected member for Milne Bay, John Guise was very much the politician, and it used to trouble Don considerably that John seldom entered discussion or expressed his view in Council, but would then very likely have quite a lot to say afterwards as a politician. This circumstance points up my earlier contention about the curious status of this body. Guise was always one to play his cards close to his chest and maybe he felt that to keep quiet in Council gave him more freedom outside. At any rate his attitude to both of us became ambivalent — again a probable political necessity.

He continued as elected member for Milne Bay through all the changes in the Legislature, was a man of great influence and one to be reckoned with, but was too much of a loner to be a trusted party leader. Over the self-government period, he was elected Speaker and brought real distinction to that office, where his gifts came into full play. At Independence, he became the first Governor General, and took up residence where we had lived for so long.

☆   ☆   ☆

In the 1950's Dosi, the cook, periodically asked time off for a meeting at 7 p.m. on a Saturday. As long as he organised someone else to do the dinner I let him go. After about the third time I became curious and asked him what it was all about. He told me that the older Milne Bay people were worried about so many young ones coming to Moresby without anywhere to live, and were raising money for a building where they could stay. I was immediately interested and kept in touch with their efforts. All our staff, among other Milne Bay people, gave regular contributions from their pay, so I backed it with a contribution myself, always admiring people who get up and do something for themselves.

After some months I asked Dosi if he would like to ask the committee to come up one Sunday afternoon for me to meet them, and we fixed a day. After a busy Sunday morning gardening, I was just coming to after an afternoon nap, when the steward on duty called me, saying the men were here. At first blank, I suddenly realised this was Dosi's day; so, telling him to bring them in and to do something special for tea, I flew off to change, as he told me they'd already cut sandwiches and got everything ready. I emerged to meet six men from various parts of Milne Bay, Dosi in his best clothes among them. I was really impressed at all they were telling of the problems, and by their constructive thinking. They had already applied for a block of land at Badili and were going to build little by little, as they got the money. I told them that people were always willing to help those who helped themselves, and that I was sure that men in the Department of Works would help with advice or even do plans and give practical help. I was particularly impressed with the chairman, Lepani Watson, from the Trobriand Islands, a leader in every way.

Time went on, they collected enough money, got substantial help from the men whom I had suggested; and, when ready to start building, were delighted that the Methodist mission in the Trobriands offered to send in a carpenter. Unfortunately they sent not only a carpenter but with him a missionary to take charge. This had not been a part of their calculations at all, and from then on they came to me with their troubles. This silly young man just assumed that it was a mission activity and took over, quite ignoring the fact that the group had originated the idea, worked for two years raising the money, got help with plans and had managed admirably on their own. I'm afraid I counselled them to stand up for their rights and exercise their authority, but it was indeed hard for them.

The building was finished all right, but the missionary remained to run it, so from then on the project waned. It was never used as they had visualised and became neither one thing nor the other. But through this activity and work for the welfare of his people Lepani Watson was recruited as a government welfare officer. Later, winning a seat in the House of Assembly, he became one of the early national leaders and a member of the first University Council. His wife was an outstanding woman, who fully supported him, and we got to know them both very well. Their eldest son, Charles Lepani, became a near neighbour of mine after independence. He is a fine-looking man of considerable ability and great charm. One of the early university graduates, he is head of the Policy and Planning office and is held in high esteem. His sister Julie, the little girl in a grass skirt at the Duke of Edinburgh's visit, is now in a senior position in the government, after attending university.

☆　☆　☆

I first met Maori Kiki through Dr and Mrs Price. Maori was the first laboratory technician trained at the Suva Medical School, and worked at the hospital with Dr Price, the chief pathologist. Through my early association with Mrs Price and her Girl Guides, I got to know many village people and the new young folk coming up, and she often talked of the Kikis. I had known Elizabeth as one of the girls training as infant welfare and maternity nurses with Sister Camillus at the little Badili Hospital, where all the Government House babies were born, so was interested in her marriage to Maori. But my admiration was caught when the two of them founded the Kerema Welfare Association, working and helping their own people. Friendship developed and one or other or both would come up to talk of this or that, and as leaders they were often guests at receptions. Don also thought very highly of Maori and respected his integrity and quiet strength.

1960 was a turning point in their lives. As laboratory assistant with the medical team accompanying the police contingent sent to Hahalis, Maori had long talks with the leaders, John Teosin and Francis Hagai. He felt, not only that he understood what they were striving for, but that he could help them to achieve their aims by more practical means and without the cultist overtones. He came back very thoughtful from this experience. After he and Elizabeth had talked it over, he approached Keith McCarthy, Director of Native Affairs, with the proposition of becoming a welfare officer in his department to work at Hutjena, the new government station near Hahalis on Little Buka.

About this time they both came and talked it over with me. I was fascinated by what they had to say and moved by their idealism. But this very idealism made me fearful for them, knowing how difficult and disappointing it can be, actually working on the ground with people. Such unexpected problems can arise, and they would have the older entrenched government men with, one set of idiosyncracies to cope with and the Hahalis people with another. However, Keith McCarthy embraced his idea and off they set, with their three children and another on the way.

They remained a year and came back subtly changed and more reticent, having experienced not only successes and failures, giving them a deeper knowledge of their own abilities, but the seeringly painful experience of public social rejection by the Sohano Club.

Maori went on working as a welfare officer attached to the Moresby district office, until he won a scholarship to the Administrative College. They lived in a duplex house at Hohola; the other half being an Infant Welfare Clinic, which Elizabeth managed to run, and look after her young family as well. She did wonderful work, helping the lonely and bewildered mothers and wives from so many different areas to face the problems and culture shock of village women who must try to fit into an urban environment. In this she worked closely with Sister Fairhall, the welfare officer and a very wonderful woman, who had worked for many years with the L.M.S. Mission.

When it was decided that a Papua New Guinea couple were to accompany the Minister Paul Hasluck to the celebration of the Independence of Western Samoa, Don chose Elizabeth and Maori Kiki. They were the first Papua New Guineans to go overseas to represent their country for such an occasion. Albert Maori Kiki was also the first to write an autobiography, a book which has had a number of reprints. At the first election after the formation of the Pangu Pati, he stood and won the seat for the Gulf electorate, later standing for and winning a Moresby seat. He became a ministerial member and, on self government in 1972, a Minister. Before his defeat in 1977 (when his electorate, now in the National Capital, was divided), he had been a very successful Foreign Minister, the Deputy Prime Minister, and had been knighted. He is now an increasingly successful businessman and does more than anyone else to assist his own Kerema people in setting up their own businesses. But the government is indeed the poorer without him.

☆　　☆　　☆

Brigadier General Diro is the Commanding Officer of the Defence Force, recently integrated into a unified service of the three arms — army, navy and air force — and working out very well. Once, when he was either Captain or Major, I was talking with him, shortly after his return from a six-month staff course at Duntroon, with men from the Pacific and south-east Asia. I asked him how he found a number of different nationalities mixed together — did they become integrated as one group?

"Yes, we integrated pretty well," replied Ted. "We definitely felt closer to other Pacific Islanders, the Malays next and then the Thais. But oh, the Indians! They argued about everything and when you boiled it down it was mostly pure semantics."

Having myself found Indians very argumentative people, I enjoyed his comment.

The year we came to Papua New Guinea, Ted, then a little boy of ten, left his village in the Owen Stanley Ranges behind Rigo and, with his parents' blessing, walked the eighty miles to Moresby in search of education. He knew no English, but presented himself to each of the few schools; but was always refused entry. He slept in the bush on Three Mile Hill, scrounged food where he could, caddied for the golfers nearby to earn a little money, and kept on presenting himself to a little school in an old, rusting, army Qanset hut at Kila Kila, run by a wonderful woman named Mrs Willis.

The little boy's persistence and his rapid acquisition of English touched her heart, and she admitted him. He was so bright, that she gave him extra coaching and he did the six-year primary course in four years, still maintaining himself by caddying, but by now living with a Rigo family. He did so well in Grade 6 that he won a scholarship to Sogeri High School and then another to Warwick School in Queensland, to do his leaving certificate; gaining that, he was one of the first four to be selected for Portsea, the army officers' training school in Victoria.

He is now a good-looking, highly intelligent man, a first-class soldier, whose troops think the world of him. His wife, Tamo, is also an outstanding person. When a welfare officer, she won a scholarship to the Home Economics Course in Suva, has made a great contribution to her country and is still doing so, both in a voluntary and a professional capacity. They have six children and she is a charming chatelaine of Flagstaff House. Ted, incidentally, is a keen, low-handicap golfer.

Chapter 17

Protest march by students against new wage scales slashing Papua New Guinean salaries.

Auxiliary Division Public Service—Future for P.N.G. Civil Servants—Discussion and Planning 1961—Amended Ordinance Passed 1963—Hasluck Goes to Dept Defence—Appreciation of his Work—New Minister Mr Barnes—New Dept Secretary and New P.S.C.—Change of Direction—Two Salary Scales Decided with Locals a Quarter Expatriate Rate—Protests and Unrest: Deputations—Arbitration Tribunal Set Up—Social Problems and Council for Social Service

Originally the Public Service of Papua New Guinea was an expatriate one. Local people were employed in the government only as "Administration Servants", But in 1956 a new ordinance made provision for an Auxiliary or Fourth Division, enabling local people to enter it at a lower standard of education. At the same time the Public Service Institute was founded, to offer part-time courses to Administration Servants, qualifying them first for the Fourth or Auxiliary Division and later, by gaining the Queensland Leaving Certificate, to enter the Third Division of the Service in the usual way.

Planning concentrated on training only. This developed steadily and soundly under David Chenoweth, who gradually lifted the Public Service Institute standards, until in 1963 a proper Administrative College was opened to its first full-time mature-age students, with himself as Principal. In the late fifties thinking began to lean toward the idea that the 1956 Ordinance should have begun a steady process of planned steps in organisation and salaries as well as in training, thus taking the Service towards what would ultimately become a Papua New Guinean one.

As early as 1959 and 1960, all the implications of salaries were worrying questions to many in the Administration, but when the Minister's intentions were sought he was adamant that there should be no differentiation. He had always stated that equal qualifications and the ability to do the same job as Australians should command the same salary. This, of course, was a great incentive. People worked hard with such high expectations, and gradually many more local people were able to draw salaries based on Australian living standards.

The service was also growing rapidly, with increasing numbers of both races. The rising pay scales in Australia, reflected in Papua New Guinea, signalled dangers ahead unless the Minister re-examined his policy. It was widely felt that the pay problem should be worked out, giving enough incentive and a high enough standard of living to local people, without saddling their country, in its future independence, with an impossibly high salary burden to carry.

Don was both worried and exasperated by the Minister's reluctance to discuss this issue. It was obvious that any change would be unpalatable. The longer it was left, the more people there would be coming up in the service and the less acceptable they would find it. However, the growing concern did lead to informal discussions with the Public Service Association, both in Moresby and in Canberra.

The President of the P.S.A. in Moresby was Peter Lalor. He had the reputation of being a radical, but Don and I both found him a most reasonable person, able to look at a problem pragmatically and seek a workable solution. He also had the true Irishman's concern for the underdog and those in trouble, and an endless stream of Papua New Guineans went to his house for help and advice, which he freely gave. At the same time he saw people as they really were and was never fooled by the meretricious or those on the make.

Informal discussions were based on current thought on re-organising the service and the alternatives which seemed to offer. These were:

1. One stream in the service and one salary, geared to the local economic conditions and paid from the P.N.G. budget; Australians to receive an allowance bringing their pay up to the Australian salary rate. The allowance could be paid either by Australia direct, or through the annual grant as part of the P.N.G. budget.
2. Two streams: a Papua New Guinean Public Service on their own salary scale, paid from that part of the budget raised from local sources, supplemented by an Australian auxiliary paid by Australia; or alternatively, Australians to become Commonwealth Public Servants, seconded to a Papua New Guinean Auxiliary.

3. One stream, but with two salary scales, according to whether the job was held by a local or an expatriate person.

The last alternative was not generally favoured. Don himself liked the first, which he thought held the best prospect for a smooth transition into the future, because Australian allowances, being paid by Australia, would be her concern only.

Discussion dragged on and Don became increasingly aware of its urgency, with time itself bringing new developments to complicate the introduction of change. For instance, he felt growing anxiety that nothing was coming forward while the Government still controlled the Legislative Council and could pass unpopular legislation — a fact he would ram home to visiting Canberra men.

In 1962 the Minister agreed at last for planning to begin, issuing instructions for a full scale "Reconstruction of the public service to make full and proper provision for the inclusion of indigenous members".

Discussions continued in Moresby and Canberra, with the Public Service Association taking a vigorous and increasingly sceptical part, because a new voice could be heard in their councils; that of John Greville Smith, another lawyer. While Peter Lalor was a man of liberal humanity, Greville Smith was an abrasive character, whose attitudes were that of aggressive trade unionism. New to the service, he began counselling against the first proposal (for one service with one salary, geared to local members, and with allowances for expatriates). He persuaded the almost exclusively European Association that it would be against their interest. Peter, with his long involvement in the country, looked for a solution equally fair to both races; but Greville Smith did not then have this viewpoint.

Eventually two firm proposals were formulated by Mr. Thomson, the Public Service Commissioner. The first was:

> An integrated service, in which indigenous and expatriate officers should be fellow members of the same service, with expatriates receiving additional emoluments in the form of expatriate allowances.

The Commissioner commented that "this proposal has the great merit of avoiding what might seem to be a racial division of the public service. It also clearly expressed the government's intention to work as one with the indigenous people, whereas any other scheme might give the impression that a separate expatriate service was being prepared, with the ultimate aim in mind of withdrawal."

The second proposal was:

> A main service, organised for local conditions and local rates of pay and the creation of an auxiliary division, which would be staffed wholly by expatriate officers.

The Minister then invited the association to examine them and indicate their preference. Though he was always firm in his own views and had no hesitation if he felt it necessary to reject the advice of those in Papua New Guinea responsible for carrying out policy, the Minister was strangely vulnerable to group pressures of a body such as the Public Service Association. All through 1963 discussion, both within the Association and with those in Canberra, dragged on without decision, and it became apparent that the chance had already gone for agreement on the solution Don and others had hoped for, namely the single service with the same basic pay for both races and for Australian salaries to be made up by expatriate allowances.

Drafting a bill finally went ahead, in time to be presented at the end of the September sitting of the enlarged Legislative Council, with government members now in a minority. All concerned then had two months to study its provisions.

On 11th November, Mr. Reeve, the Assistant Administrator (Economic Affairs), moved the second reading in the last session of the 5th Legislative Council. In his speech Mr. Reeve said:

"I would discuss the form of reconstruction which this Bill envisages. Undoubtedly, the most important departure from the present arrangements is the provision for two separate parts of one public service. This device is concerned to provide the best solution to the rather awkward problem of establishing a local service with conditions geared to a local economy and at the same time retaining, for as long as may be required, the essential assistance of an expatriate service, which, for obvious reasons, must be related to a more developed economy. Consequently, it is proposed that there shall be a local (indigene) service; consisting of First, Second and Third Divisions, and an Expatriate Division of the service, which will have three subdivisions corresponding to the First, Second and Third Divisions of the existing service. I may say that the principle of a divided service, expressed as the main Territorial Public Service, organised on local conditions and rates of pay, and assisted by an Expatriate Division, commended itself to the Public Service Association, as stated by the Minister to the Congress of that Association in September last year."

During the debate it was clear that nobody liked the Bill. The Papua New Guineans were shocked that their people, who by 1963 formed a larger part of the service, were to have lower pay in a separate section, even when they had the same qualifications as Australians. The fourteen government men had to lobby hard to put across two ideas. First, that the high Australian wage structure would be a heavy economic burden when they were an independent country. Secondly, that the Bill dealt only with economic principle; the salary rates themselves would be worked out later by the Public Service Commissioner. Eventually they saw the reasoning and accepted it with reluctance. But they were determined to exercise their new strength of numbers to change the content of the Bill.

The opposition as a whole didn't like two separate streams, as embodied in Clause 20. Lloyd Hurrell, a coffee-planter (following many years in the administration as an A.D.O.), made it known that he would move an amendment. Further, he said that, unless the administration was prepared to accept the amendment, the opposition, under Standing Order 76(c), would move to defer the Bill for six months. By then the Bill itself would lapse, because the Fifth Council would have been prorogued, and the new fully elected House of Assembly would never pass it. They made it clear that, to get the Bill at all, the government would have to accept opposition changes.

Between September and November, Don's Office Diary had recorded conferences with a variety of people about the Bill, and these doubled after the second reading opened the debate.

The government was certainly in a cleft stick. The telephone to Canberra ran hot and, when they took the attitude that it was Don's job to get the Bill through as drafted, I chuckled to hear him say: "What, with fourteen votes to twenty-two?"

Knowing that the whole matter should have been brought forward years ago, he made it clear that, if you give people power, they will certainly use it. So there was nothing the Minister or the Department could do but accept Hurrell's amendment. Being a major clause, the draftsmen then had to rewrite the whole Bill. It was finally passed on November 15th 1963, and embodied one stream of public servants, but two salaries for each job, according to whether it was held by an expatriate or a Papua New Guinean. This was so blatantly racial that it spelt trouble ahead.

Here, too, was irony and a touch of the ludicrous. In spite of the care and anxiety of those concerned with the need to work out a wise and equitable arrangement, in spite of the years of talk and discussion between Minister, Department, the Public Service Association, the Administrator, the administration and the Public Service Commissioner, so many years of procrastination meant that, when it did come forward, the P.S.A. had less liberal leadership and the government was operating with a minority in the Legislative Council. The final outcome was the solution originally regarded as the worst of the options, so that it had not even been seriously considered in the first discussions four years earlier.

Writing about all this now seems strange and highlights the paternal nature of the relationship Australia then had with Papua New Guinea. All outside discussion had been with the expatriate P.S.A. and it did not seem to occur to anyone to consult groups of local people, who were really the ones most affected.

The Bill itself could not come into force until the Public Service Commissioner had prepared the regulations, planned the reorganisation of the service and decided on the ratio between the two rates of pay for each job. It was generally felt in the administration that this should be about two thirds for a senior post, a lower ratio at the middle level and lower again for the bottom rung. But, in the event, they were to be denied the opportunity of expressing their views. Since the next step lay with the Public Service Commissioner and the Minister, there was nothing further Don or anyone in the administration could do until the Commissioner was ready to discuss progress and raise points with them, according to the usual practice.

☆   ☆   ☆

At this crucial stage, another of those "accidents of history" occurred. This was the loss to Papua New Guinea of the three top people involved in the public service reorganisation — Hasluck, Lambert and Thomson. It set off a whole new stream of events, leading to another "cause celebre", which was a major turning-point in Papua New Guinean history.

After the Federal Election of December 1963, Paul Hasluck became Minister for Defence and left the Department of Territories. Don was really sorry to lose him as his minister. The problems of personality made day to day life difficult and played their own part in events, through their effect on people. But these were small compared to the immense contribution he made over the whole range of twelve years' work. Paul Hasluck truly fathered modern Papua New Guinea.

Don held his best qualities in great respect, really enjoyed working with a man with his breadth of mind and clarity of thought, and learnt to cope with the difficult side.

I do not think nearly enough credit has been given to him for his long-sightedness and the wisdom shown in most of the principles he laid down, nor for the tenacity of his annual battle in cabinet and parliament for more money, both for development and for building up the potential and quality of the administration. He early saw how inadequate the service was for the job. It is a pity that, as the years went on he didn't keep this in mind, instead of demanding and expecting too much. As he said himself, he measured everything against perfection; but, after all, by the very nature of a public service, once recruited, nobody can lightly be dismissed; therefore it has to carry a number of inadequate people.

The curious dichotomy of Hasluck's personality, showing humanity, a poetic appreciation of beauty and perceptive insights on the one hand, and on the other the compulsive drive to lash out at others in a hurtful way, cut him off from people. This was a vicious circle. The people who constantly experienced the abrasive side of his nature put up a barrier; and Paul in his turn was hurt by this barrier and felt that neither he himself, nor what he was trying to do, was understood. Therefore the feeling he gave of having a contempt for the expatriate residents was probably a sort of protective mechanism.

These difficulties blinded people to the magnitude and quality of what he achieved, and also seemed to blind Paul himself to the extent of his own achievements. Papua New Guineans experienced Paul's best side of compassion and understanding. When he left, none of them had advanced far enough in the administration to have personal experience of his irascibility. They have remembered him as a man who worked very hard for them and who always had their welfare at heart. They still think of him and say:

"Ah, he was a good man."

Not long after he relinquished his portfolio, he gave an address to an Adult Education School in Melbourne, and he quotes from it in his book. As I read it I was thrilled and inspired, and kept thinking: if only . . . If only he had addressed people in Papua New Guinea in this way from time to time, those working there would have been given a vision to follow. Many indeed held similar views, though often inarticulately. There was such tremendous enthusiasm in many places, ready to catch fire at this kind of vision and be inspired by the deeper understanding of what Hasluck was trying to do and why. But in all my years there I never heard of any public explanation of what he was aiming at or of how he saw the future. All they had was the goad and the atmosphere of a hard taskmaster pushing them, with a 'yours not to reason why' attitude. It was so deadening to their spirit, and so hard to bear. It is sad that a man who could express his vision with such inspiration did not use this method to give the service the feeling that they were working with him.

Looking back on the twelve years that he was Minister is to appreciate the enormous contribution Paul Hasluck made to the total development of Papua New Guinea. From being just a large area of land north of Australia, with its few coastal towns and all its installations completely shattered by war, nearly half the interior unexplored, inhabited by a diverse collection of mutually hostile tribes and governed by a small handful of Australians, Hasluck brought it to be a country with its towns rebuilt and expanding, its inhabitants vitally involved with their own development, with a growing feeling that they belonged to a country as well as to a tribe, and that they themselves were participating in handling their own affairs. To bring this about, a reasonably good public service had been created, with a growing number of trained local people, while sound foundations for self-government were laid down. These foundations were not only in the development of parliamentary institutions but in the background of the whole lives of the people, in education, social development, training, agriculture, business and industry.

During his years of strenuous endeavour he must often have been exasperated by the criticism which came from the United Nations, much of it unjustified. No other country has carried out its trust to the U.N. for a dependent people with such honesty of purpose soundness of principle, or achieved so much and in such a way as has Australia. All Australians can feel a sense of pride and thank Paul Hasluck for his hard work and drive, on the lonely road in Canberra and in Papua New Guinea itself. He has earned a unique place in history for his clear-sighted perception of principles, for the quality and scope of the mind he brought to bear on all the many problems and the good judgement he showed in most of the decisions he made. Above all else his achievement in Papua New Guinea is there for all to see. A description of the country and people as he found them early in 1951, compared with the country he left at the end of 1963, speaks of its magnitude. The country itself is his monument.

☆　　☆　　☆

On the 20th December, only three days after Papua New Guinea lost Paul Hasluck as Minister, Neil Thomson, the Public Service Commissioner, retired. I have spoken before with great appreciation of Mr Thomson's qualities. In spite of his unfortunate beginning as the chairman of the Section 10 investigation, he ended with the affection and respect of the service, and he always acted in close consultation with Don.

His successor was Mr George Somers, who came from the Department of the Army. Not only had he everything to learn about Papua New Guinea, but his background in a military set-up was more authoritarian than if his experience had been in a State or Commonwealth Service.

Mr Lambert's retirement as Secretary of the Department was also due at the end of 1963, and Hasluck had selected John Gunther to follow him as Secretary. His appointment would have ensured a smooth continuation of policy and have brought more understanding of Papua New Guinea into the department at Canberra. Unfortunately the papers of appointment came onto Hasluck's desk only in his last week of office, so confirmation was left to his successor.

The new Minister, C. E. Barnes, a Country Party man from Queensland, was an extremely nice man and a fine person. However, nothing in his previous experience had prepared him for handling so complicated a portfolio as the Department of Territories, combining, as it did, the whole range of government, not only in Papua New Guinea but in the Northern Territory and several islands as well. Mr Barnes sent for John Gunther to come to Canberra for an interview. As John recounted it, they simply did not have anything to say to each other, nor had he ever had such a feeling of no communication with another person. He came away realising the unlikelihood of the appointment's being confirmed.

Instead, Mr Barnes asked Eskie Lambert to remain three months longer while he looked around. He eventually chose Mr George Warwick Smith, who had been with the Department of Trade, and who took up office at the end of January 1964.

Mr Barnes was interested in the economic development of the Territory rather than its social and political advancement. So a new Secretary with economic experience was a logical step to take. The trouble was that neither man ever clearly grasped the constitutional relationships between the Minister, the Department of Territories in Canberra, and the Administrator and administration in Papua New Guinea, which Hasluck had clearly seen and respected.

As Minister, he had been the driver of the team, the head of the household, and everybody knew it. He held the reins firmly. No one in his time exceeded with impunity the authority given or implied by the offices they held. Hasluck had a close rapport with Prime Minister Menzies, was a member of the inner cabinet, and a formidable member at that, who prepared his proposals well, was listened to with respect and always battled hard.

C. E. Barnes was new to politics, and sat in the outer cabinet. He was given Territories as his first portfolio, and from the beginning had quite a different attitude to his departmental head, expecting him to take greater responsibility. Rather than give him directions, Barnes was ready to accept the Secretary's advice and be guided by him in Ministerial decision-making.

Warwick Smith, as Departmental Secretary, in addition to his previous economic experience, revelled in taking such responsibility and exercising authority. He showed a tendency also to take over responsibility for the Public Service Commissioner, instead of leaving it where it was, with the Minister, and he tried hard to do the same with the Administrator. The new Minister did not seem to realise that he himself was abdicating his own constitutional powers and privileges by allowing the secretary of his department to assume so much.

The course taken by this salary determination was also affected by the previous experience of the third man in the team. Mr Somers had never served on or in a Public Service Commission or Board as such, though he had done similar work for the Department of the Army. But then, dealing with people under army discipline, he was accustomed both to giving orders rather than discussing things in the civilian way, and to receiving and carrying out orders himself. Therefore his whole previous relationship was quite different from that to be found in either a State or the Commonwealth Public Service. It was reflected in Papua New Guinea.

Don made his usual efforts to build up a good working relationship; but, while Somers was not unco-operative, during the crucial time he had not perceived the wisdom or the need for working closely with the Administrator. The Bill placed the responsibility for salary determination with the Public Service Commissioner and the Minister, but George Somers accepted Warwick Smith as he had previously accepted his army departmental head, taking orders from him rather than observing direct responsibility to the Minister, according to the Act. In addition, an aura of secrecy once again surrounded a vital area, and both the Public Service Commissioner and the department went to extraordinary lengths to preserve it.

George Somers was a kindly man of solid character, cautious and painstaking, but rather unaware of the way people were thinking and feeling, or of the significance of political implications; and, though he was soon to have a severe lesson, he never really grasped their true importance.

During 1964, quite an atmosphere of uncertainty was hanging over the country. Three new top people at once is a lot to absorb. And of course the uncertainty of their future salaries worried all nationals, especially the top students and the older men studying hard at the recently founded Administrative College to upgrade their qualifications.

It was during the time of waiting that this group invited me to be guest speaker at their formal dinner, held monthly during the course. The names of my hosts reads like a Papua New Guinea 'Who's who' of the seventies. Some of them were — Maori Kiki (now Sir Maori), John Kaputin, Simon Kaumi, Gavera Rea, Francis Iramu, Sinaka Goava, Joseph Nombri, Jack Karakuru, Bill Warren, Lucas Waka; Sere Pitoi (now Sir Sere), who became the first national to be Public Service Commissioner, in 1971; Noel Levi, Secretary Defence Department; Jacob Lemeki, Minister for Labour; Basil Koe, Gerry Nalau, Bernard Baruk and Cedric Tabua, all D.C.'s. I made a rather provocative speech, mainly to draw out their political ideas. We had good discussion and a most enjoyable evening, but the feeling of insecurity and a slight distrust were there, giving them a sceptical attitude.

From time to time, Don would make enquiries from George Somers, who was always reticent. However, knowing that such a reorganisation was a long and complicated technical job, I don't think he was unduly worried. It is clear from his diary that the commission was also handling other major jobs with far too small a staff. In fact he noted that they requested some secondments from Canberra to help them cope. Therefore, whenever I asked Don what was happening, because from my activities I was well aware how much Papua New Guineans were worrying, Don would assure me these were reasons why it was taking so long.

Early in September, without any prior discussion with the Administrator, George Somers informed departmental heads that the relativity of the new pay scales was to be one quarter of the Australian rate. He asked them each in his own department to work out the new indigenous salaries, from the senior posts down.

Don was angry. After raising the matter at a Policy and Planning Committee, he asked Somers to call a meeting of departmental heads. However, Somers's attitude was very much 'that's the rate, it's not for you to question it', and he showed no interest in what the administration thought about it. Naturally they all reacted with amazed concern; for they all knew what sort of repercussions there would be. Don and John Gunther, both deeply troubled, tried hard in Moresby and Canberra to get some measure of change in the decision. Mr Somers was invited to the annual D.C.s' Conference to discuss the new plans. They too were shocked and protested strongly to him. They also passed a unanimous motion pleading for a reconsideration.

These efforts had no effect whatever. On September 8th, the Administrator was officially informed of the ministerial decision for one quarter of the Australian rate and that it would be publicly announced next day. Don and John Gunther immediately made strenuous pleas to Warwick Smith, as well as to Somers, to delay the announcement at least long enough to prepare the country for its acceptance; they hoped thereby to lessen the inevitable political repercussions. They had no reason to think their representations were not being considered.

Don was aghast, therefore, to hear the announcement over the ABC news on the night of Wednesday September 9th as scheduled. He was also upset that his advice was ignored, and by the lack of courtesy shown in not informing him beforehand. As I recall it, we looked at each other in a sort of stupefied unbelief. He was more worried than I ever remember, knowing that the shock of the announcement without any preparation would bring disastrous reactions from the people. After mulling it over for an hour or so, he wrote a long personal letter to the Minister, saying how far-reaching such a huge differential between the two wage scales would be, especially among doctors and others of top rank already earning Australian salaries, and outlining the sort of political repercussions we could expect.

What most broke his heart was the knowledge that the local people would feel tricked and betrayed, and the trust so carefully built up over the years would be destroyed. He referred to this in his letter, stressing the serious effect it would have on black-white relations, but saying that an immediate announcement of a possible modification could rescue some of the ground which would otherwise be lost. He ended with a strong plea, saying that Barnes would greatly gain in stature and respect as Minister if he would announce a possible reconsideration. He posted the letter next day and hoped it would have some effect. It was neither acknowledged nor ever referred to. Don often wondered if the Minister received it.

In the meantime he had, as usual, to cope with the consequences. Howls of horror went up everywhere. It was not only Papua New Guineans who reacted, but Australians who had spent most of their lives working with the people — in D.N.A. and administration departments, teachers, doctors, medical workers, agricultural extension people and others felt that they too had been betrayed. They felt that, at one stroke, their own country had made liars of them and invalidated all they had been trying to do. In the earlier months no heads of departments or anyone in the administration, from the Administrator down — not even men like the psychologist Dr Ord and other liberal minded people working in the Public Service Commission itself — had been able to find out what was being planned or were allowed to influence decisions. And this bit deep.

A fortnight later Bob Swift was staying with us. Bob had been on the Copra Marketing Board of Angau and had then joined the department in Canberra. By now he had risen to Assistant Secretary rank, after John Willoughby's sudden death, and from then on stayed with us quite frequently. He was an easy and very pleasant guest and he always appeared to me to have a sort of boyish eagerness that was rather endearing. But this night he showed another side.

The three of us were having coffee after dinner and I was opening my mail. One was a circular on the salaries, which had come to me as a member of the Council of Social Services, and I began to look through it. Seeing it there in black and white brought home to me even more focibly how unreal and incredible it was to take three quarters of their pay. I remember looking at the teachers' salaries and thinking of my teacher friends, now men in their thirties, most with large families and living in an urban situation where they had to shop where I shopped, pay the same prices for food as I did, let alone clothes for themselves and their children. There was no way such salaries could support them even at the lowest subsistence urban level.

Horrified, I broke into a ding-dong argument with Bob, trying to demonstrate not only all the other arguments which had already been made, but arguing on the purely economic one and using a specific person, then in quite a responsible teaching job. After giving food prices I remember saying the minimum he would have to pay for a pair of shorts, a shirt and a pair of shoes — Bob's reply was that in this climate he didn't need to wear all that. Why couldn't he just wear a lap-lap?

I don't think I will ever forget my revulsion and sheer unbelief that anyone who had been involved for twenty years in the development of a people could even think like that, let alone say it. I was temporarily silenced and Don was so angry that he went out of the room. But Bob looked as pleasant and benign as ever.

I have heard many times from many people about the scenes in the various training institutions when the students heard the ABC news on the night of 9th September, 1964. They all reacted the way Don and I had, as though they couldn't believe their ears; then very soon anger set in, with its various manifestations, according to the temperament of each person. Some stamped about and even threw things to let off their rage. Some just sat glumly, some made speeches; but all performed as really angry young men and women.

But that night, in training institutions all over Papua New Guinea, in towns and villages where government employees talked in stunned little groups, something was born in the minds and hearts of the people. This was the first stirring of political consciousness. It was born in anger. Anger over an indescribably inept and stupid decision by the three newcomers whom fate brought to those three key positions at that particular time.

☆　☆　☆

Though the wage decision struck the spark, the kindling had already been laid. The men and women coming up in the new society had some just grievances, many of them springing from the inability of too many administration officers and other Australians to change their attitudes and accept the emerging leaders as person to person.

It was sad to see men who had done a magnificent pioneering job in the opening-up stage, and who were still good and right in the bush villages, being unable to adapt to an up-and-coming, thinking elite. Where they should have encouraged, too many tended to suppress. None of us can stand being patronised, Australians least of all. Yet when our time came, instead of welcoming and accepting the new leaders and the thinking young men and women, too many of us tended to fear them and put them in their place. Too many were patronising.

Another development introduced in 1963, and part of this 'kindling', was the decision of the Australian Government to form a 'special branch' in the police force to take over from ASIO, which had operated very discreetly since early post-war years. Though ASIO was responsible to its Australian director, it kept the Administrator informed.

Don was uneasy about the new development in the police, especially as they had been recruited from outside, with no knowledge or love for PNG. Hitherto D.N.A. staff had their ears pretty well to the ground as part of their ordinary job of administration: that of conveying what the government thought to the people, and the people's feelings to the government. To reinforce this aspect he had issued instructions to all D.N.A. staff, outlining the kind of information he needed and why. But I expect that the formation of the Special Branch was part of the policy of curtailment of functions for the men in the district administration. Although one knows that a modern country must have a security service, such a service does seem to lose its sense of proportion.

Don, John Gunther and others had been trying to encourage the development of a political awareness and to give help and encouragement to such groups as Maori Kiki's Kerema Welfare Society, Lepani Watson's Methodist Welfare Society and others. And so had Paul Hasluck. Resulting from a discussion he had with Maori Kiki in 1960, the groups joined together and formed the New Guinea Workers' Association, and Don made the services of Peter Lalor available to help them draw up a case of their grievances. They regarded such groups as good and healthy developments, and were delighted to see the people organising themselves. But Special Branch was highly suspicious of them and were all set to suppress the activity. When John Gunther heard of this, he simply blew up, and Don hauled them off.

It must have been about this time that Don suggested one Sunday afternoon that I go down to Ela Beach, where Oala Oala Rarua was holding a big meeting.

"Why don't you go down? You'd enjoy it."

So I hopped in the car, drove myself down and sat on the grass with the people. And I did thoroughly enjoy it. I saw a lot of my friends and was really impressed with what Oala had to say and with the orderliness and the skill with which he conducted the meeting. So I came home most enthusiastic. Wily old Don was interested in what I had to say, but didn't make much comment till he got the Special Branch report. It was alarmist. But he had my account to balance it.

This sort of thing really annoyed people like Maori Kiki, Reuben Taureka, John Kaputin, Oala Oala Rarua, Samson To Pitiliu, Lepani Watson, Toua Kapena and others, who were well-balanced men trying to do something constructive for their people. The student groups, of whom Special Branch was very suspicious, were also indignant. So it, too, helped kindle the spark which led to political awareness and development. Like other happenings at this time, Special Branch activities had quite the opposite effect from that which its officers intended.

☆　☆　☆

But to return to the night of the 9th. The news of the salary scales hit the Teachers' Training College like a bomb, and the students all decided to march to Konedobu. As far as I know, this was the first protest march. Their leader, Ebia Olewale, rang the other Training Colleges — the Medical, the Administrative and the Posts and Telegraphs — to see if they would join forces. They each decided to

make a different official approach, but many of their members joined the march as individuals, and it was a long, hot nine miles.

Word had, of course, reached Konedobu, and Don's diary records:
'September 10th: conference with P.S.C. in regard to the student
teachers from the Teachers' Training College coming in to Port
Moresby to air their grievances.' I can imagine that Don would have
spoken in no uncertain terms, because the upshot was recently described
to me by Ebia Olewale.

Ebia said that Mr Somers received a representative group in the conference room of the Public Service Institute. John Gunther and Les
Johnson, the Director of Education, sat at the side but took no part,
and seemed sympathetic to the students. All who could squeezed inside and the rest sat on the ground outside. Ebia said that Mr Somers
listened to them first and then tried to explain the situation. The
students heard him out and asked questions, which he answered, but
from what Ebia said, his answers were rather feeble and they weren't
impressed.

I asked about John Gunther and Les Johnson.

"Oh, they just sat at the side and listened. They didn't talk at all."

Ebia also told me that, the next day, Don arranged for him to come
in and see him in his office. I would think that Don wanted to see
the young man for himself and to sum him up as a person, for his
Scottish highland ancestry gave him an intuitive and very shrewd insight into character.

Ebia must have passed muster, for he tells me that Don listened
carefully to what he had to say and asked him questions. He ended
the interview by saying:

"Well, you've had your march and made your point, so I hope the
Australian Government will take notice of it."

Ebia also told me that, coming down the steps from Don's office,
a man from the Commission came up and took him over to the P.S.C.
building into the presence of Mr Somers and Mr Butler, the Assistant
Commissioner, who delivered a lecture, saying:

"Why did you organise that march yesterday? That was a very bad
thing to do."

Ebia contrasted the two interviews, saying: "Sir Donald was always
very interested in us."

The Honourable Ebia Olewale is now a busy Minister for Foreign
Affairs. To get this story, I've had a job to catch him between a visit
to Indonesia and another to Peking. It's hard to think this march was
only fourteen years ago.

Don's diary notes a number of conferences over the next few weeks
with John Gunther, Mr Somers and others about salaries and other
grievances. The march was only the beginning, for the students kept
pegging away. Some of the young lawyers gave them assistance in their

spare time, helping them to formulate their case and present it in the right way to the right authority. They remember these young men with affection, and it is interesting that two of the most involved were Fred Chaney, now a Senator and Minister for Aboriginal Affairs, and Ian McPhee, Minister for Productivity. Maybe they too became politically conscious because of this involvement over the pay scales.

At the Administrative College, men who had already had many years' experience — first as administration servants, then in the auxiliary division — were on two-year scholarships to work for the Queensland leaving certificate and then to study their chosen aspect of administration. Some were doing magistrate courses involving law, some were training in welfare work and some in straight administration. The course also included subjects broadening their general knowledge and education, the most important being Pacific History and Political Science. This latter was a study of different types of government, such as the Westminster, the Presidential, the various forms of federalism and where local government fitted into central government. It was one of the most popular subjects.

These men were probably even angrier than the teachers, but approached it differently, for they were already public servants of many years' standing. They tended to thrash the matter out and debate it, particularly the options which, as public servants, were open to them to make their protest. They decided to ask the Administrator to receive a deputation, which took place on 30th September, though a number of them had marched unofficially with the teachers to let off steam.

Maori Kiki was the leader of the men at the Administrative College. With the help of some of their tutors, notably Elton Brash and John Rumens, and the young lawyers who helped the teachers' college group, they very carefully worked on a case.

Although the long negotiations with the Public Service Association and its rather myopic attitudes had largely contributed to the delays in preparing the Public Service Bill, the Association was now not slow to recognise the seriousness of the ratio decision. It too began to support the efforts of the local officers to have the ratio changed, and for the first time began to encourage them to become members of the P.S.A.

When the administration students presented their case to the Administrator on September 30th, three others were present — John Gunther, Len Butler of the Public Service Commission, and David Fenbury, Secretary of the Department of the Administrator. Sir Maori recalled to me that they had a good discussion with these men, after which Don said:

"I accept the case, and you have presented it well. Sooner or later you will have self-government. It is good that you should find your own level now. I will pass your complaints on to the Minister."

But Sir Maori also said: "A few days later, some members of the House of Assembly came out to the college to talk to us, led by Ian Downs, and they really gave us a lecture and talked down to us as though we were children."

Ted Wolfers was there, as he was writing a thesis on political development, and a very bitter argument broke out between them when Ian accused Ted of influencing Papua New Guineans. A still indignant Maori was emphatic that they didn't need any influencing.

Sir Maori and I went on talking and reminiscing about this time, which seems so long ago, and he went on to say:

"I was trying to interest and to organise people politically, and I was alone, as there was no issue — quite unlike the African States under British rule. I was looking for an issue, so this was a gift to me personally and enabled me to get the leaders together to fight for a cause. When we had finished our study in the evenings we all used to go to my house and Elizabeth would get us food and we would talk and talk. We took it in turns to buy bully beef and it became known as the Bully Beef Club. It was this group which, a few years later, grew into the Pangu Pati."

By the time this happened in 1967, Don and I were in England, and were very interested when Robert sent us cuttings and a copy of the Pangu Pati policy. We were really impressed and we both felt in accord with it. Interestingly enough, we found that both our sons agreed with its policy too.

But to go back to 1964 and the salary scale furore. The amazing thing about all this was the unbelievable obstinacy of the men in Canberra and the new Public Service Commissioner. They simply wouldn't set a more realistic ratio. However, in justice to Mr Somers, since he was actually experiencing the reactions, he probably was developing more awareness than the men in Canberra. Don, his Assistant Administrators, many of the department heads and others who had never been consulted and who were very opposed to the ratios, found themselves in the unenviable position of being in sympathy with the public servants and students and yet being bound to uphold the Australian Government's decision. On the one hand they had to try and put the government's case to the people and at the same time to try and get a change of attitude and thinking in Canberra.

There was so much pressure that eventually Canberra simply had to give here and there, and various adjustments were literally wrung out of them. One instance was the decision that people already receiving Australian pay would not suffer any reduction while still in the position they held on September 9th. However, when they were promoted to a higher position they reverted to the local pay. Canberra thought that was an enlightened concession.

The work on the salary determinations was also associated with the drafting of the necessary regulations, so that the whole ordinance of 1963 was brought into force in September 1964, eight years after the formation of the auxiliary division. So, along with all the agitation on salaries, the total reorganisation of the service was now added . It was indeed a confusing and disturbing time. In a service which had upheld such high entry standards as the Queensland leaving certificate, they made the odd move of bringing all the cleaners, gardeners and casual manual workers into the service. It seemed incomprehensible suddenly to recruit illiterates — instead of leaving them as "administration students''. This move made the arbitration case on the salary scales (and much that came later) even more confusing, by bringing other, quite different principles into the various submissions and deliberations.

Throughout all the restlessness, Warwick Smith and Barnes remained obdurate about making any clean-cut change. So the unrest continued, with both student groups and public servants asking for deputations. Don's diary reflects it all — meeting various student groups and such people as Rarua Rarua of the Co-operative Institute and representatives of the Public Service Association, resulting in many discussions with John Gunther and Frank Henderson, the Assistant Administrators, and with the P.S.C., Mr Somers.

I note also that Mr Somers only had nine conferences with Don between his arrival and September 9th, eight months later. But after September 9th he was seeing him several times a week. There were also great comings and goings with Canberra. Such good cases were put up that the department and the Minister were forced to make many more changes in their original determination, but they would never go far enough to satisfy or quell the unrest. Finally, rather than give in, the Minister announced that an Arbitration Tribunal would be set up, which could hear whatever case the people made. As a result the country seethed, from September 1964 until the end of Don's term.

The hearing began in December 1965 ánd was not finished when he left in January 1967. During that time Bob Hawke made two visits, on the second actually opening the case. He promised and gave the resources of the trade union movement to assist the local officers to fomulate their case. The case went on and on, and affected the whole country. Other workers were affected and strikes, almost unknown before, became common. Groups such as rural workers demanded investigations into their pay and conditions.

The irony of all this was that the most illiberal and conservative-minded Minister and Secretary we had ever had, inflicted the Australian brand of trade unionism on PNG, entirely through their own obstinacy. It bedevils progress and development even now. Like many other Pacific countries, the leaders often say that unions are good. But 'the way Australians run them doesn't suit our way of doing things'. However, they're here and it's hard to see them either going or changing much.

☆　☆　☆

By the end of the fifties, as significant numbers of local people were completing their studies and being recruited into the administration and Australians were coming up in increasing numbers, the town was growing rapidly. Housing, especially for local people, was becoming an ever more pressing problem. A lot of discussion and research went on and slowly new suburbs were developing, where low-cost houses were being built for rental or purchase on a long-term basis.

Social problems and stresses were also developing. Through my work in the Girl Guides Association and other organisations, especially sport and netball, which took me frequently into the villages and housing settlements, as well as my contact with missionaries working with the people, I came face to face with many things and with poignant human troubles which would not necessarily be known to government officers. In any case, a government officer whose work might bring him into close touch with this type of problem would very likely have, somewhere above him unsympathetic men. So knowledge of the problem would stop there.

Don thus became aware of the need for him to have a proper line of direct communication between himself and the people experiencing social stresses and problems. Eventually he came up with the idea of forming a Council of Social Services, in line with a similar council in Australia (with which it eventually affiliated).

All the voluntary and service organisations and welfare groups, such as the Kerema and the Methodist Welfare Association, appointed delegates. In addition, government people (such as housing officers and welfare workers) and interested individuals (such as myself) were members. We met monthly in the Administrator's conference room under the chairmanship of Bill Johns, then President of Rotary, and many problems were brought to this council.

Our method was to appoint an ad hoc committee to study and gather the facts of such-and-such a problem, then to discuss it in full council. We made recommendations about some of these, which were sent up to the Administrator, and sometimes just presented the facts to him. Some problems, one or another of our constituent organisations could do something about. The Administrator, too, would toss problems to the Council to investigate and gather views and information for his consideration. Don valued this Council highly and used it a great deal. Under his successor it was neither used nor encouraged, so it just limped into oblivion.

Monday 28th September was our usual monthly meeting. There was a full roll-up and everybody was just boiling about the issue of the unreal differences between the two wage scales. All we could do then was to move resolutions, which we sent to the Administrator and the Minister. But later, when the Arbitration Commission was set up, we decided to make a submission to it. We formed a committee, of which I was the chairman, to work on the submission; and I did the bulk of the interviewing and drafting, greatly helped by John Langmore, then a young economist in one of the departments. He later joined the staff of the university, where he and his wife were both lecturers. The third member was Mr Parkin of the United Church, and it was he who attended the hearings and made our submission. This is the only time I took a public part in any partisan way, and I am proud that I did so.

I don't think anything in all my time in Papua New Guinea distressed me personally as much as this wage determination. To start with, I was proud of what my country and particularly of what individual men and women had done in PNG. Though, like all human beings, we had made mistakes, this was different. It made me deeply ashamed on behalf on my country. I felt it was a black stain which nothing could erase. And I still think of it that way, to this day.

When George Warwick Smith came to stay with us at the end of 1964, things were still seething, and there had been other high-handed actions. George was a very pleasant-mannered person and I must say that, though I couldn't keep from arguing with him, he was always extraordinarily generous to me. You could have a terrific argument with no holds barred, but it never got unpleasant. I remember ending an argument on this visit by saying:

"Well, anyway, I can only see one good thing coming out of all that you are doing. You are making the people so angry that you are forcing the development of political consciousness. It's coming fast. That's something no one else has been able to do."

I used to put every argument I could, and use everything I had, to try and get across to him some basic realisation of how the people felt and what the effect of his policies would be. But I don't think I got anywhere at all or managed to influence his thinking one little bit. Long after Don retired, he went on doing the same kind of things during his whole term of office, ending in the incredible Mataugan situation, which need never have happened. This in turn led to Mr Whitlam's two visits to Rabaul and his self-government speech of 1971, leading directly to actual self-government in 1973. So in a way you could call the team of Warwick Smith and C.E. Barnes the unwitting fathers of independence.

Chapter 18

Lord Casey entertained at the Goroka show, Mumu, by his host, Soso Subi the Goroka big man.

Visit of Lord Louis Mountbatten—U.N. Secretariat Visitors—
World Bank—Visit of Lord and Lady Casey—Goroka Show—
Contrasting P.N.G. Between 1951 and 1966

In February 1965, after his farewell visit to South East Asia as Supreme Commander, Lord Louis Mountbatten was to visit Papua New Guinea with his daughter Lady Patricia Brabourne and Sir Solly Zuckerman, head of Churchill's wartime scientific brains trust. I was a bit apprehensive; Brisbane friends, having stayed with the Mountbattens in England, said that things could be sticky if he was in a terse mood. Realising he could well be tired and cranky after a strenuous and probably emotional tour, I finally decided not to worry and just take no notice if he was difficult. However, he arrived in the highest of good spirits and we had a wonderful few days. Apparently he had always wanted to come to New Guinea since he had travelled in *HMS Renown* with the Prince of Wales in 1921, when an outbreak of measles on board meant cancelling their visit to Papua. He tried to come several times during the war, and now in 1965 he had finished with all his duties and ceremonies and this was his holiday.

He really was a remarkable man — very natural and with the most intense and very knowledgeable interest in everything that happens, especially the simple things like the birds and the plants and trees in the garden. He would suddenly say, "What about a swim?", just after the drivers had gone off duty. So we would all pile into the car and take off to Ela Beach, with me at the wheel. Patricia was a delight too; the mother of four children, her twins only eight months old; she was natural and outgoing.

We had the usual dinner, with a large garden party afterwards. Walking among the guests with the band playing, Lord Louis suddenly stopped in his tracks.

"That's my march. Nobody has any right to play that without my permission — that is, except the Royal Marines."

"Ah", said Don. "Our bandmaster was formerly with the Royal Marines."

"What's his name?" asked Lord Louis.

"Shacklady."

"Good God, I know him," and he strode across and greeted Tom Shacklady as an old friend. Apparently when a midshipman joins his first ship, a Royal Marine bandsman is assigned to take him under his wing and look after him. Tom Shacklady had looked after Prince Philip. So the family association had indeed been a long one.

Afterwards he told us that the Preobrajensky Guards, raised by Peter the Great and called after the village where he grew up, became the most famous Russian regiment before the 1917 Revolution. This Slavonic march, the most popular written by Donajowsky, was the regimental march. Czar Nicholas, Lord Mountbatten's uncle, gave the right to use it to King Alfonso of Spain, another of his uncles. In 1928 King Alfonso gave it to Lord Louis. As Commander of Combined Operations in 1942, he in turn gave the right to play it to the Royal Marines. And here it was being played for him by our band in Papua New Guinea. Months later Tom Shacklady brought us a regimental magazine with a story of Moutbatten recounting this incident at a reunion dinner.

Sir Solly was a round, jolly sort of person, a noted natural scientist with a lively mind and quick wit. The two men really sparked off each other and their whole visit was stimulating for us all.

☆ ☆ ☆

By now visitors were coming from United Nations secretariat and agencies such as UNESCO and WHO, in addition to the usual triennial visits of the U.N. mission from the assembly itself. Our last, shortly after the Mountbattens' visit, was led by a charming and interesting Frenchman named M. Naudy.

We found United Nations secretariat men most interesting, being in a sense civil servants of the world. I remember asking a couple of very accomplished men, one Nigerian and one a West Indian, what it was like to be working in a service with people from so many countries. Did they really develop a 'one-world' feeling or did their own separate national reactions remain uppermost? They thought awhile, then one said:

"No, I think we really do begin to think internationally and feel a team."

"But you know," added the other, "it's the people trained by the British, from the ex-British colonies, who are the backbone of the United Nations services. We are all trained to high standards. The French-trained group will argue about the philosophy of everything and most of the others don't really know what it's all about." Which reminds me of another story.

After the closing ceremony of the Commonwealth Games in Perth, to which we finally got our team of six athletes to their first international competition, Prince Philip, who opened the Games and remained there taking the closest interest, gave a party for team leaders, any Heads of State and the Western Australian organisers. I was talking to a West Indian, a Malayan and a Chinese from North Borneo, all enthusing about the Games and wishing they were held every year.

"Heaven forbid," I exclaimed, recalling the horrendous effort we had had to make. "It nearly killed us to raise the money for our six. We'd never do it every year."

They all laughed, saying smugly that their governments paid all expenses.

I asked whether the Commonwealth Games had anything over the Olympics.

"Oh, yes," said the West Indian. "Here we all speak the same language and have the same background. It's more friendly and like a family affair" — which gave me a very nice feeling.

Australia has been criticised for doing everything in Papua New Guinea herself. This was partly because, as one of the originators of the Colombo Plan, she was a donor nation. Therefore her work in PNG was regarded as part of her Colombo Plan contribution and did not entitle her to the help given to third-world countries. But by the sixties, escalating development was outrunning Australia's resources; hence her interest in seeking outside aid.

Probably the most significant of these visits was from a World Bank team, the arrangements being made in 1963 during Paul Hasluck's time. The team of five Englishmen, under the leadership of a man called Iveson, was our first encounter with the new breed of long-haired academics. They were a priceless combination of being enormously superior and deliberately casual in dress and manner, and I'm afraid they diverted me, but Don disliked their attitude. They spent some weeks travelling round the country and went off to make their report.

Don's first record of it was a conference discussion with the Assistant Administrator on August 3rd 1964. I remember how disturbed he was about this report, which did not show sufficient regard for the human elements, either social or political, nor take enough account of the economic development of the Papua New Guinea people themselves. It was mainly concerned with stepping up national earnings quickly by large-scale resource development, through the infusion of foreign capital and big company operations, concentrating on areas of good economic potential and not worrying about the low-potential areas — which, of course, included the whole of Papua and the East and West Sepik.

Don anguished over it and worried about its effect in terms of people. He was both disappointed and gloomy, seeing trouble ahead which could come in its wake. He felt it would be far sounder in the long run to put more thought and effort into an all-over spread of smaller-scale developments which would involve Papua New Guineans and include their training in technical and managerial skills. Apparently this aspect also worried the department in Canberra, and both Warwick Smith and Gutman, a new assistant secretary, tried to persuade Iveson to state in a preface that the report was purely economic and did not preclude the Australian Government from making political and social decisions. Unfortunately Iveson and his mission would not do so.

So there it was. THE WORLD BANK REPORT sponsored by the UNITED NATIONS. Sacred. The Australian Government embraced it with enthusiasm; for it did fit the economic philosophy of the new team. As part of its implementation, an economic adviser was appointed, in the person of Bill McCasker. Strangely, for such a conservative minister, Bill was by way of being one of the new breed of economists, one of the architects of Menzies' Vernon Report, shelved as being too advanced for the Australian Parliament.

Bill attacked his work with immense drive and enthusiasm, and concentrated on forming the necessary infrastructure on which the implementation of the World Bank Report would rest. He had a lively and original mind, was rather abrasive but the type which Don and I found stimulating, and we became very good friends. Bill arrived in 1966, about ten months before Don's retirement, and worked hard and enthusiastically. By the time of self-government he had achieved all the groundwork and the World Bank Report was well on the way to implementation.

Then the policy changed and the newly independent government changed the economic philosophy. Though it was very distressing to Bill and his team, which was largely disbanded, the new policy was more on the lines of what the administration had wanted in the beginning.

One area where the World Bank has made a valuable contribution is the enormous Ramu Hydro Electric Scheme, harnessing the Ramu River headwaters and supplying electricity to Lae, Madang and the Highland towns. They also financed turning the kiap roads from Lae through the Highlands into major highways, providing more up-to-date port facilities, and are now financing the first major highway in Papua, west from Moresby to Kerema, eventually linking with the Morobe road system through Menyamya and Bulolo to Lae. Its name, picturesquely linked to the ancient Hiri trading expeditions by sea between the Motu and the Kerema peoples, is Hiritano Highway, 'tano' meaning land. But these last belong to the post-independence period and long after Don's time.

☆ ☆ ☆

One of the especially happy visits was that of the new Governor General Lord Casey, and Lady Casey in May 1966. He had been up some years before as Minister for Foreign Affairs, and Don had known him well and worked closely with him in the old Liberal Party days in Sydney.

Once in 1946 or '47, having coffee on the wide verandah after lunch at the Royal Sydney Golf Club, Don noticed a lonely figure sitting by himself. It was Stanley Melbourne Bruce — Lord Bruce. He looked so craggy and distinguished, but an almost tangible air of loneliness surrounded him. There had been no mention in the press that he was even visiting Australia. Don felt the poignancy and sadness of such a notable Australian, who had been a world figure, coming back to his own country after the war, unknown and unsung. It made a deep impression.

A year or so later the Caseys were returning, after his wartime years of very distinguished service in Cairo and Washington, culminating in the Governorship of Bengal. Although it was really something for an Australian to have held such posts as a British appointee, yet here he was, another world figure returning to his country with hardly a comment on press or radio.

The thought of this really worried Don, who at the time was the Director of the Federal Secretariat of the Liberal Party. Then he had a brainwave. If Casey became President of the Liberal Party it would be just the stimulation the party needed and would bring him immediately back into public life. But of course that was easier said than done. However, he called on Lord Casey when next in Melbourne, and they had a long talk about Australian politics in general and about what they could do in particular. Then he had to sell the idea to Menzies. As a result of this and much other discussion, a proposal was put to the next party conference for Casey to form a fund-raising committee entirely separate from the organisation — a need Don had seen for some time. The idea was to raise funds whose source would be unknown to the parliamentary wing, to other members of the party or to the secretariat, thus freeing them from any sense of being beholden to any particular interest.

Casey got an excellent committee together and threw himself into the work with drive and enthusiasm, getting quite spectacular results. At the 1948 annual meeting he was elected President of the party, which brought Don into almost daily contact with him. Casey stood for the 1949 general election and was once again in parliament. Now he was Governor General. I knew Lady Casey only slightly, but we shared one or two intimate friends who talked a lot about her, which made me feel that I knew her better than I did.

Because of this long background, we anticipated their visit with extra pleasure and made sure their programme, concentrating on the up-and-coming young people, was not too strenuous. Before going to a large public gathering at Ela Beach we had a very happy dinner en famille, and he talked a lot about Moresby in 1913, when as a young engineer he had worked on the Sapphire Creek copper mine. The rusting relics are still there, halfway to Sogeri. There were no vehicles and they used to walk through the bush to Moresby. He said the path was pretty and shady; so a lot of jungle must have been cut down since then.

The next night was a buffet dinner for about sixty, followed by the evening garden party. This was our last Governor General's visit and we couldn't help contrasting this guest list with our first. Then there were not more than about forty nationals, who would have been village leaders, many with halting English and all very shy. This time, at least half the four hundred guests were nationals with achievement in politics, the administration, the church and the army behind them. They were confident and articulate.

We arranged a sitting area near the wide flight of steps on a terrace between the drive and the large level lawn we had excavated and built up on the side of the hill. Here we sat Lady Casey, where she could talk with a group of five or six, while my secretary Sue Hewitt and I moved among the guests, bringing up interesting people, one slipping out of a chair as another came in. For those on the lawn below it made a charming scene to watch, and gave people an opportunity to get the feel of Lady Casey's remarkable personality. Don, meanwhile, had been taking Lord Casey through the guests and presenting people to him.

One of the nicest times of these dos is relaxing in the living room after we have withdrawn, having a well-earned nightcap and talking it all over. Both the Caseys were marvellous at drawing people out and both were charmed at the intelligence and style of the young Papua New Guineans they had met.

One interesting sidelight about this visit was that they were very taken with Sue. Until they could find the right person, Lady Casey had borrowed an old friend from Foreign Affairs, Ruth Dobson (who is now

Ambassador to Ireland), to be her secretary. Lady Casey asked me what I thought of Sue, for Yarralumla, after Don's retirement. I said that she put her whole mind and thought into her job, was very competent and efficient, and would really look after her.

The upshot was that Sue went from us to Yarralumla. While they were in office, every now and then a card would come, with one of Lady Casey's own delightful drawings, and inside something like: 'Dear Rachel' — or even 'Dearest Rachel' — 'Thank you, thank you for giving me Sue. She is such a help and comfort to me'; then a little scrap of news, and ending 'Maie'. When the Caseys retired, with their help and influence Sue joined Christies, worked first in London and then became assistant manager in Sydney. She now manages Christies in Australia.

The main event of this visit was for Lord Casey to open the Goroka Show. They went off to Lae and Bulolo the day after our party, but as Don had a commitment in Moresby we joined them on Saturday in Goroka. Flying over the milling masses in the new showground, we landed on the strip packed with parked planes, others coming in and out all the time.

This tremendous activity took my mind back to the first Highland Show in 1956, when Robert was a patrol officer at Kainantu, at the eastern end of the same district. It was, of course, Ian Downs' idea and it was held on the sports ground. Nobody knew quite what was going to happen, but everyone worked very hard and enthusiastically. Each subdistrict put up a display of what it produced by way of new crops, traditional activities and artefacts. They were beautifully set up and displayed and must have been hard to judge, but Robert was thrilled that Kainantu won the prize.

There was an archery competition that more realistically perhaps should be called a bow-and-arrow shoot, and an Australian type wood-chop, which first mystified and then amazed the tribal onlookers, so newly graduated from stone axes. As well there were several dancing groups and various other activities to entertain and amuse. It was a lovely day, full of movement and gaiety. A good crowd of Highlanders had come, every expatriate in the valley and a few from Lae and Mt Hagen.

In the early afternoon I went to the edge of the ground to take a picture from a small hill beside a cutting, with the road some ten feet below. Then I heard a curious low sort of chant, and round the bend in the road appeared the most amazing sight. About thirty or forty men, absolutely covered all over with grey mud, grotesque mud masks covering their heads and resting on their shoulders, trotted six abreast with a curious slow, loping movement, which was quite eerie. I scrambled down the cutting to take pictures as they came up and found myself surrounded till they passed on, leaving me gasping. I then quickly clambered up the cutting to watch their arrival. They really created a sensation. It was an ancient legend from Asaro Village made into a sing-sing. No one had ever seen it or heard of it before and no one knew they were coming. They have now become famous, a group even being taken to London a few years ago, where they were real traffic-stoppers.

These things were in my mind as our plane circled on this visit ten years later, giving us a good view of the new, well-designed showground, attractively built to hold many thousands of people, with a good grandstand, seats all round the ring, exhibition halls, food stalls of all sorts and an attractive outdoor barbecue restaurant.

We arrived in time to welcome the Caseys, all of us going to the Residency to dress. Lord Casey donned morning suit with decorations and pale grey top hat; with his distinguished face and trim figure, he looked superb. Our cavalcade of cars drove round the ring to the grandstand, where all the Show Committee were waiting to greet them, the President and his wife escorting us into the stand for the opening speeches. I do not remember what Lord Casey said, but I do remember thinking that it was just right and that he held the interest of the sixty thousand people, who stopped their milling around as the pidgin translation bellowed out through the mikes.

We then got back into the cars and circled the ring again, stopping at a kunai haus wind (a thatched, open-sided shelter) for lunch. Our host, Soso Subi, who greeted us, was the original owner of the land, and he and his people had prepared a magnificent 'mumu', which was humph-humphing at the side.

He was a small, elderly man with the tremendous presence and dignity of his kind, clad in traditional dress of a foot-wide carved bark belt holding up his swinging ground-length netted billum in front and the Highland bunch of tanket leaves or 'arse grass' behind. A new moon of gleaming pearl shell was suspended on his chest, and the small fan-like circlet of exquisitely woven tiny feathers of the Goroka head-dress was held in place by a headband of giri giri, the shell money of tiny ground-down cone shells sewn on to a woven strip. The contrast between host and guest is hard to describe, but each wore his unusual raiment with equal dignity and confidence.

Drinks were handed round and it was time to open the mumu. Highland mumus are different. They make a round platform of stones, build a fire on top till the stones are red hot, place a thick pad of wet banana leaves, then pile on the food, which has been parcelled up in banana-leaf packages. Two or three pieces of bamboo tubing rest on the stones at strategic places, and the whole thing is covered with six to nine inches of the rich black Goroka earth, making a three-foot mound with the bamboos coming through the top. Now and again water is poured down the bamboo and, hitting the stones, turns instantly to steam, which makes the whole mound heave, giving off the curious 'humph' sound.

They had begun this mumu at 3 a.m. and now it was just right. There is a primaeval excitement in opening a mumu and the Caseys, fascinated, couldn't really believe that our lunch was inside that black earth. A team of young men carefully moved it away, revealing the little banana-leaf parcels, which groups of women put on large wood dishes which they placed on the table before opening them. The smell was mouth-watering, and we walked down the row of great dishes of food, helping ourselves to chicken and pork, sweet potato, taro, banana and pit-pit (the young shoots of the bamboo-like grass), all done to a turn and no flavour lost in the cooking. I doubt whether even at the great banquets the Caseys had attended the food had been more delicious than old Soso Subi's mumu.

After lunch we walked round the many fascinating displays and back to the grandstand for the parade of the sing-sing groups. I would think no sight in the world is quite like the ring of a Highland show, with thousands of highly competitive men in full regalia all trying to out-do their neighbours in the magnificence of brilliant plumage; the very ground throbbing with the rhythmic stamping of their feet and the eye caught by rows of long swaying billums and headdresses and all other sounds absorbed by the beating of hundreds of hand drums and the indescribable rising and falling of the highland voices. The Caseys were certainly entranced.

For this show it had been suggested to the people that they should end their sing-sing with each group having the floor, as it were, for a few minutes in front of the stand, to demonstrate some traditional custom.

Lady Casey was sitting between Robyn Doolan (the D.C.'s wife) and me. We were first intrigued when a little pig was let loose and ran squealing about, then alarmed when they all began shooting ar-rows at it and lastly horrified when, with a great and proud flourish, the leader disembowelled it before our eyes. We three women clutch-ed each other, wanting to look away, but couldn't. Patrol officers quickly hurried the next group on to hide the sight from us. It was so unexpected and quick and, as always after a rather frightening mo-ment, everybody in the stand began talking at once. The group was genuinely bewildered at the reaction and kept saying:

"But you told us to show you something of our own fashion." Ap-parently they had intended presenting the pig to Lord Casey.

The energetic show committee had emptied the enormous coffee store and imported not only Moresby's best band but the pipers of the Pacific Islands Regiment and the Police Band to take their turn. They had a red-carpeted dais at the end and it was a lively night, with an Australian woolshed dance atmosphere.

From Goroka, the Caseys went on to Minj, Hagen, Wewak and Madang. Lady Casey had been talking a lot about her Aunt Ellis Rowan, who was a most remarkable painter of wildflowers, birds and butterflies at the turn of the century. Spending two years from 1916 to 1918 round Madang and Nobanob, she had painted forty-five of the fifty-two varieties of birds of paradise and many butterflies and flowers, before her death at the age of 74 in 1922. The collection had been bought by the Federal Government. A series borrowed from the National Gallery was hung by Lady Casey on the stairway walls at Yarralumla, where we admired their exquisite beauty when we were staying there later in the year, for me to have the great honour of being invested with the C.B.E.

Nearly every district now has a show, the Highland ones being the most spectacular, which, alternating between Goroka and Hagen, attract tourists from other countries and folk from all over Papua New Guinea. Nothing could better illustrate the changes than a comparison between the 1956 show and the present. They are now entirely organised by a committee of Highlanders, and seem to get bigger every year. The first one had a few dancing groups, but most of the onlookers wore traditional dress and few in shirts and trousers or dresses were to be seen. Now rivalry puts hundreds of dancing groups into the arena, but the other thousands of onlookers are well dressed and move in little family groups with beautifully dressed children. They come from far-away villages in their own trucks and cars, with plenty of coffee money to spend.

1956 saw the first primary schools, but by 1966 a number of high schools were being opened, while a senior Technical College and the Secondary Teachers' Training College, now part of the university, were both in Goroka. Well-educated Highlanders could take their place easily, mixing freely and confidently with expatriates.

There's no doubt that these annual shows are a wonderful way of bringing all parts of a district together and building up a feeling of pride and accomplishment. They foster pride in old traditions, and the excellent displays put on by departments such as Health, Agriculture and Forestry show people the new ideas. The most popular are technical departments such as Electricity, Posts and Telegraphs and Broadcasting, which show great ingenuity in demonstrating how these things work.

The great contrasts between the two Goroka shows prompts me to make some other contrasts between the early fifties and the mid-sixties. While you are actually involved in the process of change and development yourself, everything seems so slow. The very nature of working in Papua New Guinea gives expatriates the kinds of stresses and frustrations they would never find in their home countries, while the local people have stresses too, mostly arising from their desire for the material benefits with which we surround ourselves and which they naturally want at once. For tribal people disappointment leads to cargo-cult thinking, and for the educated it is a long, slow grind with disappointing results in the end, giving many a sense of frustration. You need perspective to see what an incredible achievement the development of Papua New Guinea has been.

At war's end, not only was nothing left standing in any pre-war town except Moresby, but they all had been fought over and bombed by both sides. Though Moresby had suffered ninety-seven air raids, they were mainly directed at the port facilities, aerodromes and army camps, so a proportion of the houses of the pre-war population of about 350 still remained. At one time there were half a million men camped round Moresby. Quite apart from the huge bomb holes, wrecked planes, trucks and guns, half a million men can leave quite a lot of ordinary rubbish and mess.

This was what the returning civilians came back to in 1946 and 1947. It was not even like going into a new country and starting from scratch. It was starting way behind, with bomb holes to fill in and the debris of war to clean up; but by 1951 planning for rebuilding the towns on a permanent basis was well on the way and went ahead rapidly, although it was a long time before enough houses replaced the temporary houses of paper and bush material and the converted army huts.

In 1946 one third of the country was still unexplored and just a blank space on the map. By 1951, though a number of exploratory patrols had gone out and there was more idea of how many people were in the mountains, they were only just beginning to establish patrol posts and build little airstrips. There were no towns in the Highlands and only walking tracks, no roads. The Goroka and Wahgi Valley floors were both unpopulated, the people living in the surrounding mountains for security, and most were fighting with all their neighbours.

By 1966, fifteen years later, there were five good-sized towns in the highlands and a number of patrol posts had grown into small towns. The swamps in the Wahgi had been drained and thriving tea plantations were established. Coffee was well established all through the Highlands, with a policy of opening only a certain amount of land for expatriate planters, and that well scattered. The local people living around could then work on the plantations, thus learning how to do it themselves and with encouragement plant up their own land. This plan had worked extremely well. The building of roads, spoken of earlier, has made all this development possible.

So now you don't fly over an empty valley, but one studded not only with tea and coffee plantations — many of which are owned by local people — but with enough village cattle projects for the Highlands to be self-supporting in meat.

By 1966, millions of dollars were flowing into the Highlanders'

pockets from their coffee, tobacco, cattle and other enterprises —
where, as recently as 1953, roadworkers were paid in salt because
money was unknown. Good roads between Mendi, Hagen, Goroka
and Kainantu, and to the port at Lae, have brought a huge new
transport industry significantly owned and run by Highlanders.

Copra has always been the main income-earner for coastal people,
but cocoa has now been added and brings a huge income to the Gazelle,
while the smallholder blocks of the oil-palm scheme of west New Britain does likewise. Primary industry was not the only development;
for all the towns, having begun with the growth of service industries,
were now beginning to manufacture more of what is needed in a
modern economy.

Though there was not yet universal primary education, primary
schools were pretty well distributed over the whole country; all districts
had secondary schools, while training colleges for many of the
necessary skills were fairly numerous, the best reaching a high standard. The sons and daughters of fathers who in 1950 had never seen
a white man, and who were still headhunters, were getting ready for
the university.

Whereas John Gunther's cover of simple medical care was
widespread in 1951, by 1966 there were six large modern general
hospitals, each serving areas well covered with small hospitals, community health centres and aid posts, and these were well on the way
to being fully staffed by trained Papua New Guineans. By 1966, Papua
New Guinea had become part of the world link of the Seacom cable
system, and work had begun on giving it one of the most modern radio
telephone systems in the world.

The hydro-electric potential had long been recognised and not only
had the Laloki River been dammed, making a lake larger than Sydney
Harbour and so ensuring a regular water supply for the three giant
underground power stations at Rouna, but planning had begun for
harnessing the Ramu, a scheme so immense that it now supplies electricity to the whole of the Highlands, Lae and Madang.

So during this last year, although there were many problems and
much was happening that worried Don, there was also a great deal
to give him pride and satisfaction.

Chapter 19

Don leaves office and the P.I.R. pipes us onto the plane. A most moving farewell.

Don's Retiring Date of June 1967 Changed—Barnes Changes Plans re Three Top Jobs—Higher Education Commission—Gunther University Vice Chancellor—Les Johnson Assistant Administrator—Christmas Leave Darwin to Perth—Arbitration Hearing on Salaries—David Hay Appointed Administrator Elect—October and November Farewells—Departure Overseas by Ship

Some time, probably in 1963, Don had a discussion with Paul Hasluck about the tenure of his office as Administrator. This was in connection with Eskie Lambert's retirement and the proposal that John Gunther should succeed him as Secretary for Territories, and the question of who should succeed John as Assistant Administrator. Les Johnson, who had shown excellent administrative and leadership qualities since he had been appointed Director of Education in 1960, was felt to have the quality for an Assistant Administrator and also, with this experience, the possible potential for Administrator. When the time came, his record would then have revealed whether it was there or not. Don would be sixty-five in June 1966, and it was agreed between Paul and Don that he would retire on his sixty-sixth birthday, in June 1967. That would mean that, if John went to Territories at the beginning of 1964 and Les Johnson became Assistant Administrator (Services), it would have given him three and a half years experience in the top trio, including periods as Acting Administrator when Don was on leave.

It was good planning and sound thinking. Don's continuation until 1967 would also have the effect that by then he would have made sufficient superannuation payments, which would have a considerable bearing on the amount of pension he received. Actually he was only eligible for a pension at all because he had originally been recruited into the public service and had remained on secondment as Administrator, thus being able to continue paying his superannuation.

The office of Administrator, an appointment by the Governor General on advice by the Minister for Territories, had the salary fixed by Federal Parliament and carried no pension. Altering it was a parliamentary matter and therefore not easy, so it had remained static for most of Don's service.

This was becoming an acute embarrassment to the Public Service Commissioner, especially in recruiting professional people such as doctors, lawyers, engineers and architects. The rising salaries necessary to attract professional people were nudging those of the heads of departments, and heads of departments were nudging that of the Administrator.

To attract judges, it was necessary to offer higher salaries than the Administrator's. I was very amused at an acid reference in Hasluck's book to public servants of PNG who were shocked at the thought that a judge might have a higher salary than the Administrator. Don knew that, with the gradual rise caused by inflation over the years, his own salary had become inadequate long before, but there was no way he would raise the question himself. He had always been indifferent to monetary rewards, as long as he was doing the work he wanted to do; and he certainly was doing that.

So over this period he had much private amusement at the contortions of the 'powers that be'. There was a lot of unrest in the top echelon, especially in the Department of Health, where doctors were earning more than the section heads under whom they worked; Don had many a chuckle at all these Public Service Commission problems, just because Paul had such a reluctance to bring the Administrator's salary before parliament. The next amusing time came under the new Minister, when they were searching among top Canberra public servants for Don's successor. Anyone who showed any interest just laughed the idea to scorn when the salary was mentioned.

Eventually, David Hay became Administrator elect, only consenting after a considerable increase had been made, in consequence of which, after all those years, Don's own salary jumped by several thousand for his last three months in office. This salary business, and the fact that a good part of the furniture at Government House and most of the silver, glass, china, table linen and other equipment in use were our own, gave us both a sense of independence and the feeling that we were beholden to no one. We did what we did because we loved the work for its own sake, and we loved the country and its people.

But once more I have run ahead of myself, and must go back to the very sound plans Paul had made before he was transferred away from Territories to the portfolio of Defence. I have recounted in chapter 17 how John Gunther's appointment was not confirmed by the new Minister (C.E. Barnes) and that George Warwick Smith was appointed instead. John Gunther then remained as Assistant Administrator.

He had served on the Commission for Higher Education with Professor D.H.K. Spate and Sir George Currie as chairman, while Freddie Kaad was executive officer and Oala Oala Rarua his assistant. They presented their report and recommendations to the government in March 1964 and, when accepted, the Interim University Council was formed, with Professor Karmel (Vice-Chancellor of Adelaide University) as Chairman. Later John Gunther became the first Vice-Chancellor of the University of Papua New Guinea, and Les Johnson followed him as Assistant Administrator Services early in 1965.

Don missed John sadly; and, when leaving the administration, John wrote to him as wonderful a letter as one man could write to another. They had been a unique team and Don knew that, if anyone could get a new university off the ground and build it up into a going concern without much money, it would be John Gunther.

Les fitted very quickly into his new role. He brought different qualities to bear, which were valuable in the new era which was becoming evident all round us. An excellent administrator, without the intensity and drive which characterised John, he had great common sense and qualities of stability and good judgment. With Frank Henderson's agriculture background and grasp of finance, they again made a very good trio, and stood together well in coping with the changed conditions in Canberra.

Shortly after C.E. Barnes became Minister in 1964, Don had a discussion with him about the arrangements for his retirement previously made between himself and Paul Hasluck. Barnes agreed with the reasons behind the agreement and confirmed that Don would retire in June, 1967. But it did not occur to him to ask for confirmation in writing.

In December 1965 we were getting ready for a month's leave, having planned to fly first to Townsville and have a look at Mt Isa, where Don wanted to see what a huge mining operation looked like, as the first assessments of the Bougainville copper deposits had begun. We were due to leave early Tuesday morning.

On Friday night Don came home saying that George Warwick Smith had just rung to tell him that John and Margaret Overall were coming up on Sunday. John hadn't been well and they were taking a couple of weeks' holiday in New Guinea. Could we put them up

"But George, it could be only for twenty-four hours," Don had said with some irritation. "We're off on leave early on Tuesday. I couldn't put the extra on my wife when she is trying to get away. Could they come to lunch on Monday?"

We liked the Overalls, and knew Margaret's parents, Cyril and Ruth Goodman, who had been neighbours in Sydney. In fact we were with them in 1958 at the old Canberra Hotel, when John and Margaret arrived for a final interview before his appointment as the Chief Administrator of the Commission, which was to carry out the development and building of Canberra as it is today. They had shown us many courtesies over the years and we would have loved having them to stay, and were really sorry it wasn't possible. I remember tearing home from tying up ends at Guide Headquarters to find our lunch guests already there, and had to start with profuse apologies. We just had drinks and a normal lunch, talking of this and that, and off they went, while Don returned to the office and I tackled our packing and all the last-minute things. As always, it was a relief to get into the plane with that lovely glow of pleasure that for the next few weeks we could be just us — just private persons.

However, to our surprise we were given V.I.P. treatment at Townsville, including a civic reception and an interesting drive. We were particularly glad to see the foundations and layout of the new university — ours being just on the way.

Don had made arrangements with the management at Mt Isa, and during our thirty-six hours there he learnt a lot. Charles La Nauze, an engineer son of Don's cousin Barbara, detailed to show us round. Then on to Darwin for our first visit of a week. The day we left Moresby, word had come that the Minister would be there and wanted to see Don. Would we come to dinner at Government House? — then they could have a conference beforehand.

So we arrived in Darwin, went to Government House, and were greeted by everyone very happily. Don and the Minister went off for their conference, came back to join us, and after a pleasant dinner and evening we drove back to our hotel and to bed. Don was up first and when I came out of the bathroom he was sitting on the edge of his bed sunk in meditation, gazing at the floor.

"Don, whatever's the matter?" I cried, for it was totally unlike him.

"Do you know what old Barnes wanted to see me about?"

I'd quite forgotten the conference and hadn't even asked him the night before.

"He threshed about on this and that for a few minutes seeming rather embarrassed, then said — 'We've decided to retire you and thought May would be a good month'."

Don had been flabbergasted, and reminded him with some spirit of the discussion they'd had early in his ministry, when he had agreed to and confirmed the earlier arrangement made with Hasluck. Plainly he had forgotten all about it. Quite as obviously Warwick Smith's plans were behind the present move, and Barnes had the grace to be more embarrassed than ever. Don liked him so much as a person, but realised he was no match for a man like his Departmental Secretary. However, he also reminded him of the pension aspect and the difference it would make if he was retired a year earlier. It was therefore left open for future discussion.

But Don was thoroughly miserable, disgusted and upset about it, and brooded all day. He knew George wanted complete power in New Guinea and realised he wouldn't get it as long as he, Don, was there to protect the right of the PNG administration to handle its internal affairs free from Canberra control. He felt thoroughly dispirited about the way things were going in general and would have given a lot to have Hasluck back again. However, this was the new ball game and, with no choice but to play it, he tried to put it out of his mind.

We had a hot but interesting week in Darwin, a couple of fascinating days in Broome and for the first time saw the incredible northern coast of our own State. The earth was that same brilliant pinky red of the interior, softened by the sparse grey-to-green scrub, the cloudless sky a brilliant blue with a pinky haze on the horizon. The beaches were pale pink, and the vivid turquoise of the sea which washed them had a pink milkiness from the churned-up sand of the sea floor. It was ancient and looked ancient, and no wonder it had long repelled the outsiders from the lush tropical lands not so far to the north.

We had a lovely Christmas Day with our families in Perth, sitting fifteen, with four generations present. It was the last one for us with my wonderful old aunt Bessie Rischbieth, still an interesting and attractive woman at ninety-one. We visited Don's brother Bill at Leonora, then in the full flush of new mining development, this time nickel, not gold. The huge Western Mining complex was right on Glenorn boundaries, and all the young station people were busy prospecting their own properties. We then went off two hundred miles south of Perth to my sister Mary Ritson at Boyup Brook, and back to my sisters Bar and Meg, who always made us so welcome. They had built a modern house in the front garden of the home we had all grown up in, and it is a wonderful refreshment to go back to the same lovely spot, with the same Swan River lapping the same beach. Restored, we returned late in January to tackle what we knew would be a very strenuous last year.

It was a funny last year. The pace of everything was stepping up, with new and more sophisticated arrangements being made for services such as a Harbours Board, to plan and manage all the port facilities, and the Development Bank, to stimulate the financing of new private enterprise projects and particularly to facilitate loan money for Papua New Guinean enterprise and investment. At the same time the arbitration hearing went on and on. It kept everyone, from students to employers and employees, very unsettled, while discussions with the Secretary for Labour, a new department, became more frequent entries in Don's diary.

John Gunther came back from a visit to Canberra saying:

"Overall wasn't on a holiday at all, last year. He was a prospective administrator and came up to have a look."

Don was furious that he had been fed such a cock-and-bull story, and wondered if Overall knew that we had not been informed. If he didn't know, he must have thought his treatment pretty funny. You talk to people on a holiday quite differently from the way you would to your possible successor. Margaret must have thought it very odd of me not to have shown her over the house, and the false situation must have been awful for them throughout their trip. Anyway, George's approach to it certainly lost Papua New Guinea a very high-quality administrator, as he turned it down flat.

That news certainly fitted in with the Minister's bombshell to Don about leaving in May. I worried over it all the year, and when our Christmas cards went out I popped in a little note to the Goodmans, saying what we'd heard, and was it true? Ruth wrote back thanking me. John and Margaret hadn't been told that no one here knew why they'd come up, so they had thought the whole experience very strange. For Papua New Guinea it was indeed unfortunate to lose them.

By the beginning of the year, John Gunther's university planning was sufficiently advanced to recruit the first students for a preliminary year of study in order to matriculate. They furbished up the exhibition buildings at the old showground and there the students began, in great discomfort but with great elan. By mid-year Ted Kedgeley (the Registrar) and his wife Barbara had arrived, and the first professors, Don Drover of Chemistry and Gerry Nash for Law; while clearing and preparing the site for building the university itself was begun.

The University Commission had also advised starting an Institute of Higher Technical Education, which could begin with diploma courses in engineering, surveying, architecture and other practical studies, and could be upgraded to university level later on. Dr Duncanson arrived as Director and began to organise it, with his base at Iduabada Technical College. It was originally planned to be built on the university land, so that when courses were eventually upgraded to degree standard it would become part of the campus. But the new

Department of the Administrator,
PORT MORESBY.
15th February, 1966

My dear *Sir Donald*

      At the time I tender advice of my formal retirement, I want to write and say how much I have appreciated working with you over a period of nearly 14 years.

      It is proper that I should say how greatly I have valued your advice and direction on all occasions. You would be aware that there were occasions when I felt a direction or decision was wrong, but in retrospect I know of no occasion when I can say it was not sound and, in the long run, it probably gave the best result. I would hope you would think that we were complementary and that you would appreciate that if there were times when I was brash, I accepted your directions readily. There was no need for me to <u>try</u> to serve you loyally. I always had a feeling of loyalty and a desire to serve.

      I don't suppose any two people have worked for so long together in a rapidly advancing colonial situation. The years have not been easy ones, though they have been exciting and stimulating. A year or more ago, when the press were saying that you were about to retire and that I was one of the candidates for the position, I said to you then, and meant it genuinely, that I preferred to continue to serve with you as Administrator; that I had no ambitions for your position, though probably at that stage, if I had been asked to be Administrator when you retired, I would have given serious thought to it. Even today I don't know whether I would have accepted it.

      I am going to the University because this is what I want to do. In the Administration I have no sense of frustration, although I would not be honest if I said that I thought everything that was happening today was for the best. For the sake of the Territory I very sincerely hope they will keep you in your position as long as you wish to stay.

      I am absolutely certain that our new association will be most fruitful. I hope that the University, in serving the Territory, will be able to serve yourself and the Administration on all occasions.

      Dot and I will always have very happy memories of our many and varied associations with yourself and Lady Cleland, and hope we may continue to enjoy a close social relationship with you both.

      With warm personal regards.

Sincerely

Sir Donald Cleland, C.B.E.,O.St.J.,
Government House,
<u>PORT MORESBY</u>.

21st February, 1966.

        I do thank you so very much indeed for
your letter of 15th February, which I will cherish
in my personal records. I too, have enjoyed and
appreciated working with you over a period of
nearly 14 years now. At all times I knew that I
had your loyalty and support though as you say
there were occasions when we differed, but I am
very appreciative of the fact that once a decision
had been given you backed it wholeheartedly.

        You have served the Territory and its
people magnificently during the whole period of
your Service in the Territory and your contribution
will be long remembered. I am quite certain that
you will bring to bear in your new appointment all
your drive and administrative ability in developing
the University and here I feel sure you will make
a further contribution to your great record.

        We too, will always have very happy
memories of our many and varied associations with
you and Dot, and I am sure that they will continue.

        With very kindest regards,

Dr. J.T. Gunther, C.M.G., O.B.E.,
Assistant Administrator (Services),
KONEDOBU.

Farewell at Hannabada Village.

Piped onto the plane.

House of Assembly had quite different ideas and brought in a Bill to establish it in Lae instead.

As the year wore on, Don kept wishing that Les Johnson had had just a little longer experience as Assistant Administrator, to make him more obviously eligible as a candidate. He was sure he would measure up well in the top job, but the Canberra people wouldn't consider it and went on looking elsewhere. In the meantime, after some correspondence about it, Don's retiring date was fixed for January 8th, 1967, and so timed that we would fly to Madang and catch a Bank Line ship for the Middle East.

In September his successor was annouced, and Mr and Mrs David Hay came up for a three-week introductory visit. David was a career diplomat and had been High Commissioner in Canada and Australian representative at the United Nations for several years. He was an easy, likable person; Alison, his wife, was beautiful, intelligent and well groomed, but without her husband's ease of manner.

They stayed a week and we had a large party for them to meet people, and guests came to dinner every night, so that they wouldn't start their job feeling too strange. David, of course, spent his days with Don, familiarising himself with all the complexities of government, while I introduced Alison to the various organisations of which she would find herself president or patron. We had been dinning it into Canberra that the house would be very empty when we took our things, and that they would have to supply money for the Hays to furnish and equip it, so Alison had fun planning what she would do. They then went off on a fortnight's tour. We met again at the Lae Show, and could see that she wouldn't find it easy to adapt to the still quite tough conditions.

In October, shortly after their tour, we began our own farewell visits. How can I ever describe it? Through October and November we visited all of the sixteen districts, including many of the sub-districts as well. In itself this gave us an overall picture we'd never had before. It was quite an amazing experience to travel over the entire country, visiting all the main towns and government stations in the period of a few weeks, instead of over the usual course of years. It gave us an extraordinarily vivid picture of the incredible development and of the feeling of thrust and striving and movement which was so marked everywhere we went. There was no doubt but that the people were now racing into the twentieth century and were driven by a sense of urgency.

It was also an emotional experience. Not only were there big official dos, but so many little groups wanted a spot on our programme to say their goodbyes. I cannot possibly convey the impact on oneself, listening to speech after speech and hearing all the wonderful things people said, and especially getting the feeling that they really did mean it. We were so happy that people commented and seemed genuinely pleased that we were retiring in Papua New Guinea. But for this fact, our goodbyes would have been almost unbearable. Even so, for Don the impact was greater than for me, for he was laying down his life's work, and felt it very deeply.

Besides all the speeches and individual expressions of affection and appreciation, we were completely overwhelmed by their gifts, from little baskets and mats that women and girls had made, from treasured heirlooms village leaders had given Don, to the most lovely pieces of silver, crystal and china, to things like a coffee-table made by a carpentry class for our new house, or traditional bowls, pottery and carvings. The impact was almost more than we could bear, and an endearing thing about it all was the obvious pleasure people showed when they made their presentations. I can see, even now, the speech, the giving and then the sort of expectant standing back of the giver, while everyone waited in happy expectation for our reaction. We were deeply touched and it made us feel very, very humble.

One of the striking things about all these farewells was the totally different social status of Papua New Guineans. In 1951 there would be one or two big leaders at a social gathering, and they would be shy and diffident. In 1966 at least half the guests were Papua New Guineans. Often they had taken a leading part in the organisation of the function, many making speeches and all moving about among the guests with confidence. Many were well-educated men and women holding responsible positions, and Don and I felt a great sense of pride.

But we both became conscious of another aspect, which was worrying. Papua New Guineans had changed in their attitudes and abilities in a social sense far quicker than the Australians, in both the administration and private enterprise. Even though their energies were directed for so long to developing districts and bringing the people forward, with schools and training, teaching them to run their own affairs and causing them to change and develop, they hadn't realised that they themselves would have to change too. Far too many, though awfully good and helpful to the people, were unprepared, even unwilling, to meet them on equal terms without condescension.

Don wished he had observed its extent a year earlier, so that he could have thrown some thoughts into a D.C.s' conference and raised the matter round dinner tables during our travels, to get people conscious of the need and to be thinking about it. We talked about it between ourselves, but felt that our farewell visit was no time to raise the matter, and Don hoped that David Hay would have an influence in the right direction. Unfortunately, it didn't work out that way, for he and Warwick Smith had a much more 'colonial' attitude; under him the backward-looking officers and tough types in the administration were those to be advanced, and the more forward-looking people were frowned on and had a difficult time.

In November we suddenly realised that half the house staff were due for leave at Christmas and that we'd have to organise it earlier, so that the Hays could begin with a full complement. So we packed them off, arranging their return by the beginning of January. This increased the trauma of packing up, and getting ourselves out into the bungalow, while spring-cleaning the house with half a staff, meant hard work for us all.

The Moresby farewells were all left for December. Farewell parades by the army and the police, formal farewell dinners, and visits to schools and colleges. Various sports and club organisations had functions, and villages did too. Hanuabada gave us a wonderful send-off, as did Tubusereia in our very last week, where Noi Noi Vagi welcomed us and ran the programme, while Rage Tau made this speech:

"Firstly, I would thank you Sir Donald and Lady Cleland, very much on behalf of this village people for accepting our request and your visiting us. We are very grateful that you have a very keen interest in the village by paying us a visit through your many and important engagements. We are grateful too that you have done a very great deal for the good of our country and your keen interest among the people. Since the beginning of your governorship, there have been many and vast improvements in the progress of this country, in which we are very proud to be citizens.

"To you, Lady Cleland, we are also very proud and grateful that you, as the wife of the Administrator, have played a very important role in ensuring that your husband is well fed and clothed. Besides housewifery, you, Lady Cleland, have taken up many responsibilities as a leader of women's associations. We also give special thanks to you, Lady Cleland, that you have shown your interest in Tubusereia by paying us visits in the past. It is quite obvious that during your fifteen years in the Territory you, Sir Donald and Lady Cleland, have done an excellent service for us all. People of this village told me that they are sorry to lose such good leaders. They feel that this wonderful leadership should be carried on for more years. We take pride in you, because we had the feeling that you are friend of all, instead administrator or boss for all. We hope this leadership is carried over by your successors.

"We, the people of Tubusereia, feel that during your office as the Administrator of PNG have shown great interest in our village. The village and the people have changed considerable. Lot of our houses have changed from the thatched grass roof to corrugated iron type buildings. Use of tractor has improved our method of gardening. Building of the road has enabled us to visit Port Moresby regularly. Establishment of the Local

Government Council brought our water right into the village and help us manage our own affairs. Building and running of our school enable our young people to learn new things and many other things which are not mentioned.

"Finally, I hope Tubusereia people are preparing their listening equipment to hear their official guests' final voices. But before summing up, I would like the people of Tubusereia to join me in saying goodbye to our friends Sir Donald and Lady Cleland — 'Bamahuta'. In my conclusion I wish you both every success in your retirement, and may God bless you."

Vin Tobaining, the Tolai leader, made quite a different speech in pidgin at a huge and colourful gathering in Rabaul. He made a delightful pidgin listing of all the new things and changes which had come to the Gazelle. There were many other speeches, but these two together were typical of the way Papua New Guineans expressed themselves.

The climax came on Friday night at Ela Beach oval, when Toua Kapena, President of Port Moresby Local Government Council, and Bert Goodsell, Chairman of the Town Advisory Council, jointly did the honours. The oval was packed with people in little groups representing organisations, sports clubs, social groups and villages. There was a programme and speeches; the main one, by Oala Oala Rarua, brought lumps to our throats, and when after it Simon Kaumi (for the administration) and Fairfax Ross (for private enterprise) jointly presented to us a four-figure cheque from all the people of the country, Don could hardly speak to make our thanks, because thousands of people had contributed their little sums of money to it.

For an hour we walked among the people, talking to old friends and new acquaintances of all races, and feeling the exchange of warmth and affection between us. Finally we returned to the platform and waved, while everyone sang that stirring and haunting song 'Papua' as the car drew up and took us away.

Our departure was timed for 9.30 on Sunday, when the Department of Civil Aviation were flying us to board our ship at Madang. But of course Papua New Guinea just could not help but be itself when things don't easily work out to schedule. A couple of weeks earlier, word had come that the boat was a fortnight late. The Hays were due to arrive on Monday, the day after our departure, so there was nothing for it but to hide in Madang.

I was up early on Sunday, checking everything in the house and, as usual, giving myself only just time to dress, running out to find all the staff lined up beside the car, with Don having said his goodbyes, waiting in it. I took Dosi's hand and it came over me all we had gone through together over the years. I burst into tears and couldn't say one word, just mutely shook all their hands and they were weeping too. I don't often cry, but when I do I find it awfully hard to stop. About three times on the way to the airport I pulled myself together and powdered my nose, only to start again.

There were hundreds of people there, and in an enclosure on the tarmac were all the local dignitaries, most of them friends of long standing. Again I simply couldn't speak for tears and said my goodbyes with handshakes, not words. The police band was playing as our old friend Bob Cole, now Chief Commissioner of Police, accompanied Don to inspect the guard for the last time and Kay, his wife, remained with me. By then Don was nearly broken up too. Four pipers from the P.I.R. piped us from the guard to the plane, playing 'Auld Lang Syne', and there's no more nostalgic tune in the world. We were helped into the plane by their commander, Colonel Ken McKenzie, and were away.

The Clifton Bassetts met us at Madang and brought us to Smugglers Inn, a newly opened motel on the coast, where we had booked a suite with its own terrace, bordered with a stone wall lapped by the sea on one side and looking onto an exquisite, tiny, coconut-shaded beach on the other. We were alone at last, unpacked and had a lazy day. The motel assigned a servant to look after us and we were happy and comfortable.

It was strange on Monday to hear the broadcast of the welcome to our successors, the details of which Don had tied up before he left. It seemed to go off very well.

At first the Madang people left us strictly alone, for which we were grateful, and we quietly finished our thank-you letters. It was a good thing in many ways to get used to being private people in Papua New Guinea, before we set out on our travels.

Our first venture marked the difference. On Monday I went to the office to ring a taxi, but the manager wouldn't hear of it.

"Take the Kombi," he said, "take the Kombi."

I looked rather dubiously at the van, but he was insistent, so I went back and got Don. We'd never been in a Kombi before, much less driven one, and it was strange to be right over the front wheels, with the road at our feet. However, we went bowling along until we suddenly thought of yesterday: long black car, police outriders and sirens, bands, formality and piped onto the plane; today, just two people driving themselves in a Kombi van along the dusty roads — and we laughed all the way into Madang. Olga Blood saw us and came next day, insisting on lending us her Mercedes. That indeed was very nice and just like Olga, and it gave us freedom.

Evan and family were spending their leave in Papua New Guinea, had spent Christmas with Marie's brother, a planter in Bougainville, and were now in Hagen. We spoke to them on the phone and they came down to us for a few days, which was bliss indeed; so the late boat and changed plans turned out — as so often happens in Papua New Guinea — to be a great blessing. The family went back to finish their holiday in Hagen, and word came that the boat was leaving on Saturday, earlier than expected. It was strange to go on board late in the afternoon, stow our things and see how comfortable we were going to be. The director's suite had a good-sized sitting room with real leather chairs and sofa, a similar bedroom and bathroom.

Someone came to say that a lot of people were on the wharf to see us off, and we went down to talk to them. Dear people of Madang. Apparently quite a gathering had been planned for Tuesday, but the change to Saturday meant that only a few could be contacted; still there were some village people, some council leaders, public servants and townspeople of all races. We chatted and said our goodbyes, then threw the streamers they'd brought as we steamed out of Madang's lovely harbour at dusk. Agnes and Reuben Taureka and quite a number of others followed us along the shore and waved from the last point until night swallowed them. A gentle, lovely ending to the most vital, exciting and important chapter of our lives.

Don talked and worried a lot about the country at first, but gradually spoke of it less. And then one morning a couple of months later, steaming up the Nile in King Farouk's charming old baroque paddle-steamer, he suddenly said:

"Just as I was going to sleep last night, it came into my mind that for the first time I hadn't thought about Papua New Guinea all day."

I was glad. The umbilical cord was cut, and we could now enjoy the next stage of our lives.

Chapter 20

Sir John Guise, Governor General of Papua New Guinea, and Prince Charles on Independence Day.

Return to P.N.G. - Building House—Happy Family Life and new Activities—Chancellor Diocese and Pro Chancellor U.P.N.G.—70th Birthday Party—Holiday Australia: Dargie Paints Portrait—Virus Pneumonia Affects Health—Last Illness and Death—State Funeral and P.N.G. Tributes—Independence Celebrations

In 1957 the Anglican Mission subdivided freehold land it had held since the beginning of the century into an estate on the range above the Coral Sea, with lovely views overlooking the wide sweep of Ela Beach, bounded by the hills surrounding the town. With thoughts even then of retiring in Moresby, we tendered for and bought a leasehold block. When we finally made our decision we realised that we needed to give our successors plenty of time to settle down, and planned to spend a year in the Middle East and England.

We returned at the end of 1967, having arranged with David Chenoweth that, while they were overseas on six months' leave, we would rent their house, perched on Tuaguba Hill with a 300-degree view of harbour and sea. The plans for our house had already been prepared and shortly after our return tenders were called and building began early in 1968. We had great fun building stone walls ourselves, with the help of five stalwart labourers. We transformed a very steep block so that the house was built at ground level. A lower storey under the bedroom wing had a guest suite, a garden-tool room and work area for Don and a large rumpus room, which we both used as a workroom, where we each had a big table: Don with filing cabinets and bookshelves for sorting his papers and writing, and me for sewing and other jobs. It was lovely to have a place where you could just shut the door and leave a mess.

On both levels you could step straight from the house into the garden, which had wide lawns between the house and the view. It was finished by mid-year and we moved in at the end of June, 1968. Then began the happiest retirement anyone could possibly have.

Evan and Marie were now living in town near the House of Assembly, and their children, Sally (eight) and David (five), had their own room in our house, where we were most convenient baby-sitters. I don't think there is any more wonderful pleasure in life than to have grandchildren living so close that they are in and out of your house. David and Don were tremendous friends and it was a delight to see the little boy and the old man sitting together in the study, yarning away, or working together in the garden.

One of the Government House stewards, who had remained in the village and married, wrote to us before we left, saying that he would like to come and work for us when we returned. So as soon as the roof and doors were on the staff quarters, we sent for Robeibei, who came from Dobu Island in the Milne Bay province. He helped us with the landscaping and the making of the garden, his wife and the two small children coming up later. His eldest son, Lester, was David's age, and they and all the neighbour's children played together in and out of our house and garden.

Marie and I are more like two sisters than mother and daughter-in-law and Don and I had many wellings of gratitude that we were so lucky as to have such a rich and happy family life with the families of both our sons. During this time Robert was stationed at Lae, Rabaul and Goroka, so we saw Sue and Kathy going back and forth to boarding school in Brisbane each term, and they and their friends often stayed a day or so with us.

Robeibei and Nani increased their family to six and they were all very dear to us. Don always had a three- or four-year-old following him round the garden and 'helping'. Robeibei learned to drive so that he could take Don to his various meetings, while a Highland gardener used to come daily and work with him. Gardens grow so quickly in the tropics and, little more than a year after we moved in, he won the garden competition. Nothing could have given him greater pleasure and he was very proud of it.

Shortly after our return, people began approaching Don to go on boards of companies, and he ended up with a seat on the boards of a motor company, an airline and a shipping company, also one of the large old commercial and planting companies, as well as a finance institution and two in the manufacturing field. This gave him variety of interest and a wide insight into what private enterprise was doing and the contribution it was making. Having always been a professional man, this was his first actual participation in the business world, except for acting either in a legal capacity before the war or through his dealings in an official capacity as Administrator. He found the new field immensely stimulating; and, on their part, the boards on which he sat found his all-round knowledge and sagacity invaluable.

Just before Don left office, Bishop David Hand invited him to be Chancellor of the Diocese on his return. This is both a great honour and involves considerable responsibility, as the Chancellor is the legal adviser to a diocese, and he accepted it with pleasure.

Shortly after we moved into the house, Bishop Hand came to see him, saying that it was under discussion for Papua New Guinea to become a separate diocese instead of being part of the Archdiocese of Queensland. This would mean the drafting of a Papua New Guinea constitution; could Don do it? The upshot of course was that he plunged into it immediately, and it meant two years' hard and concentrated legal drafting. This, I might say, he thoroughly enjoyed and he went into it with his usual thoroughness, sending away for the constitutions of other Anglican Archdioceses. It meant constant discussions with Bishop Hand and others in the diocese, and attending numbers of meetings.

At last it was ready. I had never realised how like a constitution of a country a church constitution is. He then had to go down and present it to the Australian Synod, and this too was an interesting experience for both of us. For while Don was presenting it and taking it through, clause by clause, a programme was made for the wives, and I found it very interesting to be suddenly plunged into such a church atmosphere, with a few lay people such as myself among all the bishops' wives and representative clergy. I even found myself giving an address on the Papua New Guinea mission.

To my astonishment I found that getting the constitution accepted by Synod was only the beginning, and Don then had to draft all the canons. I had never realised that a canon is in fact an ordinance, and that the scope and drafting of it was very similar to that of a Bill or an ordinance before parliament. This took him another year of pretty constant work. It was done at last and had then to be passed, clause by clause, at the first Synod of the new Papua New Guinea Archdiocese in 1971.

☆   ☆   ☆

While Don was still engaged on the constitution, preparations were begun for the South Pacific Games to be held in Port Moresby in 1969. Various committees were being formed, and Don was asked to be chair-

University Graduations Ceremony, Sir Donald congratulating a new graduate as he presents his degree.

At the declaration of self government the two previous administrators Colonel Murray and David Hay (c) with Sir Donald.

Chief Justice Sir John Minogue, the new Administrator Les Johnson, the Vice-Chancellor Doctor (now Sir) John Gunther, Professor Karmel the Chancellor, Sir Donald as pro-Chancellor.

man of the fund-raising committee. Half a million dollars was needed to run the Games and the government had pledged to contribute dollar for dollar. So their target was a quarter of a million — quite a sum to contemplate. This meant weekly meetings of an excellent and hard-working committee, the backbone of which was Bill Johns, General Manager of the S.P. Brewery, and his accountant, Adrian Murphy. They formed district committees all round Papua New Guinea and everyone began a flurry of money-making. Don's own contribution was over a hundred handwritten letters, to everyone he could think of who had financial interests in Papua New Guinea, from big companies down to individuals, asking them for contributions. Great generosity was shown and this effort alone raised just on $100,000.

I was on the cultural committee, which had a number of sub-committees organising displays and activities to show various cultures, and I found myself chairman of the committee to build a Cultural Centre on the remainder of the reclaimed land where the main stadium, the practice oval and parking areas were being built. We wrote to various local government councils, asking them to send in materials and men to build a house representative of their area. We had a wonderful response from councils, while shipping companies and airlines helped with transport. So six quite different houses from faraway places were built.

With this going on, Hanuabada was not going to be outdone and contributed two spectacular exhibits. The construction of a sixty-foot Lakatoi, with its great crab-claw sails, in the grounds of the Centre (with the harbour as backdrop) is a story in itself. The older people of Elevala, the seafaring end of the village, remembered all the old skills, crafts and accompanying ceremonies, though the last two Lakatois had been built for the 1934 and 1935 Hiri expeditions. They taught them to the young and hundreds were involved. Then Hohodai, where the Koitapu or land people lived at the other end of Hanuabada, came into the act. Their old men began carving whole tree trunks to make a Dubu — the high platform for food displays in ceremonial feasts. All this local activity increased the feeling of excitement building up before and during the games.

By this time the Army came into the picture and put their Construction Unit to work, bulldozing an arena for dancing, while many companies and private individuals assisted generously with lighting, fencing and the hundred and one things that cropped up. The Department of Works designed and supervised the erection of a delightful complex of exhibition buildings in the style of village houses, using Kipa (sago) walls and grass thatch, but with sawn timber framework. The Cultural Centre has been an asset ever since.

The main cultural committee organised a ten-day programme of groups from different areas putting on performances, so that for ten days there were two sessions of traditional dancing each day. By that time everyone had games fever, and there's no doubt that the holding of big international events really does something for a country.

☆   ☆   ☆

Meanwhile, the university was taking shape, with solid, simple, strictly utilitarian buildings. Most imaginative use had been made of the basic construction of pre-stressed concrete beams, in such pleasing forms that the main nucleus of buildings has a harmony and integrity of design and construction that always gives me great pleasure.

During the building period the Administrative College, which had been built on part of the university land had been very generous in extending the use of their facilities such as library, dining hall and lecture rooms, as well as their newly finished staff houses. Thus the university was able to house all its new faculty and staff as well as the Gunthers themselves. The Vice Chancellor's house and a row of houses for professors were built along a ridge overlooking the campus and a very attractive village for others was built on the far side of the valley, thus enabling them to hand back the Administrative College houses. Without such generosity of a fellow institution, UPNG could never have become a working reality so soon. For office accommodation they used temporary huts near the building site.

Quite early in our retirement Don was asked to be the Pro-Chancellor of the university. Professor Karmel was the Chancellor, but as he was also Vice-Chancellor of Adelaide University he could only come up for meetings two or three times a year, and they needed someone on the spot who could be chairman of the monthly council meetings and attend to any other matters which, in the building stage, were constantly cropping up for decision.

This brought the old Gunther-Cleland team together again; and I think that, of all his retirement activities, the one which gave him the greatest satisfaction and pleasure was his association with the university. He really loved it and found it good to be working so closely with John again. It had been the vision and foresight of those two men in setting aside the land, when nobody else had even begun to think of a university, which had made its rapid and early creation possible. Don found it a tremendous privilege to take part in its shaping. It brought us into contact with the first professors and other faculty members and the first students.

What pride we all felt at the first graduation ceremony, seeing the first PNG students receiving degrees from their own University, clad in the beautiful blue gown, the colour of which had been chosen by George Buick, the Librarian, and Professor Don Drover. John and Don looked at each other sheepishly as they robed for the first time in the gold-braided gowns of office and put the black velvet Henry VIII style hats on their heads.

They were exciting years and tremendous spirit was generated by faculty and students alike, all carried along by John Gunther's own spirit and drive and his talent for imaginative innovation.

In its second year a ten-day seminar was organised which, known as the Waigani Seminar, became an annual event of some significance, attracting considerable international interest. A subject was chosen, with papers being read by UPNG and overseas academics, when a range of disciplines and a wide variety of viewpoints explored the given subject. It was a sort of cross-fertilisation, most stimulating, and it was fascinating to watch the growing participation and confidence of the students in discussion, until graduates and senior students themselves began giving papers.

John Gunther remained Vice Chancellor until 1974, when he retired. Professor Karmel had resigned (to become Chairman of the Universities Commission of Australia); Don served the remainder of his term as Chancellor, and retired about a year after John. Intermingled with all these activities he had been steadily sorting and indexing his papers, and began the book he had long planned writing.

After his retirement Don took no part at all in politics. He had bound himself to a vow of silence and absolutely refused to be drawn by press or radio to make any comments on the political or administrative scene. Though he had plenty to say to his family he never discussed things even at social gatherings. I think he was greatly respected for so keeping his own counsel.

Only once did he break this rule. He had been asked to open a conference, and we were having morning tea afterwards. It was during the Rabaul crisis, and the stand being taken by the newly formed Mataungan Association. Someone asked about it and — not realising there was a pressman there — he said:

"The tragedy is that it need never have happened."

I don't think he even elaborated much further, but a story was made of it, and it came over the 7 p.m., 9 p.m. and 7 a.m. news. Actually he was so steamed up about the ineptitude, even duplicity, with which the crisis was first precipitated, and then inflamed, that he didn't really mind. But he was more careful in the future.

In June 1971 his 70th birthday was coming up, and the family planned to give him a party. Robert and Julie were on leave in Australia, so they and the girls came up. A great many men who had served under him, some even as far back as Angau days, were still around. Papua New Guineans of long association, and people we saw frequently in the social rounds, made up to over two hundred. We had the garden lit up and speeches and cake-cutting surrounded by his grandchildren, and it was altogether a wonderful party. Don didn't look anything like his seventy years and was more like a vigorous sixty-five.

Later that year the American 'Campus Afloat' was calling at Port Moresby. Stanford University charters a ship each year for a semester, with a full lecture programme on board, and it is joined by students from almost every American university. They were to spend four days at Moresby and various reciprocal arrangements were made with UPNG. The Dean of Stanford had written inviting Don and me to travel with them to their next port, Darwin, to give some lectures on Papua New Guinea. It was a fascinating experience and I don't think we've ever sung so hard for our supper. Don was to give two lectures on government and politics and I, one on PNG art. They both went down so well that we were then beseiged, as all the other faculties wanted us to speak to them, and every minute was crammed full. The students were so interested and eager that they came up to ask questions — and very intelligent ones — at mealtimes, walking down the passages and even on the one day we found time to use the swimming pool. They also asked us a lot of questions about Australia.

Fred Chaney senior was the Administrator of the Northern Territory then. Having stayed with us while he was a senator, they most kindly asked us to stay with them at Government House in Darwin, and were wonderfully good in helping us to see places off the beaten track. We had often talked of crossing Australia from north to south, and here was our golden opportunity; we went by bus to Katherine and explored round there for four days, then flew to Alice Springs for a week, finally catching the Ghan to Adelaide. The modern Ghan inherited the very comfortable carriages of the old transcontinental trains. The two days and a night were most comfortable and full of interest.

The family birthday gift to Don was to have his portrait painted by Sir William Dargie. So after a month staying with friends and relations in Adelaide, we went across to Canberra to meet Sir William for a week of sittings. It was a fascinating experience to see so great a portrait painter at work. Of all his portraits I don't think he has better caught the essence of a person than in the one he did of Don.

Paul Hasluck was now Sir Paul, and Governor General of Australia. Hearing we were coming to Canberra, he and Lady Hasluck most kindly asked us to spend two days with them at Government House, and no one could have done more to make our stay interesting and enjoyable. Lady Hasluck was working to a writing schedule, so when we arrived on Sunday afternoon Paul met us and with the most delightful enthusiasm showed us all over the gardens and along the lakeshore to the stables, where in the dusk we fed a young filly he had bred. It was good indeed to share the obvious pleasure he got from being a squire on his domain, and we enjoyed seeing such a different side of his personality.

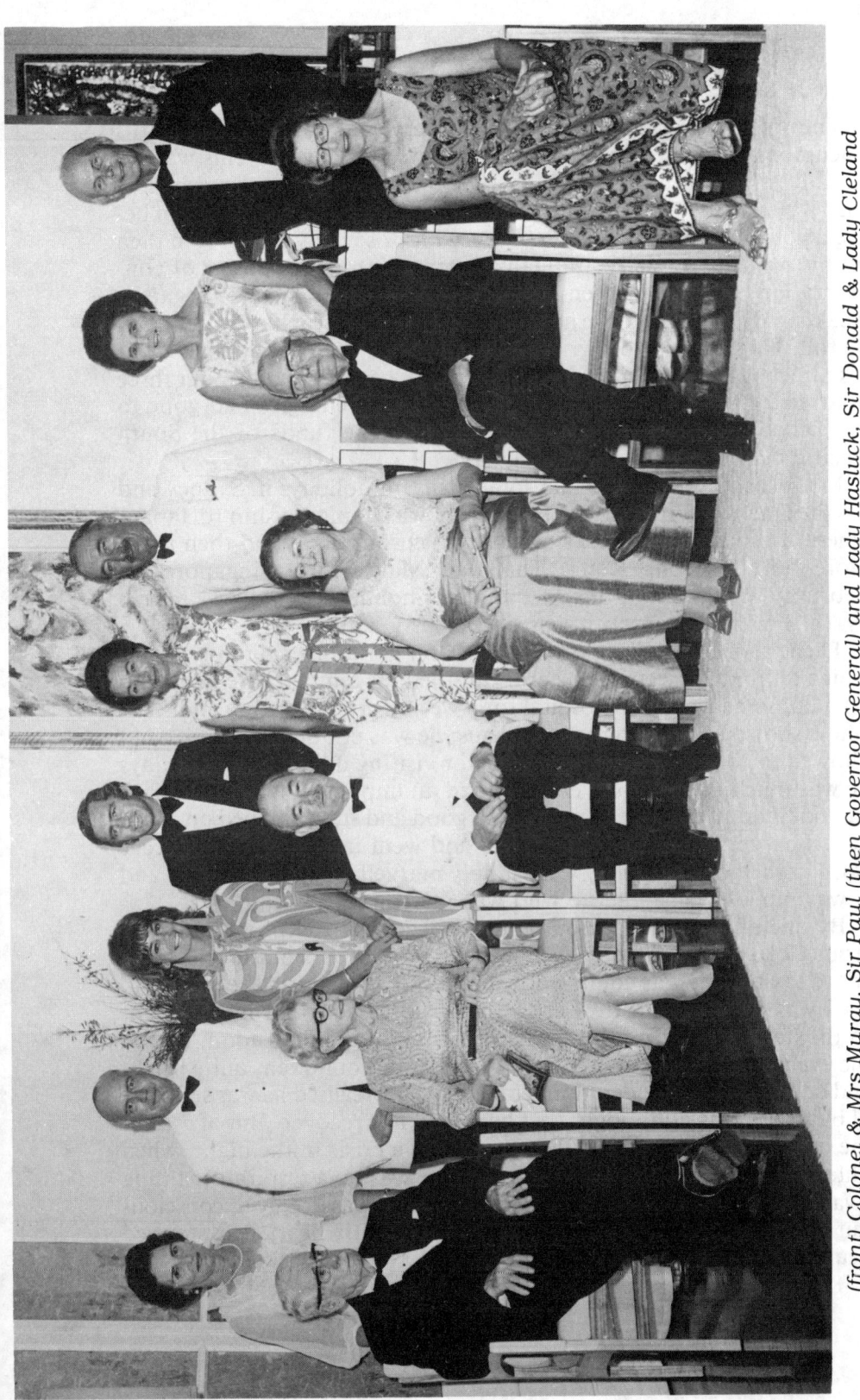

(front) Colonel & Mrs Muray, Sir Paul (then Governor General) and Lady Hasluck, Sir Donald & Lady Cleland (back) Mr & Mrs Johnson, Mr Andrew & Mrs Susan Peacock, Mr Barnes and his daughter, Mr (now Sir) David Hay & Mrs Hay. In this picture are all the Administrators from the end of World War II until self government and all the Ministers for Territories for the same period.

The following year Don had a very nasty attack of virus pneumonia,from which he never made a full recovery. This was his first illness since his coronary, over fifteen years before, and he lost the vigour and robustness which had been so characteristic. From being a young seventy, he was now every bit of seventy-two. From then on his physical capacity gradually faded. With it, his power of concentration, which had been such a valuable gift all his life, began to weaken. He had two more attacks of pneumonia, each of which took its toll. He still went on writing his book and enjoyed doing so, but his punch was gone, the book suffered and he only wrote about three quarters of it. The last of his full powers and energies had gone to the Diocesan Constitution and Canons, to the funds of the South Pacific Games and to the University.

In the last few years we had some pleasant holidays in Sydney and Perth. One we both enjoyed immensely was going by ship to Japan, where we spent three weeks at cherry-blossom time, and then spent more time in Hong Kong, Thailand, Malaya and Singapore. In February 1975 we had one of the nicest holidays we've ever had in Perth. For some reason it was particularly happy.

Then, at the beginning of August, Don got a bronchial infection, which antibiotics seemed to cure. But then his temperature kept running up, so he went into hospital for a week, for observation and tests. These showed some internal problems; he was put on a strict diet and allowed to come home, with the doctor visiting daily. For a few days he was much as usual and even chaired an important board meeting. But on Sunday evening he was not so good and stayed in bed on Monday. That night he became really ill and went into the intensive care ward at the hospital. They were simply marvellous in all they did and it was our old Dosi's niece who was matron.

By one of those miraculous coincidences of life, Robert had rung from Goroka on Monday evening, before Don's condition worsened, to say that he was coming down for a job of work in the morning. So I was able to send the car to the airport and bring him straight to the hospital, and we both sat with Don all the afternoon, and in the evening Evan was there too. We left him around ten, quite bright and doing very well under his treatment. We all realised he was seriously ill but there was no thought that he would not recover. But at 7 a.m. the doctor rang to say that there had been a crisis in the night, when phlegm blocked his windpipe, and that he was on a respirator. I rang Evan and we all went out and sat with him. He was deeply unconscious but we all felt that he knew we were there. His heart just stopped beating, a little before 9 a.m.

Though it was a terrible shock, and I will never cease missing him, we are all so thankful that he was spared the indignity of a long ill-ness or failing powers. I am also thankful that in February we had had that very happy holiday in Sydney and Perth with our relations and dear old friends, when Don had also spent a lot of time with his brother Bill. One could not believe that for both of them their lives were nearly over. For Bill had died in April.

Truly wonderful tributes were paid by this young nation, which really mourned Don. As soon as he heard the news, Michael Somare came to see me, asking if we would agree to the government's giving him a State funeral. We all felt that it would be right and fitting, and were proud and most touched. It was the first to be held in Papua New Guinea.

All the arrangements were made by the government, in close associa-tion with the family, and we came to have more and more admiration for the attention to detail, perfect organisation and care and thought of the young Papua New Guineans who were entrusted to carry it out. Don would have been proud of them.

The services, both at the church and at the graveside, were moving in a way we had never experienced or expected. The church was packed with people, both inside and out, and there had been a constant stream, especially of the older village people, paying their respects as he lay in state at the church during the day.

Afterwards, as we came down the hill into the main street, a very large crowd was waiting; while every few yards, for the whole eleven miles out to the cemetery at Bomana, little knots of people were stan-ding along both sides of the road to see him pass. Among them, many elderly men were standing stiffly to attention and saluting — old soldiers and ex-policemen who had known and served under him. But it was unexpected to see young policemen on duty along the route with tears streaming down their faces.

The cemetery is very beautifully situated at the foot of the moun-tains and with hills all around. Another large crowd (estimated at 5,000) was waiting there. I had only once before been at a graveside service but as the coffin with his darling body was lowered I could only think of the warm and kindly earth enveloping him in this beautiful place.

The Chief Justice, John Minogue, gave a wonderful eulogy at the church; then Michael Somare and our old friend Tom Critchley, the Australian High Commissioner, spoke at Bomana. Somare ended by recalling an incident when he, Michael, was Leader of the Opposi-tion. They were having a very difficult time in the House of Assembly, with both the members and the Australian Government attacking them without mercy. Even the local press was banned from the House for reporting what they said. Don was most distressed about all this and he went up and waited in his car outside the House till Michael came out. Michael told us that he had come up to him and said:

"If you chaps believe in the stand you are taking, stick to your guns."

Michael then said that by showing his faith in them Don had given them strength when they sorely needed it.

As I listened I felt: yes, that was Don. A man of few words, but always at the right time.

As we turned to go back to the cars Michael came up to me with his arms out and weeping. I nearly panicked as I saw a long line of weeping Papua New Guineans and some Australians forming up behind him, so called on all my strength to help me meet it. But the strength came from them and all the family learned the wonderful therapeutic value of the uncomplicated showing of emotion and sharing it.

In the line were people I hadn't seen for years, but whose lives had touched ours often quite closely at some point in the past — people from all walks of life: Cabinet Ministers and other leading figures, often with their wives; simple people, university graduates, young people in whose activities one of us were involved. They mostly threw themselves sobbing into my arms, their tears mingling with mine. Sir Maori Kiki, the strong and rather reserved man we had known for over twenty years through many vicissitudes, was completely broken-hearted, weeping unrestrainedly and saying, as did many others:

"He has been a father to us and now he is gone."

Don and I had always felt that we lived in an atmosphere of affection, and I knew that he had been a good administrator; but I had had no idea that what he was in himself was so widely appreciated, or that he would be so truly and deeply mourned. I feel that he himself in his modesty would have been astonished.

One of the wonderful things to be grateful for was that all the grandchildren were home for the school holidays. Evan's two were with us all the time and shared in every decision which had to be made, and Julie, Sue and Kathy came down from Goroka on Thursday, while my sister Barbara came over from Perth to be with me and represent my own dear family. Letters and flowers came pouring in and we were all uplifted and inspired by the tributes and the esteem and affection shown so widely. So many spoke of his kindness, human understanding and great personal qualities as well as the work he had done, and our loss and sadness was softened by the knowledge that these rather hidden things were appreciated by so many. We all felt bereft, but also greatly blessed.

Barbara stayed with me till after Independence, and it was the greatest comfort to have her there. They most thoughtfully sent her invitations to all the official functions and I felt that Don would wish me to attend, especially as she would be with me.

It's hard to describe just how wonderful it all was. The three main ceremonies were all very impressive, especially the lowering of the Australian flag at the stadium in the late afternoon, watched by a huge crowd. It was beautifully done and unexpectedly moving for both races. Most had tears in their eyes. I was with John and Dot Gunther. John gripped my hand and I think the three of us felt Don's presence. So many people expressed their sadness that he had not lived to see it. But had he lived, it is doubtful if he would have been able to make it. We in the family felt that his sense of timing served him even in death. The people were able to mourn him and show their respect, well before Independence a fortnight later, and before he died he knew that he was to be an especially honoured guest; for we had received our invitations and had taken pleasure in anticipating all that had been planned.

One day my sister and I had just parked the car for a ceremony at Independence when someone began running and calling my name. It was Bobby Gaigo from Tatana, a nephew of the redoubtable Dorrie Veri of the barbed wire story.

"Oh, Lady Cleland, none of our people could get to Sir Donald's funeral. It was too far and we were so sorry. But no one in the village went fishing that night. We all stayed quietly in our houses and were sorry for him."

One more little story. At a party recently I was having a long yarn with a good-looking public servant called Eki Agi. Suddenly he broke off from whatever it was we were discussing and looked at me quizzically.

"It's uncanny the way you understand us."

This rather took my breath away, but before I could reply he went on:

"Your husband did, too. He understood us and we understood him. In fact, I think we understood him better than his own people did."

I asked him what he meant.

"Oh," he said, "he was years ahead of his time."

Now it is probable that this young man did not himself know Don, except by sight or by hearing him speak. Our host, Geoff Elworthy, had lived here for nearly forty years and was very much involved with many Papua New Guineans, so later I asked him about it.

"Oh, but you don't understand," he said. "They all think like that about him. It's really remarkable."

Port Moresby
November 1978.

Glossary

Pidgin A composite language growing from the efforts of two peoples to communicate. Most of its words derrive from the dominant people's language, with the grammar and syntax of the chief users. With 700 tribal languages in P.N.G. and its increasing contact with the modern world, Pidgin is rapidly developing in vocabulary and form. It is widely used through tribal mixing in cities and towns and now developing into the national language.

Kunai Coarse man-height tropical grass used for roof thatch.

Pit Pit Another tropical grass 6–9 ft high of the bamboo family. It stems are bashed flat and woven into sheets for house walls. Young shoots are delicious food.

Lap Lap (Pidgin) Rami (Motu) Two yards of cloth wrapped round the hips. A favourite article of clothing for both men and women. It can be negligently tucked in, worn formally with a belt, the outer edge smartly pleated, or in the modern form tailored with pockets for men and darted to fit the waist for women. Its many elegant forms for men and women is developing into the National Dress.

Motu The tribe living round Moresby were the traditional traders sailing their Lakatois several hundred miles along the coast. So their language, being the trade language at the time of European contact, was taken over as the official Lingua Franca of Papua.

Lakatoi Trading ship for the annual Hiri. From three to five canoes were lashed together upon which a deck and a forward and an aft cabin was built. Two large masts were stepped and the matting sails were crab shaped. They could take some tons of cargo and about sixty men.

Hiri	The annual trading voyage, when Lakatois from all the Motu villages would sail to the Gulf of Papua. The main trade was the Motu pots for Sago, the only local food which can be stored.
Meri	Pronounced Merry. Pidgin for Woman.
Meri Blowse	A smock type top worn over a lap lap. Developed from the 'mother Hubbards' introduced by the early missionaries. It entered the world fashion scene in its Hawaiian form in the late sixties. In P.N.G. there have been some smart developments as a top, which worn with the rami or lap lap is fast becoming a national dress.
Kunda	"bush rope". The strong tough but pliable stems of jungle vines with many uses especially in house building and sailing.
Kipa	Woven sheets for house walls made from sago bark. Kipa is more durable and better looking than Pit Pit.
Wantok	A pidgin word, literally 'one talk', meaning someone who speaks the same language. Now commonly used to mean a friend or someone with whom you have an especial affinity.
Duk Duks	Originally men belonging to a Tolai secret society, wearing an almost spherical dress of large leaves threaded and hanging in layers from neck to mid calf, surmounted with a tall conical headcovering of Tapa painted with huge staring eyes.
Tolai	The vigorous people living in the Gazelle Peninsular of East New Britain. Rabaul is built in Tolai country.
Kundu	The hourglass shaped hand drums. Slight regional differences in shape, and very distinct regional differences in decoration through carving and painting.

INDEX

Fairfax Ross, 129, 230, 235
Fenbury David, 156, 270, 318
Fitzer Des, 175
Fry Tom, 219, 185
Foldi John, 275, 276, 272
Fox Jack, 76
Fox Tom and Pauline
Foot Sir Hugh, 264, 265

Gaunedi Dr Tom, 79, 290
Gazelle, 133, 145, 168, 277, 347
Gibbs Bobby, 74, 76, 288
Girl Guides, 88, 108, 194, 287, 291, 290, 321-2, 296
Glover Ted, 54, 55
Goodsell Bert, 347
Gore Judge Ralph, 183, 184, 186, 274, 273, 278
Goroka, 68, 101, 122, 136, 189, 195, 226, 232, 329, 330, 331, 332, 333
Greathead George, 67, 68
Groves W.C. and Mrs Doris, 46, 47, 48, 81
Government House, 40, 42, 43, 56, 59, 64, 87, 296
Greville Smith, 305
Gunther Dr John (later Sir John), 44, 45, 53, 93, 149, 164, 230, 232, 245, 246, 251, 253, 255, 256, 259, 266, 284, 311, 313, 316, 320, 356, 357, 363, 337, 340
Gutman Gerry, 326

Hagen, 72, 83, 289
Halligan Reg, 22, 91
Halstrom Sir Edward, 71
Hannet Leo, 295
Hanuabada, 39, 46, 62, 143, 167, 230, 346, 355
Hand Bishop David, 84, 352
Hasluck Sir Paul, 24, 28, 47, 48, 49, 55, 81, 84, 90, 93, 94, 128, 139, 141, 147, 149, 162, 163, 164, 196, 199, 205, 219, 223, 225, 226, 231, 232, 235, 238, 241, 248, 255, 256, 259, 260, 273, 274, 284, 301, 308, 309, 325, 335, 358
Hay David (now Sir), 338, 344, 345
Haviland Rupe, 101, 102, 103
Hawke Bob, 320
Herring General Ned (Sir Edmund), 19, 20
Health Dept., 45
Hewitt Sue, 328, 329
Henderson Frank 230, 337
Hicks Ted, 179
Highlands, 67, 72, 101, 327, 329, 333
Hisiu, 129
Hohnen John, 128, 232, 251
Hollandia, 139, 140
Hurrell, 237, 255, 256, 307

Iveson (World Bank), 325

Johns Bill, 321, 255, 355
Johnson Les, 252, 217, 335, 337
Johnson Syd, 202, 204, 205, 207
Judges, 100, 183, 184, 196, 198, 209, 213, 212, 214, 134
Justice, 185, 219, 221, 226, 228, 212

Kapena Toua, 316
Kaputin John, 316
Kaad Freddie, 337
Kavali Thomas, 289
Karmel Prof., 337, 356, 357
Kainantu, 69, 103
Kedgley Ted, 340
Kekedo, Mary, Walter, Roland, Rose, Jean, 292, 293
Kent Hughes Sir Wilfred, 45
Kerema, 121, 180, 181, 321
Kiap, 127, 128
Kienzle Bert, 292
Kiki Maori and Elizabeth, 251, 299, 300, 301, 312, 316, 318, 319, 362
Kirke C.P.W. 237
Keke, 63, 65, 66, 241
Kelly Judge, 234
Kwato, 127, 296

Lae, 38, 116, 243, 256, 267
Lalor Peter, 274, 304, 305, 316
Lambert Eskie, 28, 139, 148, 149, 261, 310, 311, 333, 335
Langmore John, 322
Leahy brothers, 67, 79, 128
Legistrative Councils, 32, 147, 162, 215, 230, 232, 235, 241, 224, 247, 280,
Lemeki Joseph, 51, 312
Lester Jean, 245
Liberal Party, 22, 23, 24, 28, 327
Liquor Problem, 259, 265,
de Lisle Lord, 245, 264, 267
Local Government Councils, 32, 34, 131, 132

MacArthur Gen. 406, 491, 40, 64, 91
Mann Sir Alan, 199, 200, 205, 210, 212, 213, 215, 220, 278
Madang, 52, 83, 232, 275, 332, 344, 347, 348, 349
Manus, 29, 146, 175, 176, 178, 179, 180
Marsh David 289
Marchena Dr., 98, 99
Mason Paul, 281
Mathaias 62, 63
M'boya Tom and Pamela, 90

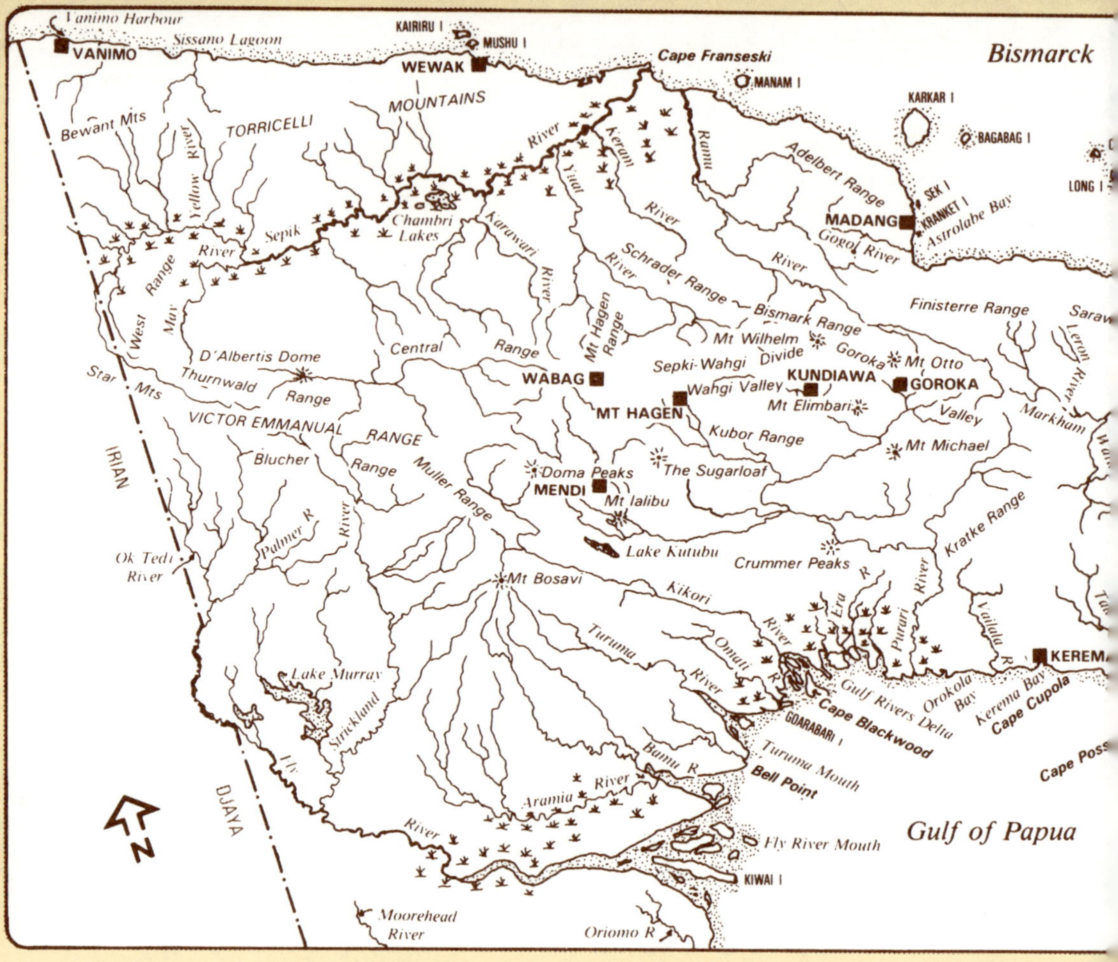

Bismarck

Vanimo Harbour
KAIRIRU I
MUSHU I
Sissano Lagoon
VANIMO
WEWAK
Cape Franseski
MANAM I
KARKAR I
BAGABAG I
LONG I

Bewant Mts
TORRICELLI
MOUNTAINS
Yellow River
West Range
River
Keram
Ramu
Adelbert Range
SEK I
MADANG
KRANKET I
Astrolabe Bay

Chambri Lakes
Sepik
River
Aarawari River
Yuat
Schrader Range
River
Gogol River
Bismark Range
Finisterre Range
Sarawat
Leron River

D'Albertis Dome
Thurnwald Range
Central
Range
Mt Hagen Range
Mt Wilhelm
Sepki-Wahgi Divide
Goroka
Mt Otto
WABAG
KUNDIAWA
GOROKA
Wahgi Valley
Valley
Markham

VICTOR EMMANUAL RANGE
Blucher Range
Muller Range
MT HAGEN
Mt Elimbari
Kubor Range
Mt Michael
Kratke Range

Star Mts
Palmer R
Doma Peaks
The Sugarloaf
MENDI
Mt Ialibu
Crummer Peaks
Eru R
Purari River
Vailulu

Ok Tedi River
River
Lake Kutubu
Eru
River
KEREMA

IRIAN
Lake Murray
Mt Bosavi
Kikori
Omati R
Orokola Bay
Kerema Bay
Cape Cupola

Strickland
Turuma River
River
Gulf Rivers Delta
GOARABARI
Cape Blackwood

DJAYA
Bamu R
Turuma Mouth
Bell Point
Cape Poss

Aramia River
River
Fly River Mouth
Oriomo R
KIWAI I
Gulf of Papua

Moorehead River

N

HIGHLANDS ROAD SYSTEM

Madang
Amele
Rai Coast
Saidor
Bogadjim

Usini
Dumpu
Gusap
Marawassa
Markham Valley
Kaiapit
Bubia
Erap
Nadzab
Lae
Labu

Kompian
Wahgi Valley
Daulo Pass
Nondugl
Gembogl
Hengenofi
Bena Bena
Goroka
Kassam Pass
Kainantu
Yonki
Leron
Baiyer River
Banz
Kerowagi
Goroka
Arona
Aiyura

Porgera
Wabag
Minj
Chuave
Watabung
Lufa
Okapa
Valley
Mumeng
Laiagam
Wapenamunda
Kundiawa
Gumine
Mt Michael
Wonenara
Bulolo
Mt Hagen
Kuta
Wau
Tambul
Edie Creek
Marawaka
Mt Kaindi

Tari
Margarima
Mendi
Pangia
Menyamya
Ialibu
Kaintiba
Aseki
Nipa
Kagua

N

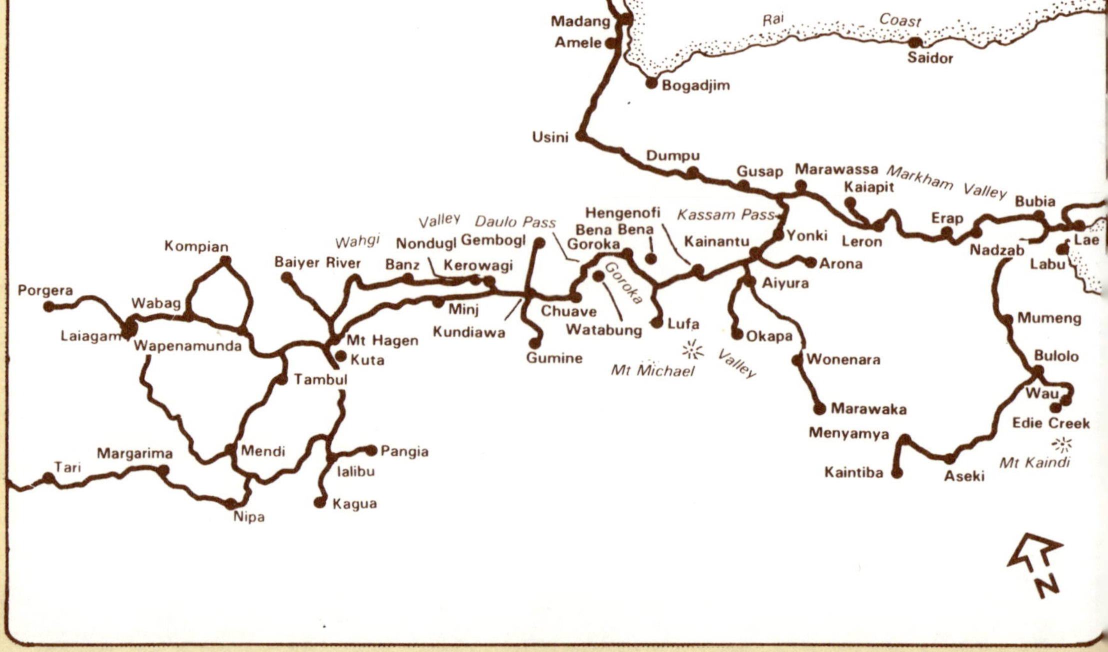